THE ANGLO-SAXON KINGDOM OF

Lindsey

THE ANGLO-SAXON KINGDOM OF

Lindsey

KEVIN LEAHY

First published in 2007 by Tempus Publishing

Reprinted in 2010 by
The History Press
The Mill, Brimscombe Port,
Stroud, Gloucestershire, GL5 2QG
www.thehistorypress.co.uk

British Library Cataloguing in Publication Data.
A catalogue record for this book is available from the British Library.

ISBN 978 0 7524 4111 5

Typesetting and origination by Tempus Publishing
Printed and bound by TJ International Ltd, Padstow, Cornwall

Contents

Acknowledgements   6

Author's Note   6

Introduction   7

The land of Lindsey   11

The foundations of Lindsey: Late Roman background   21

The arrival of the Anglo-Saxons in Lindsey   35

The inhumation cemeteries   57

The early history of Lindsey   97

Anglo-Saxon settlements in Lindsey   127

The Archaeology of Middle Saxon Lindsey   147

The Viking conquest and Anglo-Scandinavian Lindsey   161

Agriculture and industry in Anglo-Saxon Lindsey   189

The Anglo-Saxon churches of Lindsey   201

Endnote   206

Bibliographical notes   207

Index   219

Acknowledgments

This book is based on the work of many people whose efforts are gratefully acknowledged, although they may not agree with some of my interpretations. There are some individuals whose direct involvement in this project calls for special mention. Marina Elwes who, while working for the Portable Antiquities Scheme (PAS) in Scunthorpe, did many of the drawings that illustrate this book. Dave Evans, Rachel Gardner, Alan Harrison, Mike Hemblade, Naomi Field, Mick Jones, Geoff Bryant Michael Smith and Adrian James of the Society of Antiquaries Library all helped to find images. Stuart Laycock and Tom Green were always stimulating. The PAS Finds Liaison Officers who have recorded finds from Lindsey have been vital, in particular Marina Elwes, Kurt Adams, Lisa Staves, Adam Daubney, Rachel Atherton and Anna Marshall. Finally I must again thank Dianne, my wife, for her help and patience during this book's very difficult genesis.

Author's Note

Some thought was given as to how Anglo-Saxon names should be spelt, and it was decided to use modern spellings for names that have remained in use and to choose an original form for the less familiar names i.e. Alfred compared with Aldfrið.

Introduction

This is a book about the archaeology of the Anglo-Saxon Kingdom of Lindsey, not its history. This makes an advantage out of a problem: there are few surviving records of the early history of Lindsey which reflects the kingdom's isolation and the failure of its leaders to make any political impact. No foundation myth, telling of a legendary hero crossing the North Sea, was recorded for Lindsey which, in view of the contentious nature of this material, is perhaps a blessing. All we have are a few laconic statements made by people who then moved on to talk about great events in more interesting places. Bede, in his great *Ecclesiastical History* of AD 731 refers to Lindsey, but the kingdom receives no mention in the earlier chapters of the *Anglo-Saxon Chronicle*, which is concerned mainly with the kingdom of Wessex, where it was compiled in the late ninth century. Some excellent accounts of what is known of Lindsey's history are available, on which I shall respectfully draw to put the archeological evidence into its context. These, and other sources that I have used, appear in the Bibliographic Essay at the end of this work. As always in a work like this I am indebted to more people than it is possible to thank but I am grateful to colleagues who, like me, have spent years investigating the Anglo-Saxon Kingdom of Lindsey.

Lindsey had its own kings and bishops and was listed in the seventh century 'Tribal Hidage' where it was rated at 7000 hides, the same as the kingdoms of Essex and Sussex. Lindsey's autonomy was short-lived and, for much of the seventh century, control of the kingdom was contested by its more powerful neighbours, Northumbria and Mercia. The issue was finally decided with the victory of Æthelred of Mercia at the Battle of the Trent in 679 and Lindsey was subsumed into Mercia. This story would have been short if it ended in the late seventh or early eighth century with Lindsey's last king, but Lindsey continued to be seen as a separate entity even, after the eleventh century, when it was joined by Holland and Kesteven to form the county of Lincolnshire.

In the past this would have been a much thinner volume. The account of the Anglo-Saxon settlement given in *Victoria History of the County of Lincolnshire* (1906) is as short as it is despairing:

> The English conquest of Lincolnshire can only be stated as a fact; it cannot be described, for all details are lacking.

In 1934 C.W. Phillips' survey of the archaeology of Lincolnshire included a review of the Anglo-Saxon period. He too commented on the obscurity of Lindsey but began, at last, to address the legendary lack of Anglo-Saxon finds. Phillips listed five cremation and ten inhumation cemeteries, the records of which had, in the main, lain hidden in earlier literature. Knowledge continued to grow in the years after the Second World War; a thorough search conducted by Audrey Meaney for her 1964 gazetteer of Anglo-Saxon burial sites increased the number known in Lindsey to 18.

The cemeteries represent only the early part of the Anglo-Saxon period and when burial with grave goods in the field cemeteries ends, at the end of the seventh century, we lose our most important source of information. It was said that we knew more about the Anglo-Saxons dead than we knew about them alive. This might have been true of the Early Anglo-Saxon period but certainly could not be applied to the Middle and Later Saxon periods from which we had no graves; we knew nothing about these people dead or alive. Considering that the Anglo-Saxon period was almost twice the length of the Roman occupation this is astonishing. Lindsey, an obscure kingdom with little in the way of recorded history, was the darkest corner of the dark ages.

Illumination came from a number of directions: the excavation of Anglo-Saxon sites started, cemeteries and settlements have been dug and some even written up. Excavations carried out in Lincoln are being published. Elsewhere, developer-funded archaeology is producing important evidence and last, but not least, the work of metal detector users has done much to fill out the maps. When I arrived at what was then Scunthorpe Museum in 1978 the relationship between archaeologists and metal detector users or, as they were then known, 'treasure hunters' was not good, with mutual suspicion on both sides. Like colleagues in Norfolk, I saw that the intensification of agriculture since the Second World War had led to the destruction of the countryside by ploughing and realised that we had to record what responsible metal detector users were salvaging from a ruined landscape. For many years this was a lone struggle which, thankfully, ended in 1997 with the setting up of the Portable Antiquities Scheme, whose Finds Liaison Officers record objects discovered by members of the public. The results have been amazing; knowledge has increased at an unimaginable rate and our distribution maps may, at last, be starting to represent the true picture. We now know of 44 Early Anglo-Saxon cemeteries in Lindsey and the PAS database contains records of, at the time of writing, 1003 later Saxon objects and coins on which this book will draw. Evidence is coming from other sources, systematic field walking is locating new sites and the Early Anglo-Saxon Pottery Project is telling us about this most common and useful of archaeological finds. The material of this book is, in the main, not written history but the fragments that represent the lives of the people who lived in Lindsey more than 1000 years ago and who were, wherever in the world we were born, our ancestors in the ancient landscape.

While I have quoted the 'evidence' as honestly as I can, the story that I weave around it is only my interpretation and is open to revision and change. One of the most refreshing things we have seen in recent years is the abandonment of many archaeological 'truths' which have been replaced by uncertainties that are both stimulating and exciting. The converse of this is the post-modernist refusal to accept any evidence or attempt to interpret what we have found. This is both boring and destructive.

The land of Lindsey

The Kingdom of Lindsey lay on the east coast of England, in the area between Lincoln and the Humber Estuary (*1*). Unlike other, better known Anglo-Saxon kingdoms, we have the advantage of knowing where the boundaries of Lindsey lay, as they were defined by the water and marshes which surrounded the kingdom (*2*). These waters played an important part in the way that Lindsey developed, offering opportunities for trade, travel and conflict. To the north of Lindsey is the Humber Estuary, its 14 km-wide mouth opens into the North Sea towards Europe, offering a route way for both trade and attack. The Humber has a strong tidal flow with a maximum rise and fall of 7.2m but, taken on the right stage of the tide, it is navigable. Along the Humber bank are creeks or havens where the River Ancholme and smaller streams enter the estuary. These would have offered safe landing places to the shallow-draughted craft of the early Medieval Period. The Humber's main tributaries, the Rivers Trent and Ouse, and the rivers that join them, drain about 25 per cent of England and provide routes into the Midlands and Yorkshire. During the Anglo-Saxon period the Humber was seen as the boundary between Northumbria and the kingdoms of 'Southumbria'. This division, however, may not have existed during the Early Saxon period, with the Estuary acting as a link rather than a barrier.

To the east of Lindsey lay the North Sea, flanked by a deep band of coastal salt marshes which, prior to reclamation and losses to the sea during the Medieval Period, would have made landing and travel inland difficult. It can be seen from the map of Domesday settlement (*3*) that in 1086 the coastal strip and the area around the Wash were largely empty. Prior to the great storms of the thirteenth century, it is possible the Lindsey coast was protected by a line of off-shore boulder-clay islands.

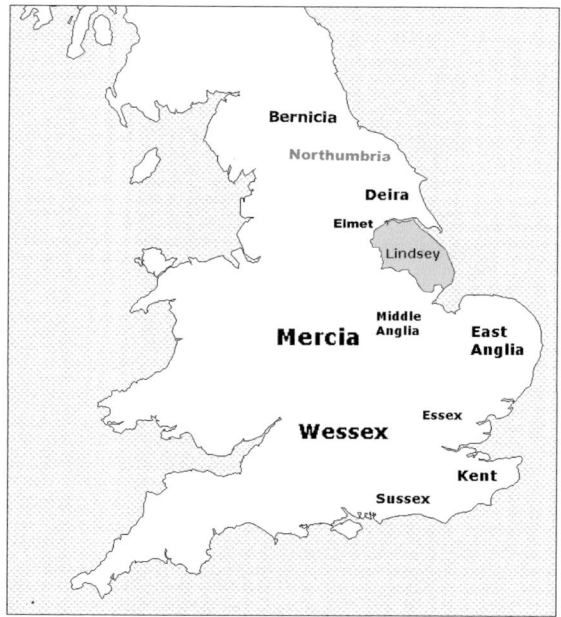

1 The kingdoms of seventh-century England, Lindsey and its neighbours. *Digital mapping by Mike Hemblade*

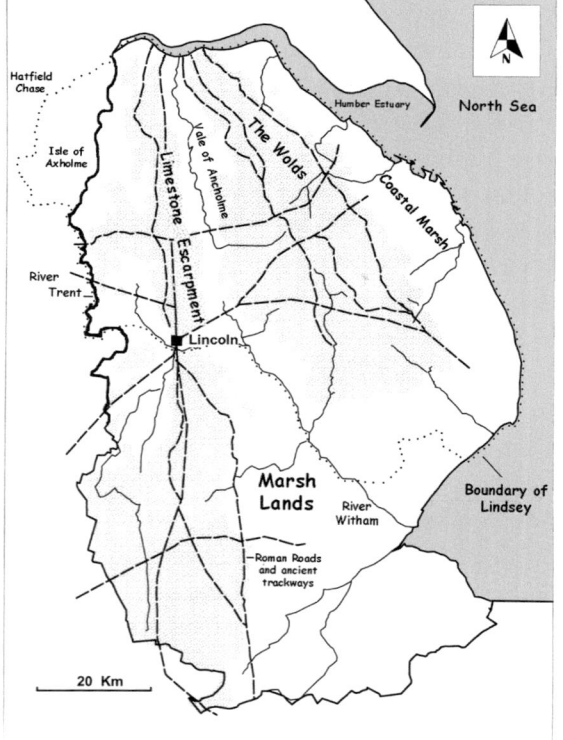

Left: 2 The geography and boundaries of Lindsey. *Digital mapping by Mike Hemblade*

Opposite: 3 Domesday Lindsey. Although compiled in 1086 Domesday gives us an insight into the way Lindsey was settled. Note for instance the lines of settlements following the spring-lines and the row of villages that lie between the higher ground and the sea, placed to extract salt from sea water. *Digital mapping by Mike Hemblade*

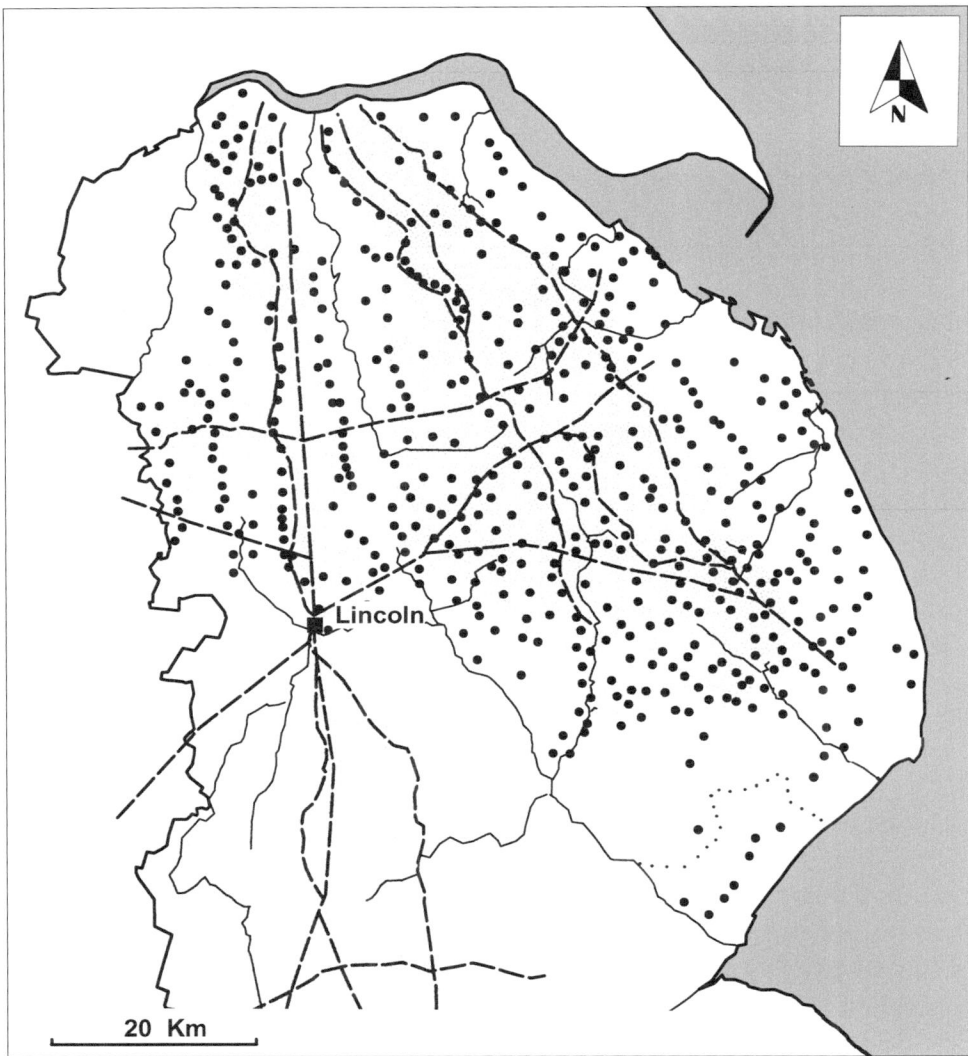

These would have provided a break-water, sheltering the coast, but in bad weather would have presented a hazard to shipping approaching the coast.

The southern boundary of Lindsey was marked by the River Witham, and the marsh lands beyond it. About 15km from the Wash the Lindsey boundary leaves the present course of the Witham and follows a meandering line to enter the sea at a point 16km to the north. It is probable that this part of the boundary follows an earlier course of the river.

To the west of Lincoln the boundary ran along the line of the Fossdyke for 6km before taking an irregular route to the Trent, just south of Newton on Trent.

As it seems unlikely that the Fossdyke was, as is popularly believed, built by the Romans, the boundary probably followed the line of the River Till. The Trent formed the western boundary for 18km before the boundary veered west to encompass the Isle of Axholme and the Humberhead levels. It then followed the River Don east, to join the Humber near Alkborough. A fixed boundary line was not needed to the west amongst the marshes of Thorne Waste as there are few better territorial boundaries than marshlands. An army can march on dry land and sail on water but after the first few miles of bog they tend to lose much of their enthusiasm.

These boundaries were recorded in the Lindsey Survey of AD 1115-18 and probably defined the extent of the ancient Kingdom of Lindsey. All of the places referred to by Bede as being in Lindsey in the early eighth century (Bardney, Barrow on Humber, Lincoln and Partney) lie within this area. The 7000 hide assessment of Lindsey in the seventh-century *Tribal Hidage* specifically includes Hatfield, an area towards Doncaster, indicating that Lindsey had always included lands to the west of the Trent. There is no evidence that Lindsey had any separate identity during the Roman period. Originally it had been part of the *Civitas Corieltavorum* based on Leicester but, by the fourth century, it was controlled by the *Colonia* at Lincoln. It could have been part of the Colonia's *territorium* but this may have extended to the south of Lincoln to include an area of Kesteven.

GEOGRAPHY

Lincolnshire is, in the popular mind, thought to be a flat county. While this image is true of the fenlands of Holland, Lindsey has a much more varied landscape. The feel of the Lindsey countryside is best evoked by the local poet, Alfred Lord Tennyson who must have had it in mind as the setting for his poem 'The Lady of Shalott':

> On either side the river lie
> Long fields of barley and of rye,
> That clothe the wold and meet the sky;
> And thro' the field the road runs by
> To many-tower'd Camelot

The rivers, the fields, the hills of the wolds and the sky are what mark Lindsey.

Lindsey is dominated by two north-south ridges; the limestone escarpment of Lincoln Cliff or Edge and, to its east, the chalk of the Lincolnshire Wolds (*colour plates 1 and 2*). These ridges are only high in relative terms, Lincoln Edge being around 60m and the Wolds rising to 170m, but set against the adjacent lowlands they give superb views over the surrounding landscape.

On the western side of Lindsey is the Isle of Axholme and Humberhead Levels. The 'Isle' consists of a range of low hills of outcropping Triassic Mercian Mudstone on which stand the present towns of Epworth, Haxey and, to the north, Crowle. The soils on the marls are fertile, but their high clay content causes drainage problems and vulnerability to drought. On the western side of the hills are large areas of blown sand which were of limited agricultural value. Around the hills are the Humberhead Levels which, until large-scale drainage was carried out during the reign of Charles I, were marshland with active peat bogs. This was a valuable economic resource used as pasture and a source of peat for fuel. The Levels would have played an important role in the development of Lindsey as they safe-guarded its western edge from incursion.

The first high ground to the east of the Trent is the Liassic Escarpment which overlooks the Trent and Humber confluence at Alkborough. Amongst the deposits forming the escarpment is the Frodingham Ironstone which was the basis of the Scunthorpe steel industry. The soils in this area are high-grade farmland and attracted early settlement. On the western edge of the escarpment the wind-blown sand has concealed some important sites, in particular the Flixborough settlement. Water is available from streams flowing west into the Trent and, in the north, east into Winterton Beck. This lies in a small valley between the Liassic escarpment and Lincoln Edge and contains some important archaeological sites, such as the Winterton Roman villa.

To the east of the Liassic escarpment the land slopes away for around 4km to where it is overlain by the limestones and clays which form the escarpment of Lincoln Cliff. This steep escarpment runs, north to south, through Lindsey reaching a height of 77m OD (Ordinance Datum) near Scunthorpe and 61m at Lincoln, 31km to the south, where it provides the Cathedral's magnificent setting. At Lincoln, on the southern boundary of Lindsey, the Cliff is interrupted by the Witham Gap, beyond which it continues, south-west, down through England. To the east of the cliff, the land dips gently down into the Clay Vale.

Parts of the Cliff are overlain by late glacial deposits of wind-blown cover sands which form agriculturally useless heathland 'warrens'. This is an unstable environment on which sand-blows frequently occur but there are areas of open pine, oak and birch woodland with some small pools and areas of bog which would have provided a source of bog iron ore. A series of streams flow down the sloping eastern side of the escarpment to the River Ancholme and provide a good water supply to the east of the cliff. The top of the Cliff is dry and dependent on wells for its water supply and it is notable that the medieval and modern villages lie, not along Ermine Street, but to the west, on the spring line (3).

Between the Cliff and the Wolds to the east lay the marshes of mid clay vale, the northern part of which is drained by the River Ancholme and the southern by the Langworth, a tributary of the Witham. The Ancholme has a very shallow gradient with a fall of only 4m over the 40km of its course and was, until the construction of the sluice at South Ferriby in 1635, a brackish tidal creek of the Humber. The marsh lands or 'carrs' that covered the low-lying floor of the vale could not be cultivated and the poorly drained flanks of the vale would be best used as pasture. With its wide marshes the Ancholme was a serious obstacle to east to west movement, effectively cutting Lindsey in two, the only crossing being at Brigg, where a gravel spit reduced the width of the marsh to 300m.

Running parallel to Lincoln Cliff are the Cretaceous deposits of the Lincolnshire Wolds that mark the eastern side of the Vale of Ancholme. The Wolds are essentially chalk upland reaching, just to the south of Caistor, a height of 170m OD, the highest point in Lindsey. Water is provided by streams emerging from the chalk to feed the rivers Ancholme and Langworth. With its succession of gently rolling hills separated by dry valleys the Wolds look a bit like Hobbiton. To the north of Barnetby, the Wolds are good farmland but until recently sheep formed the economic base. To the south the land is fairly fertile but conditions in the central and southern Wolds are varied, large areas cut by streams exposing beds of clay, sand and gravel. There are wide spreads of boulder clay on the eastern edge of the Wolds which have formed poor, thin soils.

Between the eastern side of the Wolds and the North Sea was a broad band of marshes resting on glacial tills, known as the 'clays' or the 'middle marsh'. The tills give the middle marsh a rolling topography drained by streams, running out of the clay, east into the North Sea. Fringing the coast are marine, estuarine and alluvial deposits and storm beach deposits of the Out Marsh. The soils of the Marsh range from good arable to poor heathland, with the better land to the south, all suited to mixed farming. South of the Marsh was an area of Fenland extending inland, north-west along the line of the River Witham.

THE ENVIRONMENT IN THE ANGLO-SAXON PERIOD

The landscape is only one aspect of the Anglo-Saxon environment and must be seen in the context of the climate and other factors such as sea level change and the effects of human activity. Information on the climate and the way in which it changed comes from a number of sources. Historical accounts provide useful details but have a tendency to record only dramatic events and can mislead. Scientific methods give a more objective account of past climates. The analysis of the ratio of oxygen isotopes in the cores taken from deep in the Greenland ice sheet reveals the temperature at which the snow formed and show long-term climatic changes. The shrinkage or expansion of peat deposits can reveal the level of rainfall, and pollen preserved in peat shows what flowering plants and trees were growing in the region around the bog.

At the time of the Roman Conquest the climate in Britain resembled that of today. Over the centuries that followed the climate remained fairly steady, but warmer and drier than now. These drier conditions allowed an expansion of settlement onto previously wet areas of low ground in the Vale of Ancholme, lower Trent Valley and the Humberhead Levels. A fall in relative sea level or lower tides may have aided this expansion. To the south, a dense pattern of Romano-British settlements developed on low ground around the Wash and, to the north of the Humber, settlement spread onto the flatlands around the lower River Hull. This movement onto what had been marginal marsh lands, can be matched by the wide distribution of late Roman pottery and coins throughout Lindsey suggesting that large areas were being farmed in the late Roman period.

The expansion of settlement came to an end as a result of a combination of factors affecting the East Coast during the late Roman period. Around AD 400 there was a fall in mean temperature accompanied by wide-scale changes in relative sea level around the North Sea. Flooding around the North Sea basin has been seen as one of the causes of the Anglo-Saxon migration from the continent. This flooding was probably due to multiple factors: rising sea levels, climatic deterioration, increased storminess and human activity, such as erosion caused by ploughing and a breakdown in drainage systems. This led to the abandonment of the Romano-British settlements around the Wash and their replacement with a small number of Anglo-Saxon sites further to the north. Although these moves were primarily caused by environmental changes Hays believed that social and political factors were also involved. Evidence was also found for rising water levels in Lincoln where work on several waterfront sites showed a rise in the level of the River Witham towards the end of the Roman period.

Although evidence exists for late/post-Roman flooding around the Humber, the lack of well-dated deposits makes it difficult to get a coherent picture and to distinguish general trends from local events. At South Ferriby Brickyard, Roman pottery of first-/second-century date was covered by more than a metre of alluvial clay. This sequence has been recently re-examined and a radiocarbon date of AD 70-260 obtained for a riverside road at 1.2m OD. The Roman trackway was covered by marine clays which, in turn, were covered by clays containing calcareous material washed down from the Wolds. This influx of weathered sediment during Roman or late Roman times was due to an increase in erosion which may, again, have been a result of a combination of factors. Climatic change, an intensification of cultivation, a move to a heavier plough or a change to winter wheat which would have left soils exposed to erosion, may have all played a part.

In addition to coastal flooding, the fourth-century rise in sea levels would have reduced the effective gradient of the Humber and the rivers emptying through it; the water backing up to cause freshwater flooding inland. Inland to the west on the Humberhead Levels, intensive Roman activity appears to have been terminated by flooding. The peat on Thorne and Hatfield Moors shows a change from humidified peat, deposited in dry conditions, to the non-decomposed vegetation laid down in waterlogged ground. Excavations at Sandtoft, beside the old course of the River Don, uncovered a fourth century settlement where ditches were being re-dug in an attempt to cope with flooding.

While the factors discussed above provide evidence for long-term changes in the environment, other more dramatic events may have played a part and there has been some discussion of the role played by the dust from volcanic eruptions and asteroids hitting the earth. In AD 536 the Byzantine historian Procopius recorded that '*during this year a most dreadful portent took place. For the sun gave forth its light without brightness … and it seemed like the sun in eclipse, for its beams were not clear*'. This event appears to have been referred to in other sources; the Irish Annals refer to 'failure of bread' in AD 536 and the Chinese record a famine and 'dark skies' in AD 540. Baillie's work on tree ring chronologies from England, Ireland, Scotland and Germany found that the trees showed limited growth in AD 536, improved in AD 537-8, falling again in AD 540 and 541 to recover in AD 546. The poor growing conditions would be linked to a fall in temperature and available sunlight.

The climatic deterioration during the later Roman period was not restricted to Britain, northern Europe was coming under increasing pressure. Oxygen isotope variations in the Greenland ice cap support a fall in temperature around AD 400 followed by a progressive recovery reaching a maximum in the early seventh century, but historical sources suggest that it remained cold in northern Europe. Locally, this deterioration may have been ameliorated by Lindsey's position to the east of the Pennines which gives the area a relatively warm, dry climate with an average annual rainfall of 600mm (less than Tel Aviv) and a mean annual temperature of 9-10°c. Each year Lindsey receives around 1000mm less rain and is 2-4° warmer than in higher areas to the west. This weather pattern helps ensure that crops ripen, but the area is vulnerable to drought with attendant risks of crop failure. The other factor involved in flooding is storm surge. It has been suggested that no major climatic change was needed to account for the flood levels found within York as an increase in storminess could result in a catastrophic 35ft flood every decade. It appears that the eighth century saw England with a more 'continental' environment with drier and perhaps warmer summers and harder winters. Conditions also improved in the early tenth century at the start of the 'Medieval Warm Period' with temperatures reaching a peak around AD 975. Optimum conditions continued until the around the end of the thirteenth century.

It is unlikely that much woodland survived in Anglo-Saxon Lindsey as clearance appears to have already been carried out on a large scale. The light soils of the Wolds had been cleared by the Neolithic and Bronze Age with the deforestation of lower-lying ground starting around 1800 BC. By 600 BC these areas, too, had been cleared. In contrast to most other areas, Domesday records a total lack of woodland at the northern end of the Lincolnshire Wolds and at Domesday only 3.5 per cent of Lincolnshire was wooded, half the average for England as a whole.

An important aspect of the fate of Roman Britain is what happened to the farmland; did it remain under cultivation or did it revert to natural vegetation? We can get some details of what happened from pollen analysis, but the peat deposits that interest us are the upper layers most vulnerable to destruction. Recent work has shown a sharp increase in tree and shrub pollen and a corresponding fall in herb pollen in the Humber region in the period 420-1200. This expansion of woodland may relate to a decline in cultivation during the post-Roman period. It is interesting that dendrochronology has yet to assign any tree to a felling date in the fourth century AD. This is not to say that trees were not being felled in the fourth century but that no sample so far examined has shown the necessary 50 ring sequence to give a secure fourth-century date. This suggests that by the fourth century all of the conveniently placed large trees were gone and all that was available were younger, small trees. When large timbers are again used, to build such structures as the Tamworth water mill (Staffordshire) in the eighth/ninth century, they came from trees that had begun their lives in the fifth century, perhaps in the aftermath of an agricultural collapse.

The foundations of Lindsey: Late Roman background

There is no record of any event in Lindsey between AD 314, when a bishop representing Lincoln was probably present at the Council of Arles, and the mission of St Paulinus in AD 628. These crucial years saw the transition from Roman province to Anglo-Saxon kingdom. The intention here is not to enter into a detailed discussion of the scant documentary evidence that we have for late Roman Britain. Too much ink has already been spilt over these scraps, and it is better to stay with the assured subjectivity of archaeology and save the historical speculations for later.

THE COUNTRYSIDE

Fourth-century Lindsey appears to have been highly prosperous and populous. Extensive reviews of the evidence carried out by Bruce Eagles (1979) and Ben Whitwell (1982), and of the former South Humberside by Keith Millar (1979) showed large numbers of sites, many of which can be dated to the fourth century. We have seen that the Roman period saw an expansion of settlement into new areas and, while this was explained by improving climatic conditions, it also points to an increase in population that made this expansion necessary. Romano-British farmsteads have been identified through fieldwork and aerial photography and it seems that they were generally set about a kilometre apart. Unlike the neighbouring area of East Yorkshire, Nottinghamshire and the Fens these settlements do appear to have been linked by field systems and boundary ditches and some other method of land management must have been used. Ditches are not the only way of dividing fields; excavations at Sheffield's Hill, to the north of Scunthorpe, revealed small ditches in which were spaced the traces of tree roots, probably representing a hedge with standards.

Agriculture

Agriculture formed the basis of the economy of Lindsey; indeed the region still remains essentially agricultural. The silts deposited in the river valleys were probably due to soil erosion caused by large-scale ploughing in the late Roman period. Large quantities of animal bone and spoilt grain found in fourth-century deposits next to the Brayford Pool at Lincoln suggest the large-scale processing and storage of agricultural produce. Most of the cattle slaughtered were mature and some had seen use as draught animals, probably pulling a plough. The sheep bones came from animals that were more than three years old which are likely to have been reared for wool and not killed early for meat.

Villas

Lindsey had its share of Roman villas, five of which are known on the Lindsey Wolds: Bigby, Claxby, Horkstow, Kirmond le Mire and Walesby. To the west, on Lincoln Edge, were a further eight villas: Glentworth, Greetwell (near Lincoln), Kirton in Lindsey I, Kirton in Lindsey II, Roxby, Scampton, Sturton by Scawby, and Winterton. Surprisingly, many of Lindsey's villas received new mosaic pavements during the fourth century, even those in potentially vulnerable positions near to the Humber (Horkstow, Winterton and Roxby) suggesting that no immediate threat was perceived from the sea, and some villas survived at least to the end of the fourth century.

Rural settlements

In addition to the villas and farmsteads Lindsey contains large rural settlements; Kirmington covered an area of 20ha, Owmby 30ha and Ludford 16ha. It would be wrong to call these sites towns as they lacked defences, civic buildings and planned layouts. Field walking finds show that they were densely occupied from the late pre-Roman Iron Age through the Roman period and were seemingly economically active during the fourth century. Jeffrey May's large-scale excavations at Dragonby near Scunthorpe, however, showed occupation failing before the end of the fourth century. Whatever their status, these settlements represented concentrations of population that had to be supported by local rural economy.

Communications

Lindsey was well-served by Roman roads (*2, 4*) which survived to have an impact on later settlement. The most notable is Ermine Street which still runs out of Newport Arch, Lincoln's original north gate, up to the Humber at Winteringham. Three kilometres to the north of Lincoln, Ermine Street branched, with Till Bridge Lane heading to the north-west, crossing the Trent

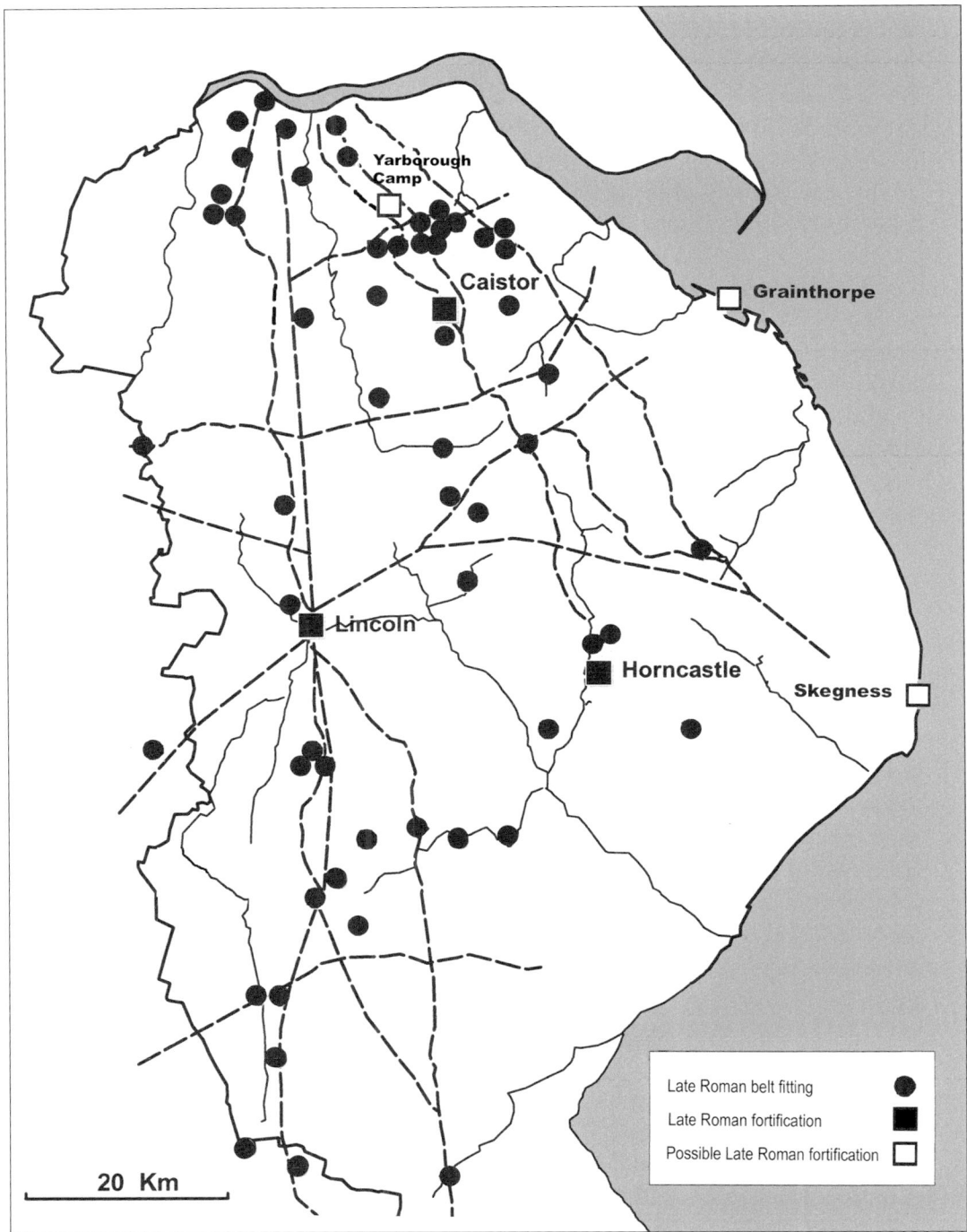

4 Late Roman belt fittings found in Lindsey and the locations of fortifications and possible for
tications. *Digital mapping by Mike Hemblade*

at Littleborough and going on to Doncaster and the north. This road allowed north–south traffic to bypass the crossing of the Humber Estuary and may have made Lindsey something of a backwater. At Owmby a road branches off Ermine Street and heads east towards the Wolds and the coast. Lindsey was also served by a network of minor roads and ancient trackways. To the west of, and parallel to, Ermine Street is the ancient trackway known as the 'Middle Street' which takes a more circuitous route along the limestone escarpment of Lincoln Edge. To the east of the River Ancholme is Caistor High Street which runs through the Wolds between Horncastle and Caistor, where it becomes Middlegate Lane up to the Humber at South Ferriby. The main east to west route passed through a gap in the Wolds at Kirmington before crossing the marshes of the Vale of the River Ancholme at Brigg.

While it is popularly believed that the Fossdyke, the canal linking Lincoln with the River Trent at Torksey, was built by the Romans this does seem doubtful. The first record we have of it is that of Simeon of Durham who records its construction by Henry I in around 1121 (*Historia Regum* ii 260). Even if the Fossdyke had been built by the Romans it needs a high level of maintenance and after a few hundred years of neglect it would have been difficult to find, let alone navigate.

Industry

Salt was being extracted from sea water during the Roman period. This is an important resource as salting was one of the few methods the Romans had of preserving meat and fish. Finds of slag blocks and quarry pits at Thealby, to the north of Scunthorpe, show that iron was being smelted. In the main, the pottery industry in Roman Lindsey catered for local markets and cannot be compared with the industrial production of the Nene Valley and Oxfordshire. Vivian Swan has listed 27 third- or fourth-century kiln sites in Lindsey. These are grouped on the Wolds south of Caistor, at the northern end of the limestone escarpment around Scunthorpe and around Littleborough and Torksey on the Trent. Only Swanpool, near Lincoln was producing pottery on a large scale and in a wide range of forms which included colour-coated fine wares and mortaria.

THE CITY OF LINCOLN

As the political, if not geographical centre of Lindsey, Lincoln was one of the most successful cities in Roman Britain. Established in the 50s or early 60s AD as a legionary fortress it became, after the army moved north in 77-8 AD, a 'colonia' for retired legionaries. The *Colonia Domitiana Lindensium* prospered; out-growing the limits of the original fortress, the walls had to be extended and the walled lower city doubled its original area with further suburbs to the south. Within the walls lay all of the buildings necessary for civilised life: a forum, basilica, baths, temples and sanitation. The legionary defences had been faced with stone in the early second century but these walls were augmented in the later third or early fourth century, being increased in thickness and their height being raised to around 7-8m. In front of the walls was a massive, 25m-wide ditch. The defences of the lower city seem to have been constructed in the third century but work was still going on in the mid-fourth. Decorated masonry from a fine building was used in their construction, which may have been an emergency measure or a way of despoiling a convenient, and redundant, pagan temple. With a total length of around two kilometres Lincoln's walls were a major undertaking but were somewhat old-fashioned, lacking the semi-circular towers seen elsewhere.

In the fourth century Lincoln probably became the capital of the province of *Britannia Secunda* and the seat of a Christian bishop who may have attended the Council of Arles in 314. The establishment of the city as a provincial capital increased both Lincoln's status and economic importance as it took on the role of regional seat of government. The governor would have needed accommodation appropriate to his status. It is possible that the forum was taken over and there is evidence for a large house in the Flaxengate area, with a basilican hall and possibly with marble wall veneers. There is also the large villa at Greetwell which may have been the governor's palace.

By the fourth century civic standards had fallen, the public baths had gone out of use and the buildings erected were of poor quality with dry-stone walling and timber framing. The number of buildings in use in Lincoln fell by more than half around the middle of the fourth century but some of these houses were imposing, one on Spring Hill contained at least 12 rooms and six large houses are known from the lower city. Behind the main street the hillside appears to have been covered with mansions and gardens, leading one to doubt if this represents urban life or just the elite looking after themselves. At this time villas were also at their most prosperous, which may reflect a flight of capital from the cities to the countryside, or a change from public to private displays of wealth.

The coin sequence in Lincoln continues to the end of the Roman period with relatively large number of coins for AD 364-78 but numbers then falling off markedly. Coins of the emperors Arcadius and Theodosius have been found beneath road surfaces in the city showing that the roads were still being maintained into the fifth century. As in other Romano-British cities, the final phase of Roman occupation at Lincoln is sealed by a layer of 'Dark Earth'. This Dark Earth marks the end of urban life in Lincoln, over-lying the remains of the latest Roman buildings, sometimes filling in between the wall bases. It contains no finds that post-date the Roman period and there are no structures within it.

Some of the dumps at Lincoln appear to have been deliberately placed, elsewhere the Dark Earth seems to have accumulated slowly, perhaps from the collapse of wattle and daub buildings. The dating evidence suggests that the Dark Earth is late Roman not post-Roman, and the condition of the pot sherds and animal bones within it make it unlikely that it was ever cultivated.

THE DEFENCE OF ROMAN LINDSEY

Fortifications

The mainstay of the late Roman defence of Britain from sea-borne attack was the forts of the Saxon Shore. These extend around the south and east coast from Porchester, on the Solent, to Brancaster, on the Wash. No forts are known to the north of Brancaster but this may not have originally been the case. The sixteenth-century antiquary John Leland describes the loss, by marine erosion, of a walled town, church and castle at Skegness 'clene consumid and eten up with the se'. This is supported by documentary evidence of the loss of Skegness church in 1525 and medieval references to 'Chesterland' or 'Casterland' in the adjacent part of the parish of Ingoldmells. These are the terms that the Anglo-Saxons used for Roman fortifications and provide a strong indication of the presence of a lost fort. Other late Roman coastal fortifications may have existed in Lindsey (4). The Roman road east from Lincoln divides, one arm going south-east towards Skegness and the possible fort, the other heading north-east towards the Humber at Grainthorpe. As this route does not appear to have served any civilian settlements, it too may have had a military function. The extension of the Saxon Shore Fort system north to the Humber would make strategic sense as it would fill a gap between the fort at Brancaster and the signal stations of the Yorkshire coast.

What is particularly interesting in Lindsey is that the Saxon Shore Fort System seems to have extended inland, with defences at Caistor and at Horncastle, closely resembling those of the Saxon Shore. At Horncastle, a 2ha trapezoid enclosure was surrounded by a 4m-thick wall faced with dressed stone, set with integral bastions and backed by a gravel rampart (5). The bastions were, it is believed, designed to accommodate *ballistae* and other pieces of artillery and would have allowed them to provide flanking fire along the foot of the walls. Caistor, too, had 4m-thick walls, equipped with bastions, surrounding a polygonal area of about 3.5 ha. The walls at Caistor were built out of undressed blocks of the local Tealby stone but we don't know if there was a backing rampart. We know little about what lay within the walls of either fortification but the scale of the defences and the relatively small size of the enclosed areas suggests a military rather than a civil function.

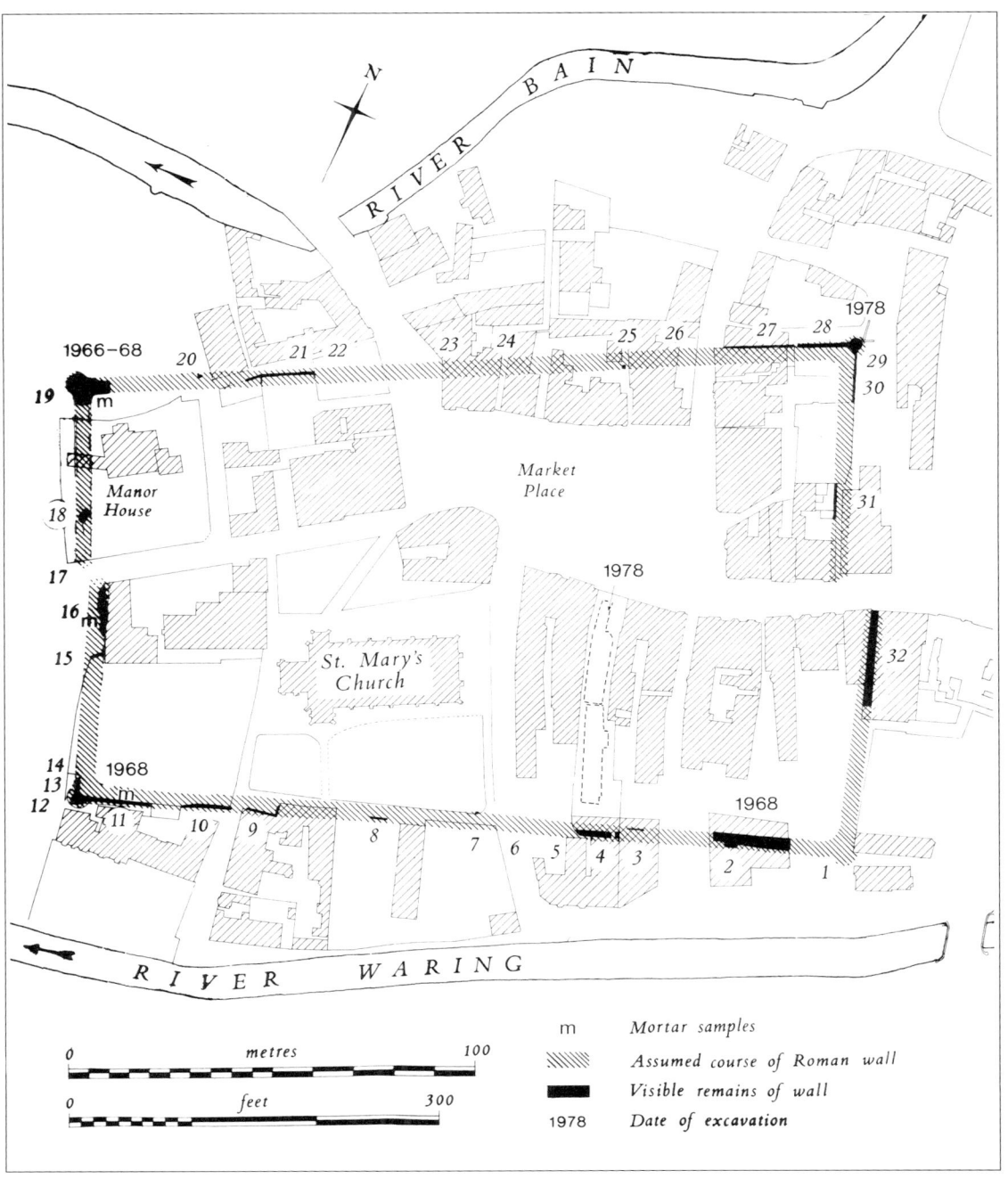

N

RIVER BAIN

1978

1966–68

20   21 22   23   24   25 26   27 28

19 m   Market Place   29
                              30

18   Manor House   31

17

16 m   1978

15   St. Mary's Church   32

14   1968
13   m
12   11 10 9   8   7 6 5 4 3   1968   2   1

RIVER WARING

m   Mortar samples
▨   Assumed course of Roman wall
▬   Visible remains of wall
1978   Date of excavation

0   metres   100
0   feet   300

5 Plan of the late Roman fortification at Horncastle. With its 4m-thick walls backed by gravel ramparts this was a formidable piece of military engineering. *Drawing by Mick Clark, courtesy of Naomi Field*

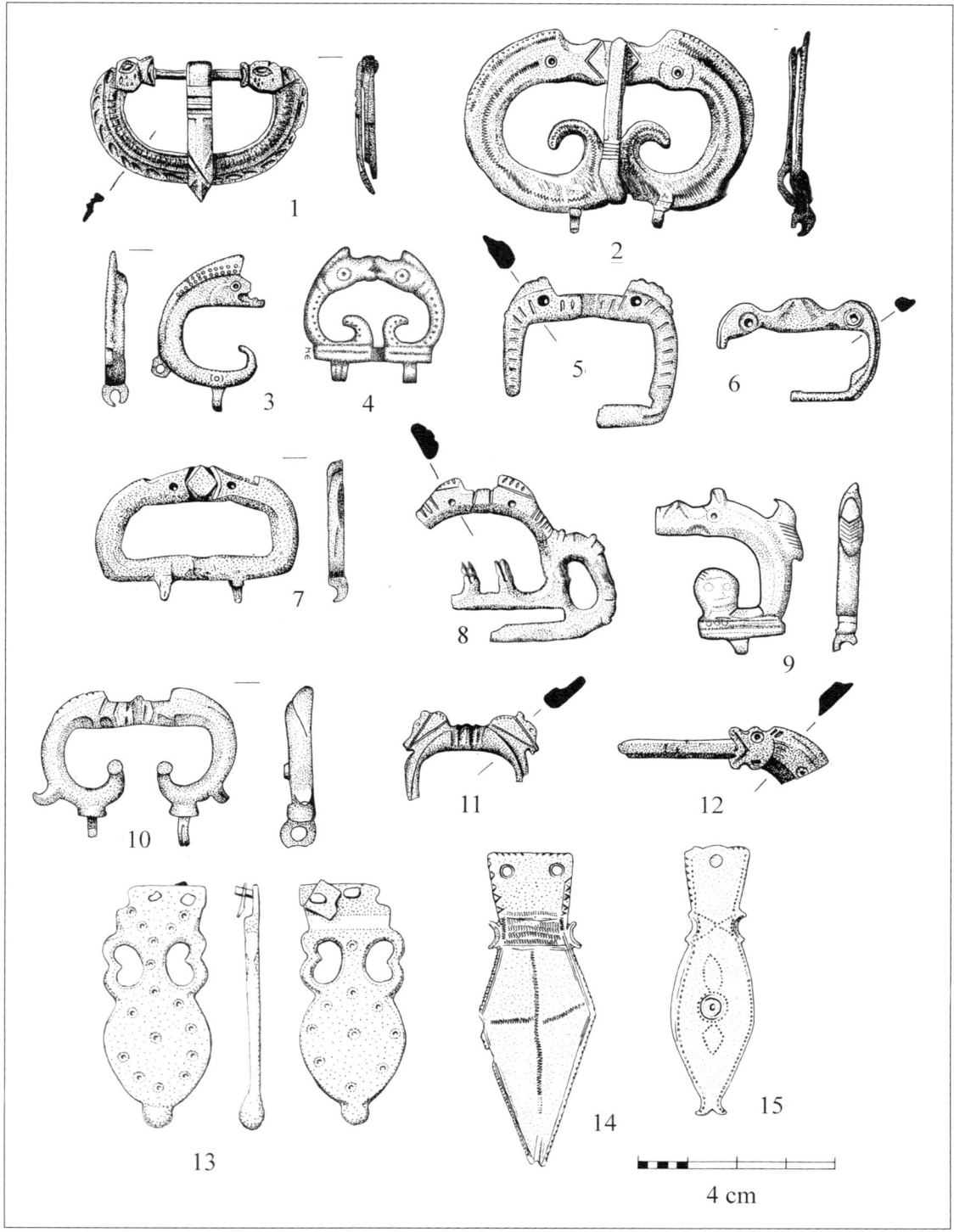

1

2

3

4

5

6

7

8

9

10

11

12

13

14

15

4 cm

A substantial civilian settlement has been found to the south of the Horncastle fortification. It has been suggested that these fortifications were collection points for the *annona*, the Roman corn tax, but the massive defences at Caistor and Horncastle do seem to be excessive for this interpretation. Caistor and Horncastle seem analogous to the Yorkshire command centre at Malton, where an earlier fort was utilised.

The defensive system may also have included the enigmatic enclosure known as Yarborough Camp at Croxton. This overlooks the major settlement site at Kirmington and is itself surrounded by Romano-British remains (see *40*). Yarborough Camp is trapezoid and the mounds on its corners might be explained as an earthen version of the bastions on a Saxon Shore Fort (see *41*, cf *5*). We know little of the final years of any of these sites except that the coin list at Caistor closes with Honorius and it was recorded in 1724 that 'many coins of Licenius' had been found at Yarborough Camp.

Soldiers and settlers?

Further potential evidence for the final years of Roman Lindsey is provided by distinctive late Roman belt fittings found by metal detector users (*6*). These buckles were first discussed by Sonia Hawkes and Gerald Dunning who, in 1961, published an important paper 'Soldiers and settlers in Britain, 4th-5th century'. They catalogued the known finds (there were none from Lindsey) and suggested that they were evidence for the settlement of Germanic *foederati* in Britain during the fourth century. *Foederati* were barbarian tribes who had a treaty, or *foedus*, with the Imperial Government allowing them to settle in depopulated frontier

Opposite: 6 Late Roman belt fittings from Lindsey:
    1. Buckle, Hibaldstow, Hawkes and Dunning Type IIIa
    2. Buckle, Dragonby, Hawkes and Dunning Type IIa
    3. Buckle, Dragonby, Hawkes and Dunning Type IIa
    4. Buckle, Stickford, Hawkes and Dunning Type IIa
    5. Buckle, Kirmington, Hawkes and Dunning Type Ia
    6. Buckle, Kirmington, Hawkes and Dunning Type Ia
    7. Buckle, Osgodby, Hawkes and Dunning Type Ia
    8. Buckle, Barrow on Humber, Hawkes and Dunning Type IIa (variant)
    9. Buckle, Dragonby, Hawkes and Dunning Type IIa, (variant)
    10. Buckle, Lincoln, Hawkes and Dunning Type IIa
    11. Buckle, Kirmington, Hawkes and Dunning Type Ib
    12. Buckle, Ingham, Hawkes and Dunning Type IIIa
    13. Strap end, Keelby, amphora-shaped
    14. Strap end, Winterton (villa) Tortworth type
    15. Strap end, Winteringham, Tortworth type
    Drawing 4 by Marina Elwes, rest by Kevin Leahy

areas of the Empire, bringing land back into cultivation and acting as guards against their less-favoured fellows. On the continent finds of these belt fittings appear to follow the Rhine-Danube frontier, supporting the interpretation of them as belonging to *foederati*. A few examples have been found in graves with weapons, a Germanic, not a Roman, burial practice. Belts were not a normal part of civilian dress in the Roman world and these buckles copied those used on sword belts, the elaborate *cingulum* worn as a badge of rank or office by soldiers and officials in the late Roman world.

These belt fittings are, we now see, commonly found in Lincolnshire, particularly Lindsey, which might suggest that Germanic settlement was taking place in the fourth century. However, while the belt fittings are based on continental originals, few, if any, of the Lindsey finds were imports and most were locally made (if not homemade) in a bewildering range of variants. The buckles have been described as exhibiting 'barbaric feeling' but are, both in form and inspiration, entirely late Classical and have nothing barbaric or Germanic about them. One should not confuse crudity with barbarism. Some buckles are decorated with human heads and birds executed in Celtic style (*6.9*), perhaps suggesting a resurgence of native tradition during the late fourth century or an influx of *foederati*, not just from free Germany, but from the equally uncivilised west. The buckles from Hibaldstow and Ingham (*6.1*, *12*) could be imports but it is difficult, on the basis of two finds, to argue for a great influx of *foederati*, however something must have stimulated the many copies.

To understand the Lindsey belt fittings it is necessary to look at where they are being found in the rest of Britain. It is all too easy to think that one's own study area contains a concentration of the finds when it is actually typical of much of Roman Britain. Fortunately, with the work of the Portable Antiquities Scheme, and of Stuart Laycock, whose tenacious research has gathered together additional data, we can now look at a representative sample. The distribution maps now show late Roman belt fittings to come, overwhelmingly, from the civilian zone of Britain, to the south and east of the Foss Way. While there are examples from the Saxon Shore Forts at Richborough and Bradwell, finds are not centred around these defensive sites nor are they concentrated around the towns of eastern England. There are two, possibly three, regional concentrations in Britain: in Lincolnshire, around the Severn and perhaps in northern Kent – all areas close to vulnerable river estuaries.

Within Lindsey the belt fittings are concentrated in the north, covering the Humber Estuary (*4*). They are not found around the Wash, as perhaps the onset of flooding was already having its impact. Isolated finds have been made in or near Caistor, Horncastle and Lincoln, but these fortified sites do not represent any foci in the distribution. The belt fittings seem unlikely to be the accoutrements of the soldiers garrisoning these fortifications. The distribution of belt fittings is rural but seems to lie along lines of communication with a concentration at Kirmington, a major undefended Romano-British settlement at the intersection of two important lines of communication. This scattered pattern of finds does seem to support the original Hawkes and Dunning 'soldiers and settlers' model with armed men settled in the countryside both to farm and guard.

Few of these belt fittings have been found in the neighbouring areas of Nottinghamshire and East Yorkshire where other late Roman finds are common. As Lindsey and East Yorkshire are geographically similar, the lack of buckles is significant and needs to be explained in some way. The people of fourth-century Lindsey enjoyed a taste for belt fittings of continental style that was not shared by their neighbours. This may reflect the area to the north of the Humber being in the military zone of Roman Britain, its coast defended by signal stations communicating back to the fort at Malton and the fortress at York. Having a garrison of professional soldiers, this area would have had no need for *foederati* or a militia. Nottinghamshire is inland and not open to seaborne attack, but Lindsey was both vulnerable and without a garrison and special precautions may have been needed.

We need to consider who would have worn these strange fittings. While we now see military-style clothing being worn by civilians both for comfort and as a fashion, this is unlikely to have been the case in the fourth century. In the late antique world the army was generally hated and it is unlikely that military apparel would be copied by civilians. Who then would have worn these sword belts?

The late Roman army was divided into two broad classes of soldiers, the *limitanei*, who were the garrison troops stationed on the frontiers, and the mobile field army, the *comitatenses*. A dearth of these buckles from Hadrian's Wall suggests that they were not issued to the *limitanei* and it seems unlikely that the elite field army was using equipment of the poor quality found in Lindsey. Perhaps a third force was present. It has been noted that in the fifth-century document known as the *Notitia Dignitatum*, the insignia of the *vicarius* who governed Britannia was not the peaceful maidens used by the other *vicarii*, but fortified citadels, suggesting that unlike his colleagues he had control of troops. The *vicarius* was a civilian and it would have been appropriate for him to recruit from the population of his own diocese. It is also possible that the buckles were worn by '*bucellarii*', the henchmen of local magnates, the recruitment of whom the authorities tried to suppress. The evidence of the buckles and forts suggests that Lindsey was militarised during the fourth century. This could provide an administrative structure that was sufficiently robust to control incomers during the fifth century and affect the process by which the Anglo-Saxon settlement occurred.

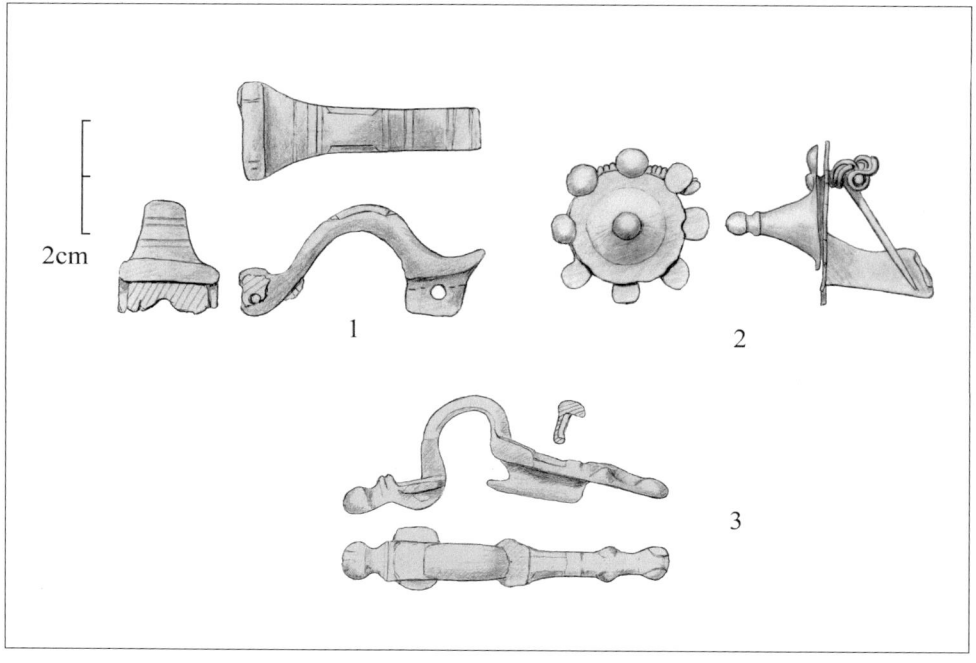

7 Early Germanic buckles from Lindsey. 1: Supporting arm brooch, Newball. 2: Tutulus brooch, Kirmington. 3: Åberg Group I cruciform brooch, Clixby. *Drawings by Kevin Leahy*

While the buckles cannot be seen as direct evidence for an influx of Germanic mercenaries into fourth-century Lindsey, we do have a small number of objects that really are early Germanic. These consist of a 'tutulus' brooch from the large settlement site at Kirmington, and 'supporting arm' brooches from the Roman roadside settlements at Hibaldstow, the Anglo-Saxon cremation cemetery at Elsham, and from Romano-British rural sites at Edlington and Newball (7). These brooches are of northern European types, probably dating from the late fourth or early fifth century. They formed part of female dress, suggesting the early presence of Germanic families at a time when Lindsey was still part of a Roman province. Equipment worn by the Germanic husbands of these women may have stimulated a local demand for the buckles discussed above.

THE END OF ROMAN LINDSEY

There are few traces of deliberate destruction in Roman Lindsey to mark the end of the Roman Diocese. Only one of Lindsey's villas appears to have met a violent end; Scampton was destroyed by fire after AD 337 but this could have been the result of an accident. The 'Dark Earth' layers that cover the last buildings in Lincoln are seen as being a late Roman, rather than a post-Roman, phenomenon. The towns and villas went out of use but we don't know the date at which this happened; in the absence of coins, sites we have dated to the late fourth century may actually belong to the fifth. At one time the great issue was 'continuity' and what survived from the Roman period. This depends on what we mean by continuity, as even when the villas were in ruins the fields surrounding them may still have been worked, but is this continuity?

Coins are one of the commonest Roman objects to be found and are important as they are datable and can show the state of the economy. Metal detecting carried out by Alan Harrison at Kirmington prior to 1979 resulted in the recovery of 4333 Roman coins of which 1511 dated from 364-388 and 102 from 388-402. Out of a total of 2763 coins from South Ferriby, 59 were of the Emperor Arcadius and 21 of Honorius, both dating to 395-402. From a total of 94 identified coins recorded from the Winterton Villa, 18 dated from 364-388 and six from 388-402, showing that occupation continued until the end of the Roman period. Activity clearly continued on these sites until coins ceased to be used in Britain. As base metal coins were not imported into Britain after c.402 and little gold or silver after 407 these sites could have been occupied well into the fifth century but, without coin dates, we cannot tell. It is notable that, of the large numbers of later fourth-century Roman coins found in Lindsey, few, if any, show any sign of wear, making it unlikely that they remained in use for long after issue. There was no attempt to produce local copies as there had been during earlier crises and, as the people in the countryside lacked both the need or ability to melt down the base metal coins, they were abandoned in vast numbers. Gold and silver coins retained their intrinsic values but the practice of clipping the edges of silver coins which, in more ordered times was practically unknown, becomes common after AD 395, an indication of a bullion, rather than a coin economy. The burying of hoards is seen as an indicator of troubled times and, of the 25 Roman coin hoards known from Lindsey, 14 date from the last 60 years of the fourth century and 11 from the preceding 280 years, pointing to unsettled times. This evidence suggests that the secession of the Roman coinage was related to a general breakdown in the administration and a loss of confidence in the provincial government, perhaps accompanied by the withdrawal of the field army.

The collapse of the coinage had implications far beyond causing inconvenience to traders. Without income from taxation the state would be unable to purchase goods and there would no longer be any reason for farmers to produce a surplus. This would have had serious consequences for the urban dwellers in Lincoln and the specialists dependent on foodstuffs grown by others. The administration needed to support civilisation would have disappeared and the semi-industrial pottery industry would, without access to a mass market, have ceased to be viable. Without coins, and with a deteriorating security situation, it would have been difficult to sell or distribute goods and production would have been for a local market only. The rural economy as represented by both the peasant sites and the villas would have fallen back to self-sufficiency. It is simplistic to suggest that an economy as complex as that of the Roman Province could have reverted to 'barter' and it is probable that production fell back to meeting only local needs together with some use of an exchange system organised by local magnates. The payment of taxes in the form of goods was a well-established practice in the Roman Empire, and surpluses could have been collected by local leaders who traded on behalf of their clients, in turn passing some of the imports back to them.

Finally, as the late Roman buckles fail to suggest any great influx of Germanic mercenaries during the fourth century, it is worth considering how the Anglo-Saxon settlers were able to take control of a highly organised Roman province. Stuart Laycock has suggested that tribalism remained a force in fifth-century Britain (as it recently was in the Balkans) and once the controlling power was removed the British tribes attacked each other. This could have allowed the incoming Germanic war-bands to exercise an influence way beyond their numerical strength. This hypothesis has much to recommend it and may well have played a part in the fall of Roman Britain.

The arrival of the Anglo-Saxons in Lindsey

The first evidence for the large-scale arrival of the Anglo-Saxons is their cemeteries. Spread across eastern England, these are distinguished by the inclusion of grave goods which were rare in late Roman Britain, and the use of cremation. The pots, brooches and weapons found with the burials can be closely linked to the Germanic homelands in northern Europe and Scandinavia showing a movement of people, or influences, across the North Sea. Two burial rites were used by the Anglo-Saxons during the settlement period. In Anglian England, to the north of the Thames, cremation was the predominant rite, but to the south of the Thames, in the 'Saxon' part of England, inhumation was more common. However in neither region was one rite used exclusively; there are cremations in the south and early graves in the north.

THE CREMATION CEMETERIES

South Elkington

Early Lindsey was dominated by the four large cremation cemeteries at Cleatham, Elsham, South Elkington and West Keal (8). Systematic work on them started after the Second World War with excavations at South Elkingon, near Louth, in 1946-7. Ploughing had revealed a patch of large flint nodules which were thought to be the remains of a Roman road. A small excavation was carried out and several near-complete Anglo-Saxon urns were found. Larger-scale work was undertaken by Graham Webster, who was then an engineer in Lincoln, but who went on to a career in Romano-British archaeology. During three weeks' digging he recovered the remains of 290 urns. South Elkington is on boulder clay making digging difficult and many urns were badly crushed. Webster wrote a

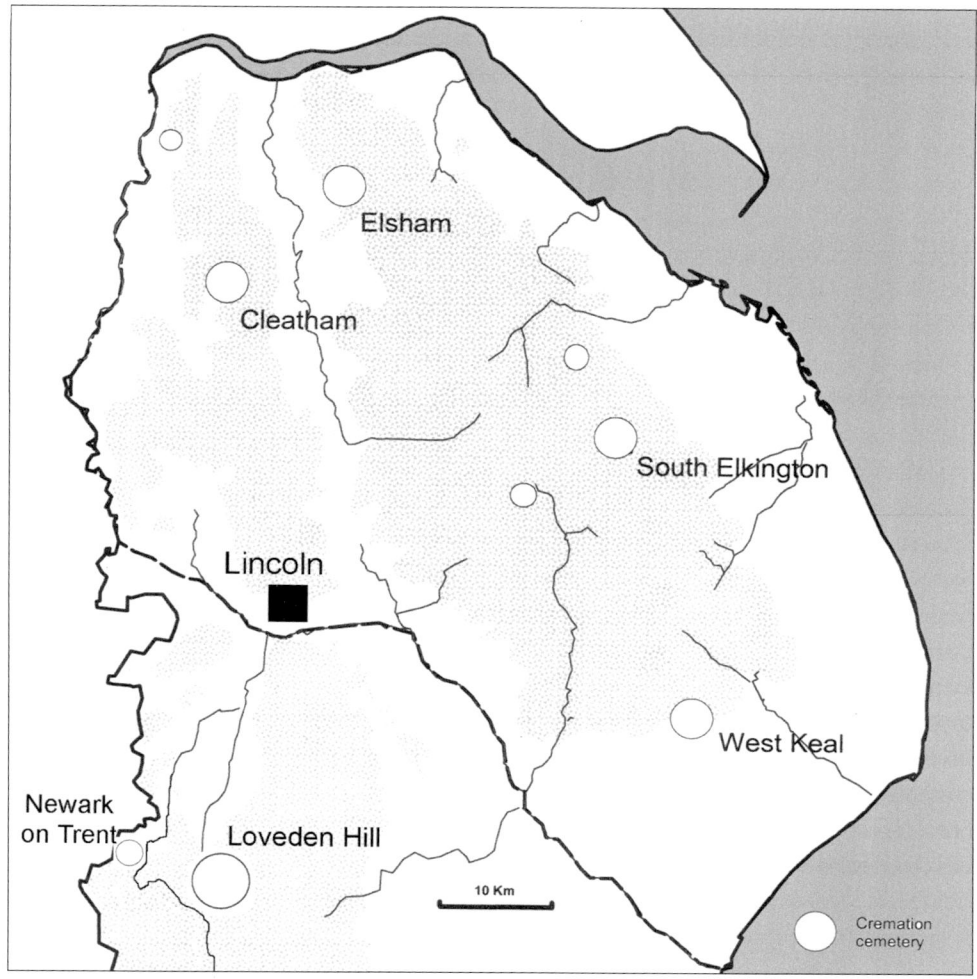

8 The locations of cremation cemeteries in Lindsey. *Digital mapping by Mike Hemblade*

report on his excavation with a discussion of the pottery by J.N.L. Myres (1952). He believed, on the basis of the area covered by flints, that about 25 per cent of the cemetery had been excavated and field walking carried out on the site in the autumn of 1998 showed this to be broadly true. Grave goods were only identified in 30 of the urns and there was no trace of inhumations on the site.

West Keal

The next discovery is the least known of Lindsey's large cremation cemeteries. Anglo-Saxon pottery and beads were recorded as having been found at Hall Hill, West Keal in the early 1930s but the real discovery came in 1954 when the farmer deep-ploughed the field and revealed a large amount of Anglo-Saxon pottery. Salvage work by Mr G.V. Taylor produced 21 urns, of which four could be reconstructed, together with many sherds. It was thought that the scatter of sherds covered two acres but that the actual cemetery was smaller than this.

Elsham

In 1975-6 Chris Knowles and Freda Berisford excavated the cemetery at Elsham in advance of the construction of the Humber Bridge approach road. Part of the cemetery lay under Middlegate Lane but it is likely that most of the site was excavated. Five inhumations and 625 cremations were found, with many urns being buried in the fill of a substantial prehistoric ditch. This excavation is not yet published but a report on the burnt bones was written by Mary Harman which the excavators kindly allowed me to use.

Cleatham

While Cleatham is the most recent cremation cemetery to be excavated in Lindsey, it was actually found before the other sites. In 1856 a road was being laid along the parish boundary between Kirton in Lindsey and Manton. Edward Trollope recorded that:

> …. the labourers suddenly turned up a group of dark-grey Saxon sepulchral urns, from fifty to sixty in number, greatly varying as to size and pattern, but filled with bones. From one of them (most unfortunately) a pair of brass tweezers were extracted, for as this article shone when cut with a knife, it was immediately pronounced by the finder to be gold, and the doom of the urns quickly followed, for henceforth they were dashed to pieces as soon as found, in the vain hope of finding more of such golden treasures.

This became known as the 'Kirton in Lindsey' cemetery although the site was actually over the parish boundary in the neighbouring parish of Manton. There might be a still earlier record of this cemetery as the 1616 Survey of the Soke of Kirton in Lindsey records that:

> One peece of waste lande there to buylde a melting hous (for ther hath bene sometimes a brasse mine as it seemeth) which piece is in length 30 yards and in bredth 30 yards granted to Thomas Sambye …

As the Cleatham site was covered with scraps of melted copper alloy this could have led the surveyor to think that the field had contained a 'brasse mine'.

The 'Kirton in Lindsey' cemetery was rediscovered in 1978 when it was found near Cleatham, a hamlet in the adjacent parish of Manton. A trial evaluation in 1979 showed that plough damage was pretty bad but a few urns had survived. A short obituary was written for the county journal and the matter rested. In following years it became clear that Cleatham was an important site. One of the urns from the 1856 find graced the front cover of J.N.L. Myres' 1969 volume *Anglo-Saxon Pottery and the Settlement of England* (*colour plate 5*) and my own interest in the Anglo-Saxon period grew. I also felt sorry for the site, we had to do something even if it was only to get a larger sample of sherds so in the August of 1984 we went back.

Cleatham was a brutally hard site. It was dug by volunteers who worked, sometimes in dreadful conditions, for no pay and with no on-site facilities. Yet when the sun shone, those long, late summer days were wonderful; no one who was there will ever forget the Cleatham excavation. The site was dug without the use of earth-moving machinery, the heavy soil being removed with picks and shovels thus avoiding the risk of an excavator blade damaging the urns, some of which barely penetrated the sub-soil. We could also collect sherds from the topsoil that were reunited with the bases from which they came.

In 1985 there was a change in agricultural practice with the farmer starting to deep-plough the field. As the cemetery was not going to survive we decided on total excavation. In the years that followed we extended our grid of 2m x 2m 'boxes' across the field following the scatter of urns. As it was vital to find the extent of the cemetery in all directions we dug beyond the edge of the main part of the cemetery and carried out intensive field walking. This showed that there were no concentrations of urns outside of the excavated area. Despite centuries of ploughing the distribution of sherds still reflected the shape of the cemetery as most of the sherds had not moved very far.

When digging finished in 1989 we had 1014 cremation burials from Cleatham but the analysis of the sherds found in the top-soil gave us a final total of 1204 urns (*9*). If we make an allowance for the destroyed urns along the southern limb of the cemetery, the graves and the '50 or 60' urns found in 1856, the Cleatham cemetery would have contained around 1528 burials. This makes Cleatham the third largest Anglo-Saxon cremation cemetery in England; after Spong Hill, Norfolk with *c*.2700 urns, followed by Loveden Hill, (Lincolnshire, but not Lindsey) with *c*.1700 urns. After Cleatham the next largest excavated cemetery is Elsham with 625 urns.

On most Anglo-Saxon cemetery sites the burials were treated in a respectful way, later interments taking place on the edges of the cemetery to avoid existing urns. Cleatham was not like that; the people who used it seemed to have a positive liking for planting their urns on top of earlier burials, usually wrecking them in the process. It is difficult to understand why they did this. It is hardly likely to

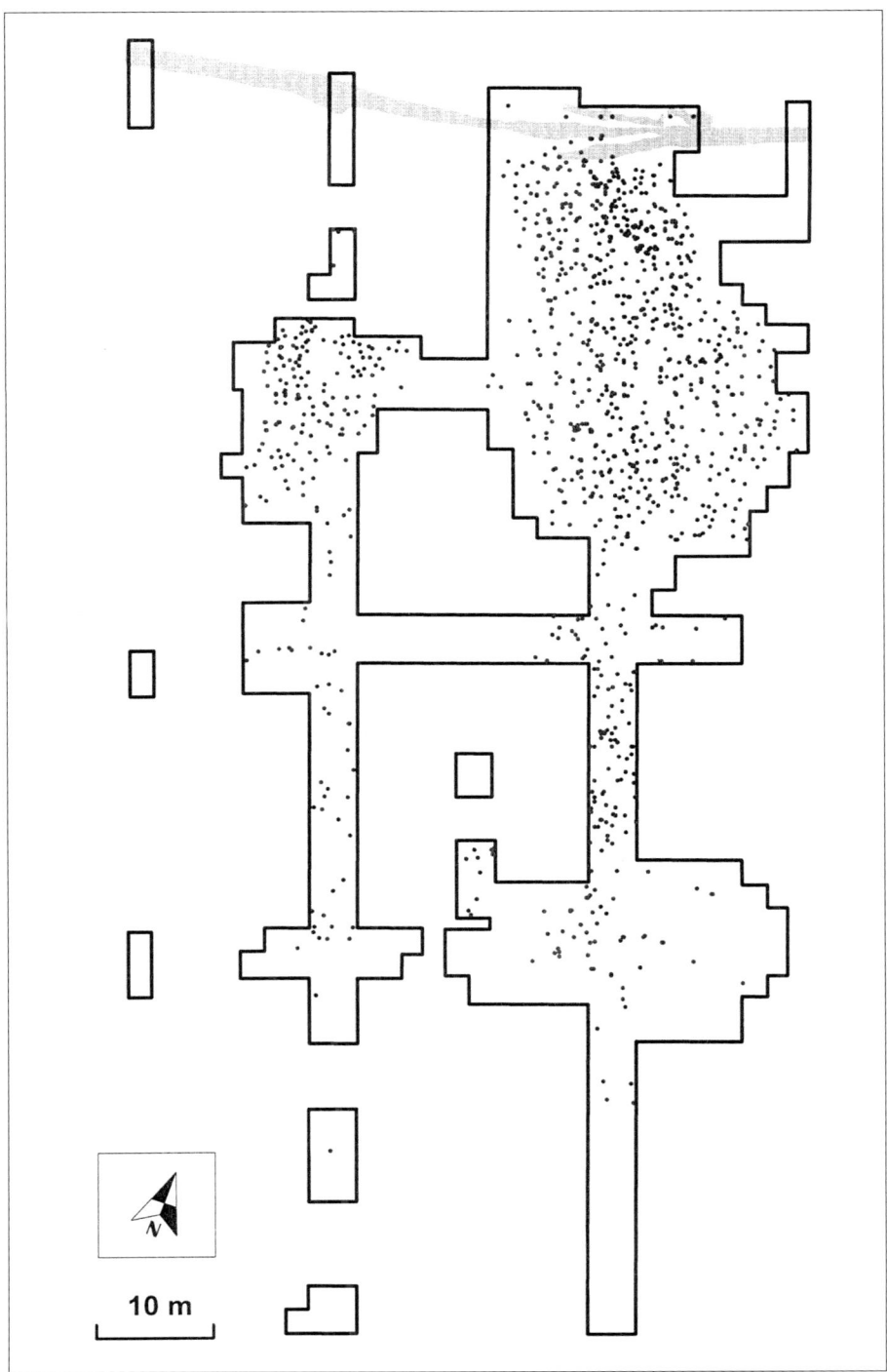

9 Plan of the urns found at the Cleatham Anglo-Saxon cemetery. *Digital mapping by Mike Hemblade*

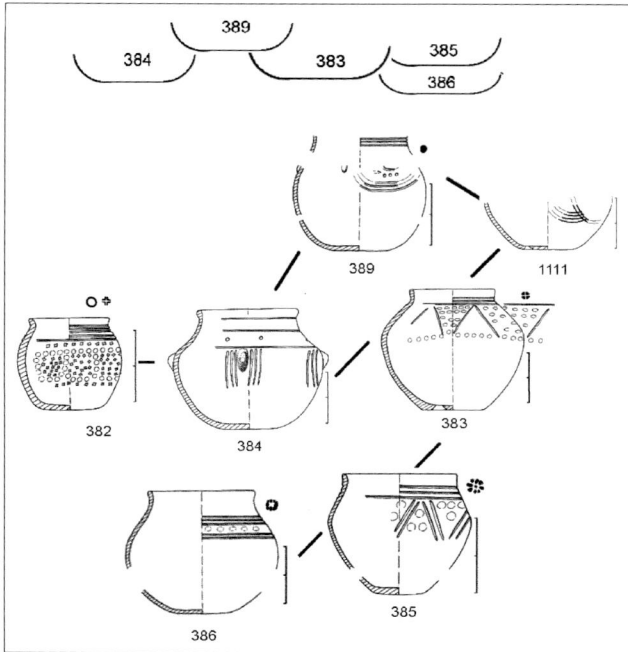

10 The interpretation of the group of intercut urns shown on *colour plate 3*. It can be seen that Urn 386 was cut by Urn 385 and both were then cut by Urn 383 and so on. These relationships are represented graphically on the lower diagram and are used to construct a matrix on which all the relationships are shown. *Drawings by Kevin Leahy*

have been accidental with up to seven urns cutting each other (*10*; *colour plate 3*). Many of the urns were covered with piles of stones that may have originally extended above the ground as a cairn; we should also remember the stone-covered area at South Elkington where, interestingly, Graham Webster reported the intercutting of urns. I feel what was happening was a mark of respect, rather than of contempt, expressing a need for families to be together in death as in life.

Other cremation cemeteries?

A lot of new inhumation cemeteries have been discovered, but there have been no new cremation cemeteries. These sites are highly distinctive and, apart from sherds, produce distinctive objects that could be found with a metal detector (copper-alloy melt and funerary tweezers). It seems likely that the four big cremation cemeteries are all that there ever were. It is possible that there was a fifth large cemetery at Bagmoor, Burton on Stather where 'Many urns' were said to have been found during ironstone mining in the 1920s, two of which survive. The size and composition of this cemetery is unknown although the discovery of an early axe of *francisca* type and a complete antler comb show that inhumations were present.

In addition to the large urn fields, Lindsey also contained small cremation cemeteries none of which have been excavated. In 1828 'more than 20 urns' were found along the line of a round barrow at Wold Newton, one of which survives. Single cremations are known from Burton Stather, where the urn may have been under a mound, and from Great Limber. Accounts of Anglo-Saxon cemeteries have sometimes been found in the most surprising places. I have a particular affection for a cemetery found in the pages of Edward Peacock's *North Lincolnshire Dialect Dictionary* which, when looking at the usage of the word 'REIGHTLIN COMB', quotes Mr John Manham of Bottesford:

> I once fun upo' th' top o' th' Holme Lordship a big broon pot, as I was digging
> for rabbits, bud when I opened it ther' was noht at all i' side but white ashes an' a
> peäsce o' an owd reightlin coämb

This delightful example of dialect records what can only have been an Anglo-Saxon cinerary urn with its cremation and a bone comb.

THE URNS

Anglo-Saxon cremation urns are amongst the most highly decorated pots made in antiquity. They were handmade with varying degrees of competence and, while some are plain, others bear a bewildering range of decoration: cut lines, stamp impressions, raised and applied bosses. They have been recognised as Anglo-Saxon since 1855 when, by comparing English urns with pots from northern Europe, J.M. Kemble was able to link them with the historically known Anglo-Saxons. He thought that the cremations were pagan burials and the inhumations Christian; a nice idea which, unfortunately, wasn't true. The chronology of the urns is crucial for our understanding of the Early Anglo-Saxon period and much effort has gone into determining it. It seems that Cleatham has now given us the key.

It is the intercutting of urns at Cleatham which allowed them to be sequenced; if one urn cuts through another it has to be later in date (*10*). If two urns are found side by side in the same pit it is likely that they were buried together and must be contemporary. By plotting out all of these relationships to build a 'matrix' it was possible to place the styles of urn decoration into five phases (*11, 12*). Attempts have been made in the past to date urns by their shape but this was found not to work, as urns of widely different shapes were found together and were clearly in use at the same time.

Importantly, once the urns were sequenced then so too were the grave goods found with them; the brooches, combs and beads, which allowed us to look at

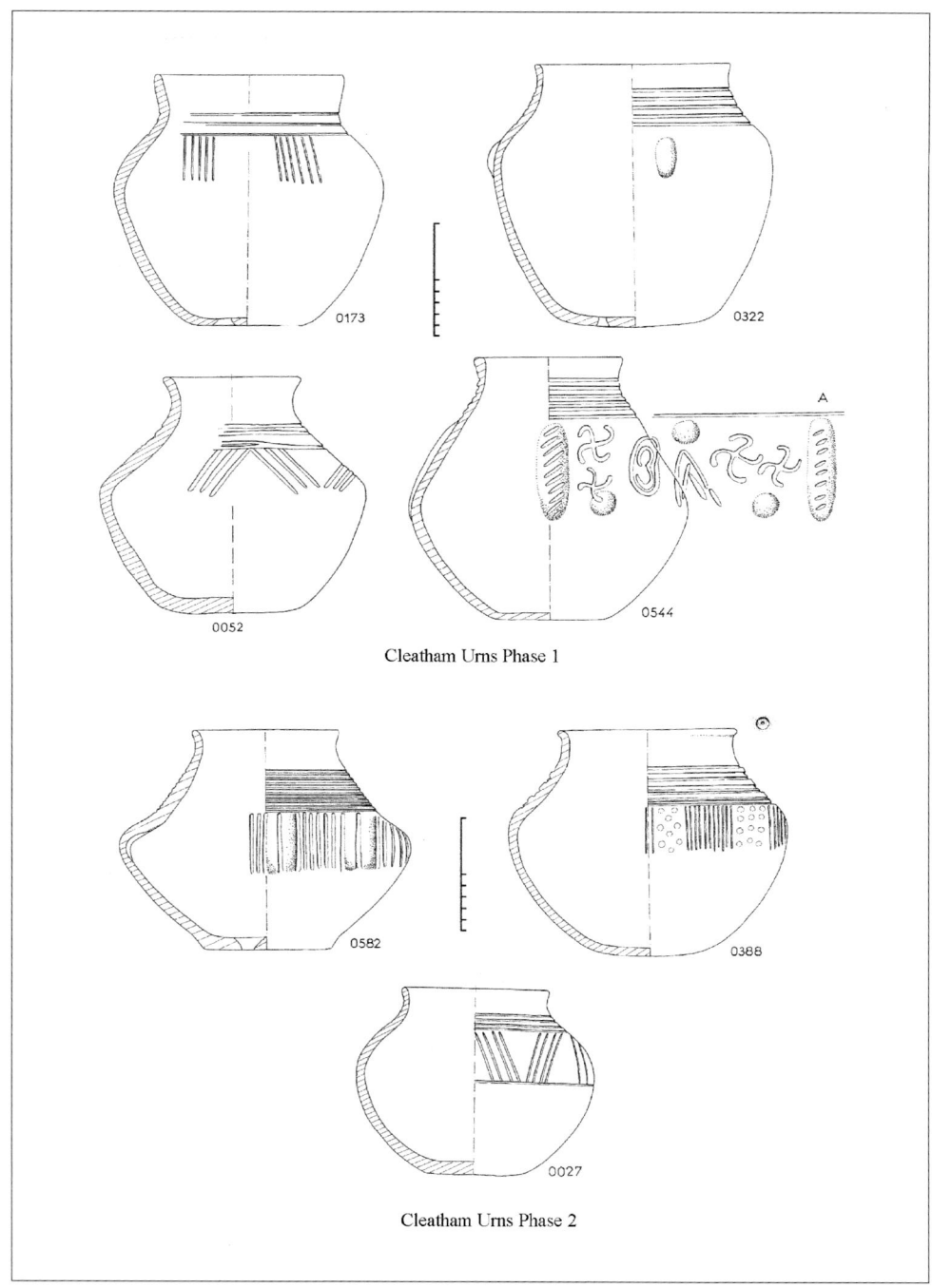

Cleatham Urns Phase 1

Cleatham Urns Phase 2

11 Decorated urns from Cleatham Phases 1 and 2. *Drawings by Kevin Leahy*

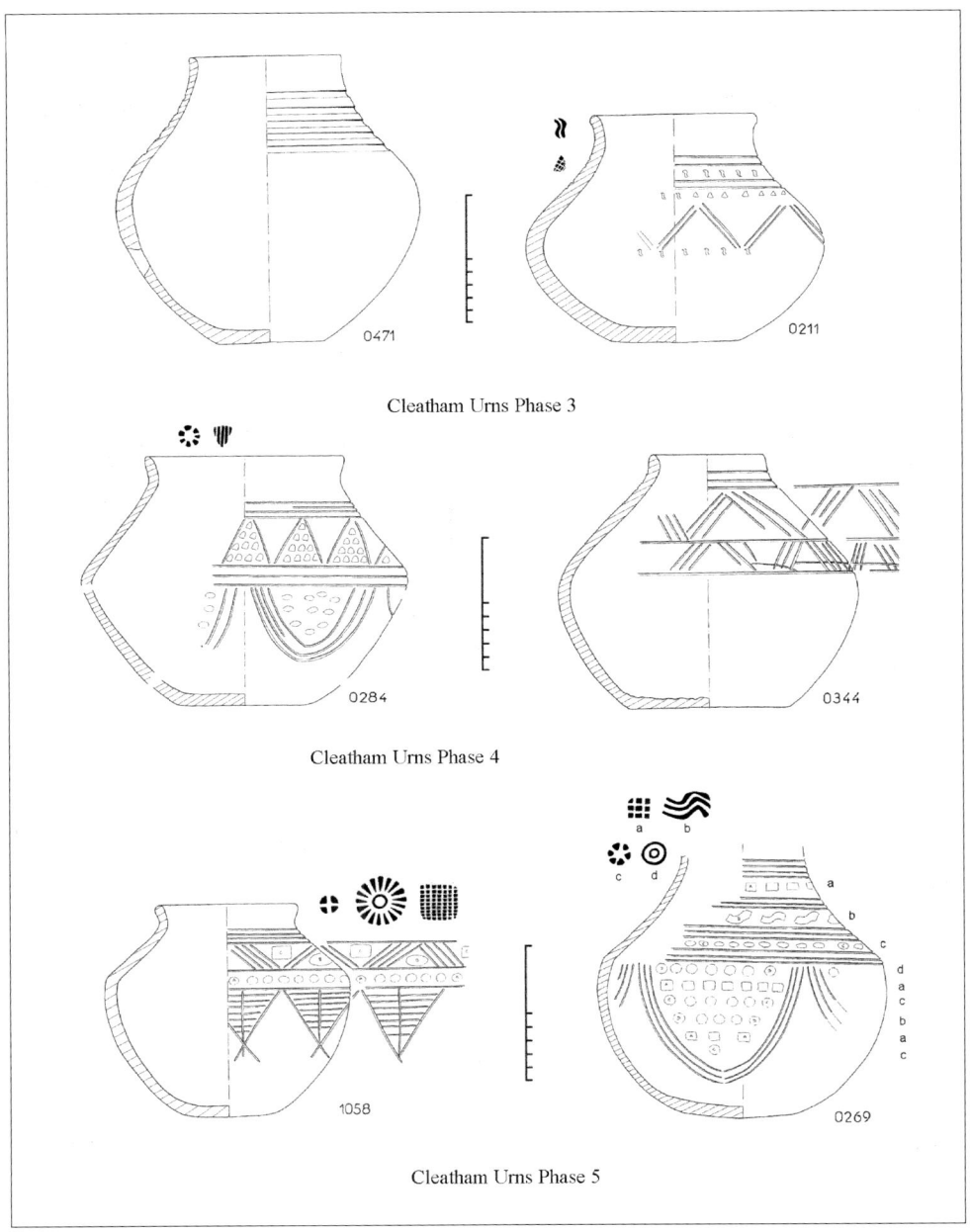

12 Decorated urns from Cleatham Phases 3–5. *Drawings by Kevin Leahy*

how the use and form of these objects changed over the course of the Early Anglo-Saxon period. This seems to work well; objects considered to be early were found in Phase 1 and objects thought to be late were towards the end of the sequence. Early 'barred' combs (*14*, Urn 458) are found in Phase 1 and Phase 2. Blue glass beads were also considered to be early and were most common in the early phases but unfortunately, they never went away and were found in the occasional urn in Phase 5. Problems exist: we don't know how much time elapsed between successive depositions and, while the sequence of urns works well, none of the phases is actually dated – when was Phase 1? It could have been as early as 420 or as late as 500. It is hoped that we will eventually be able to get high precision radiocarbon dates and finally discover when the Anglo-Saxons arrived.

FINDS FROM THE URNS

Anglo-Saxon urns contain two basic types of finds; grave goods, which were on the body as it was burned and grave-side offerings, which were placed, unburnt, in the urn by the mourners. Brooches, beads, sleeve clasps and counters were always burnt but toilet implements, tweezers, shears and razors, which are common, were never burnt (*13*, *14*, *15*). Many urns contain fragments (sometimes only a single tooth) of unburnt bone combs (*13*, Urn 288.03) although we sometimes get burnt combs as well. All of these toilet items seem to point to the Anglo-Saxons having an interest in personal grooming, shaving (*13*, Urn 961.02), plucking (*14*, Urn 598.01) and combing. The comb also had a more ritualistic meaning: at a later date a decorated ivory comb was placed in the grave of St Cuthbert. A ritual use of combs is also suggested by miniature combs (*15*, Urn 930) and we must remember that the removal of hair and eyebrows is a sign of mourning in some cultures, which might explain the tweezers. Some urns contain what appear to be amulets (*15*) and 'found' objects, like sherds of Roman pottery and the fossil (*14*, Urn 364.01). Unburnt wire finger-rings were found in one urn (*25*). Many urns contain the burnt remains of the bone, stone or pottery spindle whorls that acted as the flywheels on drop spindles (*14*, Urn 509.01) and we also see the occasional pin-beater, the tool used to beat up the threads on a loom. Other than weaving implements, tools are rare in Anglo-Saxon burials; weapons occur with inhumations but not with cremations. Some finds relate to pastimes: burnt bone counters (which are likely to have been used in a board game or for divination) were placed in some urns (*13*, Urn 265.03-06). We get the occasional knife found as an offering and whetstones, for sharpening, are also found, unburnt. The whetstone, too, could have a ritual meaning.

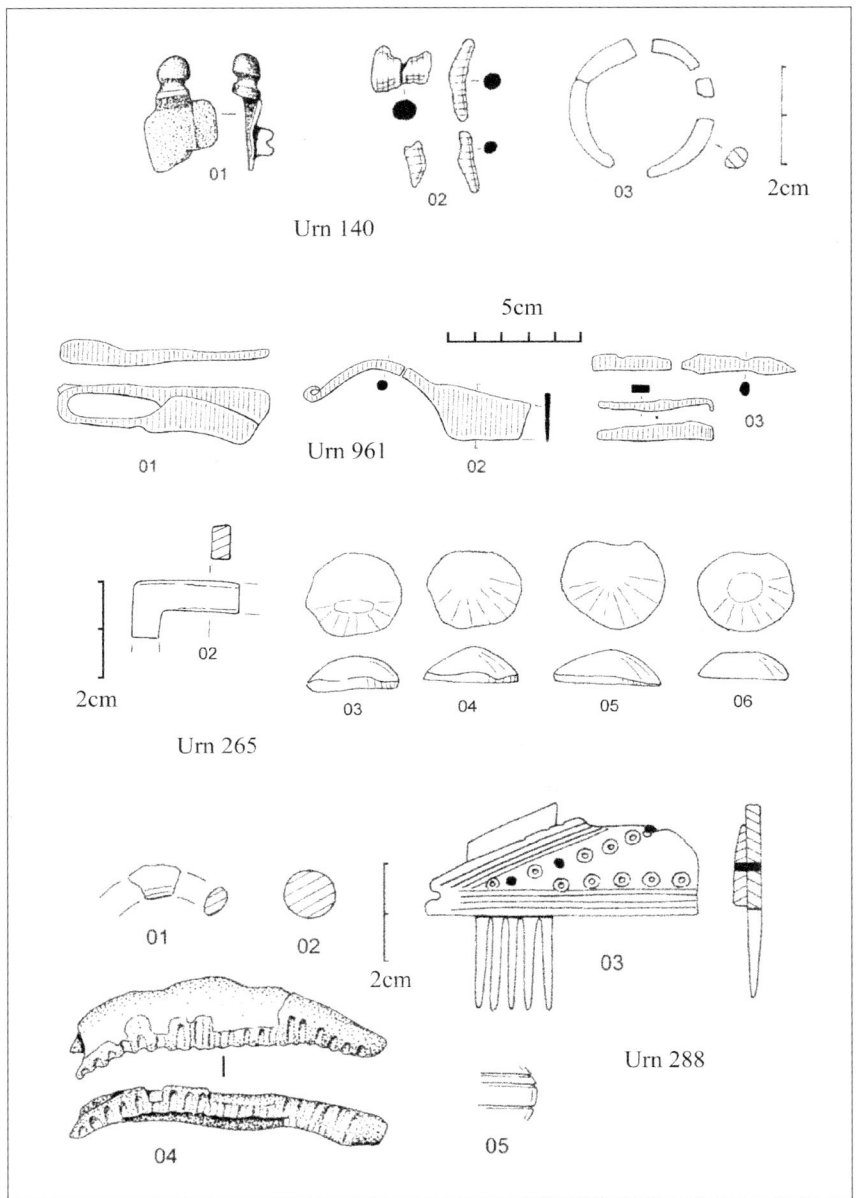

13 Typical finds from the Cleatham urns:
   Urn 140, 01 Åberg Group I cruciform brooch; 02 iron brooch pin; 03 bone ring, (all burnt)
   Urn 961, 01 iron shears; 02 iron razor; 03 iron tweezers fragments (not burnt)
   Urn 265, 02 bone buckle fragment; 03-06 bone counters (burnt)
   Urn 288, 01 bone ring fragment; 02 ivory ring fragment; 03 antler comb fragment; 04 cowrie shell; 05 antler spindle whorl fragment (all burnt except 03)
Drawings by Kevin Leahy

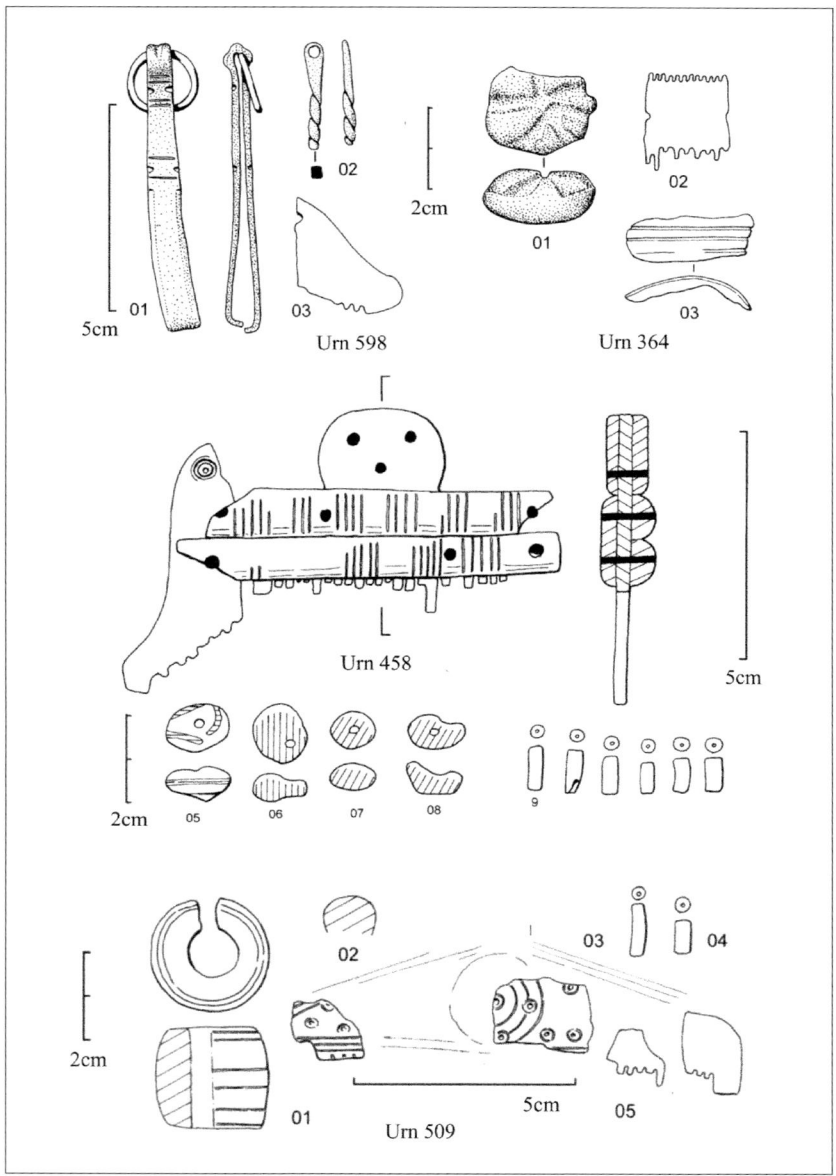

14 More finds from the Cleatham urns:
Urn 598, 01 copper alloy tweezers; 02 copper alloy toilet implement (fragment); 03 antler comb fragment (none burnt)
Urn 364, 01 fossil echinoid; 02 antler comb fragment; 03 antler spindle whorl fragment (01 and 03 burnt)
Urn 458, 01 antler comb; 05–08 glass beads; 09 coral beads (all burnt except 01)
Urn 509, 01 antler spindle whorl; 02 ivory ring fragment; 03-04 coral beads; 05 antler comb (all burnt)
Drawings by Kevin Leahy

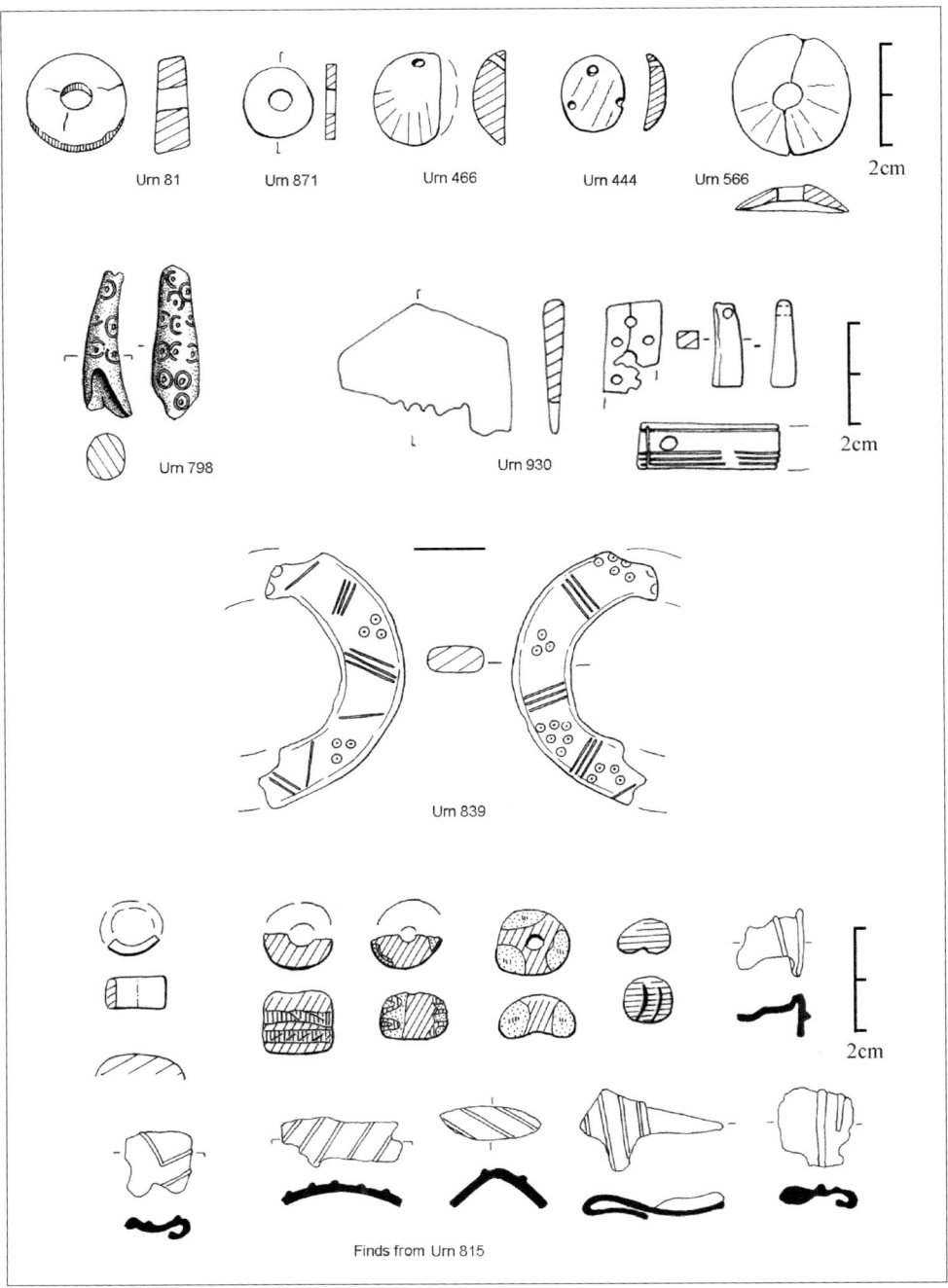

15 Still more finds from the Cleatham urns. Top row: votive pendants, all antler or bone (all burnt). Second row: Urn 798 antler 'Hercules club' pendant, burnt; Urn 930, miniature antler comb, two antler plates and a club pendant (all burnt); Urn 839, decorated ring, votive? (burnt); Urn 815, coloured glass beads (red, green, blue and yellow) and fragments of a glass 'Kempston type' beaker (all burnt). *Drawings by Kevin Leahy*

Some of the finds from the cremation urns had travelled a long way. Coral beads and cowrie shells, both of which came from the Indian Ocean, were found in urns at Cleatham and Elsham (*14*, Urn 509.03-04; *13*, Urn 288.04). Small cowries live in British waters but the large *Cypraea Pantherina* found at Cleatham must be imports. Burnt ivory was common in the urns at Cleatham and Elsham, although often only a small fragment was present. The ivory is likely to have come from Africa and formed part of rings used to support the mouths of leather or textile bags (*25*, 6). This trade would have not been direct and the coral, cowries and ivory would have passed through many hands before reaching Lindsey.

Grave goods were common at Cleatham and were found in 63.4 per cent of the urns. This is similar to Elsham where 64.9 per cent of the urns contained finds. At South Elkington grave goods were found in only 22 per cent of the urns and none of the 21 urns from West Keal contained grave goods. Cleatham and Elsham are, with Spong Hill, Norfolk (63.7 per cent) the richest cremation cemeteries, with Millgate, Newark (59 per cent) not far behind. The reason for the low number of finds at South Elkington and West Keal is not known. It may relate to the early date of the excavation and a failure to recognise comb fragments (none were recorded although they are common elsewhere) but some easily recognised objects like burnt glass beads are also less common. At Cleatham 27.9 per cent of the urns contained glass beads compared with 7.7 per cent at South Elkington. While the communities using West Keal may have been less prosperous than elsewhere, the lack of grave goods may only reflect a difference in burial practice.

CEMETERY LOCATIONS

The locations of cremation cemeteries may tell us something about the Early Anglo-Saxon settlement of Lindsey (*8*). The four large cemeteries appear to be equi-spaced, Cleatham on the limestone at the northern end of Lincoln Edge, Elsham on the northern chalk Wolds, South Elkington on the clay of the southern Wolds and West Keal on the southern edge of the Wolds. It is possible that these large cemeteries represent regional burial places, used by early folk-groupings, during the settlement period, before they coalesced to form the Kingdom of Lindsey. On the other hand, the pots and the material found in them, do look uniform and there are some clear links between the cemeteries.

Most of the cemetery sites have panoramic views over the countryside and command the landscape. The South Elkinton cemetery is on Acthorpe Top, a hill with fine views across to the sea. The cemetery at West Keal is on Hall

Hill, a spur dominating the flat fens, with a superb view to the south. From Cleatham it is possible to see across to the Trent Valley and beyond. The exception is Elsham from which the view is relatively limited. The cemeteries are all on marginal or poor quality land, Cleatham on a nasty calcareous brown earth, South Elkington on a vile clay and Elsham and West Keal on sand. This is not surprising; why give up good farm land to the dead who can't use it?

Cemeteries on boundaries

Significantly three of the cemeteries lie on parish boundaries: South Elkington lies between South Elkington and Louth, Cleatham between Manton and Kirton in Lindsey, and West Keal on the boundary between Bolingbroke and West Keal. The positioning of Anglo-Saxon burial sites on parish boundaries has been noticed elsewhere and Anne Goodier found that 17.9 per cent of cemeteries lie within 100m of a parish boundary. This is unlikely to be coincidental but we can only speculate as to why it was done; was it to keep the dead as far away from the settlement as possible? The cemeteries may have been set as sentinels; the unsleeping dead might put off intruders. The system of parishes as we now know it mostly dates from the later Saxon period but many boundaries can be very old indeed, some pre-dating the Romans.

Cleatham is also near the boundary between the wapentakes of Manley and Corringham. Wapentakes are large territorial divisions (Lindsey was divided into 18 wapentakes) which formed part of the Anglo-Scandinavian administrative system, though are likely to reflect an earlier system. Cleatham was one of three townships in the parish of Manton, the others being Twigmore and Manton itself, both of which were in Manley wapentake. Cleatham was in the neighbouring Corringham wapentake, along with Kirton in Lindsey. The inclusion of Cleatham with Kirton in Lindsey is unlikely to be coincidental. At Domesday Kirton in Lindsey was a major manorial (soke) centre with a large number of subsidiary estates. Interestingly, Cleatham is not the only cremation cemetery to be located near to an important administrative centre; South Elkington is adjacent to Louth, and West Keal to Bolingbroke. Elsham is close to the important manorial site and soke centre at Barnetby le Wold. It seems that the locations of the large cremation cemeteries retained their importance into the Late Saxon and High Medieval periods.

Cemeteries on ancient sites

Many Anglo-Saxons cemeteries lie on, or near, pre-existing monuments, both Roman and prehistoric, a topic on which Howard Williams has done extensive work. The reasons for the re-use of existing sites are probably complex but they may have emphasised the ownership of the land by showing domination over earlier inhabitants. There may have been a Bronze Age barrow on the site of the Cleatham cemetery. Edward Trollope, in his published account of the 1856 find wrote: 'Mr Richardson, in making a road on his land, had occasion to cut through a slightly rising mound …'. He went on to add: 'On the northern side of the vases (urns) a quantity of stones were found – perhaps connected with the *Ustrina* and above them from 4 to 5 feet of soil had been heaped to form a tumulus'. No sign of this mound was found during the 1980s excavations. At Elsham many of the urn pits had been cut into the fill of a large prehistoric ditch. Two late Neolithic beakers found during the Elsham excavation are likely to have come from a denuded burial mound. One side of the Castledyke inhumation cemetery was marked by a large prehistoric ditch.

The relationship between the cemeteries and Lincoln

The relationship between the cremation cemeteries and the city of Lincoln may reflect the process by which Lindsey was settled by the Anglo-Saxons. Unlike other Romano-British towns and cities in eastern England, Lincoln has no Anglo-Saxon cremation cemeteries in its hinterland. This might be explained by the city (or whatever sub-Roman power controlled the city) being able to control its surroundings in the fifth and early sixth centuries. The lacuna extends to the south of the city, there being no cremation cemeteries closer than Loveden Hill, 25km to the south, supporting the idea that Lincoln once controlled an area to the south of the city, perhaps part of its original Roman *territorium*. There are inhumation cemeteries near to Lincoln but these date to the sixth century. Elsewhere in Lindsey we do have some evidence for Early Anglo-Saxon burials close to fortified sites; the Fonaby cemetery, which is 2km to the north of Caistor, contains some early cremation burials.

LINKS BETWEEN CREMATION CEMETERIES

Regional 'potters'

Most of the urns found in Lindsey can be paralleled anywhere in Anglian England but some pots had more direct and interesting links. A number of regional 'potters' whose work occurs at more than one site have been recognised in Anglo-Saxon England. One of the first to be identified was the Sancton-Elkington potter, whose work was identified at Sancton, near Market Weighton in the East Riding of Yorkshire (then in the kingdom of Deira) and South Elkington in Lindsey. In recent years further linked pots have also been found at Cleatham (*11*, Urn 544) and Elsham. While these pots are stylistically similar it is more likely that they represent a regional style rather than the work of the same potter. A much more convincing case can be made for the Sancton-Baston

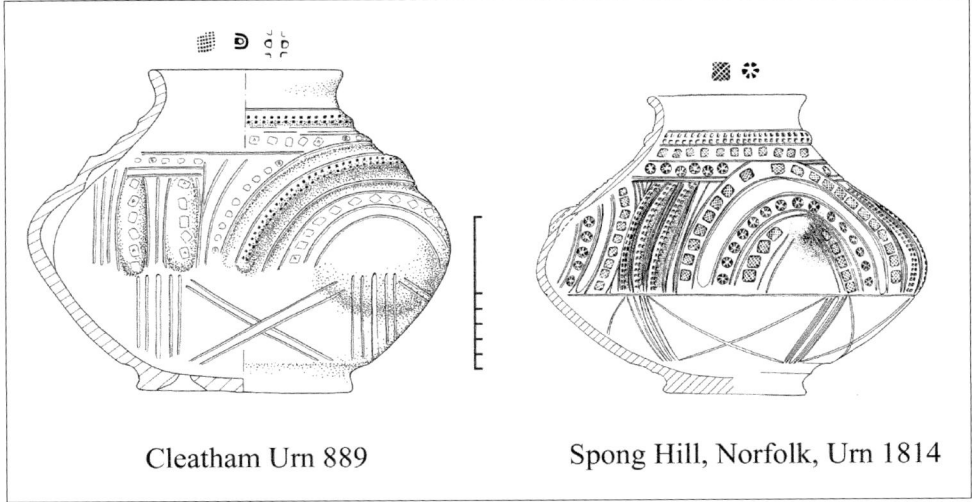

Cleatham Urn 889   Spong Hill, Norfolk, Urn 1814

16 Cleatham Urn 889 and Spong Hill Urn 1814. Although found 138km apart these vessels are identical and must have been made by the same person. *Cleatham Urn 889 by Kevin Leahy, Spong Hill Urn 1814 © Norfolk Historic Environment, Norfolk Museums and Archaeology Service*

potter whose neatly executed work occurs at Sancton, Cleatham, Elsham, and Baston, Lincolnshire, 130km to the south of Sancton. These were made using the same stamp dies but the urns were made in different pot fabrics (see below) suggesting that it was the dies that were being moved, not the finished pots. Some pots, however, appear to have been transported over long distances; Cleatham Urn 889, a highly decorated and finely made vessel, is almost identical to Urns 1814 and 2112 from Spong Hill, 137km to the south, and is likely to have been made by the same person (*16*).

There is other evidence for inter-regional links during the Early Anglo-Saxon period. All pot-fabrics contain additives (temper or filler) that make the clay easier to work and give greater strength to the finished pot. Additives include sand, limestone, sea-shell and organic materials like grass and chaff. Some pots have been found to contain crushed igneous (volcanic) rock that John Walker found to have come from Charnwood Forest near Leicester. Alan Vince and Jane Young have found pots with this Charnwood filler over a wide area of the East Midlands, including Lindsey. At Riby it was found that Charnwood pottery remained in use until the early part of the eighth century. The way in which this pottery was distributed is difficult to understand; was it finished pots or crushed rock that was 'traded'? The picture is further complicated by the discovery of acid igneous rock in both Bronze Age and Iron Age pottery which could suggest that it was a formidably ancient practice, or that igneous rock is present in the clay.

Many of the Cleatham urns contained crushed iron slag which must be linked to the 'Cinder Hills', the slag heaps that once covered fields in the parishes of Kirton in Lindsey and Manton. Pottery found around the slag points to their being Anglo-Saxon. Iron was being smelted in the area during the Roman period and slag is most common in the early urns at Cleatham, which could point to continuity. The iron deposits (probably bog-iron from Manton Warren) may have attracted Early Anglo-Saxon settlers to this location and led to the siting of the Cleatham cemetery. Unlike igneous rock, slag does not appear to have been widely used at the other cemetery sites in Lindsey; the only example seems to be the remarkable 'feeding bottle' from the Castledyke, Barton on Humber cemetery, which was made in a slagged fabric (*colour plate 5*).

The work of the regional 'potters' and the widespread use of pottery containing acid igneous rock suggests that there was an unsuspected degree of interchange between the peoples of Anglian England. This perhaps should not surprise us; the same types and styles of metalwork were used across Anglian England with similar brooches and sleeve clasps appearing in sites as far apart as Suffolk and Cleveland.

ROMAN FINDS FROM CLEATHAM

Amongst the hundreds of pots found at Cleatham were four that were clearly different as they had been made using a potter's wheel and looked Roman (*17*). In other respects they appeared to be Anglo-Saxon urns, two of them contained iron toilet sets and another, which lacked grave goods, had a lead plug in its side. It was possible to place one of them in Cleatham Phase 2, showing that they were not just used in the first years of the cemetery's use. Roman pots have been found used as Anglo-Saxon urns elsewhere in England and it had been assumed that they were simply Roman pots, found and reused. The Romano-British cremation cemetery at Gilliate's Grave, 2.5 km to the north of Cleatham, was an obvious source but none of the pots looked anything like the 'Roman' urns from Cleatham and we had to look elsewhere.

When a parallel was found it came, not from a Roman site, but from the Millgate, Newark Anglo-Saxon cemetery where Urn 262 was very similar to the Cleatham pots. A second parallel was found at Great Casterton, Rutland in a destruction layer dated by coins to after 375. The opinion was sought of a regional Roman pottery specialist who thought that the way in which the pots were made was clearly Roman but that the shape was wrong; the vessels' broad profiles looked more Anglo-Saxon. There was also something odd in the pot fabrics used; Roman potters used a fairly standard mix for their clay,

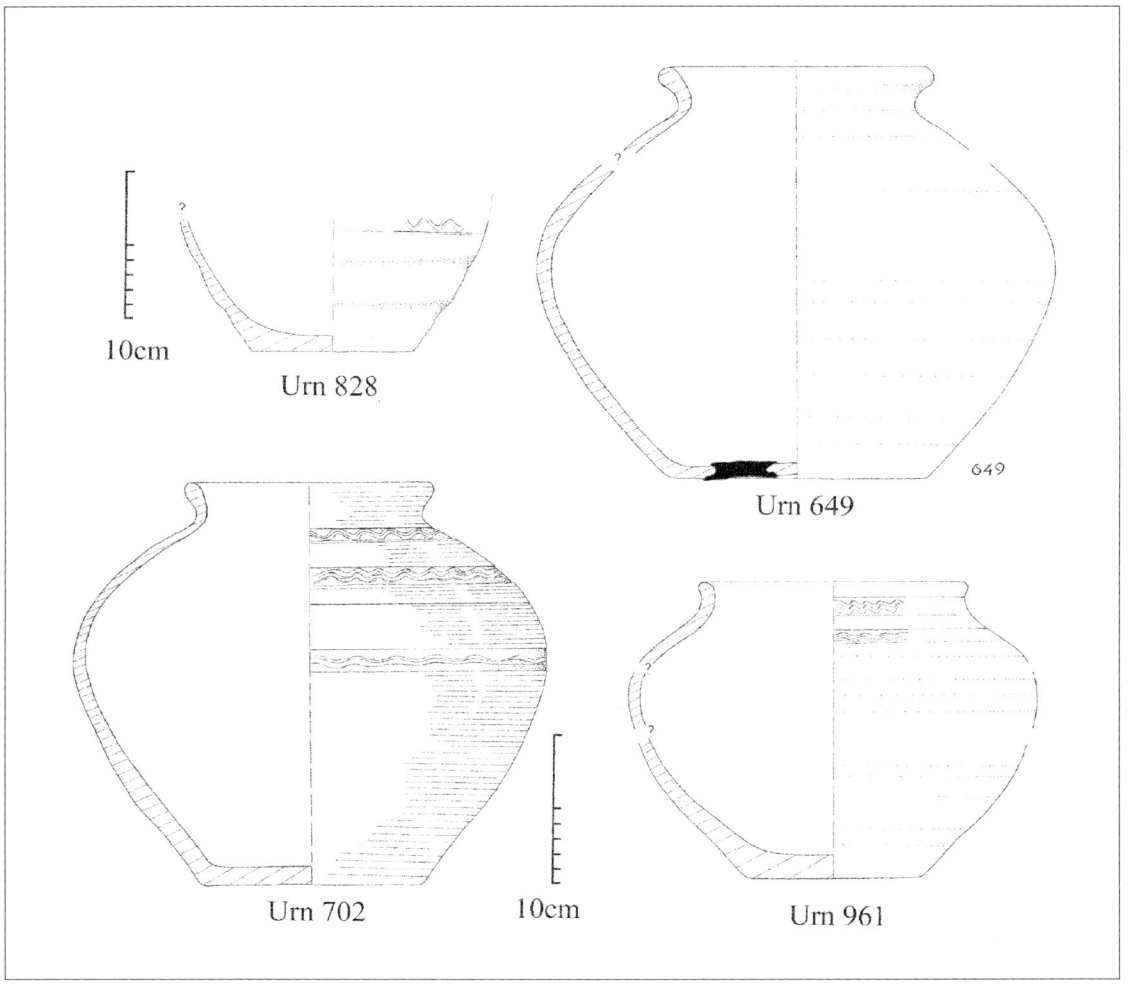

17 'Roman'-type pots found at Cleatham. When discovered these pots contained Anglo-Saxon cremations with typical grave goods. Urn 649 was fitted with a lead plug. Urn 702 was cut by other urns and could be placed in Phase 2 at Cleatham. *Drawings by Kevin Leahy*

a mix that they knew and was predictable. The Cleatham pots are all in different fabrics – the potters were no longer making the number of pots to call for standardisation. These pots probably represent the end of the Romano-British pottery industry around the middle of the fifth century. This is not a revolutionary suggestion; it would have been more surprising if the industry had stopped dead. For a while the kilns would have continued to make pots for a local market but eventually it would have not been thought worthwhile to pass on the skills and the end came. Other links may exist between Cleatham and

Newark; the great soke of Kirton in Lindsey may have originally extended south to include Newark.

Pots are not the only Roman objects to come from Anglo-Saxon cemeteries. Pendants, made from Roman coins with holes drilled through them, are not uncommon. Holes were not drilled through coins in Roman times and it can be assumed that any perforated Roman coin has seen use as an Anglo-Saxon pendant. These coins were not coming from any sort of residual circulation; at Caistor they included a brass coin of Claudius which would have been 400 years old when used as a pendant. Other Roman finds from the Cleatham cemetery include tiles and blocks of masonry from a nearby villa, used to cover the urns and placed in some of the graves. The number of sherds of Roman pottery found inside the Cleatham urns is surprising as it is otherwise not common on the site. At Castledyke unspectacular sherds of Roman pottery were found in 14 of the graves – too many for it to be coincidental – and at the Nettleton Top Anglo-Saxon settlement a concentration of Roman sherds was found on the sunken floors of buildings. It is difficult to know what these finds mean; the sherds were being collected and placed with the burials on purpose, perhaps to link the dead to perceived better times.

In view of the importance given to late Roman belt fittings (above) it is disappointing that none has been found in any of Lindsey's Anglo-Saxon cemeteries. Elsewhere in the country 31 buckles have been found in Anglo-Saxon graves: 16 were found with females and 11 with males; the remainder were undetermined. It was also found that in Lindsey there is no correlation between the buckles and the distribution of Early Anglo-Saxon cemeteries (*4*, cf *8*). There is a concentration of late Roman metalwork at Kirmington, 5km to the east of the Elsham cemetery, and a find from Hibaldstow, 3.5km to the east of Cleatham but no convincing pattern exists. This, in itself, may be telling us something; these belt fittings had nothing to do with the Early Anglo-Saxon cemeteries which represented a new and different phenomenon.

RITUALS ASSOCIATED WITH THE URNS

Most of the urns used in the cremation cemeteries were specially made for funerary use and, as Julian Richards found in his study of Early Anglo-Saxon pottery, there was a link between the urns and the person placed within them. At Cleatham the tallest urns contained most grave goods but without a report on the burnt bone it is not possible to say more than that. The best examples of urns being specially made for the individual interred within them are the Cleatham horse burials with their horse-shoe-shaped stamps (*18*). Decorated

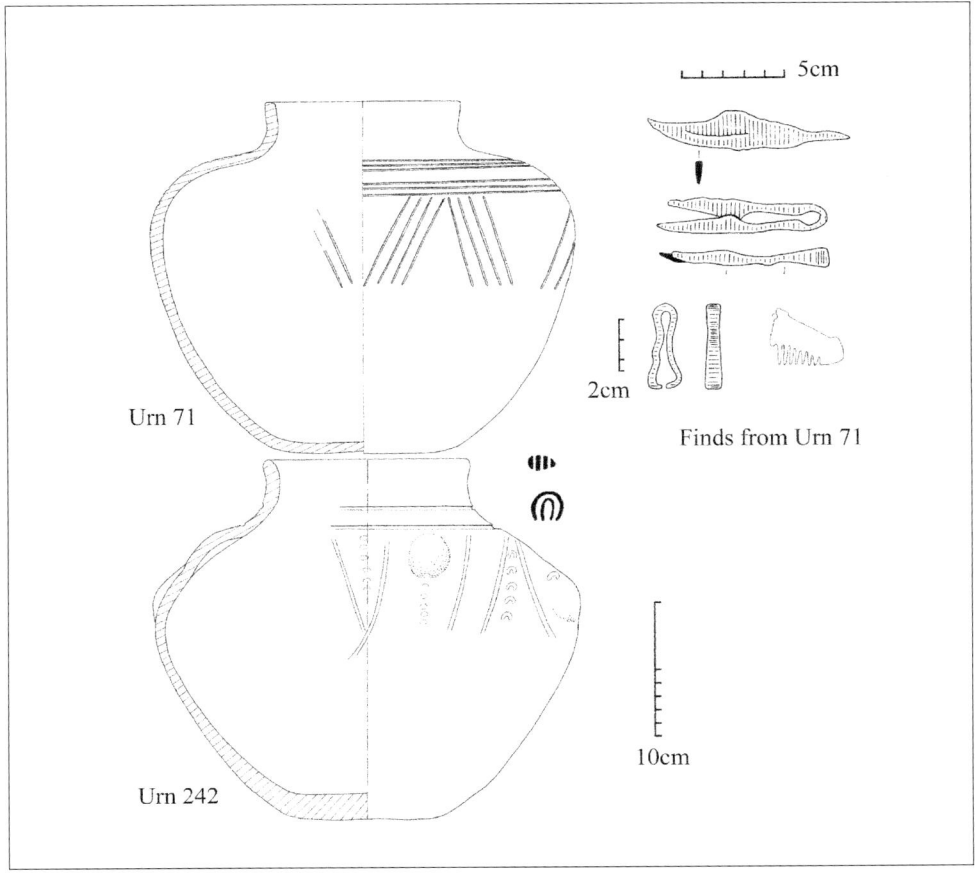

18 Double burial from Cleatham. Urn 71 was found standing on top of Urn 242 and contained burnt bones and an iron toilet set. Urn 262 contained a mass of bone from a large animal the identity of which is suggested by the stamps used to decorate it! *Drawings by Kevin Leahy*

pottery is uncommon on settlement sites; only 2.9 per cent (10/336) of the Early Anglo-Saxon sherds from Riby were decorated, a similar proportion being found on other settlement sites. Many burials were in plain pots which looked like domestic vessels, often with a band of soot around them showing that they had been used over a fire. A common practice was to chip holes through the sides or bases of urns, some having five perforations, leaving a base consisting mainly of holes. The hole was sometimes filled with molten lead to form a plug, this was not a repair but a deliberate act that is also found at the Gilliate's Grave Romano-British cemetery in second century urns. Still more strange are 'window urns' which have been found at Cleatham and Elsham. Here, the holes have small pieces of glass fitted into them to form a window. Many urns had grains of barley incorporated into the clay before the pot was fired. Burnt grain was found in the fill of some of the Castledyke graves.

With the urns and their burnt contents we are probably looking at a small part of a complex ritual activity involving the agonies of loss and bereavement, possibly coupled with a fear of the dead (*colour plate 4*). The cremation process was skilfully carried out with all of the organic material being burnt out of the bones leaving them white, unlike the Roman cremations at Gilliate's Grave which had dark grey cores. While it would have been easy to recover the burnt brooches and beads from the pyre site, it is remarkable that the tiny coral beads were found amongst the ashes. The study of the urns and finds from Cleatham has now been completed but no report has been done on the burnt bone which could tell us so much.

Animal bones in the urns
We also cannot assume that all of the bones in the urns are human. Animal bones were found with the human remains in 122 of the Elsham urns and six of the urns contained only animal bones (horse or perhaps ox). Sheep bones were the most common, being found in 48 of the urns; horse bone, found in 25 of the urns, was the next most common, followed by pig, 15 urns, and cattle in 12. It could not be determined which of remaining 10 were horse and which were cattle. The bones often came from the animal's head or legs suggesting that these were not choice cuts of meat. Bear phalanges were found in two urns and it is likely that they came from paws attached to bearskin cloaks or rugs.

Two of the Cleatham urns contained the burnt remains of horses. Urn 242 was found directly below Urn 71, a big, fine pot that contained a toilet set consisting of iron tweezers, shears and razor suggesting that it held the remains of a man (*18*). Beneath it, Urn 242 held 4500g of bones from a very large animal, almost certainly a horse. The stamp decoration on this pot consisted of horse-shoe-shaped impressions showing it had been purposely made for its occupant. Urn 639 had been placed on the top of a mass of large bones, again almost certainly from a horse. With the bones was an iron object which is difficult to identify but it could plausibly be argued that it was a fitting from a wooden saddle. Like Urn 242 this vessel was stamp decorated but in this case the stamps were in the form of a horse's foot-print with the frog in the middle of the hoof clearly shown.

The inhumation cemeteries

Cremation was the most common burial rite during the early part of the Anglo-Saxon settlement of Lindsey but we also have some early inhumations. Grave 9 at Cleatham contained an early brooch but no urn fragments, showing that the cemetery was relatively clear of urns when the burial took place. Whenever a relationship existed at Cleatham, the later graves always cut into the earlier urns; 29 of the Cleatham graves contained urn fragments or the remains of cremation burials destroyed in the digging of the grave. From the last quarter of the fifth century, cremation was increasingly supplemented by, and later replaced with, inhumation. It is not known why this happened but it follows a move away from cremation in Anglian England, described by Myres as 'the flight from cremation', perhaps influenced by rites which were predominant in southern England. Inhumation is the simpler rite; cremation involved collecting the dry wood and building and tending the pyre, a grave was often a disgracefully shallow hole. The grave goods found with the two rites are similar showing a considerable overlap between them. Fragments of late 'Florid' cruciform brooches and cowrie shells were found in Cleatham urns showing that the rite remained in use at least to the mid-sixth century.

Inhumation cemeteries are much more common than urn fields but tend to contain far fewer burials, most containing less than 100 graves (*29*). These are likely to represent family, rather than community, cemeteries. To date, 43 inhumation cemeteries have been found in Lindsey, of which six have been excavated. Many of the others are known only from antiquarian references or metal detector finds (*19*). Excavations have been carried out at Castledyke South, Barton on Humber (excavated 1989 and 1990, 196 excavated graves); Fonaby, near Caistor (excavated 1956-8, 49 identified graves); Sheffield's Hill I, Roxby (excavated 1993-1998, 43 graves) and Welbeck Hill, Irby on Humber (excavated 1962-1979, 72 graves). Graves were found during the laying of a pipeline at

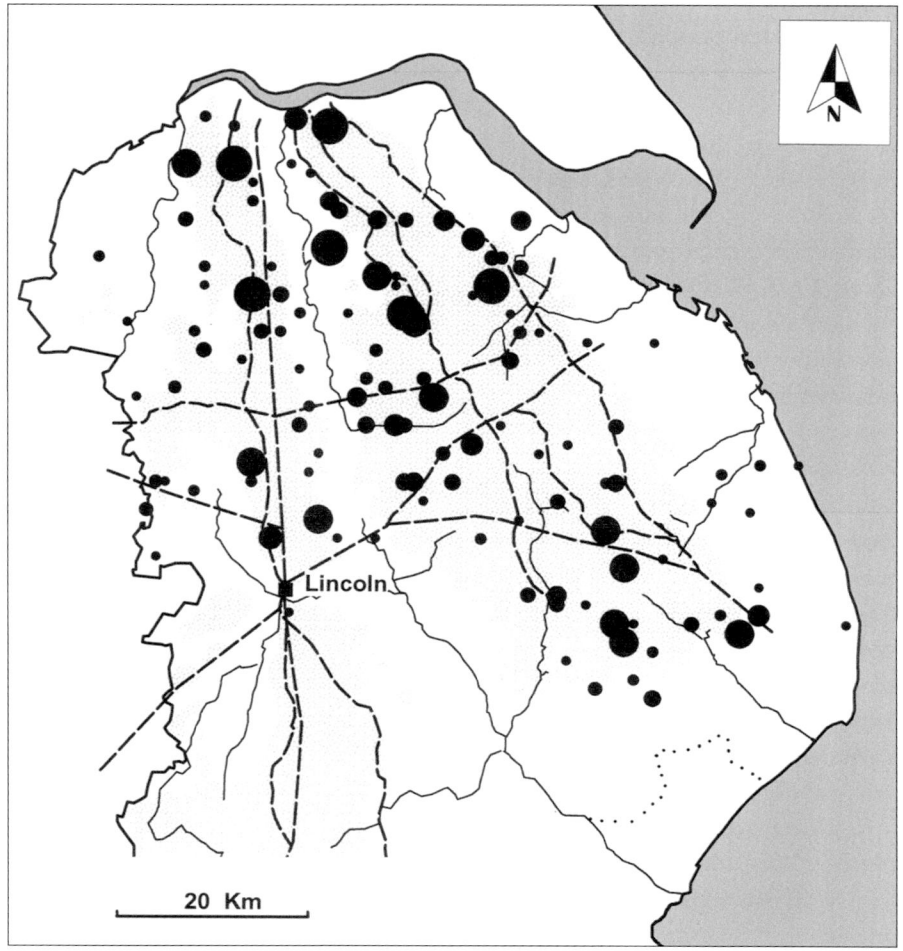

19 The distribution of early Anglo-Saxon finds in Lindsey. This includes all finds coming both from excavations and those recorded by the Portable Antiquities Scheme. *Digital mapping by Mike Hemblade*

Walesby and a rescue excavation during the 1960s at Worlaby located 12 burials. Only the cemeteries at Fonaby (Cook 1981) and Castledyke (Drinkall and Foreman 1998) have been published.

Most of the inhumation cemeteries contain a few cremations; Welbeck Hill had five cremations, Sheffield's Hill I two, and Worlaby one cremation. The large Castledyke cemetery (201 graves, including the 1939 finds) contained only one cremation in contrast to the Fonaby cemetery (49 graves) which produced 28 vessels, 12 of which contained burnt bone and a further five have the appearance of having been urns. Fonaby seems to have been a very mixed cemetery. Inhumations are also found on the cremation cemeteries; Cleatham contained 1228 identified cremations and 62 graves, Elsham, on the other hand had 625 cremations but only five graves and South Elkington 204 cremations and no graves.

As the use of cremation and inhumation was mixed it might perhaps be better to divide the cemeteries into large (regional) and small (local) rather than cremation and inhumation. However, the latter division has some basis, as inhumation is the predominant rite in the smaller cemeteries and most of the small cemeteries date from the sixth century. The move to small local cemeteries could reflect the coalescence of the original folk groupings into the Kingdom of Lindsey, with less need to support group loyalty through use of the regional burial places. At this stage the cemeteries move closer to Lincoln with the establishment of the cemetery at Welton-by-Lincoln perhaps showing that things were starting to normalise; after the settlement period an Anglo-Saxon burial could now take place near to the city. Elsewhere we have Anglo-Saxon burials associated with Roman fortified sites; in 1918 a warrior grave with a sword, spear and shield was found within the walls of Horncastle and, more recently, a sixth-century woman's grave was also found within the walls. The sixth-century Nettleton cemetery is within 500m of the walls of Caistor. The move to small local cemeteries may also reflect the change from cremation to inhumation; while it is easy to carry a pot of ashes to a central burying place, a corpse presents some problems in transportation.

THE FINDS FROM THE GRAVES

As with the cremations, the inhumations contain both grave goods, placed on or with the body, and grave-side offerings which are in the fill of the grave. The latter often cross gender; a sleeve clasp or a bead will be found in the fill of a man's grave and an iron buckle (usually worn by men) will be found in a woman's grave.

Brooches were both functional and decorative, forming an important part of Early Anglo-Saxon female dress. Finds from the graves show that the classic arrangement was three brooches, one on each shoulder and a third at the centre of the upper chest (*21*). The two shoulder brooches held the woman's tubular 'peplos'-type gown in place. This was a long tube of cloth that the woman stepped into, pulling it up to be held by the shoulder brooches. It is likely that the third brooch secured a cloak, worn on top of the gown. Two of the Cleatham graves contained five brooches, which must reflect the regard with which these women were held. The types of brooch used in Lindsey are important as they provide a guide to the cultural affinities of the people of Lindsey, representing a sort of national dress.

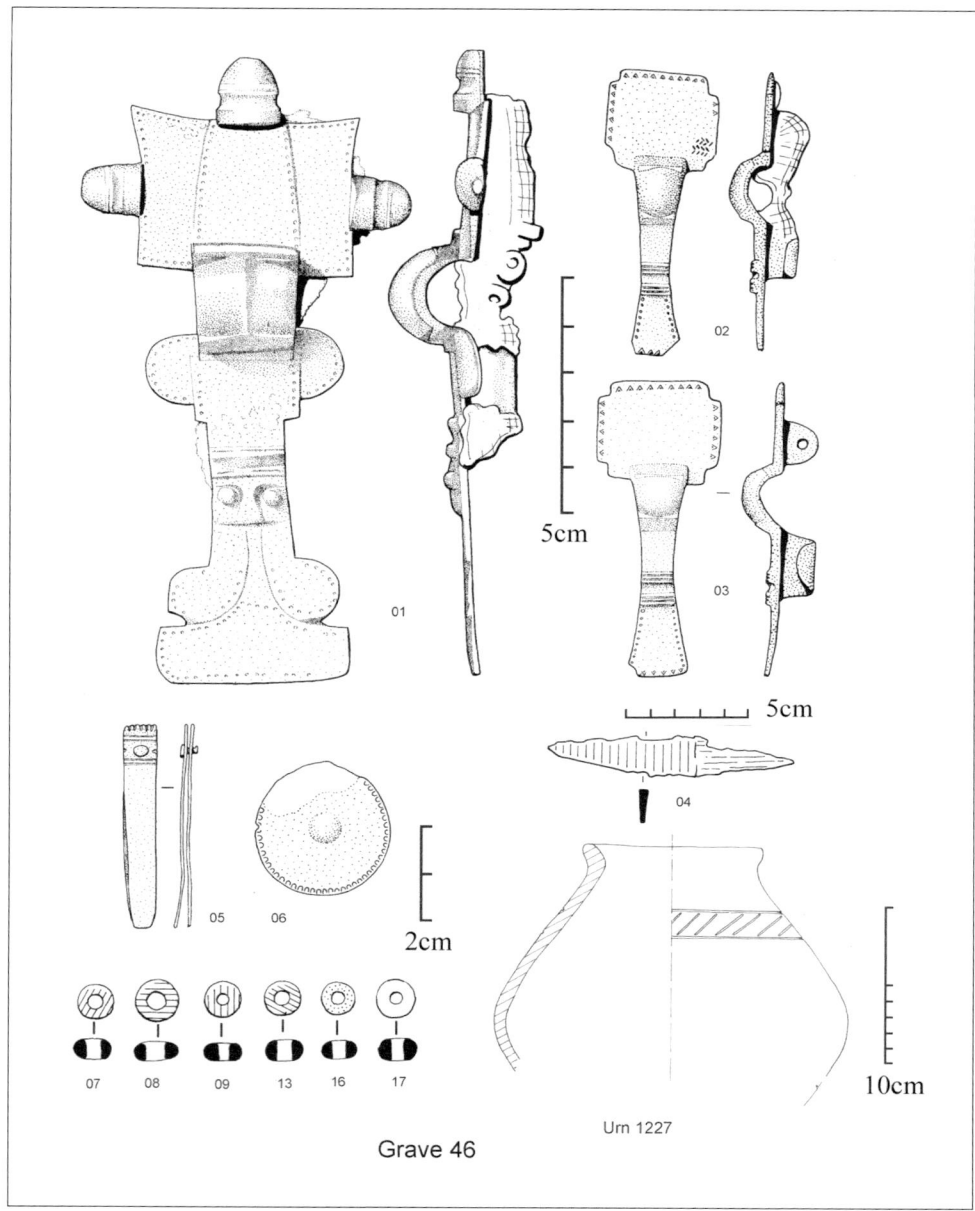

5cm

5cm

2cm

10cm

Urn 1227

Grave 46

20 Finds from Cleatham Grave 46. A typical Anglian woman's grave with two small-long brooches 02 and 03 (one on each shoulder, see figure 20) and a larger cruciform brooch in the middle of her chest, 01. Also in the grave was an iron knife (04), a copper-alloy strap end 05, a silver pendant 06, glass beads 07-17 and pot, Urn 1227. *Drawings by Kevin Leahy*

Opposite: 21 Plans of Cleatham Grave 46. This grave contained large blocks of stone brought from a nearby Roman villa. *Drawing by Kevin Leahy*

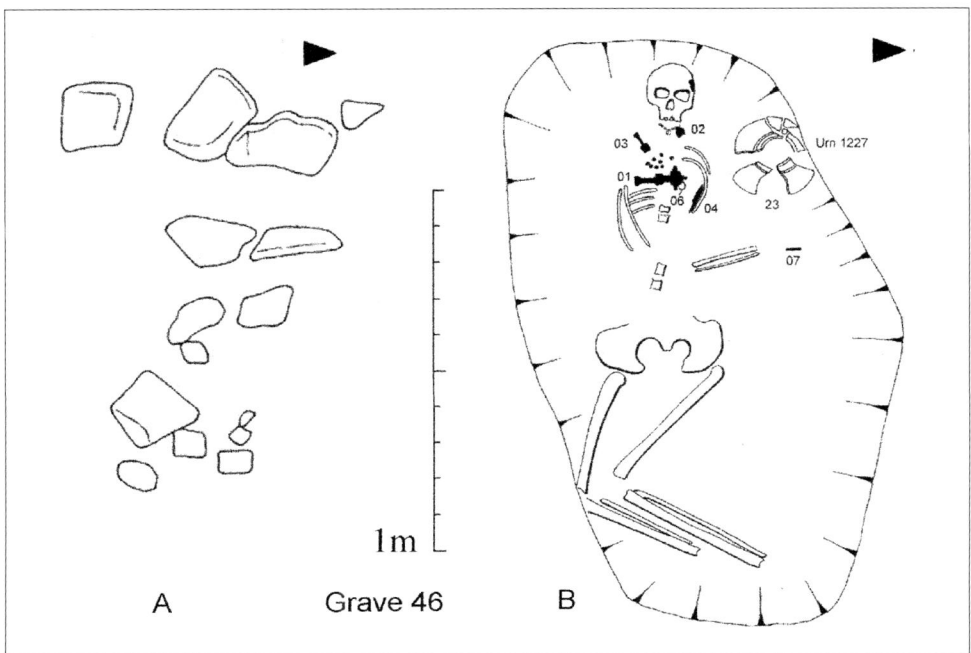

The characteristic, although not the most common type of brooch worn in Lindsey, was the cruciform brooch. These are found throughout Anglian England, an area extending from Suffolk up to Teeside and beyond. To the south, in the Saxon parts of England, women's clothing was secured not by cruciform but by saucer and button brooches. These are the areas where cremation was a minority rite, again suggesting a cultural difference. Cruciform brooches are important for our understanding of the Early Anglo-Saxon period as their form changes over time. They worked on the same principle as a safety-pin, the pin held in place by a length of wire through its coiled spring. Knobs placed on the ends of the wire gave the brooches their cruciform shape. Unlike Roman brooches, which had copper-alloy pins, most Anglo-Saxon brooches had iron pins.

The early brooches are small and have three round knobs forming the cross (*22*). As time goes on the brooches get larger and more elaborate, and the round knobs are replaced by half-round knobs. 'Lappets', small projections, appear beneath the arched bow and the cross-shaped head gets broader. The late examples are the elaborate, gilded 'Florid' brooches, often with silver panels on them and decorated with disjointed, chip-carved animals (*colour plate 7*). It is curious that the 'Florid' cruciform brooches and highly decorated square-headed brooches, while not uncommon even on small cemeteries in Lindsey, are absent at Castledyke. One would have expected to find them at this large cemetery

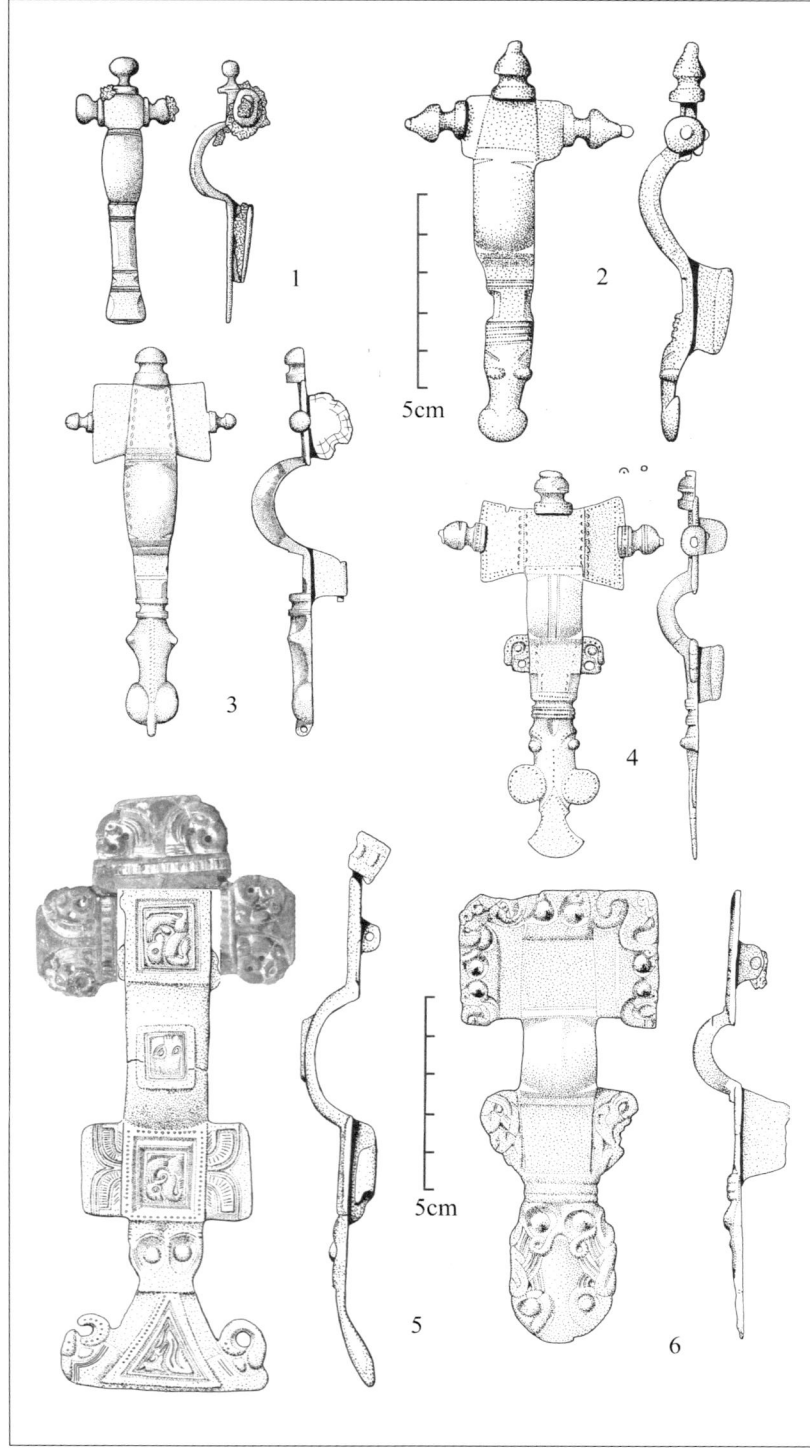

22 The development of cruciform brooches. The early brooches (Åberg Group I) were small and had round knobs (1) later examples being larger. (2) More developed examples (Åberg Group II) have half-round knob (3) and later still lappets (protrusions beneath the bow) appear (Åberg Group IV) (4). At the end of the sequence cruciform brooches of Åberg's Group V become very large and elaborate and are often gilded (*colour plate 7*). NB the Group V brooch shown as (5) was incomplete and the knobs shown come from another, but closely related brooch. The brooch shown as (6) is of a type that was described as a 'Type C2' square-headed brooch but it is now accepted that these northern brooches are related to late cruciform brooches. All of the brooches shown are from Cleatham with the exception of (6) which is from Fonaby. *Drawings by Kevin Leahy*

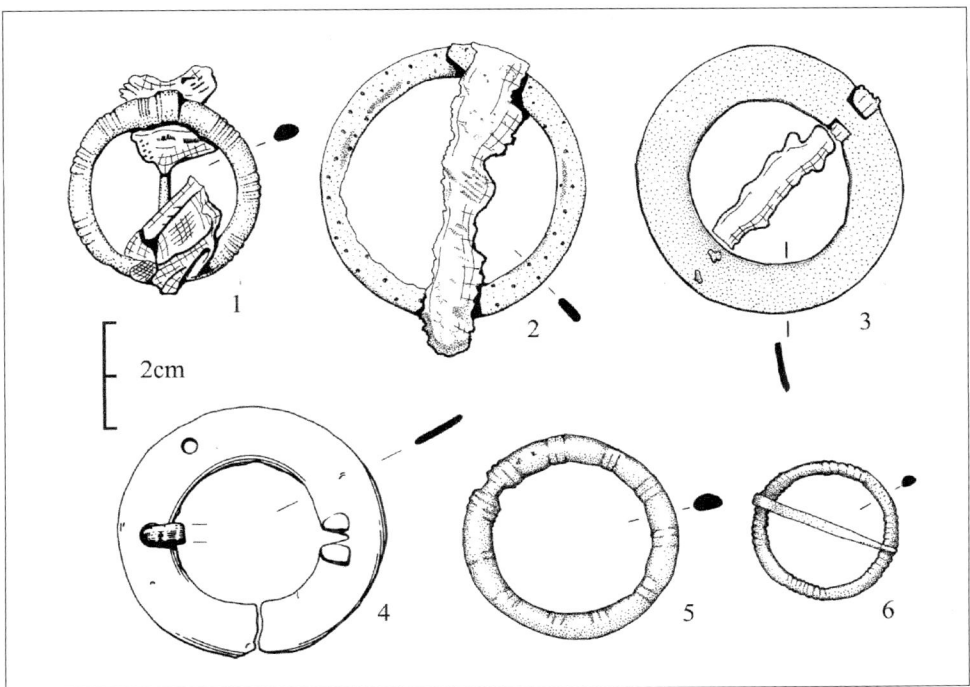

2cm

23 Types of annular brooch found in Lindsey. All copper alloy and from Cleatham except 4 which is from Castledyke. *Drawings by Kevin Leahy except 4 which is courtesy of Humber Field Archaeology*

but their absence might reflect the late date of many of the Castledyke graves. A common, and cheaper, version of the cruciform brooch was the small-long brooch (*24*). These simplified versions of cruciform and square-headed brooches are smaller and cast in one piece.

'Great square-headed brooches' (*colour plate 8*) were not used in the early settlement period and John Hines has shown that they were introduced into England with a secondary influx of people from southern Scandinavia after around 470. With them came other distinctive dress fittings, in particular sleeve or 'wrist' clasps and small shield-shaped 'scutiform' pendants (*25, 1-5; 26, 2*). Sleeve clasps usually consisted of a pair of plates that carried a hook and eye. Some early examples were made from double spirals of wire but most are either cast copper alloy or made from sheet metal, sometimes with raised decoration. Sleeve clasps were sewn to the cuffs of a woman's dress and hooked to form a fastening. They are not found in southern England and are one of the most recognisable features of Anglian dress. Scutiform pendants are made of silver and resemble small, circular shields. They sometimes have small handles on their backs confirming that they are model shields. We also have examples of 'bracteates', gold or silver pendants which

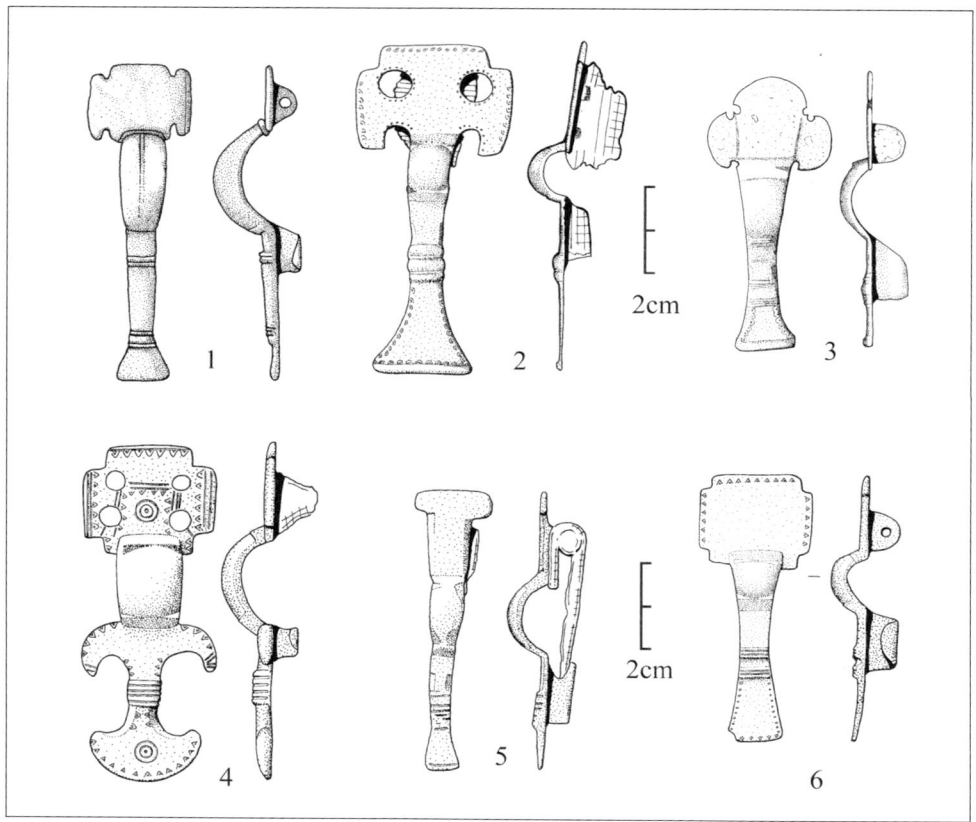

24 Small-long brooches from Cleatham, all copper alloy with iron pins. *Drawings by Kevin Leahy*

are again of northern European origin (*26*, 3-4). Other amulets have been found in Anglo-Saxon graves in Lindsey; silver-mounted beavers' teeth were found in a woman's grave at Worlaby, near the River Ancholme, the broad flat vale of which would have been perfect beaver habitat. A bone from a deer's foot was found fitted with a wire suspension loop at Welbeck Hill. Cowrie shells, which were probably associated with fertility and child-bearing, were found in urns at Cleatham (*13*, Urn 288) and whelk shells were found at Castledyke and in the lost Cabourne grave.

Annular brooches (*23*) were the most common form of dress fastening in fifth to sixth-century Lindsey. These consisted of a ring with a flat or rounded cross-section. To use one, layers of cloth were pulled through the centre of the ring and the pin passed through them. The cloth was then pulled back locking the pin against the face of the ring, securing the garment. Brooch use in eastern England has been analysed by Genevieve Fisher who found that in East Anglia annular brooches were found in 73 per cent of the graves with brooches but in Lindsey

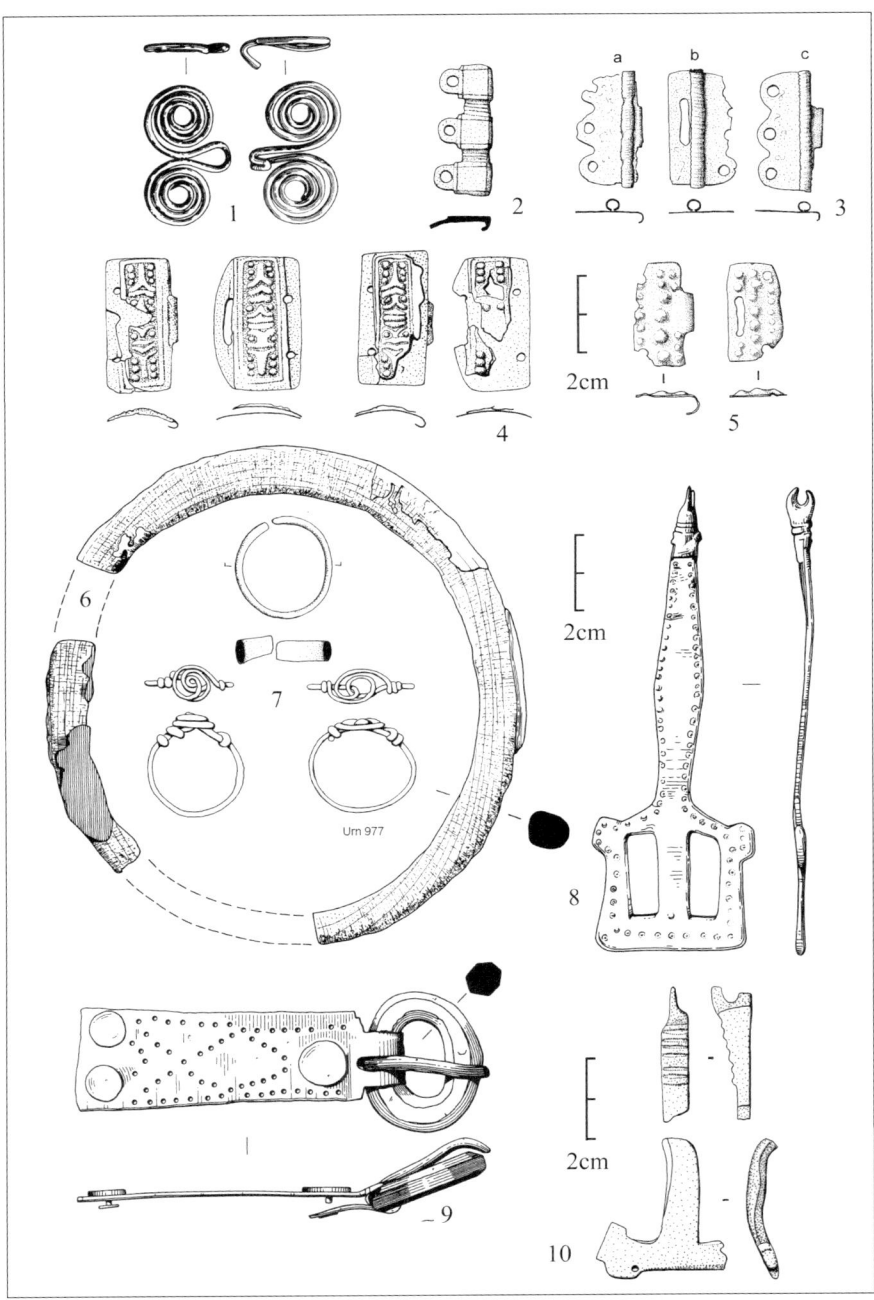

2cm

2cm

Urn 977

2cm

25 Finds from Lindsey graves. 1–5: Sleeve clasps, 1 from Castledyke, rest from Cleatham.
6: Ivory bag ring, Castledyke. 7: Copper-alloy finger rings from Cleatham Urn 977.
8: Copper-alloy girdle hanger from Castledyke. 9: Copper-alloy buckle from Castledyke.
10: Burnt girdle hanger from Cleatham, Urn 894. *Drawing of Cleatham finds by Kevin Leahy,*
Castledyke finds courtesy of Humber Field Archaeology

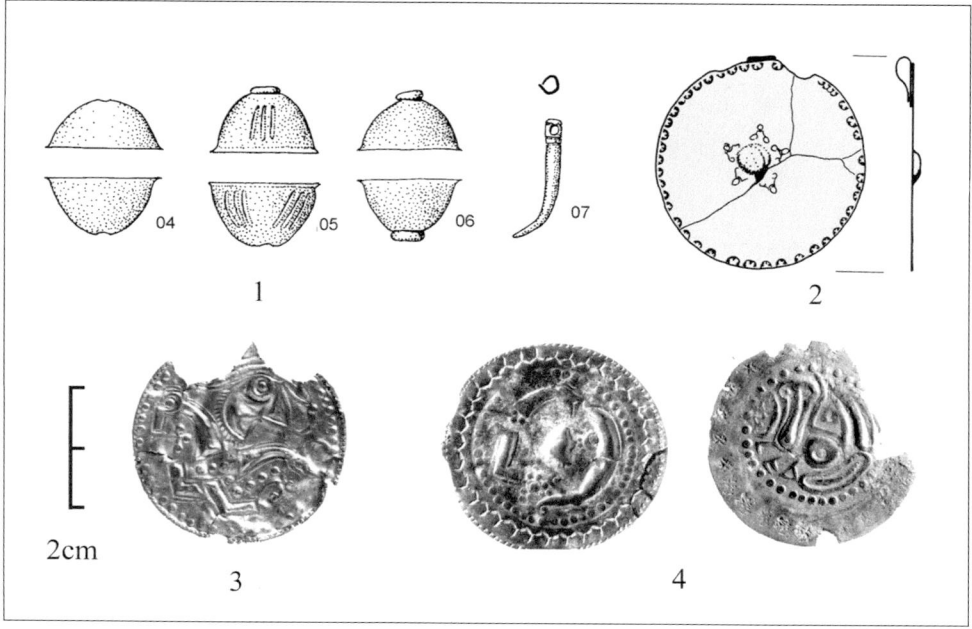

26 Silver objects from early graves in Lindsey. 1: Silver beads and 'tooth' pendant from Cleatham. 2: Shield-shaped 'scutiform' pendant from Worlaby. 3: Gold bracteate from Kirmington. 4: Two silver bracteates from the Welbeck Hill cemetery (the example on the right has runes on it). *Drawings and photographs by Kevin Leahy*

the proportion rose to 90 per cent. In East Anglia the difference was made up by a more frequent use of small-long brooches (20 per cent in East Anglia compared to 2 per cent in Lindsey). While this holds true for Castledyke, where small-long brooches were found in only 4.4 per cent of brooch graves, it was not the case at Cleatham (22.7 per cent) or Fonaby (22.2 per cent). Castledyke seems to look more towards the north and to cemeteries like Sewerby (2.8 per cent of brooch graves with small-long brooches) and Norton, Cleveland (2.3 per cent). Analytical work carried out by Catherine Mortimer on the alloys used to make cruciform brooches showed that, while at Castledyke and Fonaby a wide range of alloys were used, Cleatham seemed to follow the pattern observed in East Anglia with the brooches mainly being made from bronze.

Some 'foreign' brooches have been found in Lindsey. 'Type C2' brooches look like the square-headed type but their origin actually lies with cruciform brooches; they are in effect cruciform brooches whose knobs have been linked together (*22*). C2 brooches are most common north of the Humber and the presence of them in Lindsey shows links with the north. Southern 'quoit'/flat annular brooches have been found at Castledyke and South Ferriby and 'swastika' brooches, a form most common in the Midlands, from Castledyke and Keelby. A Frankish radiate-headed brooch, imported from the continent, was found at Searby and a fragment, with garnet inlay, at Elsham.

As well as being used as urns, pots were included in graves. At Castledyke 13 of the 196 recorded graves contained pots and at Cleatham they occurred in six of the 62 graves and in two of the urns. Eight of the Castledyke pots bore traces of soot showing that they had been used over a fire, something that was also seen on some of the Cleatham urns. Pots were usually placed in the grave between the left shoulder and the head. At Sheffield's Hill dark cylindrical stains were found in this area showing the use of leather or wooden vessels, long since decayed. Pots were common in children's graves, perhaps reflecting their dependence on adults for sustenance. One of the graves at Castledyke contained a breast- or, more likely, an udder-shaped feeding bottle (*colour plate 5*). This small vessel has an open top, tapering down to a perforated point, around which is a groove that would allow a teat to be tied into place. The bottle was found in the grave of an infant but not enough of the bones survived to say much about them. It is possible that this child was having difficulties in suckling (cleft palate?) and the bottle had been made to help overcome the problem. This is an attractive idea but there are heavy traces of wear around the teat end and while, I am told, human babies can be voracious sucklers it is more likely that this damage was caused by a succession of lambs and not a single sickly human infant. The bottle may have been seen as an appropriate offering for an infant.

WEAPON BURIALS

In comparison with the graves of women, Lindsey's Anglo-Saxon men seem to have been poorly done by. The dress fittings and beads that were such a feature of women's burials are absent, and weapons which serve as a compensation elsewhere in England, are much less common (*27*). In southern England, an average of 18 per cent of Anglo-Saxon burials contain weapons, at Castledyke weapons were found in only 6.5 per cent (13/201) of the graves and at Welbeck Hill in 6.4 per cent (5/79). Weapons are better represented at Cleatham where they are found in 11.3 per cent (7/62) of the graves (they were not included with cremations). Even when weapons are found they often do not form a full set of war-gear; there were no shields from Castledyke. The low number of weapon graves resembles that seen north of the Humber at cemeteries like Sewerby with 8.4 per cent (5/59) of the graves with weapons and Norton, Cleveland with 8.3 per cent (10/120).

The most common weapon found in Anglo-Saxon graves is the spear, occasionally accompanied by a shield; swords are rare in the sixth century but

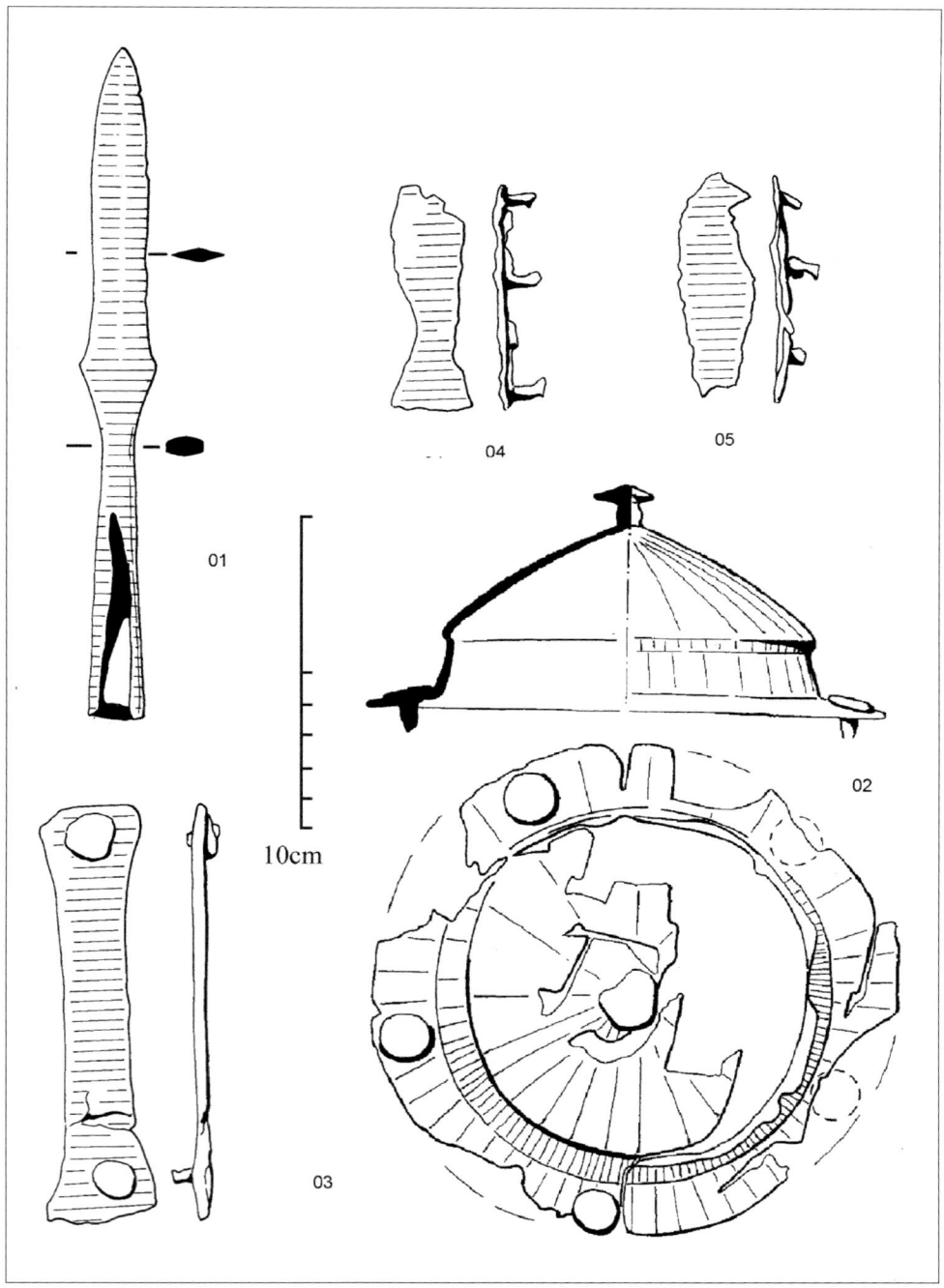

27 'Warrior grave' from Cleatham Grave 25. This grave contained a spearhead (01) and the iron fittings from a shield consisting of a boss (02), iron handle (03), and two mounts in the forms of a fish (04) and a bird (05). *Drawings by Kevin Leahy*

become more common in the seventh. The typical Anglo-Saxon spearhead can be recognised by its open or split socket; on Roman and medieval weapons the socket is usually a long, closed cone (*28*). Some spearheads are quite sophisticated; the Z-shaped cross-section sometimes used is an ingenious way of making a blade more rigid without increasing its weight. A rarer weapon is the 'francisca', a rather nasty throwing axe with a drooping blade. An attempt to catch a thrown francisca on a shield could result in it spinning behind the shield with unpleasant consequences. Franciscas are early, dating from the settlement period and we have finds from the Bagmoor cemetery and the Kirton in Lindsey villa site.

Shields are much less common than spearheads in Lindsey reflecting the shortage of true 'warrior graves' discussed above. However, some of the few known examples are of particular interest. Anglo-Saxon shields were made of wood which was, as we can see from a fine example from Sheffield's Hill, covered with leather (*colour plate 9*). In the centre of the board was a hole into which the warrior placed his fist to grip the iron handle, his hand protected by a conical iron boss riveted to the board (*27*). At the apex of the boss was a short spike which was sometimes capped with a decorated disc, as found on the shield from Sheffield's Hill which is finely decorated with animals and inlaid with garnets (*colour plate 10*). This bears traces of battle damage with a diamond-shaped hole left by a spear point on its face. To either side of the boss were gilded and silvered copper-alloy mounts in the shape of fish, which are objects of real charm (*colour plate 9*). A deep cut across the face of one of the mounts shows that it, too, had suffered battle damage. This shield had been used to fend off at least two blows and, in view of the failure to have the damage repaired, its owner may not have survived. No bones survived in the acid soil at Sheffield's Hill and we cannot see if there were any sign of injuries. A further fish-shaped shield mount was found at Worlaby and a grave from Cleatham produced both a fish and a bird which, unusually, are made out of iron (*27*).

The short, single-edged sword/knife, the 'seax', has only been found in few graves, like Stenigot and Manton, but smaller knives are very common. Knives are found with both men and women in both graves and urns. Heinrich Härke has shown that the size of knives was linked to the status of the person with whom they were buried. This seems to have been the case at Castledyke where the nine Class 3 knives, with blades longer than 130mm, were all found with adult males. There are no large knives at Cleatham, although five of the six medium-sized Class 2 knives (100-129mm long) were found with men (the other skeleton was not sexed). The remaining 41 Cleatham knives belonged to Class 1 with blades that were less than 99mm long and could not be linked to either age or sex. Occasionally traces of the handles survived on tangs of knives; the most common material used was horn, although wood was sometimes used.

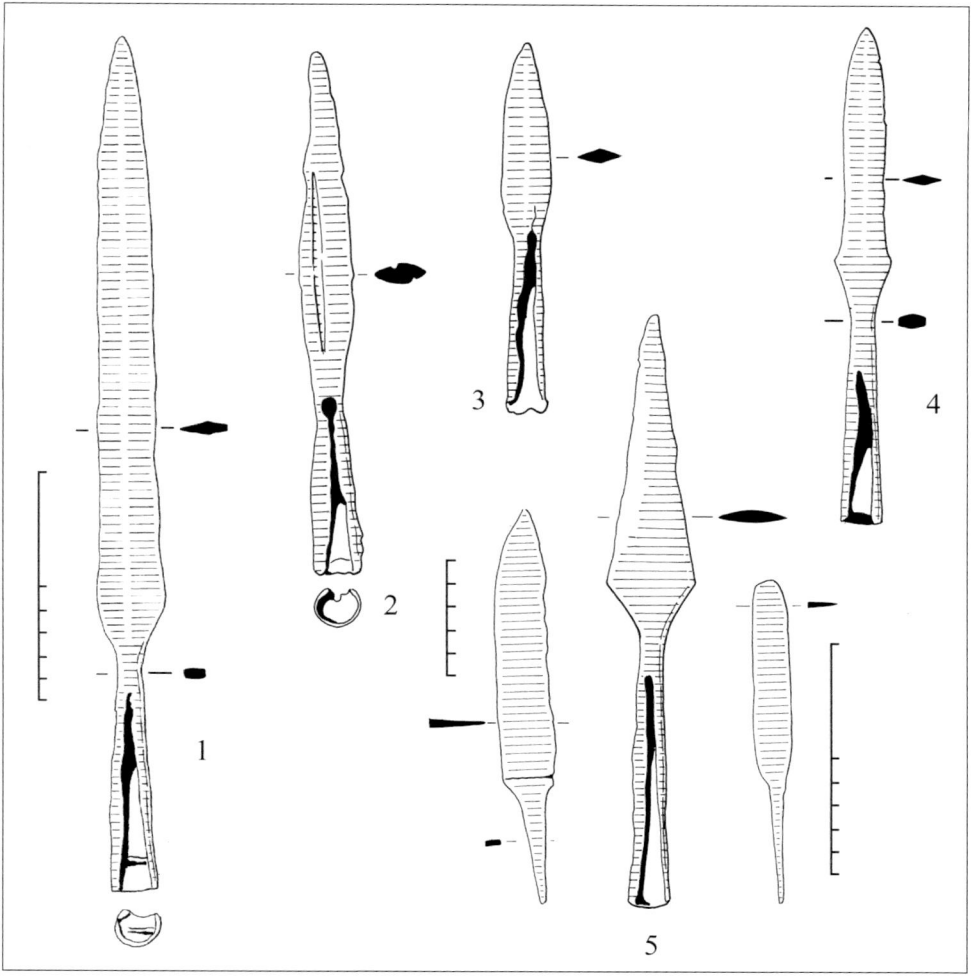

28 Typical iron spearheads from Lindsey. With spearhead (5) is an iron knife and what may be a fire steel (right). All from Cleatham. *Drawings by Kevin Leahy*

Traces of leather sheaths also survive and signs of tooled decoration are visible on some of the Sheffield's Hill knives. At Castledyke it was found that both calf and sheep/goat leather was used and that the sheath often overlapped the knife handle.

The evidence for warfare from Lindsey's Early Anglo-Saxon cemeteries is ambiguous. As is typical of northern England the number of weapon graves found in the cemeteries is low. Heinrich Härke has compared the numbers of weapon graves found in southern England with the periods of known warfare and found an inverse relationship – during times of warfare the number of weapon graves actually goes down, not up. Perhaps people engaged in conflict have better things to do with weapons than bury them. In times of peace the trappings of war become more important, the only way to show warrior status was by dressing up, even if only for the funeral. Was Lindsey engaged in warfare during the sixth century? As we have seen the kingdom had well-defined natural boundaries which reduced the problems (and opportunities) resulting from border disputes. During the seventh century Lindsey was fought over by Mercia and Northumbria but the battles that decided its fate were away fixtures. The low number of weapon graves in northern England could reflect its being a border zone where Anglo-Saxons and Britons faced each other and fighting was likely. Although Lindsey was isolated, its warriors would have been expected to support their overlord in battle and must have played some part in the campaigns.

BODY POSITIONS IN THE GRAVES

Anglo-Saxon burial involved placing the body, fully dressed, into graves, many of which seem very shallow. At Cleatham they were cut into the sub-soil to a depth of between 20mm and 950mm. Grave depths were not related to the age or sex of the person buried or to the date of the burial, but the deeper burials all contained grave goods suggesting a link with status. The preferred alignment of the graves was west-east (with the head at the west end) but there was a lot of variation. At Welbeck Hill there was a preference for a north-south alignment of the graves, west-east was the most common alignment at Fonaby but at Worlaby the graves were randomly arranged. The people using the Cleatham cemetery aspired to a general west–east alignment but were not too bothered. At Castledyke west-east alignment was again most common but north-south was also often used and continued until the end of the seventh century. It is notable that 96 per cent of graves in East Anglia have a west–east alignment compared with only 48 per cent in Lindsey, suggesting that this aspect of cultural behaviour was much less strictly observed in Lindsey.

Interesting work has been done elsewhere in England on the position in which bodies were placed in graves but so far this has proved less useful in Lindsey. Extended burial, where the body lay on its back, was used for adults at both Cleatham and Castledyke. Flexed burial, where the body lay on one side with the legs bent, was used for mature adults at Cleatham, but was most commonly used for children at Castledyke. The acidic ground conditions at Cleatham and Sheffield's Hill dissolved the children's skeletons making it impossible to see how they had been placed. It was suggested that this body position was due to Celtic influence but this seems unlikely; too many of the flexed burials are seventh, not fifth century.

On present evidence it has not been possible to see any coherent pattern in the way that bodies were laid in Lindsey.

Of all of the positions in which Anglo-Saxon skeletons are found none has excited as much interest as 'prone' burials, where the skeleton is found lying face down. Much has been written about these graves as it is generally believed that the unfortunates who received this form of burial were still alive. There were three prone burials at Cleatham and eight at Castledyke, where they were poorly furnished, and in two cases it was suggested (unconvincingly) that the bodies had been pinioned. In Castledyke Grave 166 the body of an old woman was sprawled over the body of a younger. Both burials had knives with them and it is possible that they were not simultaneous, but successive. More can be said about the prone burials at Cleatham. It looks as if the young woman in Cleatham Grave 55 had been bundled into the ground with her legs tightly folded up against her body. There were no grave goods but a segmented bead and a fragment of an annular brooch were found in the fill of the grave and may have been offerings, which would be unlikely with an execution. Cleatham Grave 31 contained the remains of a man buried face down and accompanied by an iron buckle, knife, spearhead and a sheep's jawbone. By male standards this was a well equipped grave and the possibility of live burial is reduced by the presence of the spearhead which, in Anglo-Saxon times, was the badge of a free man. The laws of King Ine of Wessex (688-726) set a higher penalty on someone giving a runaway slave a spear than a more valuable sword. It is unlikely that a spear would have been placed in the grave of an executed felon.

We can be fairly sure that the young woman buried in Cleatham Grave 11 was not buried alive as her skull and mandible were found 2.2m away, standing upright, next to Urn 115 (Phase 2), which contained feminine grave goods. Grave 11 contained no objects, but lying beside the woman's left hip was the skeleton of a chicken-sized bird. The decapitation of the young woman in Cleatham Grave 11 is not unique in Lindsey as a woman found in Grave 12 at Welbeck Hill cemetery had suffered an equally strange fate. This grave contained the skeleton of an elderly male with a fine spearhead with rings through the corners of its blade, and a small bronze-bound yew bucket. Lying over him, but in the reverse alignment, were the decapitated remains of a woman.

Grave 11 at Cleatham is not the only example of a bird skeleton being found in a grave; they occurred in eight of the graves at Castledyke, five being chickens and two geese. The Castledyke chickens were found at the right-hand side of the skeleton, as was the case at Cleatham. Burnt bird bones were found in some of the Romano-British cremation burials at the Gilliate's Grave cemetery but as one of the urns contained a coin of Trajan a direct link seems unlikely. Reference has already been made to the sheep's jaw bone found in Cleatham Grave 31;

a sheep's tooth was found in Grave 44 and what looks like a sheep's scapula in Grave 27. The latter could have come from a shoulder of mutton but the teeth hardly represent the most succulent part of a sheep's carcass. Animal bones were found in 16 per cent of the Castledyke graves where sheep were again the most common. Only one horse bone and a tooth was found at Castledyke, although two 'large ungulates' may also have been horses. Dogs were represented by a few rib fragments.

BURIAL STRUCTURES

Some Anglo-Saxon graves consisted of a lot more than a hole in the ground and we have evidence for what may have been complex structures. The ground conditions at Cleatham made it impossible to see any post holes associated with the graves but they showed clearly in the chalk sub-soil at Castledyke. Twenty-five of the Castledyke graves were associated with post holes, in 19 cases there was only a single post, five had two posts and Grave 151 may have had four posts. Elsewhere in England four post settings have been interpreted as 'mortuary houses' built over the tops of graves. The single holes found at Castledyke probably held marker posts to show the position of graves. If the idea was to prevent later disturbance it failed, as these graves were as likely to have later burials cut through them as any other. Three of the Cleatham graves contained a line of reused Roman masonry blocks down their northern sides which may represent low walls marking the position of the graves, the tops of which have been removed by ploughing.

At Sheffield's Hill two ring-ditches were found on the edge of the cemetery (*29*). These could not be described as 'barrows' as they were small, just wide enough to accommodate the length of the graves. Associated with them were three graves: two women, one within a penannular ring-ditch and another in the gap in the ditch, and a man, found with a spearhead, who was surrounded by his own ring-ditch. The women had brooches, beads and a decorated pot and although the finds from these burials were good, they could not be described as aristocratic.

Some burials were placed in coffins, the best evidence for which were found at Sheffield's Hill, where a stain showed the line of the boards, now appearing to curve as, when the planks weakened, they were pushed in by the pressure of the soil. At Castledyke traces of coffins were found in 23 of the graves but no trace of coffins was found at Cleatham although one burial was in a stone-lined cist. This grave was aligned west-east and contained the remains of a young adult male with no grave goods.

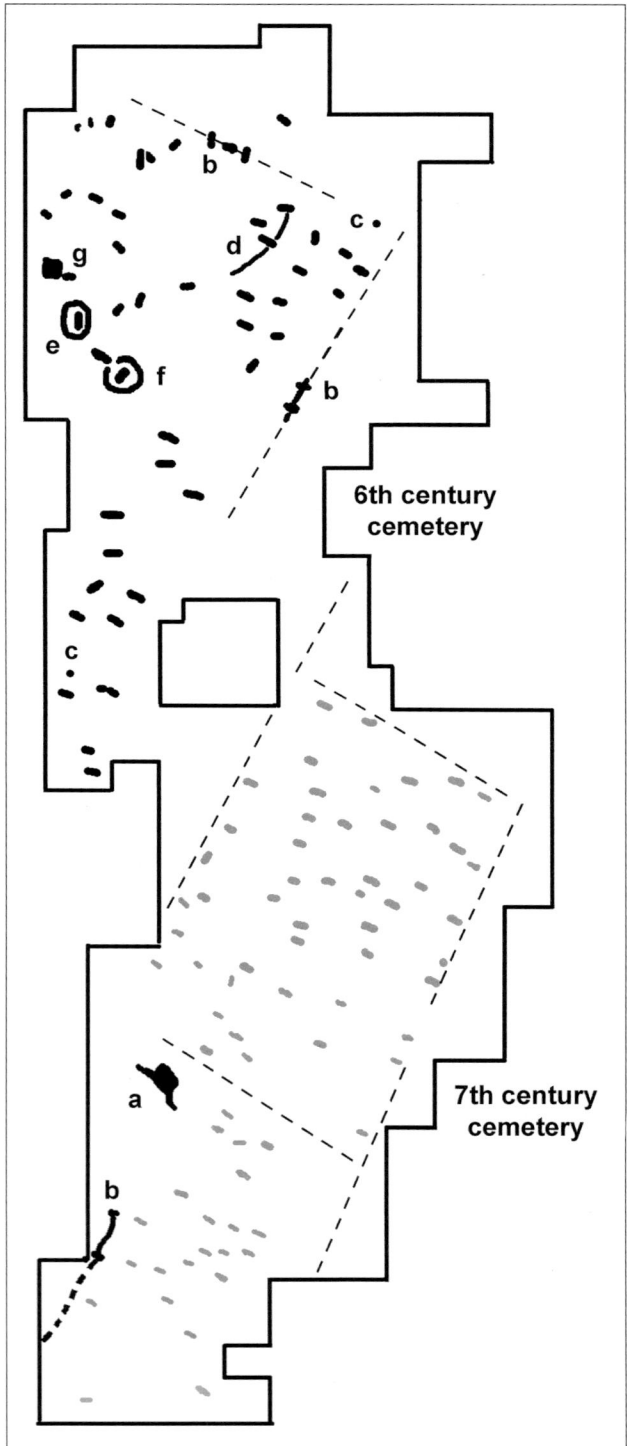

29 Plan of the Sheffield's Hill
Anglo-Saxon cemeteries.
a recent disturbance
b field boundaries
c cremation burials
d ditch
e and f ring ditches
g hearth complex

Drawing by Kevin Leahy

Stones are not uncommon in Anglo-Saxon graves in Lindsey. At Castledyke about 40 of the 196 recorded graves contained rubble and at Cleatham the use of stones in graves was still more striking (21). Twenty-six of the Cleatham graves contained blocks of dressed masonry which must have come from the Mount Pleasant Roman villa, about 500m to the south. Although at Castledyke the use of stones in graves was most commonly associated with females, at Cleatham there was no correlation between stones and the age or sex of the person in the grave. The use of stones was unrelated to finds; a rich burial might lack stones while they have occurred in unaccompanied graves. There was also no link to the date of the burial, as stones were found in graves dating to the late fifth and seventh centuries.

A number of possible explanations exist for putting stones into the fill of graves. The first – the need to hold down the protesting 'corpse' – we can reject; the practice was too widespread and is not restricted to Lindsey. Limestone blocks were found surrounding, and covering, the bodies at Loveden Hill where two bodies had a Roman stone column laid over them. The stones may have been intended to stop the dead from troubling the living and, although we should not reject what is to us a non-rational explanation out of hand, it is perhaps more likely that they were used to protect the corpse from disturbance. It was noted that at Castledyke, graves with stones in their fills were much less likely to be disturbed by later burials. It must also be remembered that England's fauna was far more interesting in Anglo-Saxon times than it is now: wolves were present and, more importantly, wild boar were common. Pigs are omnivores, excellent diggers and great opportunists, as indeed are badgers. Placing stones in the fill of a grave was probably a sensible precaution. We have other evidence for the protection of burials from scavengers. While all bone was dissolved at Sheffield's Hill other organic materials were well represented, appearing both as stains and preserved by contact with metal objects. In the upper part of the fill of some graves it was possible to see the stains left by tree branches put into the grave instead of stones. In one case the wood had been charred and the pattern left by the bark of a thorn bush could be seen.

The northern edge of the Cleatham cemetery was marked by boundary ditches which had been repeatedly re-dug, suggesting that they marked a ritual boundary. Sherds of Anglo-Saxon pottery found in them showed that they were in use at the time when the urns were being deposited, but a sixth-century grave dug through the ditches showed that they went out of use during the life of the cemetery. No boundaries were found at Castledyke although one side of the cemetery was marked by a large prehistoric ditch. Also at Castledyke, a remarkable number of graves were cut through earlier burials (30) which must have been a deliberate act as, so far as we can tell, there were no constraints on

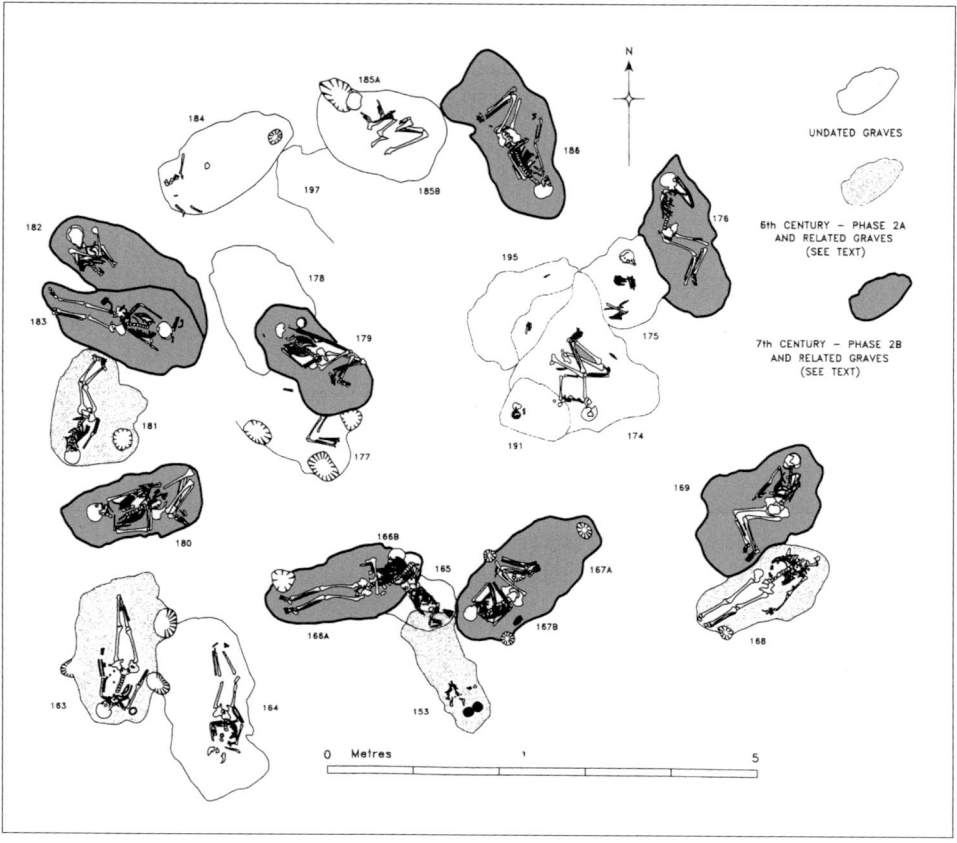

30 Grave 179 at Castledyke, a youth's grave formed the nucleus of this part of the cemetery with later burials being centred around him. *Plan by Humber Field Archaeology*

the expansion of the cemetery on three sides. The Sheffield's Hill cemeteries were located in what appear to have been Romano-British fields, surrounded by hedges (*29*).

THE HUMAN REMAINS

The bones from Anglo-Saxon graves probably bring us as close as we are going to get to the people themselves and palaeopathologists are able to tell us a great deal from the skeletal remains. It is possible to determine the sex of adults with some confidence, children are difficult to sex but, unlike adults, their age at death can be accurately determined. We can find peoples' stature, how well fed they had been, any injuries that had left traces on their bones and conditions such as arthritis. The question that usually eludes us is the cause of death; most deaths occur through diseases that leave no traces on the bones.

Of the excavated cemeteries in Lindsey, only at Castledyke were the skeletons sufficiently well preserved to be informative and it was possible to write an excellent report. The acidic soil at Cleatham had damaged most of the bones although it was possible to report on them. At Sheffield's Hill the highly acidic soil completely dissolved the skeletons, but left, in some graves, a dark stain pseudomorph of the body, like the famous 'sandmen' at Sutton Hoo (*colour plate 6*). These were probably a result of the decay of the bones locally changing the pH and causing the precipitation of mineral salts; the pseudomorphs are not casts but shadows around the bones.

Cremation is a destructive process but it is possible to get some evidence from the bones. After cremation the remains are not 'ashes' but a cracked and distorted skeleton which was broken up before being placed in the urn. Anglo-Saxon cremation was carried out with some skill, all of the organic material being fully burnt, leaving the bone white. The burnt remains are difficult to identify but in some cases it is possible to suggest what sex they were and, more often, the age at death. Mary Harman wrote a report on the burnt bone from Elsham in 1976 which remains unpublished. It has not proved possible to get the funding for a report on the burnt bones from Cleatham but Chris Knowles and Freda Berisford have kindly allowed me access to Ms Harman's work.

THE POPULATION

Of the 562 cremation deposits at Elsham, 536 were sufficiently large to be able to say something about them and challenge some of the assumptions that we tend to make about these burials. We cannot assume that one urn equals one person; 14 of the Elsham urns contained the remains of more than one person, in most cases an adult being accompanied by a child. It is very difficult to tell the sex of the person whose burnt bones are found within an urn and at Elsham Ms Harman was only tentatively able to sex 78 of 562 deposits suggesting that 37 of them were male and 41 female. In only 14 cases was she confident of the identification. It would also be unsafe to base sexing on the gender suggested by the grave goods as most male burials contain nothing that is gender specific. At Castledyke there were slightly more females than males (61 females to 51 males) and at Cleatham there were slightly more males than females (15 females to 22 males) but in both cases the differences could be made up amongst the un-sexed skeletons. A lack of males at Fonaby is probably due to a failure of the sand diggers to recognise the rusted remains of the iron weapons that were all that survived of the male graves.

It is interesting to look at how large a population is represented by these cemeteries. The 1528 burials found at Cleatham seem a lot until we remember that the cemetery was in use for at least 150 years. The ages at death of the people whose cremated bones were found at Elsham suggest an average life expectancy (having survived infancy) of 24.6 years. From this we can calculate that:

- Assuming that the Cleatham cemetery was in use for 150 years the 1528 burials represents a living population of 414 adults.
- Assuming that the Cleatham cemetery was in use for 200 years the 1528 burials represents a population of 311 adults.

This is not a massive number of people but the large inhumation cemetery at Castledyke is still more striking: the estimated 436 burials would present a population of 118 people. The many small cemeteries of around 100 graves can only have represented families. It must be recognised that these calculations are simplistic estimates, based on the assumption that the population size remained constant throughout the history of the cemetery, but they give us some idea of the size of the groups involved.

Age at death in Anglo-Saxon Lindsey
It is possible to tell how old someone was when they died as changes to the skeleton occur at certain ages, however once someone reaches maturity, growth stops and we have to rely on estimates based on things like dental wear. It was found that at Elsham 13.6 per cent of the 512 aged deposits died before the age of 13, this is likely to be an underestimate as children who died in early infancy seem to be poorly represented and different burial practices may have been used. Adolescence seems to have been a relatively safe time of life as only 5.1 per cent of the population at Elsham died between 13 and 18 years. Things got more dangerous between 19 and 24 with 18 per cent of the people dying, but death came to most people (51.0 per cent) at between 25 and 35 years. A few sturdy souls (12.3 per cent) survived beyond 35.

Most of the adult population at Cleatham were also dying between the ages of 18 and 25 (57.1 per cent females and 56.5 per cent of males) compared with Castledyke where far fewer were dying in this age range (25.0 per cent females and 12.1 per cent males). More women than men were dying between 26 and 35 years (28.4 per cent women to 17.4per cent men) at Cleatham, but at Castledyke the proportions were reversed (17.2 per cent females to 29.3 per cent males). There were no females in the 36-45 year range at Cleatham but 17.4 per cent of men died in this age range. This stands in contrast to Castledyke (where sample size was much larger) and 26.6 per cent of the women and 23.4 per cent of the men died as 36-45 year olds, and a remarkable 31.3% of the women and 34.1% of the men lived to beyond the 45 year limit of our aging techniques. The general population profile is similar to what we see in parts of the developing world like India; while the Anglo-Saxons had the advantage of living in a temperate environment this would have been off-set by the cold and damp of the long winters.

One would expect child mortality to be distressingly high during Anglo-Saxon times but the actual figures from Castledyke and Cleatham are, in comparison with other cemeteries, relatively low. At Cleatham 17 per cent of the skeletons were those of children and at Castledyke the figure was 23 per cent. Interestingly, at Castledyke, high numbers of children died as infants; the death rate was low during the six to fourteen year range, but increased during adolescence. A record of childhood malnutrition and illness is preserved in the growth pattern of the adult teeth as 'enamel hypoplasia'. While 9 per cent of the teeth showed signs of this, none was severe and it seems that females were more affected than males.

Stature

While stature is inherited, diet plays an important part in deciding if someone is to achieve their full potential height. It was notable that during the Great War the officers, coming from a more privileged class, were taller than the men whom they led. An examination of the Castledyke skeletons showed the average heights for men and women were pretty much the same as that found in England during the 1950s: 1.72m for men and 1.6m for women – they were almost achieving full stature. At Cleatham the average stature actually exceeded modern height although the sample size was small. The Castledyke cemetery contained some impressive individuals, one man was 1.89m (6ft 2in) tall and there was a 1.81m (almost 6ft) tall woman. She had worked hard, being well-built with strong muscle attachments, but was clearly female. The wide range of heights amongst the Castledyke population might suggest a population of mixed origins.

The health of the population

While most diseases leave no traces on the bones of the sufferer there are some conditions that do affect the bones. Degenerative joint disease was found in 21 of the 60 (35 per cent) skeletons from Cleatham, of which all but five were male. At Castledyke it was found on 25 of the 199 skeletons (12.5 per cent). The joint most commonly affected at Cleatham was the hip, which was damaged in 15 (25 per cent) cases compared with Castledyke where only 1 per cent of skeletons showed any sign of hip damage, a difference that is difficult to explain. Joint disease is linked to heavy work such as the cultivation of the land, most of which would have been carried out by the men.

As well as the degeneration of the joints, signs were found of spinal damage which, again, was more common in men than women. This happens in two ways: 'osteophytes', bony outgrowths on the spine which are thought to be caused by heavy stress being placed on the vertebrae during young adulthood, and 'osteoarthritis' where the vertebrae wear against each other. At Castledyke it was found that both kinds of damage occurred in the upper part of the back in women, but lower down, in the lumbar region, in men. This may be due to men carrying out heavy lifting, while Anglo-Saxon women would have spent a considerable part of their lives with their arms raised while spinning and weaving. It was notable that at Castledyke arthritis of the right shoulder occurred on 11 per cent of the 55 surviving joints which would support this interpretation.

The teeth of the people buried at Castledyke were in generally good condition with a relatively low frequency of cavities and lost teeth. This reflects their lack of sugar and, when problems did occur, these were largely confined to the older people. Tartar was common, showing that they did not clean their teeth but also that they were eating a relatively soft diet, which is also reflected in the low level of dental wear.

Cribia orbitalia is an indicator of stress caused by iron deficiency anaemia and was found in 16.6 per cent of juvenile skulls at Castledyke compared with the 25 per cent (1 of 4) at Cleatham, although the numbers at Cleatham are too small to be meaningful. The five eighth-century children found at Flixborough nearly all showed signs of *Cribia,* which Simon Mays has suggested may have been caused by internal parasites preventing the uptake of iron from the food, or some other chronic condition.

Three of the skeletons at Castledyke had lesions on their ribs showing that they had suffered chronic chest infections. These may have been due to tuberculosis, a disease that was probably more common than these examples suggest. An eighth-century woman found at Flixborough had a calcified lymph node, which Mays thinks may have been due to tuberculosis. As is usual in Anglo-Saxon cemeteries there was little sign of cancer amongst the remains. This is not surprising as usually only the lesions caused by secondary cancers will leave any trace on the bones. One of the Castledyke skeletons had two small growths on her(?) skull but these are believed to have been benign.

Injuries

A few of the surviving skeletons from the Lindsey cemeteries show signs of injury. At Castledyke an elderly man had suffered a broken jaw and a middle-aged woman had suffered a small depressed fracture of her skull, probably caused by a blunt instrument, but unlikely to have killed her. The skull of a young/middle-aged man from Castledyke had been trepanned, a 35mm x 10mm hole being cut into his head. This was done for a variety of reasons both medical and ritual; it could have been related to a condition like migraine. There are signs that the wound had healed. Other skeletons show signs of the bumps that occur in everyday life; there were five broken collar bones at Castledyke and two at Cleatham, one of which had healed well but the other had suffered an infection and the bone had eventually healed 50mm too short. A middle-aged man at Cleatham had suffered at least three broken bones in his life: a 'Colles' fracture to the right arm which, like a broken collar bone, is usually the result of falling on to an outstretched arm. He also had a fracture to the right tibia and fibula which had led to the shortening of the leg and which in turn, may have led to problems with the spinal column.

A young adult male at Cleatham had suffered a broken forearm that had become infected and only healed with difficulty. The arm had atrophied showing that the limb had gone out of use. He was found with his arm positioned across the body, with a small iron fitting on it, which may have been part of a brace or sling supporting the weak arm. Injuries of this type are known as 'parry fractures' as they occur in defending against a blow. At Castledyke these fractures were most common on women. Broken ribs were found and fractures to the lower leg occurred at both sites.

Occasionally we see long-forgotten tragedies, a grave at the Walesby cemetery contained the remains of three children, placed together in a confused way after, perhaps, dying in an epidemic. At Castledyke the grave of a 35-45 year old woman was found with the skeleton of her unborn baby still lying in the abdominal area. Measurement of the baby's bones showed that it died around the 37th week of gestation and, as it had not yet descended, it is unlikely that the mother had died in childbirth. It is more likely that she had died of a complication of pregnancy such as toxaemia.

At both Castledyke and Cleatham there was a good correlation between the biological sex determined by the osteologist and the gender, as represented by the grave goods (brooches with women, weapons with men). This is of interest as there has, in recent years, been some discussion of cross-gender burials where men were found with the sort of grave goods usually found with the bones of women. I must admit to some scepticism about this issue. Just because feminine dress fittings are found with what appear to be the remains of a man it does not necessarily mean that he was wearing a dress. The cross-gender grave side offerings (beads and clasps found in the graves of men, iron buckles with women) found in the Cleatham graves show that objects could cross the sexes.

What does the work on the bones tell us about the life of the people of Anglo-Saxon Lindsey? It does tend to contradict the commonly held impression that life was brutish and short. While life was clearly hard for these people the remains found at Castledyke and Cleatham cemeteries suggest that the people were relatively well fed, with few diet-related problems and with most people almost achieving full stature. There were few signs of violence and it is likely that the incidence of injuries was no more than would be found now. One thing that is clear is that we are not looking at the remains of a pampered aristocracy, these were hard-working peasants. Six of the men with degenerative joint disease had been buried with spearheads; their status as 'warriors' had not removed them from the labours of agriculture. While most of the sixth-century graves contained something in the way of grave goods and some would pass as rich, none of them could be described as aristocratic and one must wonder where the aristocracy were buried. The idea that we are looking at an egalitarian society is attractive but unlikely, someone must have been in control. Perhaps they were still in Lincoln?

SUB-ROMAN SURVIVAL?

One of the most interesting pieces of evidence we have for early Lindsey is negative. Looking at the large cemeteries like Cleatham and Castledyke it might be thought that they represented a large population but, as we have seen, spread over 150 years they don't seem to be that impressive. If we take the demographic estimate a little further and extend it to the whole of Lindsey some interesting observations may be made. Lindsey contains 49 known Anglo-Saxon cemeteries of which five are large (Castledyke, Cleatham, Elsham, Elkington and West Keal), the others being much smaller. Let us assume that:

- Castledyke contains 436 burials
- Each of the four cremation cemeteries contains, like Cleatham, 1528 burials
- All 44 of the smaller inhumation cemeteries contain 150 graves (probably an overestimate)

The Anglo-Saxon cemeteries of Lindsey therefore contain a total of 13,148 burials which could mean:

- Assuming that burial took place over 150 years, the 13,148 burials represent a population of 3562 adults.
- Assuming that burial took place over 200 years, the 13,148 burials represent a population of 2672 adults.

These figures are highly speculative but they do serve to show that the size of the population is inadequately represented by the cemeteries. There must have been a part of the population that does not appear in the burial record. If the number of cemeteries was to be doubled, tripled or quadrupled, the population represented would still not be sufficient to prevent large-scale woodland regeneration in the post-Roman period. Left alone fields will return to woodland in around 50 years and there is some evidence for farmland falling out of use in the sub-Roman period. Dendrochronology points to some spread of woodland following the departure of the Romans and recent work has shown there to have been a sharp increase in tree and shrub pollen and a corresponding fall in herb pollen in the period AD 420-1200 suggesting a decline in cultivation. This is evidence for the reversion of farmland to its natural state in the post-Roman period but not on the massive level that would result from a population fall to only 3562 adults. At Domesday, Lindsey had a population of about 60,000 souls and we should be looking at that order of figures. We can see the Anglo-Saxons through their highly distinctive burial rites; the unmarked graves of the missing thousands have vanished. This can happen; the total number of burials known from Roman Britain gives a population of around 2000 and not 3-6 million as suggested by other evidence. I think that the missing thousands were the descendants of the people of Roman Lindsey who remained in place, working the land as they had always done, their unmarked burials impossible to find or recognise.

ARCHAEOLOGICAL EVIDENCE FOR BRITISH SURVIVAL

It is only in recent years that we have started to see evidence for the survival of British culture in Lindsey. Most of it is coming to light through the success of the Portable Antiquities Scheme in recording metal detector finds. As Lindsey was considered to be part of the pure heartland of Anglo-Saxon England the discovery of this material means that we have to revise our view of the English settlement. The invisibility of the British population is usually taken as a grim fact and it is worth reviewing the evidence from Lindsey.

Penannular brooches
A penannular brooch consists of a ring with a gap in it, through which a long pin is passed before the ring is turned to lock the pin against the back of the ring (37). Nine penannular brooches have been found in Lindsey all of which belong to Elizabeth Fowler's type F1, being distinguished by their pseudo-zoomorphic terminals (resembling animals' heads) which are sometimes inlaid with red enamel. These brooches are decorated with close-set ribbing which extends only half-way around the ring, stopping before it reaches the back. Many of them have pins with a neat bead-and-reel fitting where they encircle the ring.

The dating of these brooches is uncertain but a fifth- to sixth-century date seems likely in Lindsey.

Nationally, penannular brooches have a clear northern and western distribution, finds being concentrated around the Severn Estuary and the Roman Wall. The cluster of finds in Lindsey represents a striking departure that must be explained (*38*). While some of the Lindsey penannular brooches are imports from the north or west (or products of a very mainstream local tradition) others seem to be locally made copies, showing an active local tradition of making and wearing these British brooches. Finds are concentrated in the northern part of Lindsey with examples from the Cleatham cemetery and two from the neighbouring Mount Pleasant Farm. A further example was found in a sixth-century grave at the Sheffield's Hill cemetery. There are three examples from Kirmington which might indicate sub-Roman survival at this major site where sixth-century finds are rare.

Hanging bowls

The other type of post-Roman, British metalwork to be common in Lindsey are 'hanging bowls', 12 examples of which have been found in Lindsey (*38*). These are made from sheet copper alloy and are usually fitted with three suspension rings, attached by decorated fittings, with some bowls also having decorated discs in their centre and under the base (*39*). While hanging bowls are usually found in Anglo-Saxon graves, their decoration is late Celtic in style and consists of whirling watch-spring spirals and curving designs quite unlike the disjointed animals and interlace used by the Anglo-Saxons. Coloured enamel was laid in the plain areas between the spirals to give a striking contrast. Although enamelling was commonly employed in Roman Britain it was not used in the Germanic homelands which, again, points to the bowls being made by the British. On the hanging bowls from Manton Warren and St Paul in the Bail, Lincoln, the enamel was supplemented by the use of *millefiori*, slices of multi-coloured glass sticks. The decoration on the Manton bowl contains 115 pieces of *millefiori* which came from ten glass rods, linking it to the largest bowl found in the great Sutton Hoo ship burial. They must have come from the same workshop.

Most hanging bowls are stray finds or lack data, but finds from excavations tell us something about the way in which they were being deposited. During the excavation of the important early church at St Paul in the Bail in Lincoln (*42*) a stone-lined grave was found. No skeleton was found, the bones having been carefully removed, perhaps a 'translation' in which the bones were given a more appropriate re-burial elsewhere, a process carried out for people who were considered to be saints. Hidden under a stone at one end of the grave was the bowl, missed when the grave had been cleared (*39*). Oddly, for what must have been a prestige object, its three suspension mounts only look like each other in general terms and the discs in the base are different again. It appears that the St Paul in the Bail bowl had been fitted with mounts salvaged from other bowls, it had been repaired and was clearly old when buried in what is likely to have been an important seventh-century Christian grave.

Reference has already been made to the seventh-century 'boy warrior' found within Grave 179 at the Castledyke South Cemetery, Barton on Humber. As well as having a sword, this young man was buried with a hanging bowl, lying by his left shoulder. The bowl was plain with no decoration, the mounts being simple discs (*32*). This is the second hanging bowl to have been found at Castledyke, another example was disovered during the excavation for an air-raid shelter in 1939, when five burials were found. These bowls were also plain but had simple kite-shaped suspension mounts and came from an area of the cemetery that contained important and exotic objects such as a gold bead, scales, a die for making foil mounts and the remains of a continental metal vessel. A hanging bowl was also found with weapons in a seventh-century grave at Bracebridge Heath, to the south of Lincoln (*34*).

A bowl was found in Grave 20, an otherwise undistinguished burial at Cleatham (*31, 12*). This had been stripped of its three mounts, all that remained were three patches of solder and some setting-out lines. On the side of the bowl is an inscription scratched on in runic letters. While these can be transcribed as '? E D I H' the meaning of the word is unknown. This grave contained the remains of a woman, the only other find being a small annular brooch, suggesting a seventh-century date. While it has been argued that hanging bowls were seventh century, burnt fragments were common in sixth-century urns at Cleatham.

Hanging bowls have then been found with the remains of both men and women and, on two occasions (Castledyke Grave 179 and Bracebridge Heath) were associated with weapons. The hanging bowls found in Lindsey occur in a remarkable range of sizes, forms and decorative styles suggesting that they were the products of an active tradition, not of a single workshop. While we have some fine examples, the simple nature of many of the bowls and the burnt fragments found in the Cleatham urns suggests that their use was not restricted to the aristocracy. Their function remains unknown.

Celtic burial rites?

There are some aspects of the Anglo-Saxon graves in Lindsey which might point to 'Celtic' or sub-Roman influence. The inclusion of the bones of domestic fowl in six graves, and geese in two, at Castledyke reflects a Romano-British rite. The most striking example of a late Roman-style burial in Anglo-Saxon Lindsey is the decapitated, prone corpse found with bird bones in Cleatham Grave 11 which looks late Roman on three counts. The unaccompanied male burial in a stone-lined grave at Cleatham resembles the 'long cists' seen in the north and west, but our lack of knowledge of late Roman burial practice in Lindsey limits what can be said about them. However, Roman burials of this type have been found just to the south of Lincoln at Navenby. Further indication of sub-Roman survival comes from the Roman-style urns found at Cleatham which indicate that the Romano-British pottery industry survived, in some form, into the fifth century.

THE END OF PAGANISM: SEVENTH-CENTURY CEMETERIES

The sixth century saw the gradual replacement of cremation by inhumation, with new cemeteries appearing in which graves predominated. At Cleatham and Fonaby the new rite was used in parallel with cremation but the Elsham and South Elkington cemeteries, where there were few inhumations, may have been abandoned.

The 'Final Phase' cemeteries

In the seventh century a new type of cemetery appeared which is typified by Sheffield's Hill II. Sheffield's Hill I is a typical sixth-century cemetery with the 47 graves irregularly aligned and scattered across the field (*29*). Grave goods were found in most graves, some being well equipped, but none could be described as rich. In the seventh century things changed: Sheffield's Hill I was abandoned and a new cemetery was opened, in the adjacent Romano-British field, 10m to the south. In the new cemetery the 72 graves were aligned west-east and were laid in rows. The grave goods had changed; the cruciform, square-headed and small-long brooches were no longer used, sleeve clasps were abandoned, weapons became still more uncommon and buckles, if worn, were small. Polychrome beads, which had been popular, were replaced by plain, monochrome varieties. Still more striking was the allocation of grave goods; in the fifth and sixth centuries some people had more than others but everyone was basically getting the same sort of things. In the seventh century most graves had little in the way of grave goods but there were a small number of graves with rich finds, gold and garnet jewellery, amethysts and swords (*colour plate 12*). Something had changed.

The disappearance of the big brooches and the sleeve clasps, and their replacement with small annular brooches and pins suggests that the women were dressing in a different way (*31*). Some new object types like work boxes and iron chains, worn at the waist, appear (*33*). There was a movement away from 'Anglian' dress towards a single style being adopted throughout Anglo-Saxon England, a style of dress that was introduced from Christian Frankia but

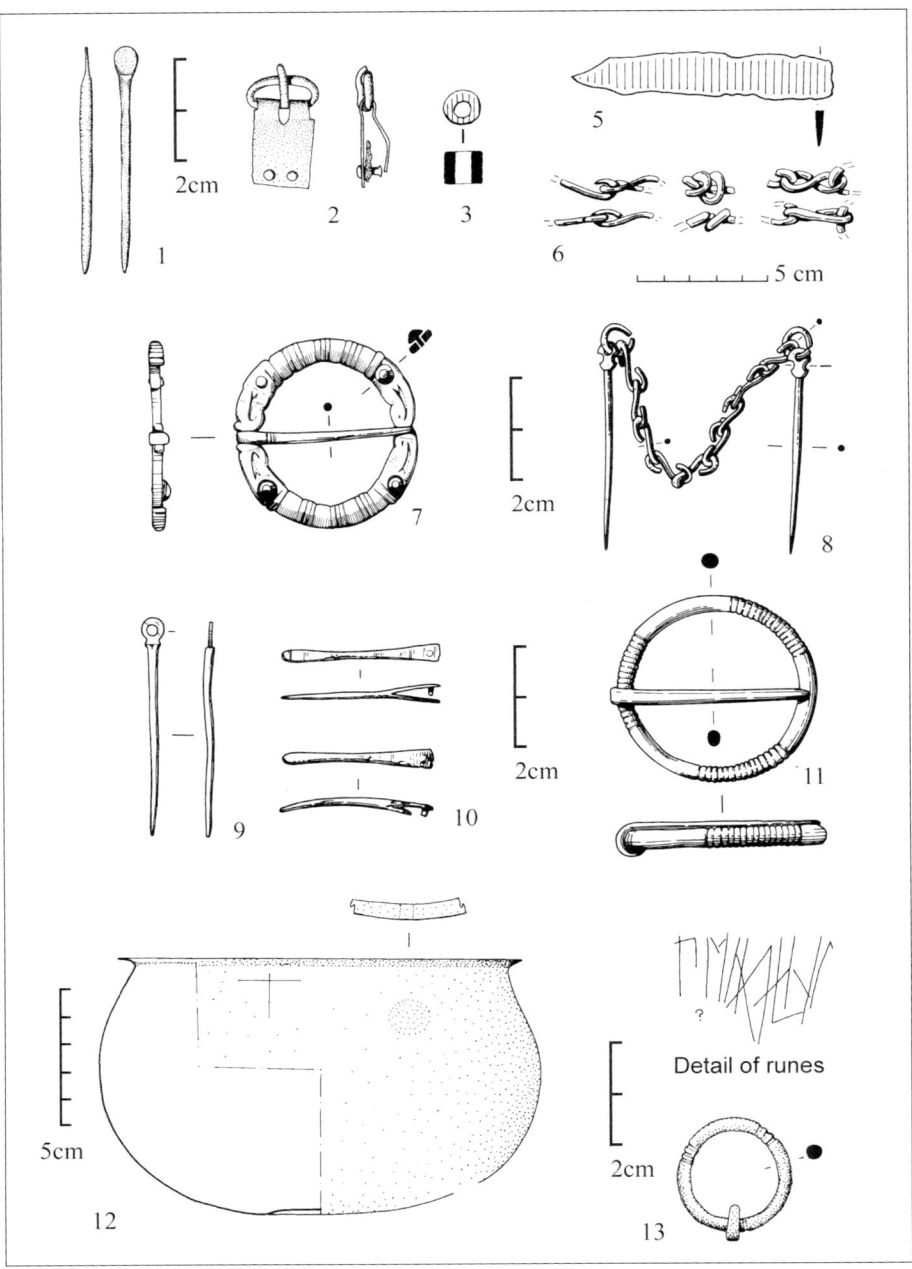

31 Finds from seventh-century 'Final Phase' graves in Lindsey. 1–6: Group of finds from Cleatham Grave 50; 1: silver pin; 2: small copper alloy buckle; 3: plain glass bead; 5: iron knife; 6: fragments of an iron chain; 7: Silver brooch decorated with birds' heads, Castledyke Grave 106; 8: Linked silver pins, Castledyke Grave 46; 9–10: Pin and strap ends, Castledyke Grave 15; 11: Silver brooch, Castledyke Grave 138; 12–13: Hanging bowl with runic inscription and annular brooch, Cleatham Grave 20. *Drawings of objects from Cleatham by Kevin Leahy; from Castledyke courtesy of Humber Field Archaeology*

ultimately originated in the Eastern Mediterranean. Sheffield's Hill II may not have been a Christian cemetery but it was certainly influenced by Christianity. The use of grave goods in Christian burials is not a problem; contrary to what is commonly believed, there is nothing in Church Law that forbids the use of grave goods. We only have to look at the finds from the grave of St Cuthbert, now at Durham, who was buried with a gold and garnet cross, a liturgical comb, a portable altar and a Gospel book.

These late graves contained some imported material. Castledyke Grave 1 contained a wheel-thrown pottery jug with a trefoil mouth, a type found throughout Merovingian France and Germany (*colour plate 5*). Nine examples are known from England, all of which come from Kent with the exception of one from a seventh-century grave at Bruncliffe in Derbyshire. While the Kentish jugs came from the Pas de Calais region it seems likely that the Castledyke find was brought across the North Sea from the Rhine. Castledyke also produced a handle and foot ring from a Frankish bowl of a type previously only found in Kent and we have finds of 'Coptic' bowls of the type found in the Cabourne grave (below).

Sheffield's Hill II is typical of what is known as a 'Final Phase' cemetery. These represent the final phase of the pagan Saxon cemeteries in eastern England that were first recognised in Cambridgeshire by Tom Lethbridge. He excavated cemeteries that contained few grave goods and, as his work progressed, he realised that these cemeteries were not poor but dated to after the conversion of the Anglo-Saxons to Christianity. In his report on the cemetery at Shudy Camps he summarised what defined these cemeteries:

- Most of the bodies were unaccompanied by grave goods.
- No object of typical pagan form had been found, with the possible exception of two annular brooches reused on chatelaines and a few Roman coins.
- Both weapons and brooches were absent and belts, if used, were narrow.
- The cemetery appeared to date from a time when the ordinary pagan cemeteries closed.

The idea was taken further by E.T. Leeds who used the term 'Final Phase' for the title of the last chapter of his 1936 book *Early Anglo-Saxon Art and Archaeology*. He extended the range of these late burials, adding examples from Kent, Derbyshire, Wiltshire, Yorkshire, and Lincolnshire. In Lindsey, he placed the cemeteries at Riby Park and Searby in this group.

Excavations since the last war, particularly at Chamberlain's Barn, Beds and Winnall, Hampshire have helped fill out what we know about the Final Phase cemeteries and led people to think about them. Boddington gives the following summary of Final Phase Cemetery attributes:

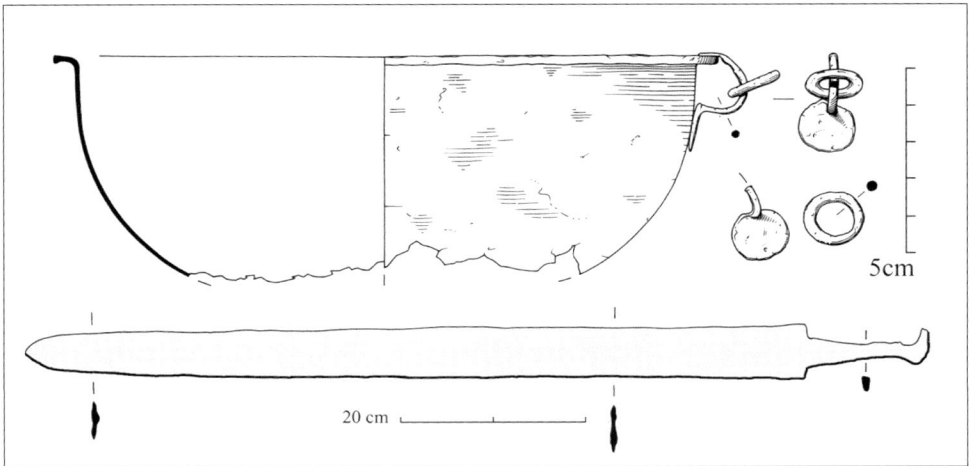

32 The finds from Grave 179 at Castledyke; a hanging bowl and a sword. *Drawing by Humber Field Archaeology*

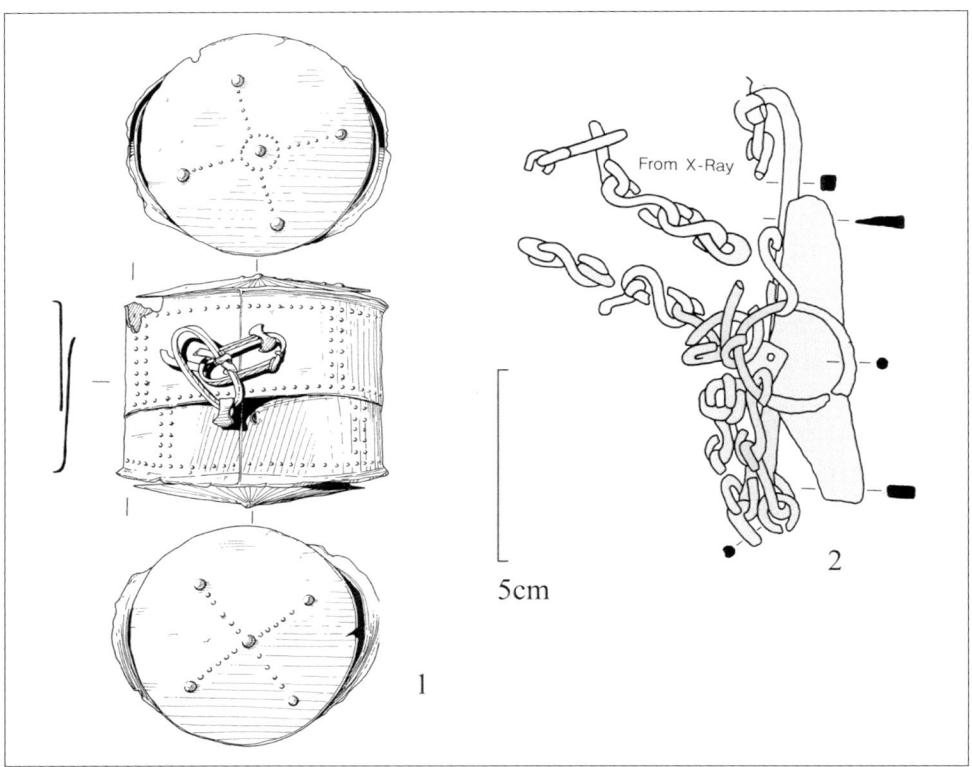

33 Finds from Castledyke Grave 183, the copper-alloy work box, iron chain and fire steel are typical of the seventh-century 'Final Phase' burials. *Drawings courtesy of Humber Field Archaeology*

1. New cemeteries established under Christian influence.
2. These cemeteries are close to the settlements, whereas their pagan predecessors tended to be further afield, often on boundaries.
3. Burial is entirely by inhumation, cremation being absent.
4. The graves are consistently west-east.
5. Some graves are in, or under, barrows.
6. The proportion of graves without artefacts, or with only a knife, is high.
7. Artefacts are predominately small dress fittings or small personal tokens.
8. Weapons are rare.
9. Some objects, notably cross forms, have a possible Christian significance.

The other aspect of the Final Phase cemeteries is the general decline in the use of grave goods, but with some graves being very rich. This is likely to be a result of the rise of a local aristocracy during the seventh century, with wealth being concentrated into fewer hands. This can be seen at Castledyke with Grave 179, which contained the bones of a youth aged around 14-16 years, together with a sword and a bronze bowl (*30, 32*). The grave was dug through an earlier spear burial which, as weapon burials are not common in Lindsey, seems deliberate and it is likely that a point was being made. This young man's grave acted as the nucleus for later burials, with graves being dug around him; he was clearly seen as being someone of importance. Even in the Anglo-Saxon period it is unlikely that this youth had managed to make a great reputation for himself as a warrior; it is much more likely that his status was inherited and not achieved. He was admired, not through what he had done, but because of who his parents were.

Unlike Sheffield's Hill there was no sign of 'cemetery shift' at Castledyke with the start of Final Phase burials; they continued to dig graves through each other as they had always done. There was also no sign of cemetery shift at Cleatham, although the seventh-century graves were clustered together in the north-eastern corner of the site. None of the Final Phase graves at Cleatham could be described as rich, although there was some interesting material, including the garnet-set buckle in Grave 15. It was reported that the burials found in 1916 by soldiers practising entrenching at Riby Park were arranged in regular rows. Both the layout of the cemetery and the find of an amethyst bead show it to have been seventh century, but an urn, often thought to have been in this grave, was found in the preceding year and was probably not associated.

Single graves
The other type of burial typical of the seventh century are single graves, some of which lay beneath mounds. These, again, are likely to represent an elite whose status was reflected in their graves. It is unfortunate that, to date, no example of a

single grave has ever been properly excavated in Lindsey and that all we have are casual finds. In the 1920s a 'warrior grave' was found by quarry workers around 700m to the north-east of the Cleatham cemetery. Little is known about this grave but it seems that human (and possibly horse) bones were found, but not kept. What does survive are the grave goods which consist of a sword, a 'seax' or single-edged short sword, a spearhead, two knives and an iron bridle bit, representing an important seventh-century group. This grave was on the parish boundary between Manton and Hibaldstow. In 1939 the important Manton hanging bowl was found further along this boundary, and this too, is likely to have come from a mound.

Our knowledge of other single or mound burials is also sparse but we are left with some tantalising evidence. What may have been a mound burial was found in 1915 at Asgarby, on the Clay Wolds above Bolingbroke, near to the West Keal cremation cemetery. The finds consisted of a sword, a shield boss, a knife, three plates decorated in Anglo-Saxon Style I, a D-shaped buckle, fragments of an amber glass-lobed beaker and pieces of bronze. The sword and shield boss no longer survive, probably never having reached the British Museum; the lobed beaker has been described as a 'fragmentary piece of doubtful affinity'. The sixth-century date of the decorated plates suggests that the finds came from a cemetery found in Asgarby in 1811 from which the British Museum received beads and two cruciform brooches. A more convincing mound burial was found in 1954 when a field overlooking a tributary of the River Bain at Stenigot was deep ploughed. On cutting through a low mound of chalk rubble the remains of three adults were found with a bronze cauldron, a seax with scabbard fittings, an iron fire-steel, a knife and what are likely to have been the iron bindings from a bucket.

Other barrow burials in Lindsey seem, on consideration, to be still more dubious. The 'barrow' at Cock Hill, Burgh le Marsh has a superb setting next to a possible Roman road and on the edge of the Wolds overlooking the coastal marsh land. A small trench dug in 1933 had produced a seventh-century buckle plate and an incomplete skeleton. This was thought to be a barrow but when in 1976 a raised footpath was laid next to the mound medieval pottery was found beneath it and it seems to overlie medieval ridge and furrow fields. It could be the site of a post mill with the human bone coming from the graveyard of a nearby church. There are also problems with the 'King's Barrow' at Bardney which local tradition holds to be a royal burial of eighth-century date. The name 'King's Barrow' is of recent date and seems to be a fine piece of creative etymology in which the old name for the field 'Coneygarth' was linked with the German *Koenig* (king) and not the more likely, but less interesting, rabbits. The barrow was trenched in 1912 but nothing was found except the traces of an earlier 'unscientific' excavation.

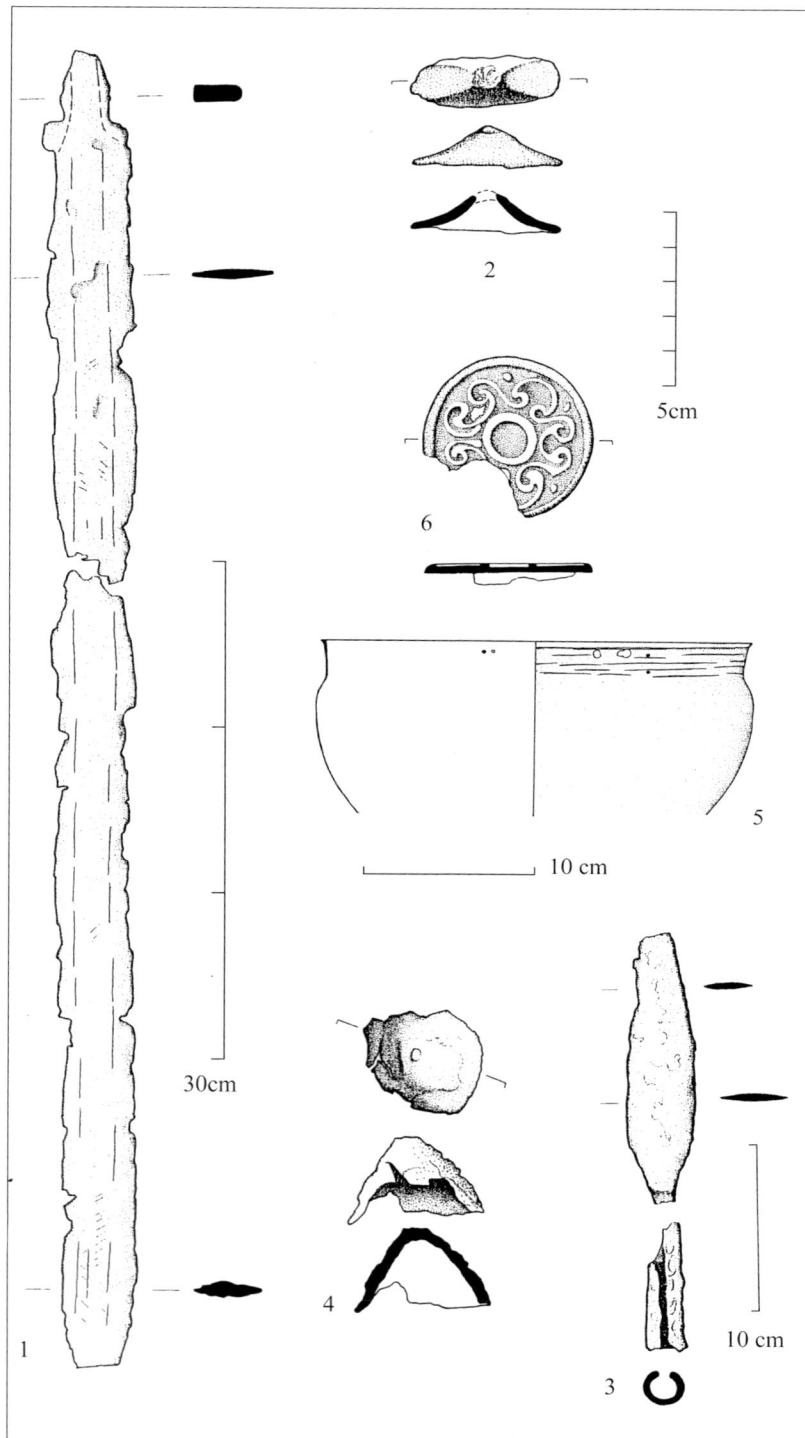

5cm

10 cm

30cm

10 cm

34 Finds from the Bracebridge Heath warrior grave. An iron sword with a pattern-welded blade (1), fitted with a copper-alloy pommel (2). With it was an iron spearhead (3) and a fragment of a shield boss (4). The copper-alloy hanging bowl (5) was fitted with an enamel decorated mount (6). *Drawings by Marina Elwes courtesy of Lindsey Archaeological Services*

Bracebridge Heath lies just outside of Lindsey but it is of some interest. The grave (*34*) was found during the laying of a pipeline along the boundary between two parishes making it probable that, like the Manton graves, it was originally marked by a mound. The finds consisted of a sword with a copper-alloy pommel of early fifth-century date, a spearhead, a hanging bowl and what may be the apex of a seventh-century shield boss. The sword had a pattern-welded blade, a process that involves twisting and fusing together strips of iron for decorative effect; a process also used to make two fine swords found in seventh-century graves at Sheffield's Hill. The most common surviving element of these swords are the pommel caps which have a characteristic 'cocked hat' form and the pyramid-shaped fittings that were used to attach a sword scabbard to the belt (*47,1*). Both pommel caps and pyramids are usually made from copper alloy but we have a superb set of gold hilt fittings from Market Rasen (*colour plate 15*). It is possible that these gold hilt fittings came from a grave, they were found in the up-cast from the scouring of a river and there are a number of ways in which the sword could have found its way into this river. The findspot is on a parish boundary and the sword could have been in a barrow, later destroyed by the movement of the river. Alternatively, it may have been deliberately thrown into the river, a practice that occurred from the Bronze Age onward. Finally, it could have been lost in a skirmish, as many early medieval battles were fought at river crossings. The Market Rasen fittings, the delightful boar's head crest from Horncastle (*colour plate 16*) and the drinking horn mounts from Holton le Moor (*colour plate 11*) show us something of the quality of material available to the aristocracy in seventh-century Lindsey.

A chance to examine a single grave was lost with the discovery, by metal detector users, of an important burial in the Cabourne area. The grave contained a copper-alloy Coptic bowl, a glass 'palm' cup, a set of slide keys, an iron spoon or ladle, a whelk shell and a spearhead. There does seem to be a contradiction here as spearheads are usually found with men and keys with women and, although they could have come from the same grave, it is possible that there was more than one burial. As the excavation of this important burial could have told us so much it represents a tragic loss.

Caenby, a king of Lindsey?

The burial found beneath a large mound at Caenby, may have represented Lindsey's Sutton Hoo but unfortunately it had already been damaged when it was excavated in 1849. At that time the mound was still very large with a diameter of around 110ft and a height of 8ft (larger than the mound covering the Sutton Hoo ship burial). A body was found in a sitting position on the original ground surface and was accompanied by a sword,

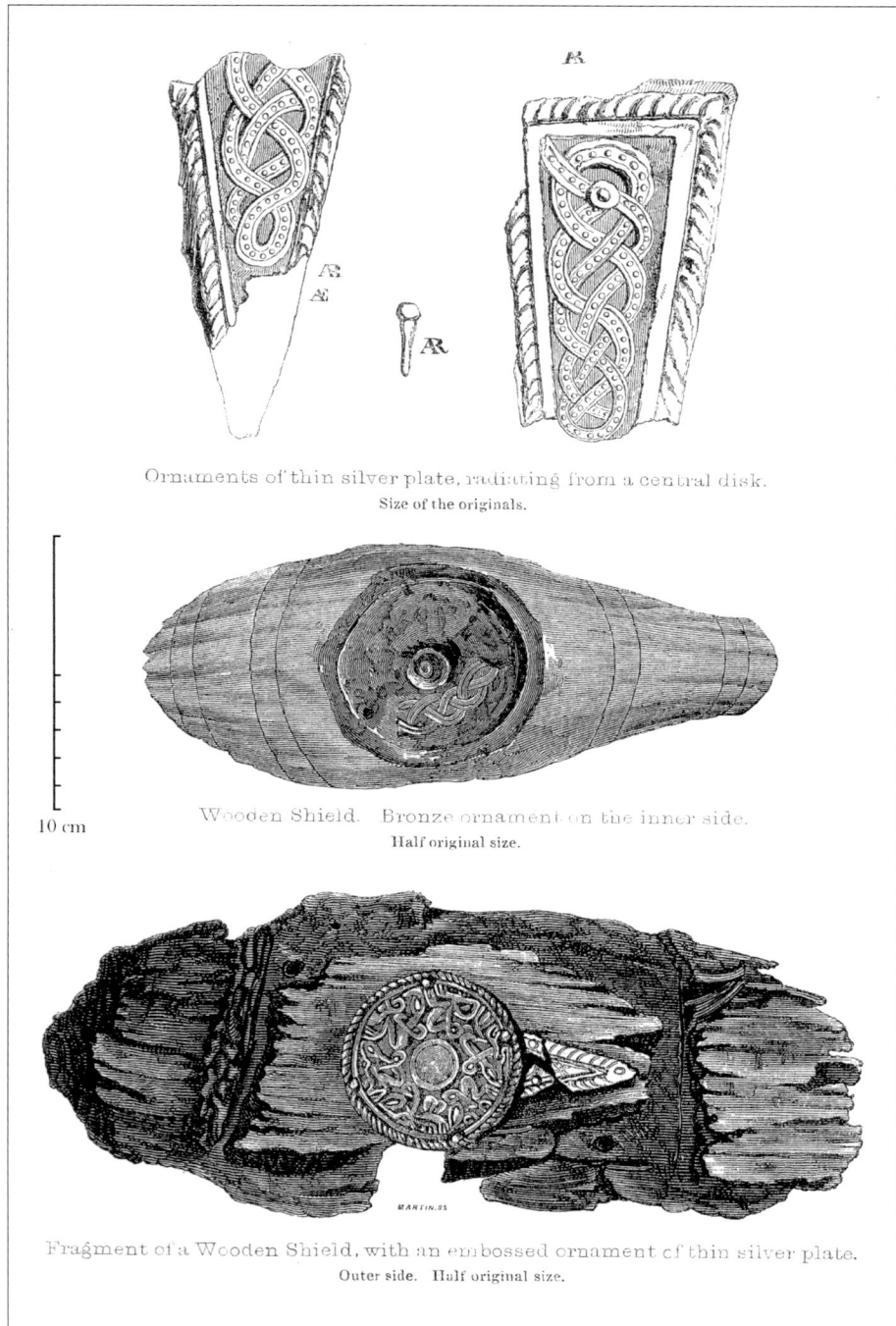

Ornaments of thin silver plate, radiating from a central disk.
Size of the originals.

10 cm

Wooden Shield.   Bronze ornament on the inner side.
Half original size.

Fragment of a Wooden Shield, with an embossed ornament of thin silver plate.
Outer side.   Half original size.

35 Page of illustrations from Jarvis' 1850 account of his excavation of the great Caenby barrow. The origin of the wooden mounts is uncertain, they could have come from a chest, a bed or a chair.
Drawings courtesy of the Society of Antiquaries of London

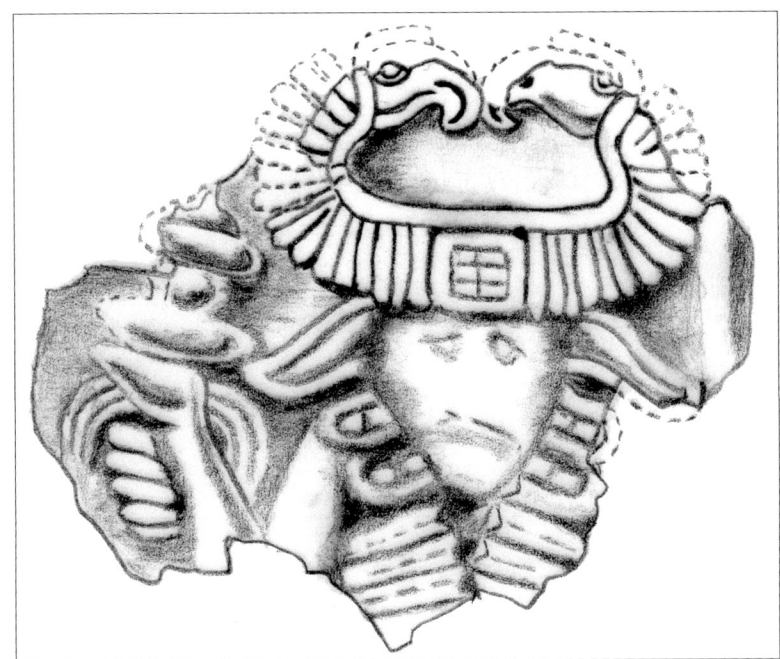

36 Foil mount from Caenby showing the head of a warrior wearing a horned helmet. Foil mounts of this type were found on the helmet from the burial in Mound 1 at Sutton Hoo. *Drawing by Dianne Leahy after Bruce-Mitford, 1978*

a shield and a series of fine metal mounts (*35*). The surviving metalwork from Caenby reflects the importance of this burial and included a decorative foil showing a figure wearing a horned helmet closely resembling the mounts on the Sutton Hoo helmet (*36*). Other seventh-century mounts may have come from a horse harness but could have adorned a box, chair or bed. We must, however, await the re-evaluation of these finds before we can assess their importance.

Paul Everson has discussed the location of Caenby within Lindsey which makes it a convincing site for a royal burial. At Caenby, Ermine Street, running north from Lincoln, was crossed by an east-west route-way which Everson has suggested is ancient as it forms the boundary between the parishes of Harpswell and Hemswell, breaking the run of strip-like parishes that typifies the limestone scarp. He suggested that the place-name 'Harpswell' comes not from the Old English *hearpere* (harper) but from *here paeð* (an army path which was, in the Anglo-Saxon period, a royal route). The road continues west to the Trent near Gainsborough, meeting it where there is a break in the marshes. It seems that Caenby, or the adjacent Spital in the Street (in Hemswell parish, *spital* means ho*spital*) was a meeting place and market during the Medieval Period and earlier. The hospital was first mentioned in the later twelfth century but its earlier name seems to have been *Herwik* meaning, in Old English 'army camp', supporting the *here paeð* interpretation of Harpswell. Hemswell, Harpswell and Kirton in

Lindsey were linked both administratively and ecclesiastically. All were included in the great soke of Kirton in Lindsey, and the Chapel of St Edmund which is likely to have had an Anglo-Saxon origin, was under the patronage of Kirton. The association of what is clearly an important site at Caenby/Spital with Kirton in Lindsey might further reinforce the status of the Cleatham cemetery.

1 Lindsey landscape, the Wolds near Horncastle. *Kevin Leahy*

2 Lindsey landscape, the view from the Cleatham cemetery, looking west from Lincoln Edge towards the Trent Valley. *Kevin Leahy*

Left: 3 Digging at Cleatham,
a group of seven urns being
uncovered. It was the intercutting of
the urns that allowed the cemetery
to be phased. *Kevin Leahy*

Below: 4 The Cleatham cemetery
in the sixth century. What we
uncovered is only part of what is
likely to have been complex ritual
the details of which we cannot even
guess. *Painting by Dianne Leahy*

Above: 5 Pottery from Anglo-Saxon
cemeteries in Lindsey, from left to right:
Imported Frankish jug from Castledyke,
feeding bottle from Castledyke, urn found
at the Cleatham cemetery in 1856 and urn
from the Elsham cemetery. *Kevin Leahy*

Right: 6 A pseudomorph of a body from
the Sheffield's Hill cemetery. The decay of
the skeleton in the fiercely acid soil caused
minerals to be deposited leaving a shadow
of the bones. *Kevin Leahy*

7 'Florid' cruciform brooch from Scampton. This brooch came from a ploughed out cemetery and was found in seven pieces over a six year period. It is made from copper alloy and is decorated with Anglo–Saxon Style I animal art and has been gilded with silver (or tin) plates added to its edges. Sixth century. *Kevin Leahy*

8 Great square-headed brooch from Scampton, also found in pieces. Faces are concealed in the elaborate design. Sixth century. *Kevin Leahy*

9 Fish-shaped copper-alloy mount from a shield from Sheffield's Hill. The mount is one of a pair. It has been gilded and had silver (?) plates added at its ends. The brown material behind it is part of the wooden shield board and the black material is part of the leather with which the shield was faced. Sixth century. *York Archaeological Trust*

10 Copper-alloy mount from the apex of the above shield. It has been gilded and is inlaid with four garnets. The lozenge-shaped mark at 3 o'clock was left by the point of a thrown spear. *York Archaeological Trust*

11 Silver–gilt drinking horn mounts from Holton le Moor. These objects came from an important object which can be paralleled by finds from the 'royal' burial at Taplow, Berkshire. It is a very fine example of Style I decoration. First half of the sixth century. *Lisa Staves*

Above: 12 Gold pendant, two gold beads, two amethyst beads and two glass beads from Sheffield's Hill. This group of objects was found in one grave and shows the sort of material being worn by the better class of woman in the seventh century. *Kevin Leahy*

10cm

13 Gold and garnet pendant in the form of a stylised insect from near Horncastle. This pendant is a good example of cloisonné garnet work in which the cut garnets are set in thin walled gold cells. These cells were lined with impressed gold foil to scatter the light and give the stones life. Pendants in the form of insects are known on the continent but the fitting looks English (see the gold beads on *colour plate 12*) and we may be looking at a continental object that has been mounted locally. Later sixth to seventh century. *Kevin Leahy*

14 Gold pendant cross from Newball. This object is important as it is the first definitely Christian find that we have from Lindsey. It is hollow and may have contained a relic. Though this cross appears to us to be upside down, this has been noted on other objects of the period that bear crosses. The cross would, however, have been the right way up when the wearer raised it to her face. Seventh century. *Lisa Staves*

15 Gold sword hilt fittings from near Market Rasen. These fittings are decorated with an elaborate design of sinuous animals executed in filigree gold wire, and are set with garnets. They show the quality of metalwork available in Lindsey during the early seventh century. *Kurt Adams*

16 Silver-gilt mount in the form of a boar from Horncastle. This delightful object is only 40mm long, the boar's tusks are clearly shown and the eyes are marked by garnet. Behind the head the body is compressed into a small space but the limbs are still visible. Parallels from elsewhere suggest that this object came from the crest of a helmet. Later sixth to seventh century. *Adam Daubney*

Above: 17 The Flixborough excavation. This view of the site shows some of the complex of Middle Saxon buildings in the process of being recorded. Many of the buildings were rebuilt on a number of occasions making for complicated archaeology. *Kevin Leahy*

Opposite above: 18 Finds from Flixborough excavation. These objects have been gilded and are decorated with the animals and interlace characteristic of the eighth century. *Kevin Leahy*

Below: 19 The Witham pins. Found in the River Witham at Fiskerton in 1826, these objects represent one of the masterpieces of Middle Saxon decorative metalwork. They are silver gilt and some of the animals have blue glass eyes. Interestingly they are not a set, no two of the disc heads are the same and, while the artistry of the discs is superb, the linking bars could have been done in the dark. Eighth century. *Illustration courtesy of the British Museum*

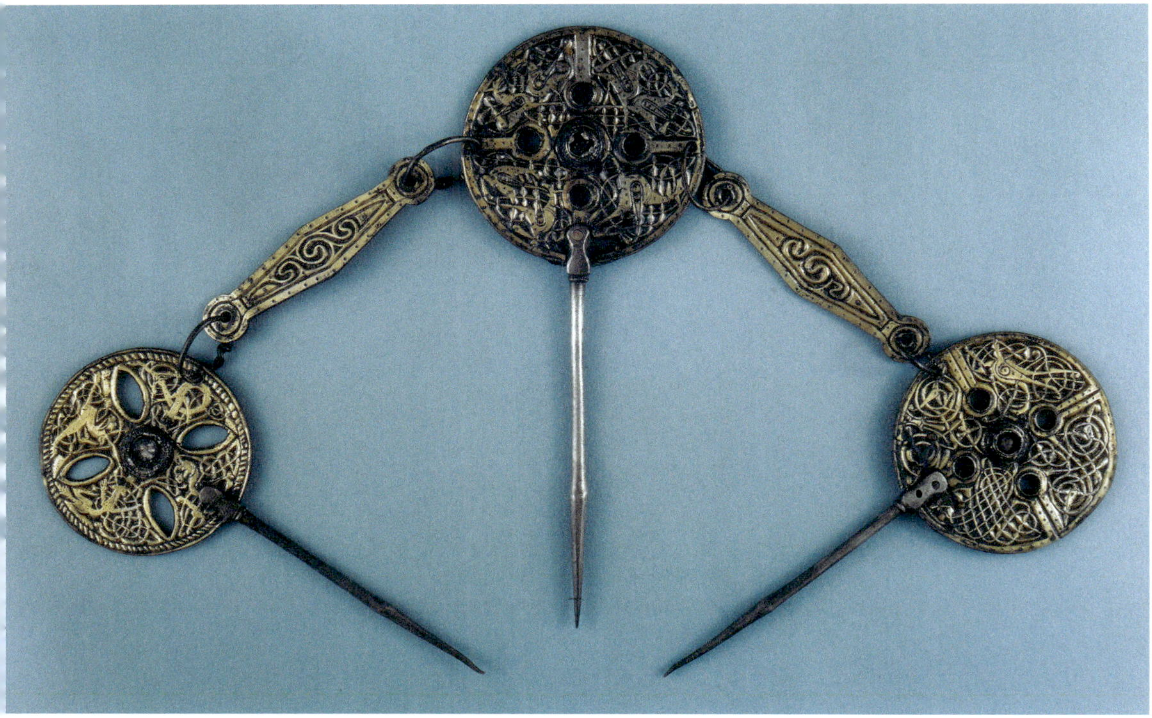

20 Inscribed lead plaque, silver stylus and alphabet ring from the Flixborough excavation. These objects and the many other styli provide important evidence for literacy on the site at Flixborough. Eighth century. *Kevin Leahy*

21 The Flixborough tool hoard and the lead vats in which it was found. When discovered one lead vat was upside down over the other forming a closed container. Other tool hoards have been found in lead vats. Eighth to ninth century. *Kevin Leahy*

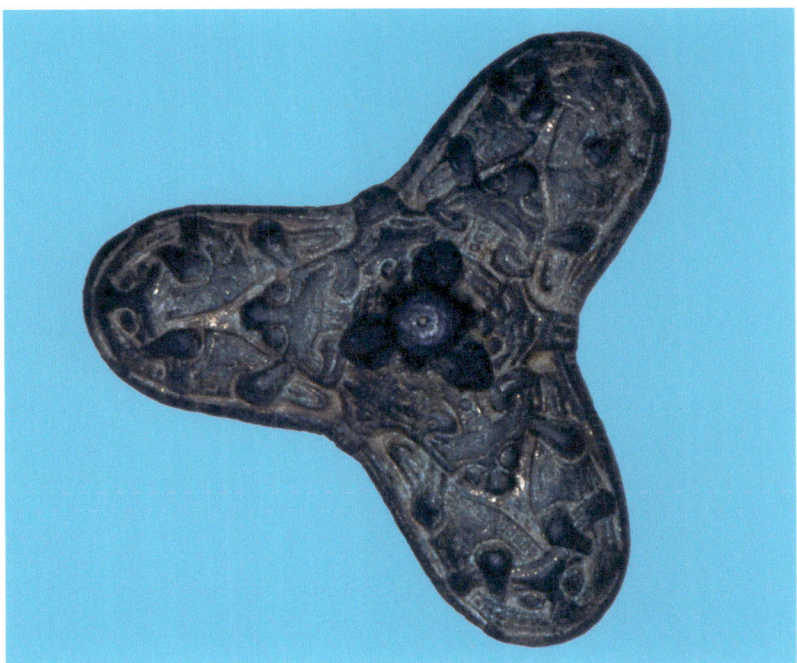

22 Viking trefoil brooch from Stallingborough. A superb example of the Viking Borre style this object is covered with a complex mass of intertwined animals. Later ninth to early tenth century. *Kevin Leahy*

23 Lead weights set with fragments of decorative metalwork and an Anglo-Saxon silver penny. These finds from Torksey are representative of the many objects of this type. Later ninth to early tenth century. *Kevin Leahy*

Above: 24 Silver ring from Theddlethorpe. This massive ring is decorated with the large stamp impressions that are typical of Viking silver work, diameter 26mm. Later ninth to early tenth century. *Steve Thompson*

10mm

Above: 26 The Anglo-Saxon tower and baptistery of St Peter's Church, Barton on Humber. It was here that Thomas Rickman first showed that Anglo-Saxon buildings survived and how they could be recognised. This photograph shows the strip work and the distinctive forms of the windows in the three lower stages. Later tenth century. *Kevin Leahy*

Opposite below: 25 Anglo-Saxon silver penny of Edward the Confessor struck by the moneyer Othbern of Lincoln. During the late Saxon period Lincoln was one of the most important English mints. *Lisa Staves*

27 The past forms the present. Aerial photograph of Barton on Humber illustrating how the streets still follow the line of the Middle Saxon ring work. St Peter's is the building with the light-coloured roof at about 4 o'clock. *Photograph courtesy of David Lee*

The early history of Lindsey

There are few historical references to Lindsey but the little we have are useful in providing a context for the archaeology. In the past archaeology has been seen as the servant of history, filling in the gaps and being forced into an historical framework. Neither discipline has primacy; the evidence for the early Medieval Period is so thin that they need each other. Lacking early records we have to grasp at mere mentions of Lindsey. Our most important references are a genealogy of Aldfrið, King of Lindsey, and the inclusion of the kingdom in the Tribal Hidage, a seventh-century tribute assessment. There are references to the kingdom in Bede's 'Ecclesiastical History' and later mentions of Lindsey when it had become part of Mercia.

THE GENEALOGY OF ALDFRIÐ, KING OF LINDSEY

This pedigree is our most important evidence for the kings of Lindsey. It appears in a document known as the *Anglian Collection,* which was probably compiled in Northumbria between 765 and 779, and contains the pedigrees and regnal lists for six Anglo-Saxon royal dynasties: Deira, Bernicia, Mercia, Lindsey, Kent and the East Angles. Four copies of the *Anglian Collection* survive of which the earliest, a Mercian copy dating from the first half of the ninth century, is in the British Library. The section containing the genealogies is headed 'Here are the genealogies of the kings reigning in different places in the parts of Britain'.

The genealogy starts with Aldfrið and lists his forebears back in time. Each man's name is followed by his father's name with the generative -ing:

Lindfeana (Lindsey)

Aldfrið	Eatting (the son of Eatta)
Eatta	Eanferðing
Eanferð	Biscoping
Biscop	Beding
Beda	Bubbing
Bubba	Cædbæding
Cædbæd	Cueldgilsing
Cueldgils	Cretting
Cretta	Winting
Winta	Uoding
Uoden	Frealafing
Frealaf	Frioðulfing
Frioðulf	Finning
Finn	Goduulfing
Godulf	Geoting

This list is both illuminating and frustrating. The pedigrees in the *Anglian Collection* are standardised at 14 generations from Woden, son of Frealaf, the common mythical ancestor of the Anglian kings. The Lindsey genealogy differs in that it includes only 11 generations back to Woden but then goes on to extend Woden's pedigree for a further five generations through *Frealaf, Friothulf, Finn, Godulf* and *Geot*. Sir Frank Stenton suggested that this addition was due to the compiler of the *Anglian Collection* having a particular interest in Lindsey, perhaps being a Lindsey man. However, a more plausible explanation is that these early, mythical, generations at the foot of the Lindsey list were originally shared by all of the genealogies tabulated in the document. That the Lindsey genealogy shows only 11 generations is difficult to explain. The standardisation of the other genealogies in the *Anglian Collection* is suspicious and is likely to have been forced; Lindsey, as the exception, gains in credibility, although Aldfrið's genealogy may have been shortened merely to accommodate the earlier, mythical generations.

None of the individuals on the pedigree can be dated with any degree of certainty. Stenton equated Aldfrið with the *Ealfrið rex* who witnessed a charter of confirmation made by Offa of Mercia between 772 and 796. This was important evidence as Offa was a man known to object strongly to any sub-king encroaching on his (Offa's) royal prerogatives. If Offa allowed this man to call himself king, then king he was. The charter also gave us our single date for anyone in the Lindsey genealogy; he must have been around in 772-96. Unfortunately it is now believed that the name on the witness list should read, not *Ealfrið Rex*, but *Ecgfrið Rex* and refers to Offa's son, and brief heir, Ecgfrith. Ecgfrith was anointed King of the Mercians in 787, nine years before his succession in 796 and would have been correctly styled *rex*. Stenton had also suggested that the name *Biscop* on the genealogy came from the title 'bishop' and must post-date St Paulinus' mission to Lindsey of AD 628. However, as Sarah Foot pointed out, *Biscop* is a perfectly acceptable Old English name and we have no need to look for an external origin. The other genealogies in the *Anglian Collection* close with historic personages whose dates are known, Edwin of Deira (616-33), Æthelred of Mercia (675-704) and Æthelberht II of Kent (725-62) but this wide range of dates offers little help in dating the reign of Aldfrið. Dr Foot tentatively suggested a *floruit* for Aldfrið around the last quarter of the seventh century to the first quarter of the eighth century. The only other evidence for King Aldfrið was a series of silver coins bearing the inscription *Ealdfrið*. It is now accepted that these are better attributed to Aldfrið of Northumbria (685-704) and that the kings of Lindsey did not issue coins. Myres drew attention to Winteringham and Winterton, two parishes near the Humber which contain the personal name *Winta*, who might have been the *Winta* listed on the genealogy. Attractive as this idea is, it is impossible to prove and must remain a matter of speculation.

THE TRIBAL HIDAGE

Further evidence for Lindsey's existence as a kingdom is provided by its inclusion in the seventh-century tribute assessment known as the *Tribal Hidage* where the *Lindesfarona* are assessed, along with Hatfield, at 7000 hides:

Lindisfarona syfan Þusend hyda mid HæÞfeldlande

The [land of] Lindsey with Hatfield Chase [is assessed at] seven thousand hides

David Dumville has suggested that Hatfield had been part of the Kingdom of Elmet and that it had been added to Lindsey for administrative purposes, which appears reasonable – Hatfield is separated from Lindsey by marshes and is not geographically part of the kingdom. While the accuracy of the *Tribal Hidage* is open to doubt, the assessments must have at least reflected some reality and provide an indication of the economic importance of Lindsey in relation to other kingdoms. Lindsey (with Hatfield) was one of six kingdoms rated at 7000 hides which placed it, along with Essex and Sussex, in the second tier of the 35 kingdoms listed. It is notable that Lindsey, alone amongst the 7000 hide kingdoms, has a regnal list, in spite of the much better charter evidence for other kingdoms, such as the Hwicca. Lindsey's 7000 hide assessment was far less than the massive 30,000 hides of Mercia, or the 15,000 hides of Kent but greatly in excess of the 600 hide rating of the North and South Gyrwe in the Fens or the 300 hides of the Gifle and Hicce. An assessment of 7000 may, however, have been symbolic, as '7000' was the measure of land allocated to Beowulf by King Hygelac and might be seen as an appropriate holding for a nobleman.

There is general agreement that the *Tribal Hidage* is a tribute list compiled during the seventh century and probably during the last third of that century. The list is mainly concerned with the Midlands suggesting that it is a Mercian compilation. Mercia heads the list and is described as 'the area first called Mercia' indicating that it was compiled after the period of Mercian expansion. Nicholas Brooks, however, has argued that it dates from one of the periods of Northumbrian ascendancy during which the northern kingdom was able to demand tribute from Mercia. The inclusion of Lindsey and Elmet in the *Tribal Hidage* supports it being a Mercian creation from a time when Mercia controlled these two peripheral areas. No other parts of Northumbria are included within the *Tribal Hidage* and, if this had been a Northumbrian assessment, these two parts of the Northumbrian core kingdom would also have been omitted. Whatever the political situation at the time of this assessment the important fact is that Lindsey was included in this list of kingdoms or tribes.

THE HUMBRENSES

J.N.L. Myres raised the possibility of the existence of a Humbrensian tribal grouping based around the estuary, perhaps including Deira, Elmet and Lindsey (*1*). The names of the three kingdoms have Celtic roots and may have been sub-Roman British kingdoms before passing under the control of the English and certainly we have good evidence for a Celtic survival in Lindsey (see above). Elmet, which approximated to the West Riding of Yorkshire, is known to have survived as a British enclave into the seventh century. Barbara Yorke has drawn attention to parallels between the administrative structures and religious practices in Lindsey and those of Deira and Elmet, again suggesting that they may have shared a similar early development based on the survival of late Roman organisation. It is also worth noting that Kristensson has found that the dialect of medieval Lindsey is seen as part of a northern linguistic group while that of Holland and Kesteven is more closely linked with the Midland dialect of English.

The term 'Northumbria' first appears in Bede's *Ecclesiastical History* (completed in 731) and it has been argued that the concept of the Humber as a dividing line was his invention. Although the word 'Northumbrian' (*Nordanhymbri*) would have been useful to him, Bede failed to use it in his earlier works and, in the preface to his *Ecclesiastical History*, he was, as Myres points out, concerned to explain the meaning of 'Northumbria', suggesting that it was new to his readers. The word 'Humbrenses' occurs in late seventh-century sources with, amongst other accounts, Ecgfrid being described as '*rege Hymbronensium*' (*ibid* 252), suggesting that he was king of the Humber region which, at that time, was considered to include the tributary rivers of the estuary, York and, almost certainly, Lindsey. As St Paulinus' mission to Lindsey in 627/8 is likely to have been an off-shoot of the saint's mission to Northumbria it seems that Lindsey was, at that time, under the domination of King Edwin. This need not have prevented Lindsey having its own king but he would have been *sub regis*, semi-autonomous, paying Edwin homage, tribute and giving military assistance. Myres ventured that it was the irrevocable loss of Lindsey in the second half of the seventh century that led to the formation of Northumbria as a region and turned the Humber into a boundary. Attractive as this hypothesis is, valid criticisms have been levelled at it and the case is far from proven.

Some claims have been made for cultural links across the Humber during the Early Anglo-Saxon period. Urns made by the Sancton/Elkington and Sancton/Baston potters are found both in Lindsey and in Deira to the north of the estuary. While the Sancton/Baston urns are stamp-linked and probably represent the work of one potter, the Sancton/Elkington pots look more like a potting tradition than the work of an individual. Brooches of the northern C2 'square-headed cruciform' type occur in Lindsey with finds from Fonaby (*22*, 6) and Cleatham but the type also occurs further south. Although Lindsey was under the domination of Deira it is unlikely that the three Humber kingdoms ever formed a single polity and the apparent cultural links across the estuary are more easily explained as a shared Anglian cultural tradition.

THE SEVENTH-CENTURY WARS

At the time of St Paulinus' mission to Lindsey in 627 the kingdom was under the control of King Edwin of Northumbria, probably reflecting a long-standing relationship. This relationship came to an end with the defeat and death of Edwin at the Battle of Hatfield Chase, to the west of Lindsey, in 632. The victorious Penda of Mercia and his ally Cadwallon of Gwynedd moved north to devastate Northumbria, only to be halted by Oswald of Bernicia's destruction of Cadwallon at Rowley Burn near Hexham in the final months of 633. The succession of King (later Saint) Oswald resulted in a period of peace, during which Northumbria again controlled Lindsey. Oswald died in battle against the pagan king Penda of Mercia at *Maserfelth* (probably Oswestry) in 642 and the fortunes of the two kingdoms fluctuated in the years that followed. Mercia was dominant for some years after *Maserfelth* but, in 655, Penda was defeated by Oswiu of Northumbria and Mercia (and Lindsey) were again under Northumbria's control. This ended in 658 when a revolt, centred around Wulfhere (one of Penda's sons), expelled the Northumbrians from Mercia. In 679, Mercian forces under Æthelred achieved a final victory at the Battle of the Trent. At some time after this battle Lindsey was settled as a Mercian province. It is possible that Lindsey's own royal line ended around this time and the kingdom was administered by a Mercian ealdorman.

We know little of the part played by Lindsey in the struggles between Mercia and Northumbria. Although it lies on the boundary between the two protagonists its isolated, island-like position may, to a large extent, have insulated Lindsey from the conflict. The major frontier battles between the two warring kingdoms (Hatfield Chase, 632; Trent, 679) were fought, not in Lindsey, but to the west on the road from Lincoln to Castleford, sparing Lindsey the suffering caused by the passage of an invading army and, indeed, the depredations of 'friendly' forces. It is impossible to gauge the sympathies of Lindsey during these times but some indication might be provided by the action of the monks at Bardney. Fifty years after Oswald's death in 642 the saint's niece Osthryth, Queen of the Mercians, decided to have his remains translated to Bardney. The monks refused to accept them because 'although they knew him to be a saint they pursued him dead, with ancient enmities, as one sprung from another province who had taken rule over them' (Bede, H.E. III, 11). This may simply be a hagiographic device to introduce a nice miracle into the story (a beam of that light shone from the coffin up into the sky all night) but there could have been some real ill-feeling. The 'other province' from which Oswald had sprung need not have been Northumbria but could have referred more specifically to Bernicia, Lindsey feeling an affinity with the neighbouring kingdom of Deira.

PLACE–NAMES IN LINDSEY

A further source of evidence for early Lindsey comes from place-name studies. This represents dangerous ground for the non-specialist, being the preserve of a small number of scholars with an arcane knowledge of early languages and the way in which they develop and interrelate. As an archaeologist, all I can do is to attempt to evaluate this evidence in archaeological terms. Students are well served by the English Place-Name Society's volumes which will cover most of Lincolnshire wapentakes. This detailed work has been summarised in Cameron's useful 1998 publication, *A Dictionary of Lincolnshire Place-Names*.

Lindsey has few surviving Celtic place-names but these are of great interest. Unlike most Romano-British cities, Lincoln retained its Roman name in a recognisable form: *Lindum colonia* = *Lin-coln* which comes from the Celtic/Latin name for Lincoln. The first element is the British *linn*, 'a lake or pool' probably referring to the Brayford Pool below the city, coupled with *-coln* from *colonia*: a city originally set up for retired soldiers. Lincoln is the only Roman city in eastern England to have given its name to an Anglo-Saxon kingdom, which may reflect the way in which the Anglo-Saxon settlement happened and the place of the native population in the society that then formed.

The second element of the name Lindsey, 'ey', appears to be the Old English word for an island, *g* which has led to the belief that Lindsey itself was considered to be an island. There is some justification in this as it was surrounded by water and marshes. More recently it has been argued that the Anglo-Saxons' use of the word *g* was restricted to relatively small islands and that the island may have been Wigford, just to the south of Lincoln, which was enclosed by the River Witham and the Sincil Dyke. The archaeological evidence fails to support this as secular settlement does not recommence in the Wigford area until the tenth century. It has also been proposed the *g* may be the steep hill on which Lincoln stands, rising like an island out of the surrounding landscape. I prefer *g* to refer, as was originally suggested, to the whole of Lindsey, which was, from the earliest times, what was meant when the word was used.

As is typical of eastern England only major elements of the Lindsey landscape kept their early names. A local feature like a hill or stream is easily renamed but with something like the Trent, passing through many peoples' lands, it was impossible to get a consensus. The River Trent was referred to by Ptolemy in *c.*AD 140-50 as the *Trisantonia* and we can trace the development of the river-name from the British *Trisantonia* > primitive Welsh: *Tihanton* > Old English (Bede): *Treenta*. The name may have originally meant 'wanderer'. It is no surprise that this great river retained its original name. It is impossible to suggest a convincing origin for the name 'Humber' and Kenneth Cameron thought the name to be, not only pre-Anglo-Saxon but also pre-Celtic. Likewise the Lindsey village of Swallow is likely to have a pre-Celtic name, originally referring to a stream. It is likely that the names of the rivers Ancholme and Witham are of Celtic origin although of uncertain etymology. There is little else in the place-name evidence to suggest the survival of an identifiable British population. Walcot, in Alkborough parish, may refer to *Walh* or 'Welsh' but the word could have been used in its alternative meaning of 'slave'.

Place-names containing the element *wic*, as in *wich* m-type names are seen as an indicator of a Romano-British survival into the Anglo-Saxon period. *Wic* is a word derived from the Latin *vicus* which, during the Roman period, was the term used for the smallest unit of self-government in the provinces. In Old English *wic* had a variety of meanings including: port, street, dwelling place, dairy farm and place where salt was extracted. It is the association of *wic* with the early element *h m* which allows this group of names to be separated from the ports and dairy farms. *Wichams* are thought to represent something which the Anglo-Saxons identified as a Roman settlement and indicate some form of survival. These place-names usually occur near Roman roads and settlement sites. There are three *wichams* in Lindsey: East and West Wykeham and Wykeham, a deserted medieval village in Nettleton parish. East and West Wykeham are near Ludford, where the Roman remains covered an estimated 16ha and are less than 2km from Roman roads and 5km from the Sixhills Anglo-Saxon cemetery. The Nettleton Wykeham is near the Roman walled site of Caistor on the Wolds and 1.2km from the ancient trackway of Caistor High Street. Near Caistor are the Nettleton and Fonaby Anglo-Saxon cemeteries and in 1987 an Anglo-Saxon settlement was found at Nettleton Top, 1km to the north-west of Wykeham. It cannot be argued that the Lindsey *wichams* indicate any sort of coherent Romano-British survival, but they suggest that, during the early period, some settlements existed which were identified using a Latin word.

It is considered that the earliest Anglo-Saxon settlements are those containing the element -*h m*. This is based on the distribution of -*h m* place-names and it being compounded with early, and not late, elements. Some problems exist in recognising the early -*h m* place-names as it can be difficult to distinguish between -*h m*, a settlement, and *hamm*, land in a river-bend, a river-meadow or dry ground in a marsh. This is a highly specialised argument but fortunately the -*h m* place-names of Lincolnshire were included in Dr Cox's study and were accepted by him. It is satisfying that both Cleatham and Elsham have place-names containing the early -*h m* element, the first element of Cleatham coming from *clæte*, a burdock. That the site should be named after this plant causes no surprise. The burdock, *Arctium sp.* is a large, 1.3m-high biennial which grows on waste ground and can still be found at Cleatham. It is edible but its most notable feature is the dried seed capsules, which cling to clothing in a way likely to make any visit memorable. Elsham contains, as its first element, the Old English personal name *Elli*. Apart from these two cemeteries there is no direct correlation between pagan Anglo-Saxon burial places and -*h m*, -*ingham* or -*inga*- place-names.

Cox was able to identify 15 -*h m* place-names in Lindsey, representing 3.2 per cent of Domesday place-names. This is far less than in Suffolk, where they form 11 per cent of the place-names, and Norfolk where they represent 9.6 per cent of Domesday place-names. It is likely that this is a result of the renaming of parishes following the Danish conquest in the ninth and tenth centuries (*64*). *H m* place-names appear relatively equi-spaced in Lindsey but are absent along the Humber and Trent banks, where early settlement might have been expected, and there are no examples on the Isle of Axholme. The only possible candidate, Burnham, is likely, on topographical grounds, to be derived from *-hamm*. There is a strong link between *-h m* place-names and Roman roads, and the sites which are not on or near Roman roads appear to be on the line of ancient routeways. Cleatham lies 2.5km to the west of Ermine Street and the Elsham cemetery lies across the line of the ancient Middlegate Lane trackway.

On the eastern edge of the Lincolnshire Wolds is Wyham, which contains the element *w oh*, the Anglian dialect word for a pagan shrine. Early versions of the place-name Widun, 1086 and Wihum, 1115 show that it does not contain the early *h m* element. *W oh* place-names are not common and Wyham is the only example in Lindsey. The other Old English word for a holy place was *hearg* but the two words seem to have been used differently. *W oh* tends to be used for places on low ground and along lines of communication, suggesting that they were personal or wayside shrines. Wyham is on the western edge of the Wolds where they meet the marsh, and is near the possible Roman road leading to Grainthorpe. If it was only a minor shrine it seems odd that its name should have survived.

PSEUDO-HISTORY?

Most of history consists of accounts of kings and battles. We have seen that we have an account of the kings of Lindsey (at least we know they existed) but what of the battles? We don't know much about the earlier period but there is evidence to suggest that something interesting was going on.

The end of Roman Lindsey was a complicated business which cannot be seen in the simple terms of an Anglo-Saxon invasion. The fourth-century buckles and the fortifications at Caistor, Horncastle and possibly Yarborough Camp suggest that Lindsey had a militarily competent Romano-British population who were able to control Anglo-Saxon settlement (see *4*). The lack of early cemeteries around Lincoln, a city that both kept its name and gave its name to the kingdom, suggests a robust administration (see *8*). While Lincoln survived, it is unlikely that anything remained that resembled a Roman city. It was probably the headquarters of one of the people Gildas described as '*tyrani*'.

In addition to this we have evidence for a British survival; there seems to have been a large section of the population not represented in the Anglo-Saxon cemeteries and there is archaeological evidence for British culture in the form of the hanging bowls and the penannular brooches (*37-39*). The genealogy of Aldfrið, King of Lindsey, contains a British name, *Cædbæd*, suggesting links at

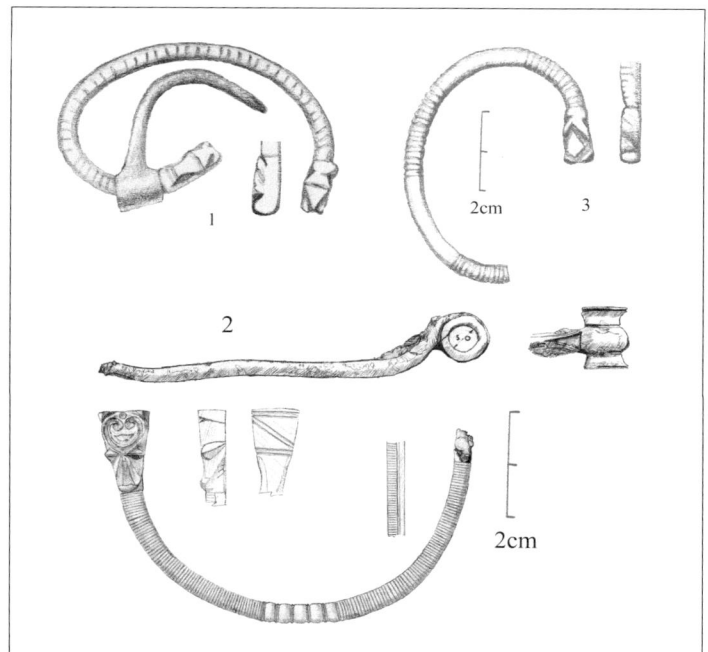

37 Copper-alloy
penannular brooches of
Fowler's Type FI. These
brooches are probably
of sixth-century date
and suggest the survival
of a Romano-British
population.
1: Brooch from
Winteringham. 2: Half
of the ring and the pin
from a brooch from East
Ravendale. The pseudo-
zoomorphic terminal is
inlaid with enamel. 3: F1
penannular brooch from
Kirmington. *Drawings 1
and 3 by Marina Elwes, 2
by Michael Smith*

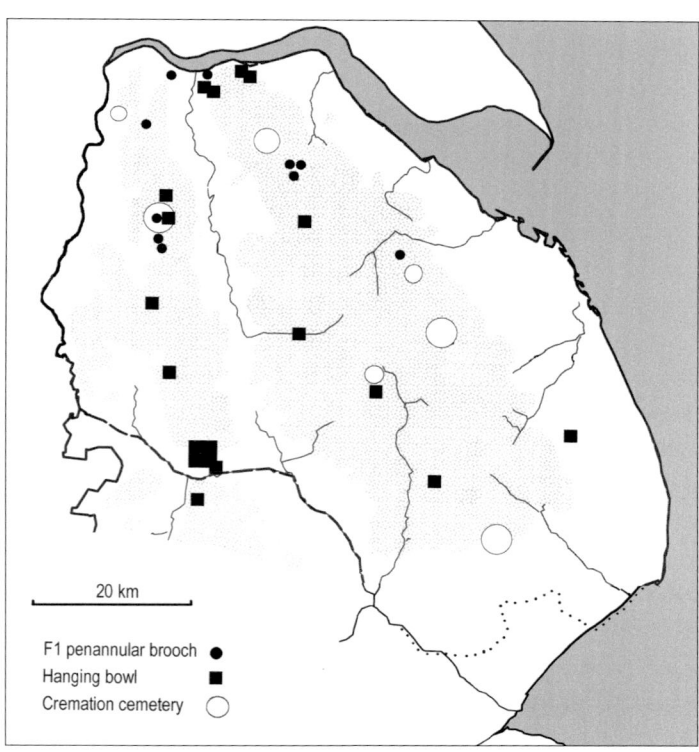

38 Distribution of F1
penannular brooches and
Celtic hanging bowls in
Lindsey
*Digital mapping by Mike
Hemblade*

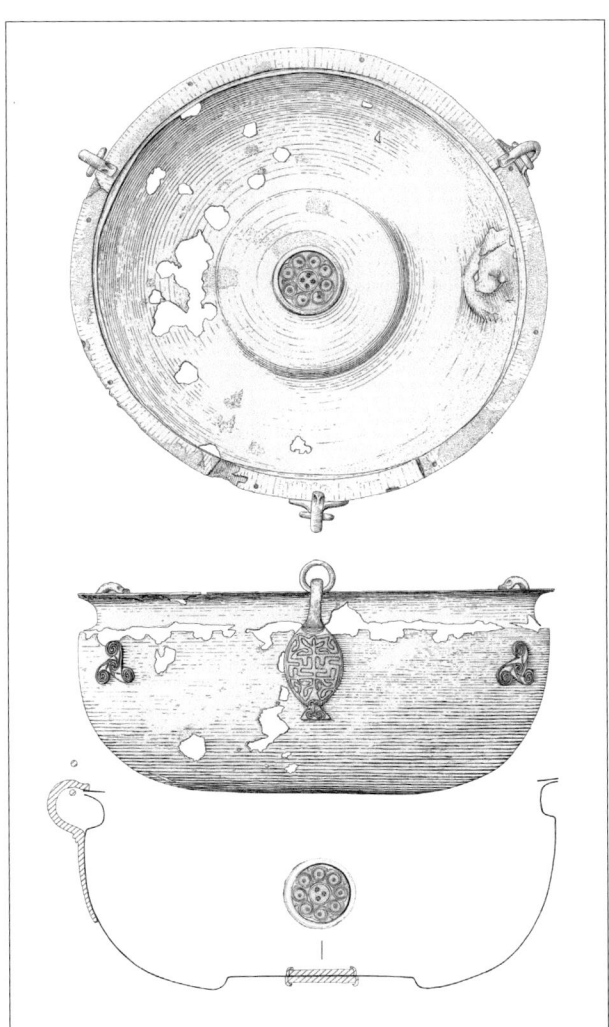

39 Hanging bowl found in the stone-lined cist on the site of the church of St Paul in the Bail, Lincoln. *Drawing courtesy of the City of Lincoln Council*

the highest level of society. Genealogies were political documents and were manipulated, but descent was important in early medieval aristocratic society and the kings of Lindsey were not ashamed to have a '*walh*' in the family.

Arthur, King of Lindsey?

There is a context for this British/Anglo-Saxon interface which lies in the Arthurian legends. In recent years, however, a number of people, J.B. Reavill, Tom Green and myself, have begun to look at the evidence and found it possible to argue that the Arthurian legends might best be placed, not in Wales or Cornwall, but in Lincolnshire. Documentary evidence for King Arthur is thin and of uncertain value but we must try to use what little we have. The first direct reference we have to Arthur is in the *Historia Brittonum* which was written around AD 830 and is often attributed to *Nennius*. Chapter 56 records that:

> Arthur fought against them [the Anglo-Saxons] in those days, together with the kings of the Britons, but it was he who was the leader in battles [dux bellorum]

This shows, for what it is worth, that Arthur was seen as a war-leader who, if he was a king, was a king amongst other kings. The *Historia Brittonum* goes on to list Arthur's 12 battles:

> The first battle was at the mouth of the river which is called Glein. The second and third and fourth and fifth upon another river which is called Dubglas and is in the district Linnuis. The sixth battle upon the river which is called Bassas. The seventh battle was in the Caledonian wood, that is, Cat Coit Celidon. The eighth battle in Fort Guinnion in which Arthur carried the image of St Mary, ever Virgin, on his shoulders and the pagans were turned to flight on that day and a great slaughter was upon them through the virtue of our Lord Jesus Christ and through the virtue of St Mary the Virgin, his Mother. The ninth battle was waged in the city of the Legion. The tenth battle he waged on the shore of the river which is called Tribruit. The eleventh battle took place on the mountain which is called Agned. The twelfth was on Mount Badon, in which nine hundred and sixty men fell in one day from one charge by Arthur, and no one overthrew them except himself alone. And in all battles he stood forth as victor.

> Translation from Leslie Alcock, *Arthur's Britain*, 1971

We have a date for the last of Arthur's battles, that of Mount Badon which Gildas, a contemporary historian, said took place in the year of his own birth, which is considered to have been around AD 500. While referring to the battle as 'almost the most recent but not the least slaughter of the gallow's crew' Gildas makes no mention of Arthur. If Mount Badon took place around AD 500 the other 11 Arthurian battles must then have taken place in the latter part of the fifth century.

The locations of these 12 battles has been much debated, often on the basis of doubtful philology, but Tom Green has looked at the text in detail and found that location of the battles in *in regione Linnuis* is best interpreted as Lindsey. Recognising that the *Historia Brittonum* was compiled more than 300 years after the event by someone with his own political agenda it seems odd that Lindsey is even mentioned; its profile was never high and the reference suggests that someone knew, or thought that they knew, something. It is difficult to place any of the other Arthurian battles in Lindsey, the 'River Glein' where Arthur fought his first battle might be Brigg (properly called 'Glanford Brigg') but the River Glen in the south of Lincolnshire is a better candidate. Green has suggested, on philological grounds, that the battle of Mount Badon could have been fought at Baumber near Horncastle. This is possible but proof, or a strategic context, seem lacking. No case can be made for Arthur's ninth battle fought in the city of the Legion (*urbs legionis*) being Lincoln, as there had been no legion garrisoned in Lincolnshire since the first century. Various suggestions have been put forward for the location of this battle but York seems plausible and would place it in the Humber region.

We have another 'historical' reference to late Roman activity concerning Lindsey which comes from Geoffrey of Monmouth's *History of the Kings of Britain* which was finished around AD 1136. Geoffrey wrote:

> Soon afterwards the Picts assembled a huge army, crossed the borders from Albany, and began to ravage the northern parts of the island. As soon as this was announced to Vortigern, he collected his own soldiers together and crossed the Humber to meet the Picts. When the two sides came together, the Britons and their enemies fought bitterly with each other, first on one flank and then on the other. In the end, however, the Britons did not have much battling to do for the Saxons who were present fought so manfully that the enemy, used until now to being on the winning side, were forced to retreat almost immediately.
>
> Once he had won this victory with the help of the Saxons, Vortigern increased his gifts to them, to their leader Hengist he gave many lands in the neighbourhood of Lindsey, so that he could maintain himself and his fellow-soldiers.

> Tranlated by Lewis Thorpe

While this appears to be important evidence it must be recognised that Geoffrey of Monmouth's *The History of the Kings of Britain* is not an unimpeachable source and was looked upon as the *Da Vinci Code* of its time. Much of what Geoffrey wrote, such as his account of Britain being founded by Brutus, a refugee from Troy, was arrant nonsense and even in the twelfth century scholars were accusing him of having made it up. However there is more to his work than this; Thorpe noted that most of the people and places to which Geoffrey refers existed; his background is twisted almost beyond recognition but there is something there. Geoffrey tells us in his introduction that 'Walter the Archdeacon' gave him 'a certain very ancient book, written in the British language'. Did he have a source that is lost to us? It is possible, but while there is no apparent reason for the inclusion of Lindsey in the *Historia Brittonum* Geoffrey did have a possible motive for mentioning it in his history. Part of *The History of the Kings of Britain, The Prophecies of Merlin* had been commissioned by Bishop Alexander of Lincoln and Geoffrey may have wanted to add a little local interest.

There is no river *Dubglas* in Lindsey. The word means 'blackwater' and it would seem to be an appropriate name for the River Ancholme which was, until the early seventeenth century, a tidal creek of the Humber. The name Ancholme was seen by Ekwall as coming from the British word '*an-*' (marsh) combined with '*colne*', a word sometimes used for rivers. This seems to be appropriate for the muddy Ancholme which presents a formidable obstacle in the landscape and cuts Lindsey in two. It is at its narrowest at Brigg where an ancient trackway makes a crossing. This is a location of great strategic importance and was briefly fortified during the Civil War. If any place was to be the site of multiple engagements it is Brigg (*40*).

This is all highly speculative and, after raising the issue of King Arthur having fought at least some of his battles in Lindsey, I have to admit that I don't believe it, or at least I don't believe the details. I think that the Arthurian legends are a composite, set in a political/military situation brought about by the collapse of Roman control. There is good evidence that this situation existed in Lindsey and may even have been reflected in the *Historia Brittonum*. The story was probably embellished with events from elsewhere in what Rachel Bromwich describes as the 'old north' being added to the list of Arthur's battles. Lindsey looks a much better setting for the Arthurian legends than Wales and the west, where Arthur might have struggled even to find Anglo-Saxons to fight.

To describe this military situation in terms of Anglo-Saxons versus Britons is to put forward a simplistic (Hollywood) interpretation of what was happening. The Anglo-Saxons no doubt fought the Britons but the Britons also fought each other, assisted by the Anglo-Saxons who, on occasion, were also at each others' throats. The concept of 'national identity' didn't come into it, loyalties were much more personal and locally based. At a later date we have only to remember the unholy confederation of the Christian British King Cadwallon with the pagan Anglo-Saxon Penda, which defeated and killed the Christian Anglo-Saxon King Edwin.

If we have so much evidence for British survival why don't we speak Welsh? In the past we have perhaps seen Roman Britain from the perspective of the villa owners, prosperous and sophisticated. It wasn't like this for most of the population of Roman Britain and by the fourth century most of the people would have felt little affection for Rome, and affiliation with the incoming Anglo-Saxons might have seemed a better bet. As the great historian J.M. Kemble wrote in *The Saxons in England* (1849): 'The mass of people, accustomed to Roman rule or to the oppression of native princes, probably suffered little by a change of masters,

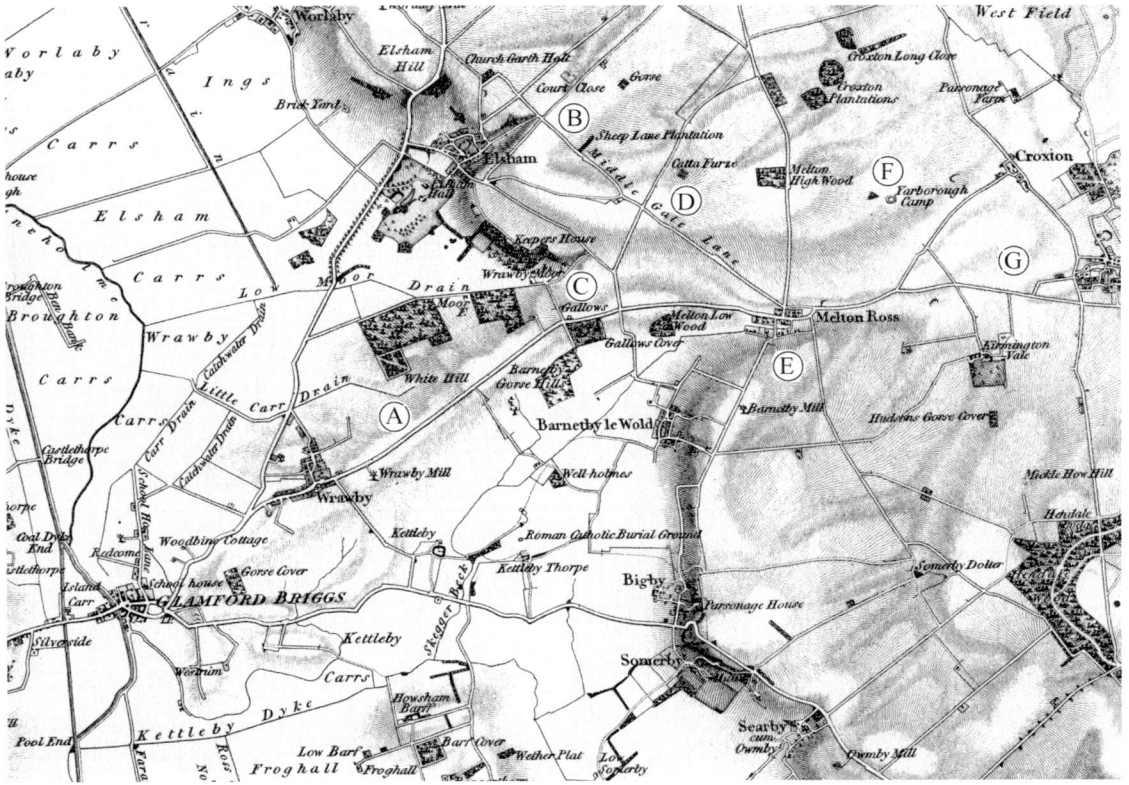

40 Anglo-Saxon sites around Melton Ross and Barnetby le Wold. A: The natural causeway across the Vale of Ancholme. B: Site of the Elsham cremation cemetery. C: Site of the Melton Ross gallows. D: The Middlegate Lane ancient trackway. E: Site of the Melton Ross productive site. F: Yarborough Camp. G: Site of the Kirmington Romano-British settlement

and did little to avoid it'. For most people, tramping in the mud behind a plough, the view of the ox's backside remained depressingly familiar.

Camelot?

The route to the east from Brigg passes through a gap in the Lincolnshire Wolds at Kirmington (*40*). On the northern side of this gap, in the parish of Croxton is 'Yarborough Camp', a 0.62ha trapezoid earthwork enclosure made up of a bank with a mound on each of its corners and a surrounding ditch (*41*). An entrance on the eastern side of the monument was emphasised by building the bank on top of a natural scarp thus creating an impressive façade. Fieldwork has revealed intensive Romano-British settlement to the east of the camp but on a different alignment. This need not trouble us; civilian interests would have been secondary to the need of the army to use the escarpment to produce an impressive frontage.

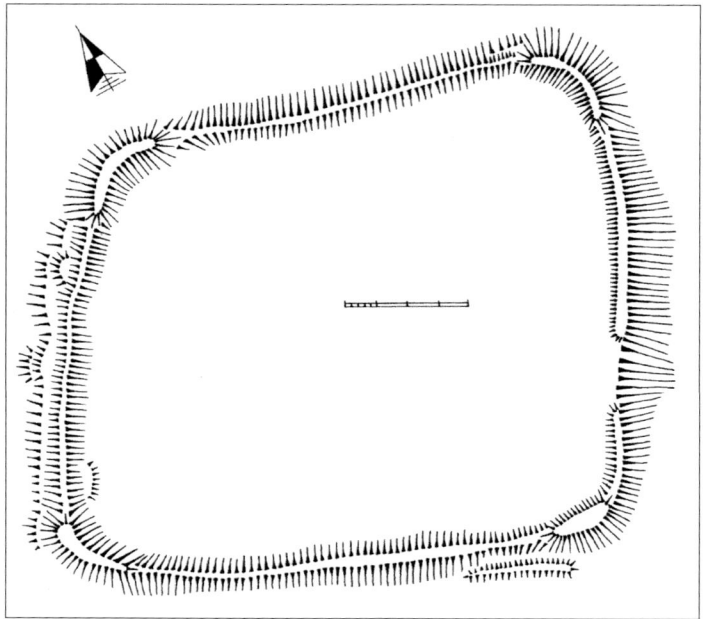

41 Plan of Yarborough Camp. *Based on a survey carried out by Kevin Leahy and G.C. Dyson*

Yarborough Camp is difficult to date on morphological grounds. The English Heritage scheduling notice describes it as a 'large univallate hillfort' which is unlikely as there are few other hillforts in Lindsey, though it might be paralleled by the rectangular Iron Age Enclosure at Weelsby Avenue, Grimsby. The corner mounds at Yarborough Camp are unlike anything found on Iron Age hillforts and might be an attempt to copy the bastions seen at Caistor and Horncasle. The only parallel that exists for Yarborough Camp is Countess Close, overlooking the confluence of the Trent and Ouse at Alkborough. This, too, has corner bastions and Roman pottery has been found in the enclosure. Medieval pottery has been found in the ditch but could relate to a reuse of the site.

Yarborough Camp was first described in 1724 when it was visited by William Stukeley. He recorded:

> Two miles west of Thornton (Curtis) is a great Roman camp called Yarborough which surveys the whole hundred dominated from it, and all the sea coast. Vast quantities of Roman coins have been found here: Mr Howson of Kennington (Kirmington) has pecks of them, many of Licinius.

No Roman coins have been found at Yarborough Camp in recent times but, in 1967, the site was visited by archaeologists who were excavating at the Dragonby Iron Age/Roman settlement. They found four sherds of pottery, one Bronze Age, two Romano-British grey ware and a sherd of Early Anglo-Saxon gritty ware. There is also a record of the bases of two Romano-British pots being found in the south corner of the enclosure.

Perhaps the most significant thing about Yarborough Camp is its name. 'Yarborough' comes from the Old English word '*eorburgh*' (earth fortification; the name of '*Arbor* Low', the Derbyshire henge monument, shares the same origin). *Eorburgh* is the term that the Anglo-Saxons used for pre-existing earthworks, they tended to refer to their own works simply as '*burh*'. The Anglo-Saxons' interest in Yarborough Camp was not merely antiquarian; it gave its name to the large Yarborough wapentake and must have acted as the folk-moot, where the people of the wapentake assembled. The camp retained its role as a communal meeting place to at least as late as 1536 when it was a mustering point for the Lincolnshire Rising. Wapentakes were district assemblies of freemen and, while the name is Scandinavian, the institution is far older, with most of the Lindsey wapentakes having English, not Scandinavian, names. Yarborough Camp is not the only earthwork to have given its name to a wapentake in the Humber region. The great prehistoric ring-work at Thwing in the East Riding of Yorkshire (Deira) was reoccupied during the Middle Saxon period with buildings and a cemetery. Thwing is in Dickering, that is 'dyke-ring' wapentake, and the place-name Thwing may come from '*thing*', the Old English word for a meeting place.

Two kilometres to the south-east of Yarborough Camp is the important Romano-British settlement site at Kirmington. Cropmarks show the presence of a Roman fort on the site, presumably from the conquest period. Metal detector finds made on the site prior to the implementation of the 1979 Ancient Monuments and Archaeological Areas Act show that occupation continued through the fourth century with a concentration of 'military' belt fittings and three late Celtic penannular brooches. There is very little evidence for Early Anglo-Saxon activity at Kirmington, a pattern also seen at the other large Romano-British settlements in Lindsey, Owmby and Ludford. It would be wrong to assume that the site was abandoned; sub-Roman pottery is as yet poorly known and, in the absence of coins, we cannot tell if a site was occupied. Perhaps there was activity on the site in the sixth century. Three and a half kilometres to the west of Yarborough Camp is the Elsham cremation cemetery which, unlike the other large cemeteries in Lindsey, is not on a parish boundary and lacks a commanding position. Elsham could represent Anglo-Saxons placed to control the Kirmington Gap and the crossing of the Ancholme during the settlement period.

Was Yarborough Camp Camelot? I think that it is possible, but there were a lot of alleged Camelots. Ken Dark has shown how, in the west of Britain, the sub-Roman population retreated into defended hill-top sites, Cadbury/Camelot in Somerset being the best known example. By the standards of the early Medieval

Period, Yarborough Camp has a good historical background. It seems to have been fortified, or refortified, in the fourth or fifth century using a blundered version of late Roman military architecture. It defends a highly strategic point in the landscape covering both north-south and east-west routes. In describing the Lindsey landscape I quoted Alfred Lord Tennyson's 'The Lady of Shalott':

> On either side the river lie
> Long fields of barley and of rye,
> That clothe the wold and meet the sky;
> And thro' the field the road runs by
> To many-tower'd Camelot

Perhaps the poet sensed more than he knew. Whatever its origin, Yarborough Camp is a monument of national importance that should be seen and cherished by all.

CHRISTIANITY COMES TO LINDSEY

The conversion of the Anglo-Saxons to Christianity is usually taken to mark the start of the 'Middle Saxon' period, which ends with the Viking conquest of much of England in the later ninth century. As we don't know when the people actually became Christian it is better to use the end of the field cemeteries as a rather negative starting point. At least this shows when Christianity was becoming established.

ST PAULINUS' MISSION

The first recorded event in the history of Lindsey is Bede's account of the mission of St Paulinus to the kingdom c.AD 626. Paulinus had arrived in England with a party of clerics sent in 601 to assist St Augustine's mission to Kent. In 625 he travelled to Northumbria with Ethelburga of Kent when she married King Edwin who, while not a Christian, seems to have been sympathetic and eventually accepted Baptism. Early in his mission Paulinus visited Lindsey and preached at Lincoln, where his first convert was Blæcca the 'Prefect of the city of Lincoln'. Bede, writing around 731, recorded an account given to him by Deda, who was Abbott of the monastery of Partney and who had known an old man who 'had been baptised at noon by Bishop Paulinus in the presence of King Edwin together with a great crowd of people, in the river Trent near a city that the English call Tiowulfingacæstir [probably Littleborough].' Remarkably, he went on to give a physical description of St Paulinus who 'was tall, with a slight stoop, black hair, a thin face, a slender aquiline nose, and at the same time he was both venerable and awe-inspiring in appearance'. Paulinus built a stone church in Lincoln 'of remarkable workmanship' in which he consecrated Archbishop Honorius following the death of Archbishop Justus in 627. This building was in ruins by the time that Bede was writing, but its walls were still standing and 'every year miracles of healing are performed in this place, for the benefit of those who seek them in faith'.

This short account tells us quite a lot, although it also raises questions. The fact that St Paulinus went to Lincoln shows that the city was not deserted and that something was still going on there. Blæcca, who met Paulinus, was described by Bede as *præfectumque Lindocolinae civitatis*. Bede's use of the title 'præfectus' is interesting. It could be a survival of a late Roman honorific title, but the word also appears in other texts, which can tell us what it meant to the Anglo-Saxons. In early West Saxon charters '*ealdermen*' are referred to as '*praefecti*' which was sometimes translated as '*gerefa*' (reeve). Blæcca does not appear on Aldfrið's genealogy but this does not mean that he was not a king of Lindsey; the genealogy is not a king list and Blæcca could have belonged to another branch of the royal house. Blæcca's name alliterates with some of the other names included on Aldfrið's genealogy (*Bubba*, *Beda*, *Biscop*) suggesting that he might have been a member of Lindsey's royal house. Bede refers to Lindsey as *prouinciae Lindissi*, the first land on the south bank of the Humber, bordering the sea. *Prouinciae* is a term which he generally uses for independent peoples but he occasionally uses it for sub-divisions of kingdoms; units that he elsewhere describes as '*regiones*'.

The church of St Paul in the Bail

The earliest and most enigmatic church in Lindsey is that of St Paul in the Bail (*42*) that stood in what had been the forum of the Roman Lincoln. It lay beneath its Victorian successor and a succession of medieval and Anglo-Saxon churches and graveyards. There were three early buildings, a rectangular timber structure, one end of which may have been divided off by three or more post holes, possibly marking the line of a chancel. This may have been a church but we cannot be sure. The south side of this building had been destroyed when the larger apsidal-ended church was constructed. This building was 8m wide and may have been 20m long. It was orientated east-west, putting it on a slightly different alignment from that of the forum in which it stood. All that remained of the building were the foundation trenches for its walls, which, along its southern side, still contained the stone packing to secure a wooden sill-beam. The nave was separated from the semi-circular apse by a trench; this contained a

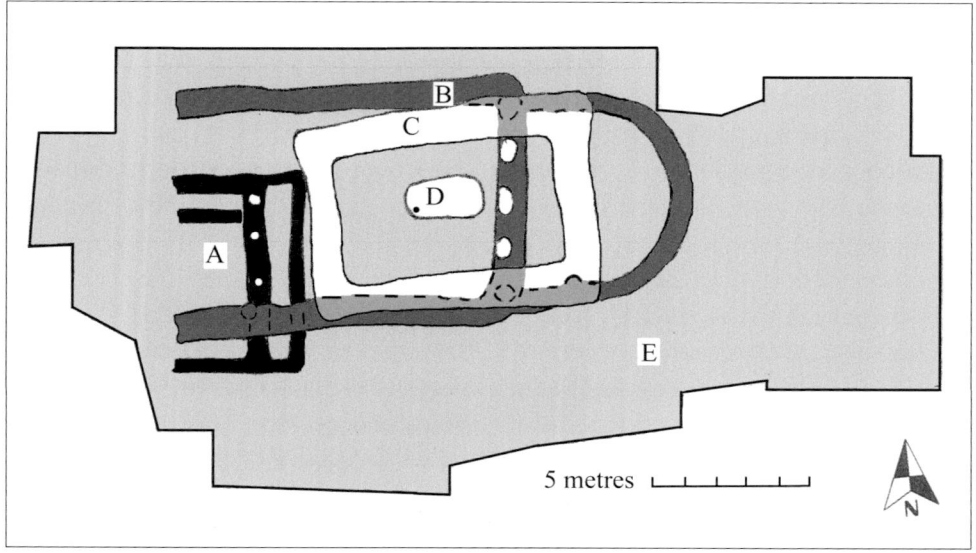

42 Church of St Paul in the Bail, Lincoln. A: Foundations of a possible Romano-British church. B: Foundations of the apsidal church. C: Foundations of single-celled structure. D: Cist grave containing hanging bowl. E: Area of excavation. *Plan by Kevin Leahy after Steane et al 2005*

row of five post holes in front of which was an empty, stone-lined grave in which was found the hanging bowl (*39*). After the demolition of the apsidal church it was replaced by a rectangular structure which seems to have been built around the grave containing the bowl. A fragment of carved stone was found during the excavation which Everson and Stocker have suggested came from a decorated sarcophagus that once held an important burial.

The dating of this sequence is very important; was this the church that St Paulinus built in 627/8 or is it late Roman? When it was first discovered, parallels were drawn between the form of the apsidal church and the seventh-century churches of the Kentish group, which like St Paul in the Bail, have a row of columns across their apses. This, together with the grave with the hanging bowl, provided convincing evidence that this was the church referred to by Bede. The trouble is that Bede leaves us in little doubt that Paulinus built in stone and that the walls of this building still survived at the time he was writing. Bede had a local informant in Deda and we must accept what he said. A coin of Arcadius 388-92 was found on the latest forum surface within the apsidal structure, which may indicate that the church was in use *c*.390.

Other than the bowl, the only other dating evidence was the skeletons from the graves associated with the early buildings and samples from eight of them were sent for radiocarbon dating. The results were unexpected; the earliest graves, which appeared to post-date the church, were placed in the fifth to sixth centuries suggesting that the church pre-dated Paulinus. The interpretation of these dates is contentious, and Mick Jones and Alan Vince differ on the dating. Jones thinks that the church is late or sub-Roman while Vince would prefer a seventh-century date on architectural grounds. The dates do seem to present a coherent pattern and what we have at St Paul in the Bail is a sequence of Christian religious practice from at least as early as the Early Anglo-Saxon period through to the eighth or ninth century. If the smaller, square-ended building is Roman, and a church, the sequence must have started earlier. After the conversion, the first churches would have been built for the bishops either in former Roman cities like Lincoln or as chapels attached to royal households. The apsidal church at Lincoln could have held more than 100 worshipers making it unlikely that it was a royal chapel. If it was not stone-built (as seems likely) we have not found Paulinus' church and we must look elsewhere in Lincoln. Alan Vince has ventured that there were a number of pre-Conquest churches in the upper city; St Mary, St Paul in the Bail, All Saints, and the church of St Clement, which may also be early. This would make the upper city look like a diffuse monastery, like Bardney (see below).

LATE ROMAN CHRISTIANITY

While Bede makes no mention of any surviving Christian community in Lindsey at the time of St Paulinus' mission, it is worth looking at the evidence. The radiocarbon dates from burials at St Paul in the Bail suggest that Christianity existed in the city prior to 627 but this need not trouble us; Bede's hero would have gained little credit from preaching to the converted and the form of Christianity being practised in seventh-century Lincoln may have been unorthodox. Christianity was a powerful and cohesive force which would hold together something of the earlier administration, and its survival in sub-Roman Lindsey would affect the development of the Anglo-Saxon kingdom. Unfortunately, we know little of Christianity in late Roman Lindsey and the sub-Roman period. It is likely that a bishop from Lindsey attended the Council of Arles in AD 314, although there is some ambiguity regarding this. There are four entries for Britannia, the first clearly refers to York, but the second and third both seem to refer to London. It is thought that the third entry, *Adelphius episcopus de civitate Colonia Londiniensium*, should refer to 'Adelphius bishop of the city of *Colonia Lindensium*', i.e. Lincoln.

There are some finds that may relate to Christianity in Roman Lindsey. A fragment of a fourth-century lead baptismal font has been found at Walesby. This was originally cylindrical with a diameter of 900mm and a height of 550mm.

43 Forgery of a coin of Magnentius and medallions cut from similar coins, each showing part of the chi-rho monogram. *Harrison collection. Image by Kevin Leahy*

It is decorated with a large Chi-rho monogram (the two initial letters of the Greek word *Christos*) and a figurative panel showing what may be a baptismal scene. This seems to show the rite being carried out by '*affusion*' where water is poured over the adult candidate's head. Two fragments from a lead box were found within the Roman defences at Caistor. This was badly crushed, but had splayed sides originally being 600mm sq at its base, increasing over its 360mm depth to 760mm sq at its rim. It was decorated with peltae and crudely executed figures wearing tunics, above which was the inscription '*Cunobarrus fecit vivas*', Cunobarrus made this may you live (happily), a formula that has been seen as potentially Christian.

Some of the motifs used on mosaics, while originally pagan, may have been adopted by the Christian Church. Orpheus occurs at Winterton and Horkstow and was equated with Christ, and the peacocks and grapes shown on the latter mosaic are also seen as Christian symbols. Even if the Christian interpretation is valid the Empire was, by the mid-fourth century, Christian and the villa's owners would have been at least officially, Christian. Some oblique evidence for Christianity in the countryside comes from finds of small medallions cut from large brass coins of the Emperor Magnentius, which were distinguished by the Chi-rho emblem that dominated their reverse (*43*). These are by far the most common coins to be cut up in this way and they may have been touch-pieces, showing Christianity as a superstition in the countryside. It is interesting that, while in his diatribe *De Excidio Britanniae* (The ruin of Britain) the mid-sixth-century monk Gildas accuses his contemporaries of many things, paganism was not one of them. Sub-Roman Britain may have been substantially Christian.

THE DEVELOPMENT OF CHRISTIAN LINDSEY

St Paulinus' mission to the north came to an end with the defeat and death of King Edwin at the hands of Penda of Mercia (pagan) and Cadwallon of Gwynedd (Christian) in 632. Following the battle, Paulinus 'escorted' the widowed queen and the royal children back to Kent leaving James, his deacon, to accept the glorious crown of martyrdom in York (embarrassingly for Paulinus, James was not harmed and lived to a ripe old age). Oswald, who replaced Edwin as King of Northumbria was also a Christian, having been converted to the Celtic brand of the Faith while an exile in Scotland.

The Bishops of Lindsey

An attempt was made to cement peace between the two warring kingdoms by the marriage of Penda's son Peada to the daughter of Oswald's successor Oswiu, on condition that he became a Christian. Around 653 he returned to his kingdom of Middle Anglia taking with him four priests. In 655, Diuma, one of these priests, was consecrated as Bishop of Mercia and the Middle Angles, a massive diocese that extended from the Thames to the Wash and as far west as the Severn. No mention is made of Lindsey and it is likely that, due to the ascendancy of Northumbria at that time, Lindsey was under the control of a northern bishop. In 669 Chad was consecrated 'Bishop of the Mercian race and Lindsey' with his see at Lichfield. Chad, like Diuma, was an Irishman, these early bishops all being Irish or Irish-trained, an important consideration as the Irish Church differed from the Roman Christianity introduced through Kent by St Augustine.

The duties of the early bishops were enormous; until the tenth century there was no system of parish priests and the bishops were expected to visit each part of their diocese at least once a year, preaching, teaching and giving the sacraments. Considering the size of the diocese this was impossible. It was also impossible to get these bishops to give up their gargantuan dioceses and the power that went with them. Archbishop Theodore failed to get sense to prevail after the death of Bishop Chad in 672 and Winfrith was appointed to replace him, only to be sacked for 'disobedience' some time before 676. He may have objected to a proposed division of his diocese. A better opportunity came in 678 when the great Northumbrian prelate Wilfrid fell out with King Ecgfrith and went into exile (he supported Queen Æthelthryth's desire to remain a virgin). Wifrid's enormous Northumbrian Diocese was divided into three; Deira and Bernicia, (the two kingdoms that formed Northumbria) and, to the south, the Diocese of Lindsey.

The first Bishop of Lindsey was Eadhæd in 678 but, following the Northumbrian loss of Lindsey in 679, he returned north and became Bishop of

Ripon. He was succeeded as Bishop of Lindsey by Æthelwine who was Bishop for 14 years and Edgar who was elected in 693 and died in 729 at the age 90. Cyneberht who succeeded Edgar died in 731. He was followed by:

	Accession	Death
Aluwioh	733	750
Aldwulf	750	765
Ceolwulf	765	796

Later bishops can only be dated by the appearance of their names on the list of witnesses to charters:

	Accession	Death
Eadwulf	796	836 x 839
Beorhtræd	836 x 839	862 x 866

Bishop Eadbald, who witnessed a charter in 866 and Bishop Burgheard, who was around in 869, may have been bishops of Lindsey but it is impossible to be sure. Other possible bishops have been suggested but Peter Sawyer is doubtful about them. Arthur Owen has suggested that St Herefrith of Louth may have been a Bishop of Lindsey martyred by the Danes when the bishopric of Lindsey came to an end. The bishopric was revived twice in the tenth century; Leofwine, who was described as the successor to Beorhtræd, witnessed charters of Eadred and Edgar, first appearing in 953. He eventually became Bishop of Dorchester uniting the diocese with Lindsey. Bishop Sigeferth of Lindsey witnesses five charters between 996 and 1004. He was probably followed by Ælfstan who witnessed charters in 1009 and 1011.

What sort of people were these early clerics? After Eadhæd's short time as Bishop of Lindsey he was replaced, successively, by Æthelwine and Edgar who between them held the diocese for 50 years. Both men had trained in the highly ascetic Irish tradition and Bede records the abstinence practised by Edgar who 'never ate more than once a day during Lent, taking only bread and the thinnest of milk'. Bishop Æthelwine of Lindsey was the brother of Abbot Ealdwine of Bardney and their sister Æthelhild was abbess of the unnamed monastery near Partney. Bede records how this abbess called to see Queen Osthryth while she was at Bardney; these people were clearly members of the aristocracy.

We have little archaeological evidence for the conversion; the church of St Paul in the Bail has already been discussed but we have a few finds, the best of which is the small seventh-century gold cross found at Newball (*colour plate 14*). This is plain, but the small window in its face suggests that it contained a relic. Some of the gold pendants from the Final Phase cemetery at Sheffield's Hill include cross elements in their designs and they too may be Christian (*colour plate 12*) as may be the increasing use of west-east graves.

Syddensis civitas: where was the cathedral?

The location of Lindsey's cathedral is an interesting question; bishops were generally known by the name of the city that housed their cathedral – Canterbury, York, Lichfield – but Bede refers to the Bishop of Lindsey as just that, bishop *in prouincia Lindissi*. A cathedral was built by Cyneberht, the fourth bishop (this is described simply as being '*in urbe*', in a city) for which Bede composed an inscription to go over the apse dedicating it to an apostle. The first mention we get of the location of Lindsey's cathedral is in 803 when Bishop Eadwulf of Lindsey attended a church council and was described as *Syddensis civitatis episcopus*. This in not a great help; where was *Syddensis civitatis*? Various places have been suggested: Caistor, Horncastle, Louth, Stow and, of course, Lincoln. Lincoln is the most likely candidate, *Syddensis civitatis* means southern city and Lincoln lies on the southern edge of Lindsey but why this odd name should have been used is not known. The inscription that Bede wrote for the cathedral itself presents a problem as he dedicated it to an apostle, ruling out both St Mary (the dedication of the present cathedral) and St Martin, and leaving St Peter at Pleas in the lower city as the most likely candidate. William the Conqueror granted the churches of Caistor, Kirton and Wellingore to Bishop Remigius, an act that likely restored to him what were probably ancient rights. It was recorded that Wellingore had belonged to the church of St Peter at Lincoln, that is St Peter at Pleas. Peter Sawyer has pointed out that if Wellingore was an episcopal minster then its mother church would have been the cathedral.

David Stocker has speculated that *Syddensis civitatis* was the monastery at Bardney. This is an interesting idea that could fit the evidence. The use of the word '*civitatis*' need not be a problem. As well as the cities of man there were also the cities of God; Bede used the word to describe Cuthbert's retreat on the island of Farne which was hardly a great metropolis. Bishops could take their titles from a principal monastery, (Lindisfarne for Bernicia) or a royal centre (York for Deira). One might wonder if, in the absence of a local king (after 679 Lindsey was probably controlled by a Mercian Alderman) the bishop would, at first, be monastery-based (as in Ireland). The bishops of Lindsey would have attended the Mercian kings' court but their names are infrequent on the lists of witnesses prior to 770. Stocker has suggested that the monasteries seem to be paired with aristocratic sites (Bardney – Lincoln; Hibaldstow – Kirton in Lindsey; Barrow – Caistor or Barton) and that the bishops had dual lives, dividing their time between a monastery and the peripatetic royal household.

LINDSEY'S MONASTERIES

Monasteries were one of the most important aspects of Anglo-Saxon Christianity, with extensive estates and strong links to the highest levels of society they were able to exercise great power and influence. It is unfortunate that there have, with the possible exception of Flixborough, been no excavations on any of Lindsey's Anglo-Saxon monasteries, although, through the works of Bede and other sources, we know the locations of some of them (44). The first monastery that we know of in Lindsey was at Bardney which was founded towards the end of the seventh century by the King and Queen of Mercia, Æthelred and Osthryth. Following her assassination around 704 Osthryth was buried at Bardney and Æthelred himself eventually retired to Bardney as its abbot, a post he held until his death in 716 when both were enshrined as saints. Bardney's great claim to fame was that it housed the relics of the sainted King Oswald and it continued to be an important royal monastery. In 792 the shrine of St Oswald was enriched by King Offa of Mercia.

Little is known about the layout of Lindsey's Anglo-Saxon monasteries but their sites and settings have been discussed by David Stocker. Bardney was built on what was effectively an island overlooking the River Witham, down stream from Lincoln. Island or peninsular sites were often used for Anglo-Saxon monasteries. The 'island' at Bardney was large, measuring 5x1.5km and was linked to the high ground by a narrow neck of land in its north-east corner. Across this is a ditch, the Scotgrove Dyke, which looks recent but may have been re-cut. Bardney is believed to have been destroyed by the Danes in the ninth century and then refounded as a Benedictine priory in 1087. There is some early eleventh-century sculpture in the village, pointing to religious activity on the site during the hiatus. There is some doubt as to where on the island the Anglo-Saxon monastery lay as tradition said that the medieval monastery was not on the same site as its Anglo-Saxon forebear. When Leland, the antiquary visited Barndney in the 1530s he was told:

> the monkes hold opinion that the old Abbay of Bardeney was not in the same place wher the new ys but at a graunge or dayre of theyrs a myle of.

The island's ancient road layout is based, not around the medieval monastery, but around the high ground on which the modern village and parish church are set. Stocker has suggested that difficulty in locating the Anglo-Saxon monastery is due to there being no one site for it as the whole island was the monastery, with a number of separated churches, one of which became the site of the medieval monastery. There are medieval references to at least three churches or chapels

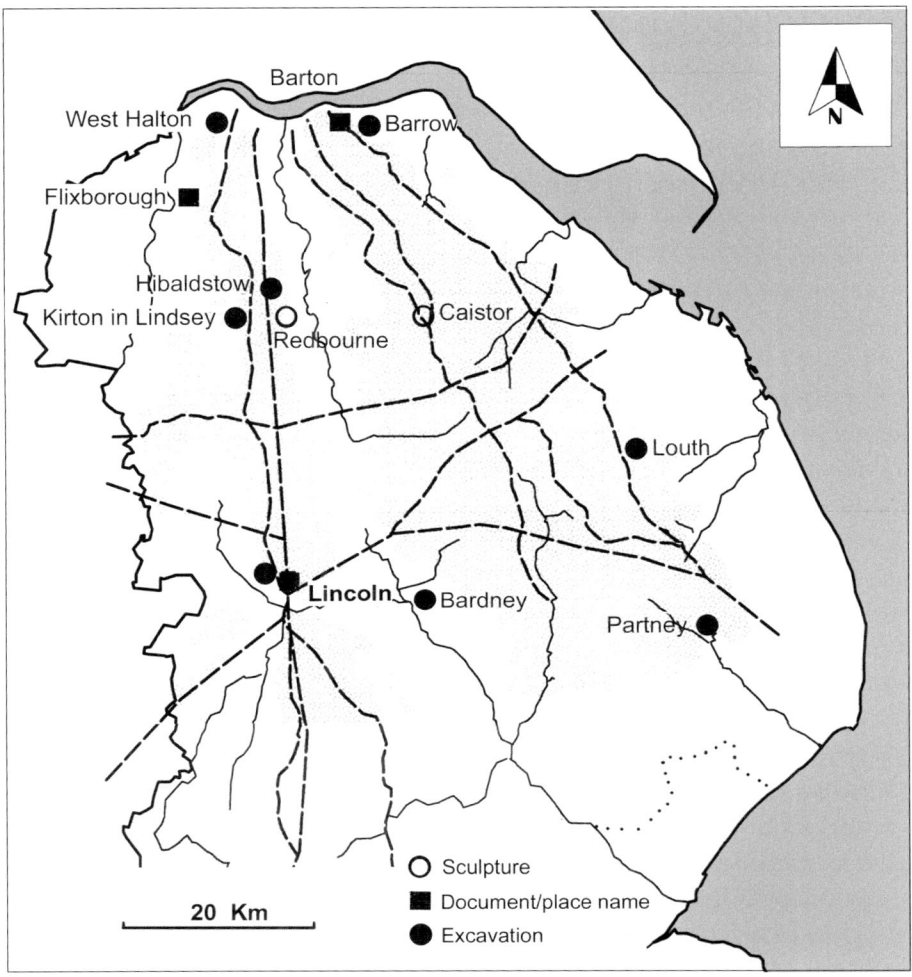

44 Locations of Anglo-Saxon monasteries in Lindsey

on the island; near the abbey was the old parish church of Ss Peter and Paul, the relationship between it and the abbey being confused, suggesting that they were old. In addition to the parish church there were the medieval chapels of St Leonard and of St Andrew and possibly a third chapel. The chapel of St Andrew lies in the centre of the island at the crossing of the ancient roads. In addition to these there are hints of other churches on the island. There has been some discussion as to whether Bardney was a 'double house', that is a monastery that contained both monks and nuns. This type of establishment was well known in the Anglo-Saxon period but, as Peter Sawyer has pointed out, Bardney was ruled by an abbot, while double houses were in the charge of an abbess.

A case could be made for an unnamed monastery near Partney (Skendleby?) being a double house. Bede recorded how, one night, a male guest was possessed by a demon and started to have convulsions. Someone ran to the abbess's gate to fetch her, Abbess Æthelhild opened the monastery door and went, with one of the nuns, 'to the men's dwelling, where she called a priest and asked him to come with her to the patient'. When the priest's exorcisms failed Æthelhild remembered that she had some earth onto which the water used to wash St Oswald's bones had fallen. She sent a serving woman to get the casket containing the earth and as soon as they were brought into the house the demon left the man. The reference to the 'men's dwelling' has been taken as evidence that this was a double house but, unfortunately, Bede uses the word men, not brothers suggesting that, while there was a priest, there were no monks.

At Bardney we see a number of the recurrent features of Anglo-Saxon monasteries: they are on islands, or something that was like an island, with multiple churches spread over a wide area. The refoundation of Bardney in 1087 also follows a pattern; the sites of a number of Lindsey's Anglo-Saxon monasteries were reoccupied in the Medieval Period, and their origins and sanctity remembered. Stocker also pointed out that some of these early monasteries were on sites where there had been activity in prehistory. The fruitless excavation of the 'King's Barrow' has already been discussed above (page 91); it is extremely unlikely that it covered the grave of abbot/King Æthelred.

The other Lindsey monasteries referred to by Bede were Partney and Barrow. We only know of Partney because two of its abbots, Deda and Ealdwine, were known to Bede. Stocker has shown that Partney follows the same pattern as seen at Bardney; it is on an island near a river (in this case the Lymm) and there is evidence for the church of St Nicholas and the chapel of St Mary. Both were referred to when Gilbert de Gant granted Partney to Bardney Priory after the conquest, perhaps restoring a relationship that had existed in the seventh century.

In 669 King Wulfhere of Mercia gave Chad, his bishop, an estate of '50 hides' at *Adbaruae*, that is, Barrow on Humber. This was a substantial grant; the size of a 'hide' varied according to the quality of the land, but was generally around 120 acres. The Barrow Monastery did not get off to a very good start, Chad died in 672 and in 674 Mercia lost control of Lindsey following Wulfhere's defeat at the hands of Ecgfrith of Northumbria. After the Battle of the Trent in 679 Mercia regained, and then retained, control of Lindsey. Bede wrote that St Chad built a monastery at Barrow (perhaps the first church to have been built outside Lincoln) 'where up to the present day traces of the monastic rule that he established survive', an ambiguous comment if ever there was one. Chad's episcopal see was at Lichfield where he died and it is unlikely that he spent

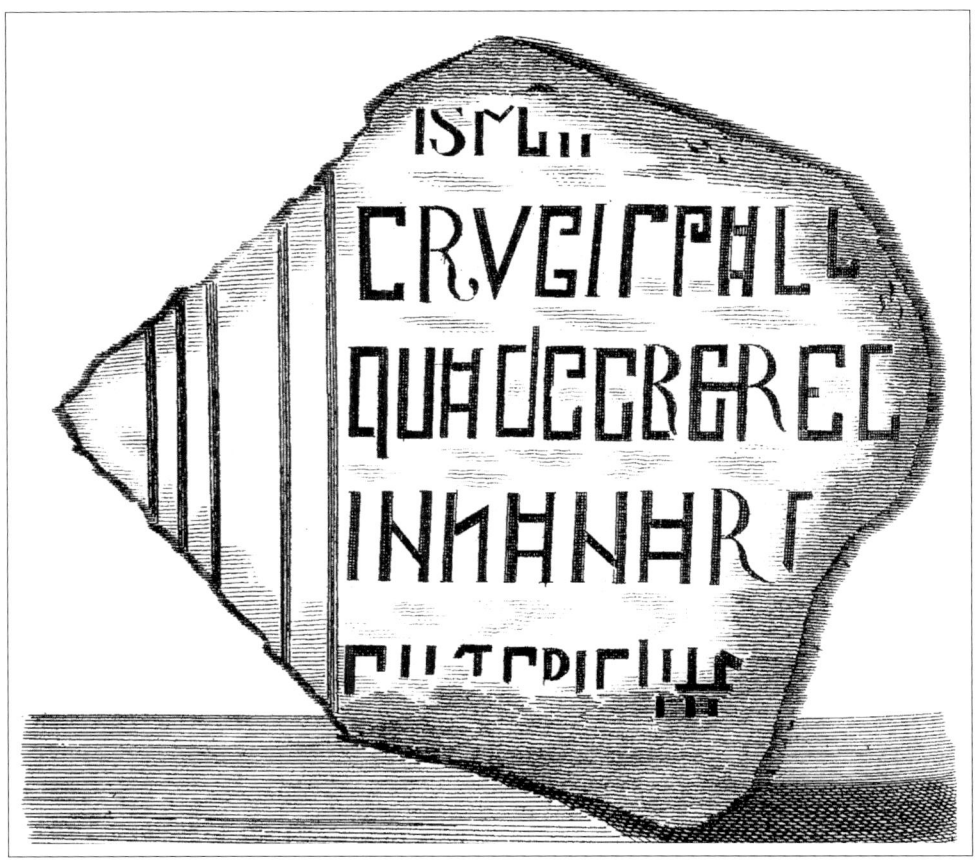

45 Inscription on stone found in 1770 on Castle Hill in Caistor but now lost. There is not much left of the inscription, but John Higgitt in Everson and Stocker (1999) suggested that it read:
-[ID]-
CRVCISPOLI[.]-
QVODE[G]BE/RE[C]-
INHONOR[E]-
[..........ID]-
This appears to be a reference to a man E[G]BEREC- and the dedication IN HONOR[E]- suggests that the fragment came from a church dedication of eighth- or early ninth-century date. Height 12 inches (300mm)

much time admiring the view of the Humber. One person who we know to have visited Barrow is the former Bishop Winfrith of Mercia who had been dismissed for 'disobedience' some time before 676. En route to Rome (no doubt to lodge a complaint) he was badly beaten up in Gaul and had then retired to Barrow. David Stocker has commented that the 'island' on which the Barrow monastery stands is much smaller than that used elsewhere and has suggested that a larger piece of raised ground to the north of Barrow might be a more likely location. I feel that the area of the town known as the 'Island' remains the most likely location. Human remains are constantly being found in this area and the whole site seems to have been a cemetery. While not all of the skeletons are Anglo-Saxon this location was clearly seen as being special into the Medieval Period. We are fortunate that a charter based on what we believe to have been Wulfhere's original grant has survived. Having been destroyed, presumably by the Vikings in the 870s, King Edgar sold the 50 hide monastic estate at Barrow to Peterborough Abbey in 971 for 40lbs of silver and a gold cross. The boundary given in this charter can (mostly) be defined and it seems to have included the two parishes of Barton on Humber and Barrow on Humber.

There is documentary and archaeological evidence for a number of other possible Anglo-Saxon monasteries in Lindsey. Bede refers to Hygbald as 'a very austere and holy man who was an abbot in the province of Lindsey'. It was recorded that he was buried at a place called '*Cecesey*' near the River Ancholme. To the west of the Ancholme is a group of churches dedicated to St Hygbald: Manton, Scawby and Hibaldstow; the word 'stow' means a holy place or a place of assembly. No site is known but, looking for the features that characterised Bardney, Stocker identified two islands between Hibaldstow, Redbourne and the Ancholme, one of which was the site of a medieval priory. Redbourne Church contains a fragment of what is likely to be eighth-century sculpture that could have come from a monastic church. There are other possible monasteries; in 792 Abbot Æthelheard of Louth was appointed Archbishop of Canterbury. The location of the Louth monastery is not known, but the site of the Cistercian Abbey of Louth Park lies about 2km from the town, is near to a river and was almost surrounded by marshes. Winghale Priory at South Kelsey may also have been an early minster; it was on an island by the River Ancholme and Anglo-Saxon metalwork has been found on the site. A better case can be made for Caistor on the Wolds where a fragment of an inscription was found in 1770 (and subsequently lost). The inscription is too truncated to be read but is likely to have been the dedication of an altar (45). It was executed in a highly competent monumental fashion using elongated rune-like Roman lettering of a style that probably dates from the eighth century. The present church contains some features surviving from earlier structures, in particular a substantial crossing, and the lower part of the west tower seems to include the remains of an earlier building. There is evidence for a second church dedicated to St Mary, which lay about 50m away from the surviving church of Ss Peter and Paul. This all suggests that there were a number of churches within the Roman walls, forming a monastery.

Anglo-Saxon settlements in Lindsey

Having spent so much time on the cemeteries it is important and refreshing to look at where, and how, the Anglo-Saxons lived. Lindsey has not yet had a settlement and its landscape examined to the same extent as at West Heslerton to the north of the Humber, or a study carried out like that in the Fens to the south. However, a good start has been made and we are starting to see the Anglo-Saxon settlement pattern in Lindsey. In 1999, the North Lincolnshire Museum started a community archaeology project, now supported by the Heritage Lottery Fund. This involves large-scale, intensive field walking with all finds being recorded using a Global Positioning System. Work has been concentrated in four areas: the limestone of Lincoln Edge, the Triassic hills of the Isle of Axholme, the Chalk Wolds and the Liassic escarpment overlooking the Trent at Alkborough.

The four study areas have yielded quite different results. Results were best on the limestone around Kirton in Lindsey and Manton where we have found a surprising number of Anglo-Saxon sites. These consist of small scatters of Early Anglo-Saxon pot sherds, often associated with iron slag. Larger sites exist on Manton Warren and to the south of Kirton in Lindsey, where field walking produced more than 1400 sherds of Anglo-Saxon pottery. The evidence from this area is impressive but can it be typical with a major cemetery (Cleatham) lying between the two parishes? On the Wolds we have looked at the parishes around the Elsham cemetery but so far we have found surprisingly little trace of Early Anglo-Saxon settlement, although good evidence for Romano-British activity is being found.

Evidence for Early Anglo-Saxon settlement has been found in both of the other study areas. A concentration of pot sherds marked a major site at Owston Ferry on the Isle of Axholme. This, along with a number of small scatters of pottery and finds of Early Anglo-Saxon metalwork from Belton, show that there was Early Anglo-Saxon settlement to the west of the lower Trent and that the river was not a barrier. Field walking around Alkborough produced evidence for Early Anglo-Saxon settlement which is, as elsewhere, associated with Romano-British pottery suggesting some continuity of land use. These small sites might best be interpreted as non-nucleated settlements; homesteads rather than villages. The existence of the 'homestead' sites could also relate to the small inhumation cemeteries now being identified. We have made a start in understanding the Early Anglo-Saxon settlement pattern in Lindsey and trends are starting to emerge. The one thing that can already be said is that there is far more evidence for Early Anglo-Saxon settlement than we would ever have guessed.

EXCAVATED SITES

Only a small number of Anglo-Saxon settlement sites have been excavated in Lindsey. A building excavated at Willoughton in 1937 was dated by associated pottery to the Anglo-Saxon period. It was described as a 'hut' and, although no structural elements were found, it was said to have had a paved floor. This seemed highly unusual but it can now be paralleled by the large Middle Saxon *Grubenhäus* (or 'activity area' as the excavators described it) found during pipe laying at Belton (see below). In 1954 fieldwork at Sandy Knobs, Salmonby had produced a sub-rectangular area of compacted soil measuring 8ft x 12ft. Both this and a nearby structure of sleeper beam construction were associated with Anglo-Saxon pottery and both baked and unfired 'green' loom weights. In 1972 work at Salmonby revealed a sunken-floored building or *Grubenhäus* associated with Anglo-Saxon pottery and green clay loom weights. Soil marks suggested that there were at least six other buildings in the vicinity. Four sunken features and a large quantity of undecorated domestic pottery were found at Irby on Humber near to the excavated cemetery at Welbeck Hill. The association of a settlement with a cemetery is not known elsewhere in Lindsey, although the scatter of sherds found around the Sheffield's Hill cemeteries could come from a settlement. Limited excavation carried out at Normanby le Wold produced large quantities of Middle Saxon Maxey-type ware but the only structural evidence was a yard or path. A *Grubenhäus* and some ditches and fences were found at Cherry Willingham which are likely to represent an Early/Middle Saxon settlement.

In 1986-7 excavations at Nettleton Top revealed three *Grubenhäuser* with pottery and loom weights, both baked and green. While these could have been part of a larger settlement destroyed by sand extraction, it is possible that we found all there was, and that it was a homestead, not a village. At Nettleton Top two pits containing charcoal and burnt ironstone were found. Similar pits have been found on other Anglo-Saxon settlement sites and are likely to have been slow-cookers in which meat was baked by surrounding it with heated stones. In addition to the *Grubenhäuser,* the people of Anglo-Saxon Lindsey would have used hall-type buildings constructed using earth fast posts or, in the case of Salmonby, sleeper beams. A seventh-century building with earth fast posts was found at Flixborough but we lack other examples, due, probably, to the difficulties involved in identifying post holes other than on a controlled excavation.

An interesting feature of these Early Anglo-Saxon buildings is that, with the exception of the *Grubenhäuser,* they are unlike the buildings used in the Germanic homelands where the 'long house', accommodating humans at one end and cattle at the other, was used. Why this change occurred is unknown, perhaps the milder climate meant that cattle could be wintered outdoors. In some respects the Anglo-Saxon buildings resemble those used in the Romano-British countryside.

MIDDLE SAXON SETTLEMENTS AND 'PRODUCTIVE SITES'

In the early 1980s numismatists recording metal detector finds saw that some locations were yielding large numbers of Middle Saxon coins and small non-ferrous objects. These they called 'productive sites' and, while the term is hardly an accurate label it has become established and, in the absence of anything better, we still use it. There is no agreed definition of what makes a productive site; how many finds does one need for a site to be 'productive'? It is also likely that the term covers a wide range of different types of site: trading centres, aristocratic residences and monasteries, and we don't know what we are dealing with, even on excavated sites like Flixborough. We work more on the basis of tacit agreement than definition but this may not be a bad thing; to define is to proscribe and we don't have enough information to begin to make divisions. There are a number of productive sites in Lindsey, some of which can, for reasons of security, only be known by parish or general location. This is a far from satisfactory situation but fortunately it is possible to discuss some of the more important sites in detail.

The large number of coins and metal objects found both as single finds and from 'productive sites' lead Mark Blackburn to suggest that Lindsey was one of the most wealthy regions of England in the eighth and ninth centuries (*63*). This prosperity was probably due to a number of factors: the agricultural potential of the area is good and it has access to resources from both the rivers and the sea. Communications were excellent; the sea allowing both coastal trade and access to Northern Europe and the rivers of the Trent and Ouse systems providing routes inland. As an ancient kingdom Lindsey was able to develop cohesion and economic links. The finds from the other areas of Lincolnshire present a different picture. Little Middle Saxon metalwork has been found around the Wash in the Parts of Holland. The lacuna in Holland is supported by a low population density at Domesday and, until reclamation started in the Medieval Period, the area was poorly developed.

While finds have been made in Kesteven to the south-west of Lindsey productive sites are, with one exception, absent. This site is in the Sleaford area and has yielded very large numbers of early coins and some small metal objects. In view of the large number of continental coins found and the site's location on the eastern edge of Kesteven, it is likely that it was a trading centre; a market or fair site where merchants gathered. The lack of productive sites elsewhere in Kesteven may relate to the area's heavy soils and high level of woodland or to its isolation on the edge of Middle Anglia. While finds are now being recorded to the south and west of Lindsey in South Yorkshire and Nottinghamshire, the amount of material being found in Lindsey remains outstanding.

The regional distribution of productive sites is of great interest but we can only understand them by looking at individual sites and by drawing on every available source, attempting to place them in their historical and geographical context. So far it has only been done in detail for the Flixborough and Melton Ross/Barnetby le Wold sites but useful parallels can be made with the productive site to the north of the Humber at South Newbald.

It is interesting to look at the pattern of finds from these sites, Flixborough being excluded as this mass of material would unbalance the figures. From Lindsey we have 94 objects that can be dated to the eighth century and 171 to the ninth. While the quantity of finds is higher in the ninth century the general quality falls. In addition to these we have 316 objects that can only be dated to the eighth or ninth century, these are mainly pins but with 20 hooked tags and some pairs of tweezers. This all seems to point to a high level of prosperity in Middle Saxon Lindsey.

Melton Ross

The Melton Ross site lies at the point where the east to west route through the Wolds and across the Ancholme crosses Middlegate Lane, the ancient route running up the western side of the Wolds. A parallel may be drawn with South Newbald, which lies at the point where the Roman road north from the Humber at Brough divides, one branch going to Malton, the other to York. Katharina Ulmschneider has discussed the strong correlation between productive sites and lines of communication pointing to economic importance, something that

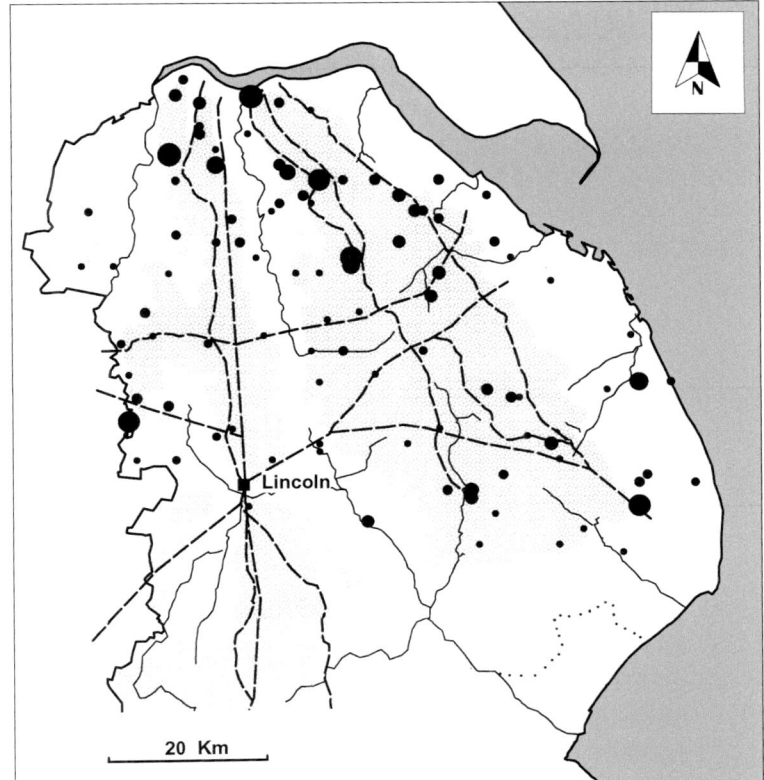

Right: 46 Distribution of Middle Saxon finds in Lindsey. *Digital mapping by Mike Hemblade*

Below: 47 Finds from the Melton Ross site.
1: Pyramid mount from a sword scabbard, seventh century. 2: Fragment of a gilded copper-alloy mount, originally in the form of a cross, eighth century. 3: Silver-gilt decorative mount bearing an animal and interlace, eighth century. 4: Silver-gilt pin bearing the figure of a bird. *Drawings by Marina Elwes*

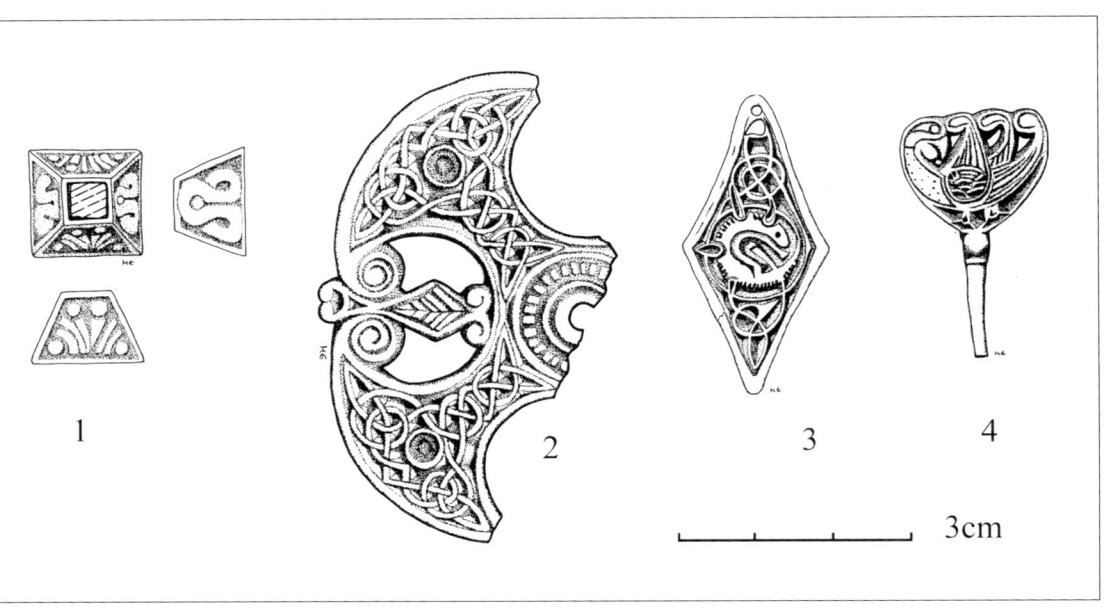

seems clear from figure *46*. The Melton Ross site was found by metal detector users, one of whom, Gary Parkin, realising the importance of the site, had his finds recorded and obtained information from other people. In all, 90 items of Anglo-Saxon metalwork were found, of which 37 were Early Anglo-Saxon. Forty-nine pieces of Middle Saxon metalwork were recorded and four items of later Saxon date (*47*). Unfortunately, few of the coins were seen but photographs show that they included Frisian *sceattas* of Series E, *sceattas* of Series J and R, Northumbrian *stycas* and broad pennies of Coenwulf of Mercia (796-821) and Æthelred II (986-1016).

The Melton Ross site appears to be only relatively productive, but Mr Parkin was only able to search a small part of the site as he did not have access to the main area. However, the high quality of some of the metalwork from Melton Ross shows it to be an important site. There was some overlap between the scatters of Early and Middle Saxon metalwork but the main concentration of early activity was to the west, where there was a cemetery. The Middle Saxon finds came from an area covered with fragments of animal bone, pottery and pieces of lead melt, which is typical of these sites. As seems to be the case on other productive sites in Lindsey the quantity of metalwork increased during the ninth century but the quality fell. A small number of tenth- to eleventh-century objects and finds of Late Saxon Torksey and Stamford ware pottery show that activity continued on the site at a lower level in the Late Saxon period. The Domesday entry for the site and the presence of Ross Castle, an imposing thirteenth-century moat, show that Melton Ross retained some of its importance.

The detector finds are not the only archaeological evidence for the settlement at Melton Ross. Aerial photographs show a series of enclosures defined by parallel ditches (*48*). Enclosures of this type were first recognised at Butterwick, a site in a bend of the Gypsy Race, the main stream on the Yorkshire Wolds. At Butterwick small rectangular features within the enclosures are likely to represent *Grubenhäuser*, the sunken-floored buildings used in the Anglo-Saxon period (*49*).

When we start to look at the location of the Melton Ross site things start to fall into place (*40*). While being close to the village of Melton Ross the finds actually came from the neighbouring parish of Barnetby le Wold, the site lying on the parish boundary. This is not the only instance of a productive site being cut by a parish boundary; the boundary between Newbald and Hotham actually steps out of line in order to cut the site, a deviation described in a royal charter of 963. The boundary between Barnetby and Melton Ross steps out of line just to the west of the site. On the map, the parishes of Barnetby and Melton Ross form a coherent triangle bisected by the parish boundary. Other productive sites in Lindsey lie on, or near parish boundaries. The parish

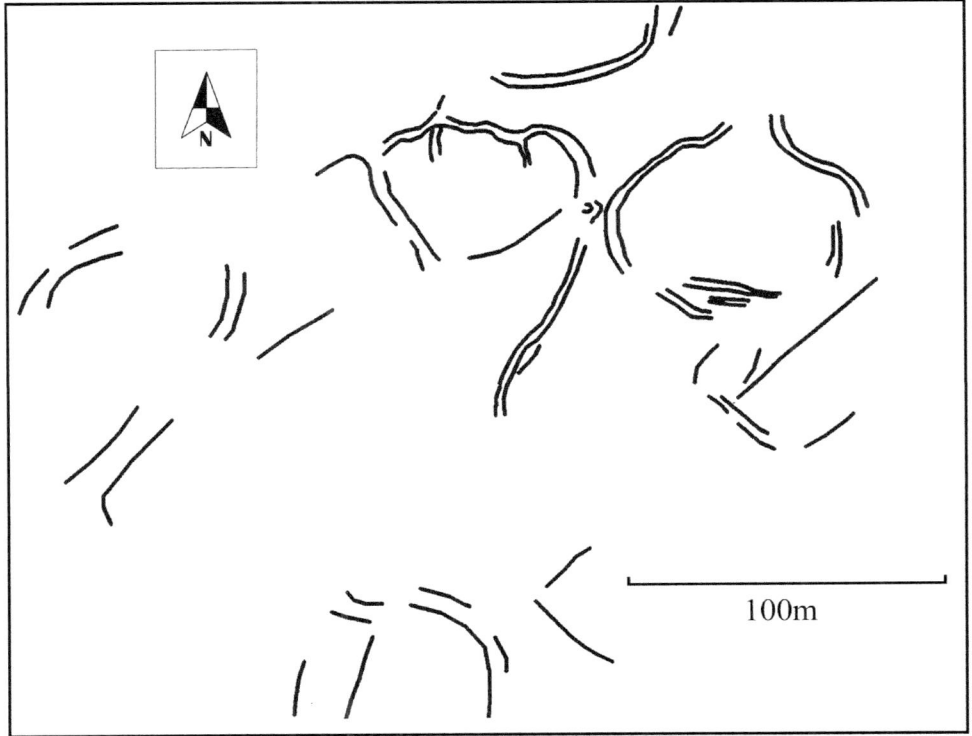

48 The 'Butterwick'-type crop marks observed at Melton Ross. *Plotted by Mike Hemblade*

system came into use in the tenth and eleventh centuries when landowners built churches on their estates and allocated tithes to support them, parish boundaries often followed the limits of those earlier estates. We have seen that three of the four large cremation cemeteries in Lindsey are on parish boundaries and it is possible these divisions continued to be seen as important. Elsham, the only cremation cemetery not to be on a parish boundary, is on Middlegate Lane, 3.5km to the north of Melton Ross. There is also the correlation between the large cemeteries and places that went on to become important manorial centres. The Domesday Survey valued Melton Ross at £6 in 1066 but by 1086 its value had risen to £8. It had a church and a priest. Like Melton Ross the value of Barnetby, (the other half of the original triangular estate) had risen from £15 in 1066 to £20 16s in 1086. It had half a church but, more importantly, it was a 'soke centre' with holdings in the port of Barton on Humber and, interestingly, at Riby, another productive site.

The diversion near the Melton Ross productive site is not the only place where the parish boundary steps out of line, as it once extended to the west along the line

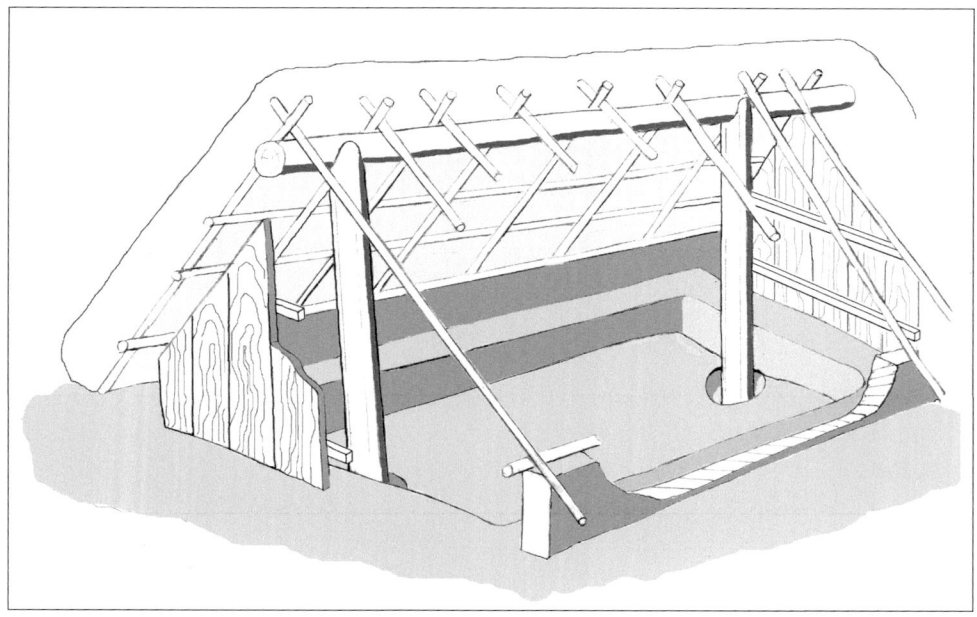

49 Possible recnstruction of a *Grubenhäus* found at Nettleton Top. *Drawing by Kevin Leahy*

of the road to the Ancholme crossing (*40*). At a point where the parishes of Melton Ross, Barnetby, Elsham and Wrawby meet there stands a gallows. This useful public amenity is no recent innovation, its location being marked on the 1824 Ordinance Survey, and the Hundred Rolls of 1276 refer to a '*furc*' at Melton Ross belonging to Robert de Ross. *Furc* appears in a number of contexts amongst which are *furcae suspensivae* in 1317 and *furcae judiciales* in 1296 and 1305. More details are given of the Melton Ross *furc* which is described as *antiqui conquest* showing that it dated back to before the Norman Conquest. Excavations carried out on the site of the Melton Ross gallows by the University of Sheffield failed to locate any human remains but severe plough damage would have destroyed any graves.

There are other significant sites in the area around Melton Ross. In the parish of Croxton, but adjacent to the north-east boundary of Melton Ross, is Yarborough Camp which is likely to have retained its importance as the folk moot of the eponymous Yarborough wapentake. The church of St Mary, Barnetby le Wold is inconveniently placed outside of the village and contains an interesting carving over the top of one of the windows. This consists of a single piece of stone on which is carved what looks like a cat, its tail forming a simple knot-like interlace. It is usually dated to the twelfth century on the basis of the form of the window opening but it could be dated to the eighth or ninth century and have been reused from an earlier church.

It would seem that at Melton Ross we have all of the features of the Anglo-Saxon State; the administration which met at Yarborough Camp, the judicial function at the gallows, commerce and communications along the roads and possibly, ecclesiastical at the church. Amongst the finds from the site is a seventh-century pyramidal sword mount (47) which would have been aristocratic. There is also an eighth-century cross-shaped open work mount of the type found at Whitby where it was thought to have a religious function. The Melton Ross site was important and retained some of this importance up to the conquest.

Riby Cross Roads

Another Butterwick-type site has also been found at Riby Crossroads, 11km to the east of Melton Ross. Here the Barton Street trackway (now the A18) and the Caistor to Stallingborough road (the A1173) cross, placing the site on lines of communication. In 1991 the laying of a gas pipeline gave the Humberside Archaeological Unit a chance to excavate a 5m-wide transect across the site. It was found that most, if not all, of the ditches and post holes on the site were Anglo-Saxon. Some pits contained early to Middle Saxon pottery but most of the ditches contained just Middle Saxon pottery with a few residual sherds of earlier wares. Five shallow depressions were found that may have been *Grubenhäuser* but the lack of internal post holes makes this doubtful. Found within them was pottery, animal bone, loom weights and an early eighth-century coin. A few coins from Riby have been recorded on the Early Medieval Coin Index, in addition to which there have been rumours of Anglo-Saxon coins, including gold, being found. As we have seen above, Domesday Riby was linked to the soke centre at Barnetby le Wold which was, in turn, linked to Melton Ross.

Belton

While not a productive site, work carried out by Northern Archaeological Associates at Belton on the Isle of Axholme has revealed traces of buildings that have not survived elsewhere. The site was discovered during the construction of a pipeline across the Isle of Axholme. Two Middle Saxon *Grubenhäuser* were found, one measuring 5.7m x 4.6m with post holes at each of its ends and stakes around its sides which may represent revetment. The second building was more unusual and consisted of a shallow pit, the base of which was covered with burnt stones and gravel. It was seen by the excavators as being atypical and was described, not as a *Grubenhäus*, but as an 'activity area'. Both structures contained Middle Saxon finds including metalwork (bone and copper-alloy pins) a loom weight, Northern Maxey-type ware, but no Ipswich ware. Joining sherds showed the two structures to be contemporary. A third 'building' consisted of a series of pits and two ditches; these were not at 90° to each other and may not have been part of the same structure.

DEFENDED SITES

In addition to the 'Butterwick'-type sites and the monasteries we have a number of Middle Saxon defended sites in Lindsey. Defences were constructed during the early Medieval Period, sometimes on a large scale like Offa's Dyke, the Wansdyke and King Alfred's *burhs*. Yarborough Camp, the most important defensive work in Lindsey has already been discussed as being late/sub-Roman. Countess Close at Alkborough may also fit into this period. A massive ditch, 4.8m wide and 2.4m deep was found beneath the medieval chancel of St Peter's church, Barton on Humber (*85, colour plate 27*). This formed part of 183m x 137m enclosure that can be seen in the layout of the lanes and streets to the east of the church. While this is difficult to date it is probably Middle Saxon.

Place-names containing the element '*burh*' ('a fortified place') provide further evidence of defences. These have been discussed by Barrie Cox who identified at least 12 of them in Lindsey and suggested they had been constructed during the wars between Mercia and Northumbria in the seventh century. This does not seem likely as the main battles of this conflict were fought outside Lindsey. The locations of the *burh* place-names do seem to follow a pattern but fail to make strategic sense when considered in terms of the Mercian wars. There is a line of *burh* place-names down the Wolds – Habrough, Stallingborough, Ludborough, Burgh on Bain, Burwell and Burgh le Marsh, which could relate to the settlement period or could have been during the troubled years of the Viking conquest. Barton on Humber is strategically located and Flixborough and Gainsborough would have been well placed to guard the Trent. The pattern of early modern streets in Gainsborough suggests that, as at Barton, they were curving around a large circular feature, which, alas, is now gone (Naomi Field, pers comm.). Other place-names with possible military connections are Harpswell and *Herewichil* in Kingerby parish which could relate to the '*here*', the Old English word for army.

The tenth-century manor at Goltho (Bullington) appears to have been surrounded by a rampart and ditch, 2.1-2.4m deep and 5.4m wide, which had largely been removed by the Norman ditch. This might be paralleled by the ring work that Caroline Atkins recognised during her survey of the Barrow on Humber motte and bailey which was also partly covered by the motte for which it had formed the first bailey.

At Goltho the work of Guy Beresford showed the development of a Late Saxon manor, sealed beneath the remains of a Norman motte and bailey (*86*). A range of building techniques had been used with the posts set both in pits and continuous trenches. The earliest structures on the site had close-set posts that were not paired across the building and could not have been linked in pairs by tie beams.

These posts must have been joined by a wall plate on which the roof was constructed. The buildings had been divided into rooms by a cross wall and there was evidence for paired doorways, set opposite each other in the long walls.

The main complex at Goltho consisted of a hall and other buildings constructed around a courtyard and surrounded by the rampart and ditch. These buildings included a hall, and a series of 'bowers' or detached private rooms. Finds from the other buildings around the courtyard led to them being described as a 'weaving shed' and 'kitchens'. The hall had slightly bowed, long walls and was divided into three rooms: a hall, an ante-chamber and a small extension at one end. It was 'stave-built', a method which uses close-set timbers joined together to form the walls. This makes extravagant use of timber, calling for a large number of staves, each around 460mm wide. There were three doors in the hall, an opposed pair into the ante-chamber and one into the far end of the hall. An extension was entered through a door linking it to the ante-chamber. The floor was made out of trampled clay and seems to have been kept clean, the eastern end of the hall was 460mm higher than the rest of the room to form the 'upper' end where the owner would have sat. In the middle of the raised area was a hearth built out of cobbles. Over the years the hall underwent a number of rebuilds on the same plan.

Like the hall and later bowers the Goltho 'weaving sheds' were stave-built and had been rebuilt on four occasions. Their interpretation as weaving sheds is based on the material found around them. Associated with the weaving sheds was a pit which served as a latrine. The first of the kitchens seems to have lacked any sub-surface features, its walls must have been made of rammed clay so that no post holes were needed. Only its clay floor and an area of burning marked its position. There was a single door and in the middle of the floor was an oven, which now consisted of a 100mm-deep hollow filled with the burnt daub that had once formed it sides and top. While this site was identified as Goltho, Paul Everson has convincingly argued that it was, in fact, Bullington. I would also believe the chronology to be shorter than was suggested with post-Roman occupation starting in the tenth, not the ninth century.

FLIXBOROUGH

The Flixborough site was discovered in 1933 when 'Roman' pottery and loom weights were found close to the site of a church belonging to the deserted medieval village of North Conesby. In 1988, the then Humberside Sites and Monuments Record received a planning application for a sand pit on the site. Knowing of the earlier finds, a watch was kept when extraction started and 11 skeletons were found, all in very poor condition; some had been in coffins with iron fittings of the type used for Anglo-Saxon burials (*88*, 10-12). On the strength of this and the finds from a trial excavation, English Heritage sponsored a 12-week excavation. We were still digging 20 months later, the work on site being carried out, with great skill, by a small team from the Humberside Archaeological Unit (now Humber Field Archaeology).

The Flixborough excavation produced a massive amount of Anglo-Saxon material, the whole site seemingly dominated by the rubbish dumps. These contained 15,000 finds including metalwork, pottery, glass and more than 5 tonnes of animal bones. If the site was monastic the amount of bone does not equate with the bread and skimmed milk diet enjoyed by Bishop Edgar. Although the Flixborough excavation has not yet been published Dr Christopher Loveluck, who now manages the project, has published an interim account of the site on which this synopsis will draw, along with my own observations of the excavation and preliminary examination of the finds.

Flixborough buildings

An important feature of the Flixborough site was its degree of preservation. At some time after its abandonment it had been covered with a layer of blown sand, 2m deep on the western side of the site and tapering out to the east, which protected the remains. The buildings at Flixborough were well preserved, original floor surfaces survived and it was possible to trace paths and yards made of limestone rubble. There may have been around 40 buildings but the full area of the Flixborough site was not excavated as the ends of buildings were seen in the east face of the sandpit. It is also likely that the material in the dumps covering large areas of the site had been brought in from elsewhere. It had been hoped that the rest of the site lay on the top of the scarp to the east but extensive trial trenching failed to produce anything.

Some of the Flixborough buildings were of respectable size; the largest measured 20m x 6.5m, perhaps with more than one storey, but other buildings were less than 10m long (*colour plate 17*). All of the Flixborough structures were post-built, no *Grubenhäuser* were found, although the evidence from Belton and at the Bail in Lincoln show sunken-floored buildings were in use during Middle and perhaps Late Saxon periods. Not all of the Flixborough buildings were standing at the same time and some had been rebuilt on four occasions. All that survived of most of them were the post holes and wall trenches that had once held the wall posts of timber buildings. In some cases flat stones on which the posts had been seated were found at intervals along the wall trenches. One building may have had its wall posts set into a sill beam resting on a gravel foundation. This building had a clay hearth at one end and had been divided into two rooms, associated with it were four burials which lay along its walls, the bodies extended and aligned west-east. There were two further burials outside the building. With one exception these graves contained the remains of children aged between three and twelve years old. The exception, found in one corner of the building, was a woman aged between 20 and 30 years at death with the remains of a perinatal infant at her feet.

Some method must have been used to fill in the gaps between the posts forming the walls of Anglo-Saxon buildings. Burnt daub was found at Riby and Flixborough showing that clay had been used to complete the walls. The gaps between the posts had been filled with wattles made from thin twigs or split wood over which the clay, mixed with straw, was laid to form the walls. On occasion the clay was baked, either from when a building had burnt down or from a fire following a building's demolition, preserving the impressions of the wattles.

Window glass and lead glazing 'cames' were found at Flixborough and dated to around the late eighth or early ninth century. The small panes of glass were nibbled to shape with pincers and mounted in the H-sectioned lead cames. The use of glass in windows was an important social indicator. Amongst the many iron objects found during the Flixborough excavation were large numbers of 'fittings', many of which may have been architectural or come from furnishings.

What was the Flixborough site?

The interpretation of the Flixborough site has been the source of some debate. In some quarters it has been taken as an established fact that it was an Anglo-Saxon nunnery; other interpretations have been more cautious. The Flixborough buildings are not like the small monastic cells identified at Whitby and Hartlepool, but larger buildings have been found on monastic sites elsewhere (Whithorn and Hoddom) and a monastic interpretation of the site cannot be excluded on these grounds. There is nothing amongst the massive quantity of finds from Flixborough that can definitely be said to be Christian. This need not surprise us; with the exception of sculpture and stone grave markers even the historically attested Anglo-Saxon monasteries have failed to yield much that we can say, without doubt, is of a Christian nature. The decorated mounts from Whitby (an example of which was found at Melton Ross; *47, 2*) may have once been attached to a shrine or book. Carvings have been found on or near two of Lindsey's possible monasteries, Redbourne and Caistor, but from the rest there is nothing other than scanty history and suggestive topographical settings. The major shrines that once graced Lindsey are long gone; St Oswald's remains were moved from Bardney to Gloucester in 909 and the bones of St Herefrith were taken from Louth by the monks of Thorney Abbey, Cambridgeshire, in 970s. The empty grave at St Paul in the Bail (*42*) may have contained the remains of a saint but they have long since been removed, either for safety, or translated to a richer setting. The only archaeological evidence we have for Flixborough being a monastery is the remarkable number of styli, the lead inscription and a ring bearing the first half of the alphabet, A to L (*59; colour plate 20*). It is probable that the alphabet ring was one of a pair, its counterpart bearing the other half of the alphabet. It is likely that it was an amulet; in a society where writing was something mystical, to carry with you the letters that could form the whole of the Bible must have had a magic of its own.

There are 27 styli from Flixborough which are made from iron (*88*, 4), copper alloy and, in one case, silver (*colour plate 20*). These were found in deposits dated to the late eighth to early ninth century which seems rather late for the golden age of Anglo-Saxon monasticism, but this is the date at which the styli were finally deposited, not when they were made and used. Styli were used for writing on waxed tablets; a shallow recess in the face of the tablet was filled with wax and the text scratched onto it with the pointed end of the stylus, any errors being erased with its flat end. Writing tablets were used for practising writing and for preparing drafts, which were then copied onto the expensive vellum. The large number of styli found at Flixborough shows that the level of literacy was high and we may be looking at evidence for a school, which would have been attached to a monastery. It is sad to relate that analysis of the cattle bones found on the Flixborough site came from adults or sub-adults; there were very few of the calf bones which would have supported the manufacture of vellum on the site, although the crescentic knife (*88*, 7) is of a type used in the preparation and working of skins.

A find of major importance was the inscribed lead plaque which has 12 nail holes around its edge, five of these damaged in a way that suggests that it was torn away from a surface to which it had been nailed. Cut with a V-shaped chisel on its face are four lines of text:

+ALDUINI ∴ ALDHERI∴.
HAEODHAED ∴ EODUINI ∴
EDELGYD ∴ EONBERECHT
EDEL NUN [or UIIN?]

(The final line is on the edge of the plaque and is difficult to read.)

Michelle Brown, who has studied the plaque, has written that the inscription lists seven Old English personal names, six men and one woman, some of whom might tentatively be linked to historically known individuals:

ALDUINI	Abbot Ealdwine of Partney
HAEODHAED	Eadhæd, Bishop of Lindsey
EDELGYD	Æthelhild, abbess of the unnamed monastery near Partney?

We cannot be sure that these are the people who are referred to on the plaque. They are historically recorded to have been alive around 700 and, by parallel with the lettering used in manuscripts, the plaque should be later eighth century in date. This need not exclude links between the plaque and the people. Michelle Brown noted that the form of the inscription (an initial cross followed by a list of names) is the format that was used on a list of charter witnesses or in a book of benefactors. This must have been a list of people who were important to the Flixborough community and the plaque could have been fixed to a reliquary.

Since the discovery of the Flixborough plaque two further examples of inscriptions on lead have come to light; at Kirkdale in Yorkshire a small lead fragment bore a partial inscription suggesting that it came from a grave. The other lead inscription was discovered in Lindsey during excavations at St Helen's Church, Cumberworth; a small lead plaque bearing a Latin inscription was found above burials which had been dug through the timber buildings that preceded the stone church. Elisabeth Okasha has transcribed the inscription as:

+xpi ex hoc signo [-----] expiatum [-----] exiguum squalorem m[...t]
[u]olutum qu[i] in uirt[ute] [cr]ucis mundum de morte red[em]it
ta[r]tara disrupit aut celestia pandit

+ though this sign of Christ [---] the small foulness [accusative] [-----], he by the power of the cross redeemed the world from death, shattered hell or threw open heaven.

This looks like a funerary cross although there is no name on it, but this might have been on a second cross. Dr Okasha dated it to the tenth to eleventh century by the style of the lettering.

There is a historical context for a monastery at Flixborough. In 672 Queen Æthelthryth (also known as Etheldreda or Audrey) left her husband King Ecgfrith of Northumbria to become a nun at Coldingham, Yorkshire (it was his support for this decision that led to St Wilfrid being sent into exile). Æthelthryth had retained her virginity despite having been married twice: first to Ealdorman Tondberht of the South Gyrwe (an Anglo-Saxon people in the Cambridgeshire area) and then to Ecgfrith to whom the impossibility of an heir must have been a problem. In 673 she left Northumbria and fled to Ely where she settled and founded the important monastery. On her journey south she crossed the Humber at Winteringham with her maidens, Sewara and Sewenna and fled to a nearby village 'almost surrounded by marshes' (*Liber Eliensis*). In return for the hospitality she received from the people of this place she had a church built. The twelfth-century *Liber Eliensis*, when discussing the life of Ely's founder, recorded that

Æthelthryth founded two monasteries in Lincolnshire, one was at *Ætheldreðestowe* which David Roffe has argued is at Stow Green near Threekingham (Kesteven). The other was at *Alftham* which was probably West Halton.

This presents some problems as, although the location described in the *Liber Eliensis*, 'almost surrounded by marshes', sounds like the typical setting for an early monastery (Ely itself was on an island) it does not fit West Halton which is not directly on a river. According to Margaret Gelling the *halh* element of the place-name means a 'nook, a corner of land', which can mean land between rivers or in a river bend. This would be appropriate for West Halton which lies in the angle formed by the Trent and Humber. There is some supporting evidence; the dedication of the church at West Halton is to St Etheldreda and, while the existing structure is largely a product of a drastic restoration in 1876, the original church was visited on 29 May 1697 by Abraham de la Pryme who was curate at Broughton, nearby. He said of West Halton:

> This town tho' it bee but little now is nevertheless of great antiquity. It's [*sic*] parish is very large, which [is] also a good sign of its antiquity. The church is now faln to ruins, but appears to have been very stately, magnificent, and larger than anyone for a great many miles round about it.

West Halton then had a large and magnificent church – it had once been important.

De la Pryme's reference to the size of the parish is also interesting. It is not now that large but it has an odd shape, like an elongated 'L', one arm of which almost reaches the Trent. This shape could be due to it having been the original minster for this corner of north-west Lindsey and, as parishes were created in the tenth century, they were removed from this large 'mother parish'. West Halton is what was left behind. Originally, there was a part of West Halton parish that was not attached to the main area, Halton Old Park, and that lay next to the Anglo-Saxon site at Flixborough. Further links exist; in 1455 there were complaints about the failure of the parson of West Halton to serve the chapels of St John the Baptist and Holy Cross at Flixborough, which could be an ancient obligation. The Flixborough site is next to a circular graveyard that once surrounded the Church of All Saints in North, or Little Conesby, which was demolished in 1778 but had been drawn in 1776 by John Snape. He shows a simple two-cell structure of probable Norman date although an earlier origin cannot be excluded. We have seen that the presence of multiple churches is a feature of monastic sites and that three churches or chapels in a small area at Flixborough might support the presence of a monastery.

Like West Halton, the Flixborough site could not be described as an island, being on the escarpment overlooking the River Trent, now 1.4km to the west. It is possible that the two sites were originally part of a group of linked monasteries and that *halh* or nook in Halton was not the present parish but the whole of the area, down to, and including, Flixborough, 7.5km to the south. West Halton is in the nook/angle between the Trent and the Humber but touches neither river; the word *halh* only really becomes appropriate if the whole area is considered and not just the parish of West Halton.

So what then was Flixborough? David Stocker has suggested that Anglo-Saxon monasteries and royal sites were paired (Lincoln/Bardney) and that we could be looking at a Flixborough/West Halton pairing with Flixborough or, more accurately, Conesby the 'king's settlement', carrying on the aristocratic link into the ninth century. Anglo-Saxon royal sites have been excavated such as Cheddar and Yeavering, both of which, in total, yielded less in the way of metal objects than were found at Flixborough on a quiet day. We don't need large numbers of finds for a site to be aristocratic. Large numbers of objects were found on the monastic site at Whitby but other Anglo-Saxon monasteries have produced few finds (Jarrow and Hartlepool). While Flixborough is productive, it must be said the finds from the site impress more by their quantity than their quality. There are many fine objects but nothing that has the assured grace of the Witham pins (*colour plate 18*, cf *colour plate 19*).

What then do the objects themselves tell us? (See examples in figures *50*, *51*, *52*, *55* and *58*.) The finds from Flixborough look feminine, with large numbers of pins and small dress fittings, but this need not mean anything; we saw in the Early Anglo-Saxon period how little material survived in the graves of men, whose clothing was not secured by copper-alloy fittings. Finds of tools on the site show the presence of men but then there is a lot of evidence for weaving which was a feminine activity. There is nothing in the way of war-gear from the site. While we might be wrong to expect finds of helmets, swords and spearheads we might have hoped to see *something*; the Anglo-Saxon aristocracy was a warrior society. Metal detecting on much smaller sites like Melton Ross (*47*, *1*) and Welton le Marsh has produced weapon fittings.

We have oblique evidence of a further monastery in Lindsey at a place called *Donemuthan* which was attacked by the Vikings in 794. The River Don where the attack took place is usually thought to have been at Jarrow where there is a River Don. However, Parker has argued that the Northumbrian river only became known as the Don in recent times by a process of backwards historical naming. He suggested that it is possible that the attacked monastery was at the mouth of the Yorkshire Don, a channel of which, on Morden's map of 1695, enters the Trent almost opposite Flixborough.

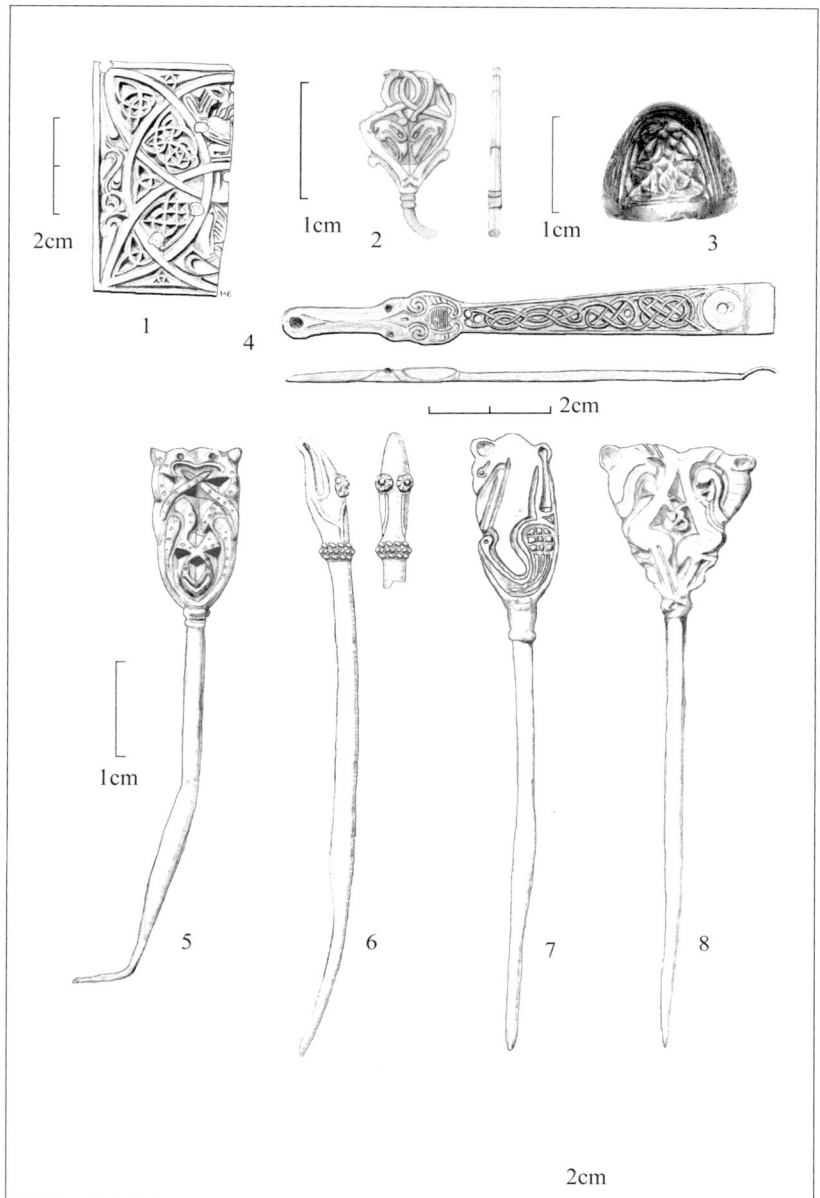

50 Middle Saxon metalwork, eighth century. 1: Gilded copper-alloy mount, with animals and interlace, Horncastle. 2: Silver-gilt pin-head, two confronted birds and interlace, West Ravendale. 3: Silver gilt cone, interlace, Louth. 4: Gilded copper-alloy mount, silver plug in end of nose, animal had red glass eyes, Flixborough. 5: Silver-gilt pin, confronted animals and interlace, hipped shaft, Flixborough. 6: Silver-gilt pin in the form of an animal's head, Hatfield. 7: Silver-gilt pin in form of a gryphon's head, Flixborough. 8: Silver-gilt pin with tooling marks, Flixborough. *Drawing 1 by Marina Elwes, rest by Kevin Leahy*

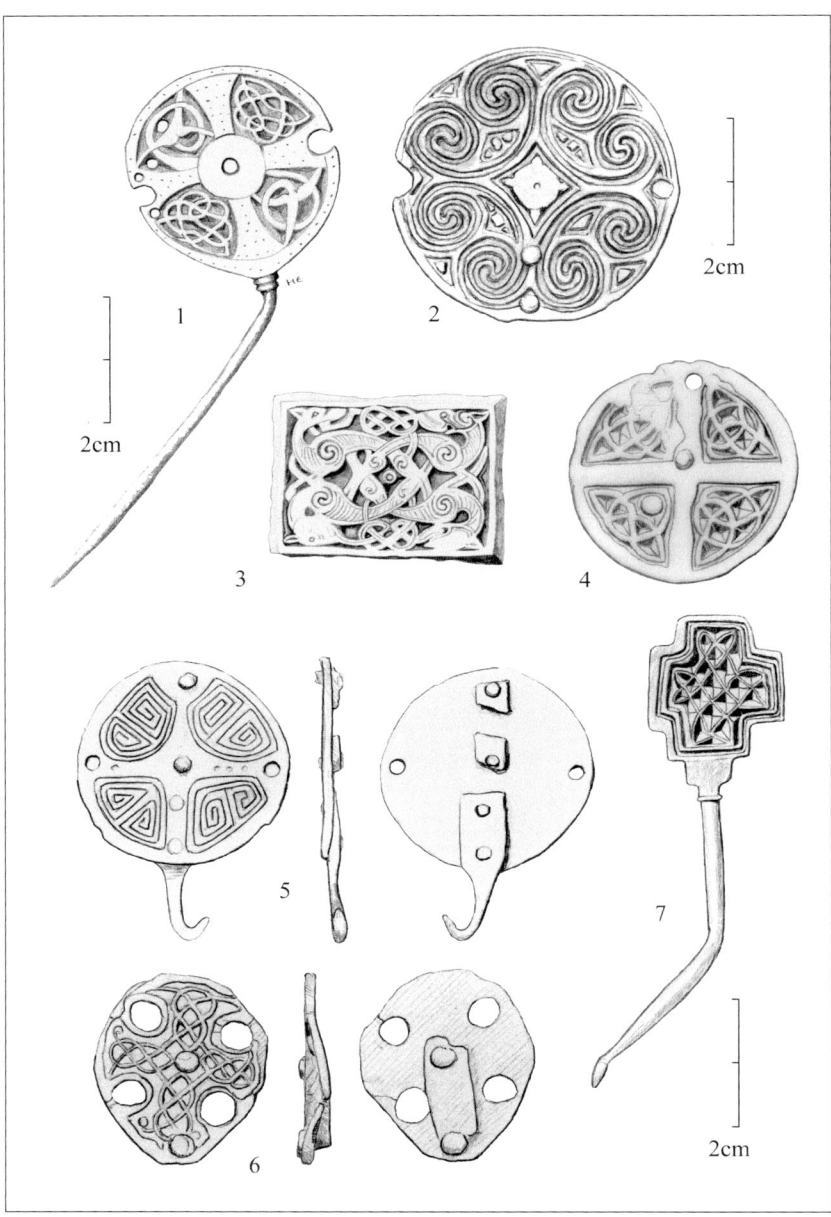

51 Middle Saxon decorated pins, eighth century. 1: Silver disc-headed pin with animals and interlace, Horncastle. 2: Gilded copper-alloy disc from a triple pinset, Flixborough. 3: Copper-alloy Pressblech die for making foil mounts in Hiberno-Saxon style, Stickford. 4: Gilded copper-alloy pin head, Flixborough. 5: Gilded copper-alloy pin (or brooch) with 'Greek key design', Welton le Marsh. 6: Pin head with interlace, no gilding, Welton le Marsh. 7: Copper-alloy pin with gilded head in the form of an interlace decorated cross, West Ravendale. *Drawings 1 and 3 by Marina Elwes, rest by Kevin Leahy*

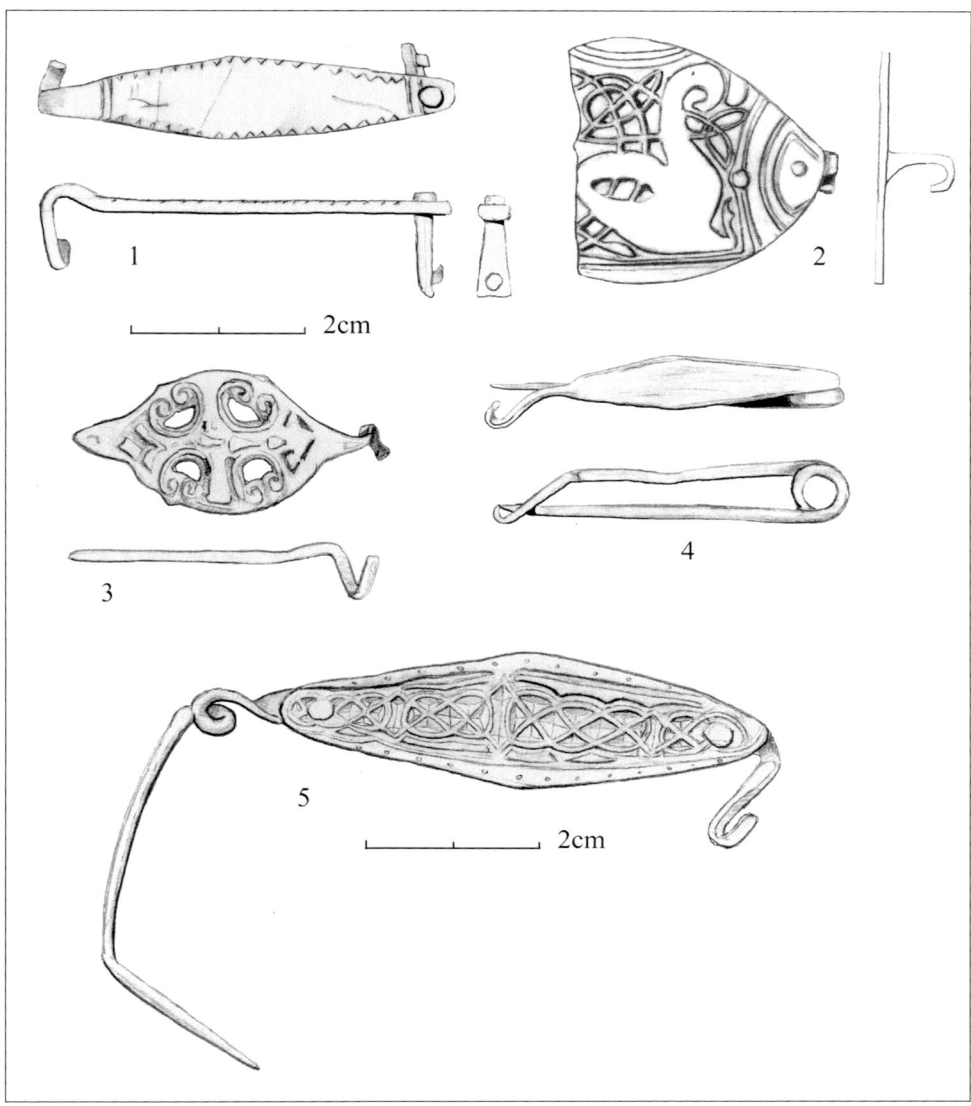

52 Middle Saxon strip brooches, eighth to ninth century. 1: Copper-alloy strip brooch, Flixborough. 2: Copper-alloy brooch decorated with animal interlace and cut down from a larger object, Riby. 3: Openwork copper-alloy strip brooch, Louth. 4: Copper-alloy strip brooch, Flixborough. 5: Gilded copper-alloy strip brooch with interlace decoration, Mablethorpe. *Drawings by Kevin Leahy*

The Archaeology of Middle Saxon Lindsey

Until recently the Middle Saxon period was, from an archaeological point of view, practically unknown. The historical records are better for the eighth and ninth centuries but, in the absence of the rich pagan cemeteries, the amount of archaeological evidence that we have is minimal. This paucity had implications for our understanding of the Middle and later Saxon periods, which seemed almost nonexistent. Even at this time there were hints that the limited picture was incorrect; there were some superb finds, two of which, the eighth-century Witham pins (*colour plate 19*) and the Witham bowl (*54*), came from Lindsey.

In the last 25 years there has been an explosion in our knowledge of the Middle and later Saxon periods. This has come about through two agencies: the use of metal detectors in the countryside and the advent of large-scale excavations on sites of the period. In Lindsey we have been fortunate enough to have been able to learn from both sources; we started recording detector finds at an early date and some important excavations have taken place on sites in the former kingdom. The database of the Portable Antiquities Scheme together with the records that I made before the start of the scheme contain more that 600 items of later Saxon metalwork from Lindsey, in addition to which we have more than 900 non-ferrous finds from the Flixborough excavation. We are now beginning to see the richness and density of the Middle Saxon culture (*46*).

The quality is varied; some pieces like the silver-gilt Witham pins (*colour plate 19*) and Witham bowl (*54*) are of outstanding artistry. There are some copper-alloy objects which are elegantly designed, like the plate from Horncastle or the mount decorated with an animal's head from Flixborough (*50, 1, 4*). During the eighth century the most common style of decoration consisted of interlace and animals. On finer work these were combined, with parts of the animals being extended and interlaced (*53*). Sometimes the animals were given small glass beads as eyes

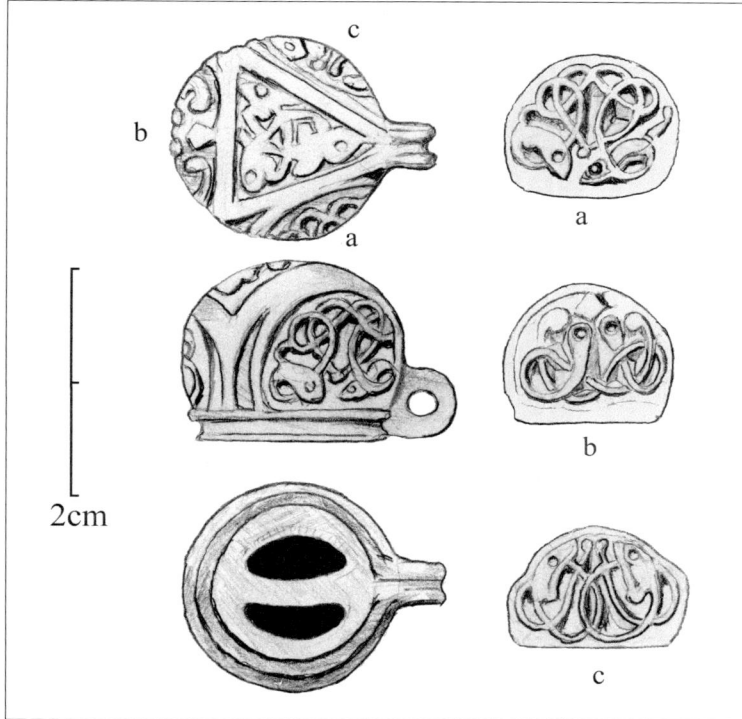

53 Silver-gilt 'pomade' from Wrawby. It is interlaced with animals, some of which have retained the blue glass beads forming their eyes. The function of this object is uncertain; it is hollow and has a suspension loop and could be interpreted as a pomade that was filled with sweet-smelling herbs. *Drawing by Kevin Leahy*

and much of this metalwork was gilded, often to great effect. On poorer work the interlace was used alone (*51*, 4; *52*, 5). In addition to the animal interlace we see some use of spirals (*51*, 2) and Greek key-like designs (*51*, 5). The most popular layout for the decoration on these pins and brooches was based around crosses, probably reflecting the community's Christian beliefs. While there is nothing in the decoration surrounding the crosses that appears Christian, similar motifs were used in illuminated manuscripts and they were clearly acceptable to the church.

The lower quality of some of the metalwork is interesting as it suggests that the use of these pins and brooches was not restricted to the aristocracy, and that the lower orders also had access to it. It is also interesting that many of the objects show signs of repair or reuse; even the discs used on the Witham pins had been reused. Other objects have traces of replacement fittings on their reverse (*51*, 5) or have been cannibalised from larger objects, as on the brooch from Riby (*52*, 2). As well as the fine pins with decorated heads there is a bewildering range of simpler dress pins which are found in large numbers on Middle Saxon sites, 485 being found at Flixborough alone. These pins are not easy to date and cover the eighth and ninth centuries. Some are clearly early; the linked pins from Flixborough (*55*) can be paralleled by finds from seventh-century graves.

54 The Witham bowl. This remarkable object was found during drainage works on the River Witham in 1816. It is now lost, having last been seen in 1868, but fortunately the Society of Antiquaries had commissioned the drawings we now see. The bowl was, and perhaps still is, silver-gilt and, with a diameter of around 150mm, was relatively small. If the drawn section is to be relied on, it was cast, not beaten to shape. Its decoration used a range of techniques; millefiori glass, filigree and casting. It is odd in having four, not the usual three, mounts. What are we to make of the figure of the startled Brontosaurus in the centre of the bowl surrounded by four attendant sabre-toothed tigers? Its head is set above the level of the bowl's side so its blue glass eyes could be seen peering over the rim. If there is any object that shows the quality of the metalwork available in middle Saxon Lindsey it is this. *Illustration courtesy of the Society of Antiquaries of London*

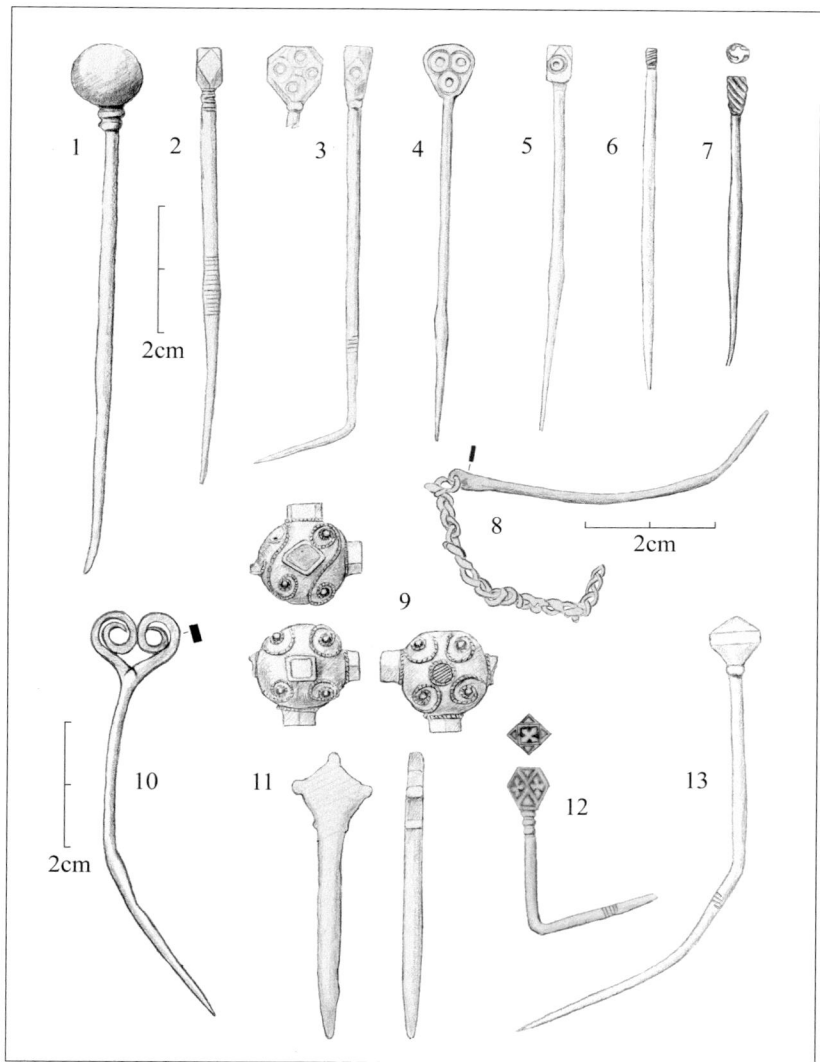

55 Some of the forms of pin in use in Middle Saxon Lindsey, showing characteristic features like hipped shafts and incised lines around the shafts. All copper alloy except 9 and 12 which are silver. All from Flixborough except 9, from Mablethorpe, 11 from Osgodby and 12 from Swallow. *Drawings by Kevin Leahy*

1-5, 7, 10 and 13: Standard forms.

6: Has no head but the top of the shaft has been roughened to take a glass head.

8: An early form that also occurs in seventh-century graves.

9: Can be paralleled by a find from Flixborough, its hollow, silver-gilt head is fitted with bosses surrounded with filigree and granulation. Each boss was filled with a small piece of red or white glass.

11: An Irish kite-headed pin of a type introduced into England by the Vikings. These are more common in Yorkshire than in Lindsey.

12: Silver pin inlaid with black niello.

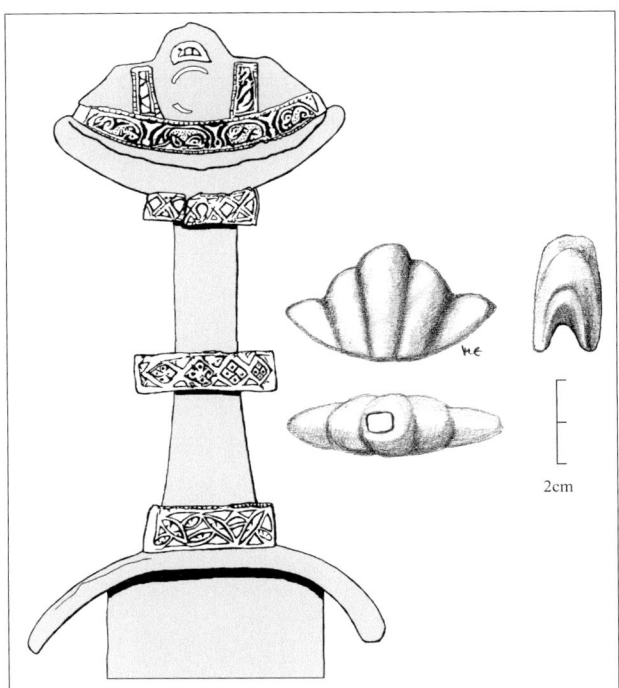

56 The Witham sword. This weapon has an iron hilt inlaid with silver and niello. The design is in the ninth century 'Trewhiddle style'. With it is the copper-alloy pommel cap from a similar sword found at Alkborough. *Sword drawn by Dianne Leahy, pommel by Maina Elwes*

The little silver pin from Swallow bears ninth-century style decoration (55, 12) and the kite-headed pin from Osgodby (55, 11) is an Irish type introduced into England by the Vikings and will be of tenth- or eleventh-century date. Most pins are made from copper alloy although some silver and iron were also used. There were some composite pins, originally with glass heads, like the one from Flixborough (55, 6). Many, but not all, Middle Saxon pins have a collar around their shafts just below the head. Hipped shafts, which expand part way down their length, are common, as are areas of grooving around pin shafts which must have helped hold them in place. Many pins have sharply bent shafts which again may relate to the way in which they were worn. Unfortunately, in the absence of graves we have little idea who was wearing these pins, brooches and strap ends or how they were wearing them.

We have little evidence for the manufacture of objects like these; a crucible fragment was found at Flixborough. One pin from Flixborough appears unfinished, its surface covered with rough file marks and with the interlace between the two animals botched (50, 8). However, in spite of the rough finish, the face of this object has been gilded and it must have been seen as complete. The thick metal plate from Stickford (51, 3) is a *Pressblech* die used for making foils, decorated in what looks like Hiberno-Saxon style.

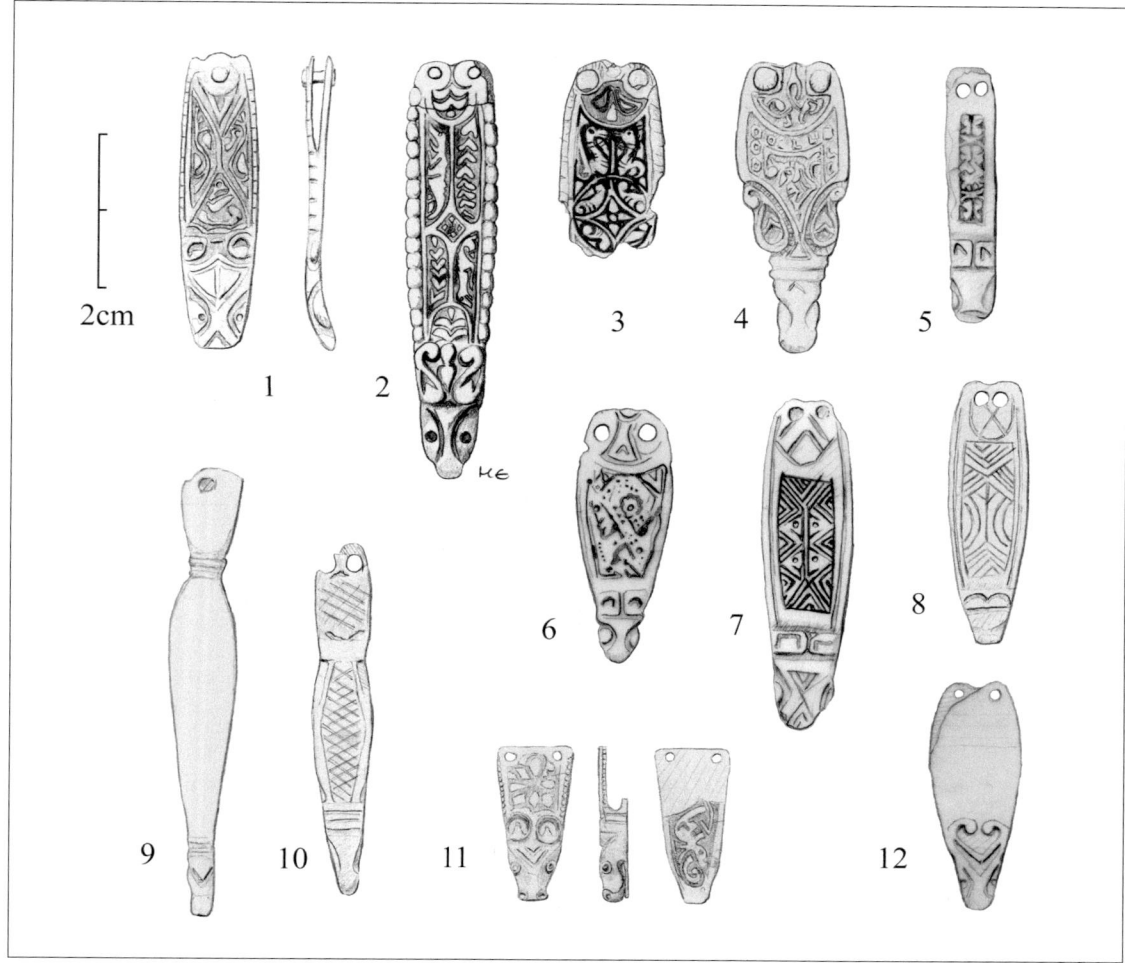

57 Typical ninth-century strap ends from Lindsey.

  1: Caistor, decorated with a leaf-tendril design, may be base silver.
  2: Melton Ross, copper-alloy with silver rivets, good Trewhiddle style inlaid with niello, animal
    has blue glass eyes.
  3: Torksey, silver, very fine Trewhiddle style inlaid with enamel. Fragment very thin and represents
    only the face of the strap end.
  4: Welton le Marsh, some signs of silver inlay, but design difficult to resolve.
  5: Torksey, copper-alloy, neat little strap end with Trewhiddle decoration but no inlay.
  6: Winterton, copper-alloy with silver inlay, a crude, blundered version of a Trewhiddle animal.
  7: Bardney, copper-alloy, no inlay, geometric decoration.
  8: Caistor, copper-alloy, geometric decoration, incised.
  9: Stallingborough, plain 'bow tie' strap end but still has an animal head terminal.
  10: Welton le Marsh, copper-alloy with lattice decoration.
  11: Torksey, silver with niello, animal with blue glass eyes, high-grade workmanship.
  12: Winterton, plain strap end.
Drawing 2 by Marina Elwes, rest by Kevin Leahy

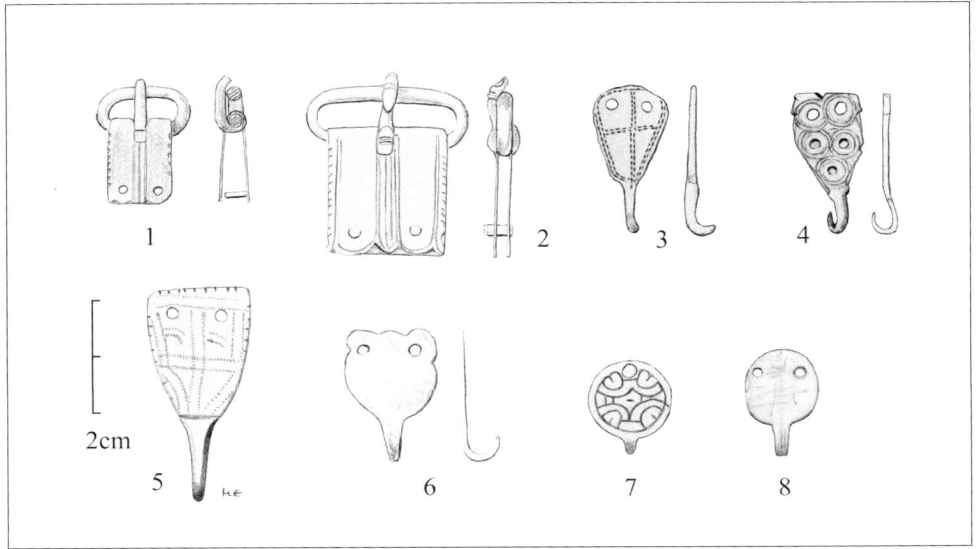

58 Middle Saxon buckles and hooked tags. 1–2: Buckles from Flixborough. 3–8: Hooked tags from Harpswell (3), Torksey (4), Bielby (5), Flixborough (6), Aylesby (7) and Bardney (8). *Drawings all by Kevin Leahy*

The ninth century brought a change in fashion, the gilding which typified the eighth century was no longer used. It was replaced by extensive use of silver, and silvering which, for effect, was often inlaid with niello, a black silver sulphide. This was used in what is known as the 'Trewhiddle style' where the area to be decorated was divided into small panels and filled with animal, plant or geometric motifs (*56, 57*). As before, the decoration is better executed on some pieces than on others, but there seems to have been a general fall in the standard of workmanship. The Trewhiddle style is most often seen on strap ends, some of which are delightful (*57*). It is not known how strap ends were used; they may have been worn on cross-garters around the legs or perhaps employed anywhere where it was necessary to secure clothing. The other dress fitting commonly used were hooked tags (*58*). These, again, are difficult to date but it seems that the triangular form is eighth century (some long, narrow examples being found in seventh-century graves) and the small round examples are late, being made in Lincoln in the tenth century.

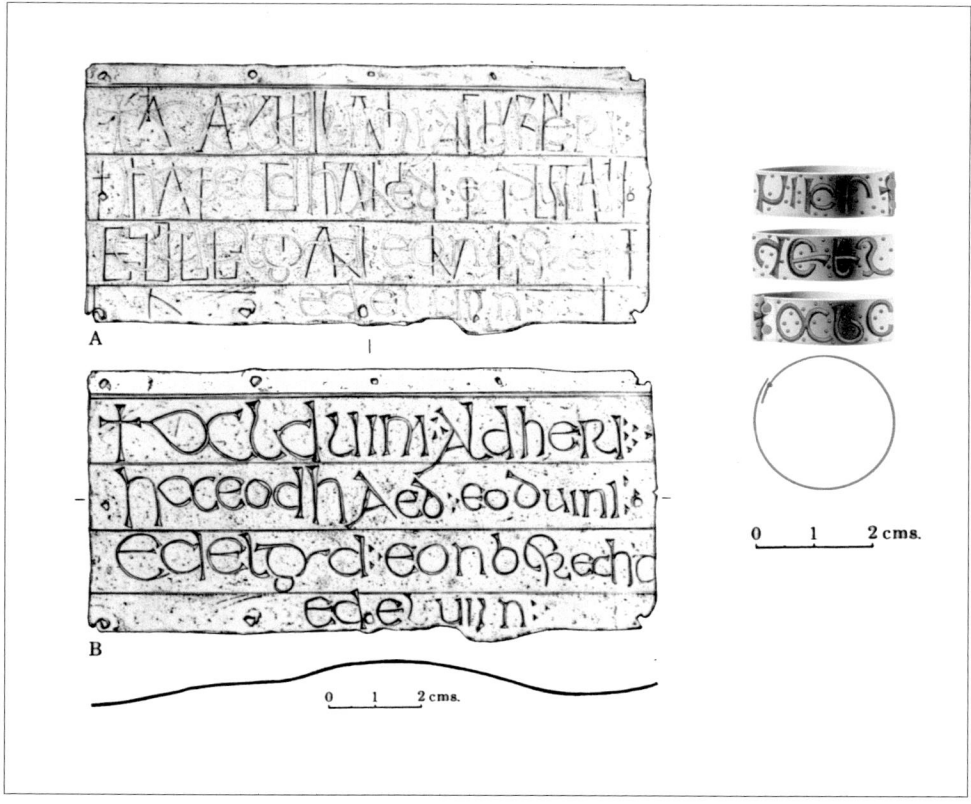

59 Inscriptions on the lead plaque and alphabet ring, Flixborough. Inscription B was written over the top of inscription A. *Drawings courtesy of Humber Field Archaeology*

MIDDLE SAXON POTTERY

In Lindsey the Early Saxon gritty wares were replaced by Maxey-type wares during the early eighth century. This pottery gets its name from a site in Northamptonshire where it was first recognised, but, unlike Ipswich and Stamford wares, it was not made at this type site. Maxey-type ware is undecorated and was handmade using a coil method. Its fabric contains large quantities of crushed sea shell and, although it looks crude, was well fired. There appears to have been two main types of Maxey-type ware, the earliest are thin-sided, finely coiled vessels with a fabric tempered with large amounts of finely crushed shell. They have flat bases and their sides, although fairly straight, are curved into bucket and barrel shapes (87). Later Maxey-type pots have thicker walls and are tempered with larger shell fragments. Coiling is coarser and pieces of shell can be seen on the exterior of the pots. Bowls are more common and some of the pots have turned-out rims instead of the flat-topped form found on the earlier group. One of the distinguishing marks of these pots are pairs of triangular, ear-like lugs, set each side of the rim to hold a handle.

Crushed sea shell temper/filler was added to the clay to improve its working properties and add to the strength of the finished pot. Because of the crudeness of Maxey-type pottery it was assumed to be homemade but Alan Vince has shown that Jurassic fossil shell was being used. These pots must have been made along the limestone ridge that runs down the length of the Midlands, and then distributed throughout the region. It looks like they were the work of specialist potters. At Flixborough, Maxey-type pottery was being used alongside imported Ipswich ware.

MIDDLE SAXON TRADE

Imported material

In addition to the large amount of Middle Saxon metalwork being found we are also seeing objects that had been imported and show active contact with the continent. The most common finds are small silver coins known to numismatists as 'Series E and D *sceattas*' and to the rest of us as 'porcupine' *sceattas* (the degenerated head of the Roman emperor looks like a porcupine). These date from the late seventh to early eighth century and came from the area of the Rhine; to date, 61 of them have been found in Lindsey. In addition to the coins, we are seeing metalwork of continental type, particularly 'Ansate' brooches (*60*) of which we have 27 examples. These brooches were made from copper alloy and are often decorated with ring-dots and transverse ribs. We also have five strap ends decorated with Carolingian acanthus-leaf designs dating from the eighth to ninth century (*61*). The distribution of this material (*62*) lacks any real foci although finds tend to lie along lines of communication; the largest group, the four finds from Elsham, were found near Middlegate Lane. Neither Lincoln, Torksey nor Flixborough seem to figure in the distribution of metalwork although there are 13 continental coins from Flixborough.

The continental imports most common at Flixborough were fragments of lava quern stones which were being imported from the Mayen area of the Eifel Mountains in Germany. Quern stones from this source are not uncommon on Middle Saxon sites and have also been found at Riby and Goltho. These may have been the 'black stones' referred to in a correspondence between the eighth-century Mercian King Offa and Charlemagne. The Riby excavation also produced sherds from a wheel-thrown grey ware bowl of a type found in late

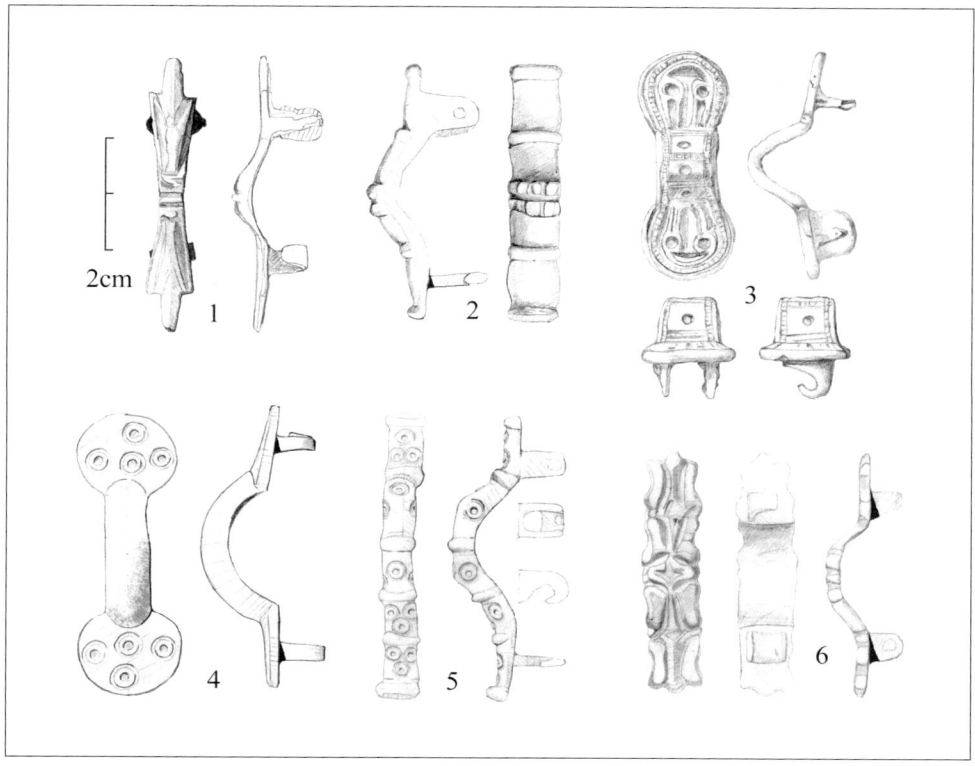

60 Continental 'Ansate' brooches from Lindsey. 1:'North-east Lindsey'. 2: Withcall. 3: Spilsby. 4: Manton. 5: West Ravendale. 6: West Ravendale. *Drawings all by Kevin Leahy*

seventh- or eighth-century graves in north-west France and Belgium. Some imported pottery was found at Flixborough but not enough to suggest that the site was as a 'wic', one of the early medieval trading centres like Ham*wic*, Ips*wich* or Yor*vik*.

One of the most important types of 'imported' Middle Saxon pottery found in Lindsey is Ipswich ware. This was produced in the Suffolk town between around 650 and 850 and has been studied by Paul Blinkhorn. It was handmade, using the coil method, but with the rims often finished by turning the pot on a slow wheel. Ipswich ware was well fired and has a sandy, grey fabric looking disconcertingly like Roman grey ware to the untutored eye. It has a wide coastal distribution from the Humber to Kent and has been found on excavations at Riby, Holton le Clay and Flixborough where it appears in the late eighth or early ninth century. Amongst the Ipswich ware from Flixborough are sherds of large, stamp-decorated pitchers which, outside East Anglia, tend only to be found on aristocratic sites. Although not decorated, an Ipswich ware base found at Riby

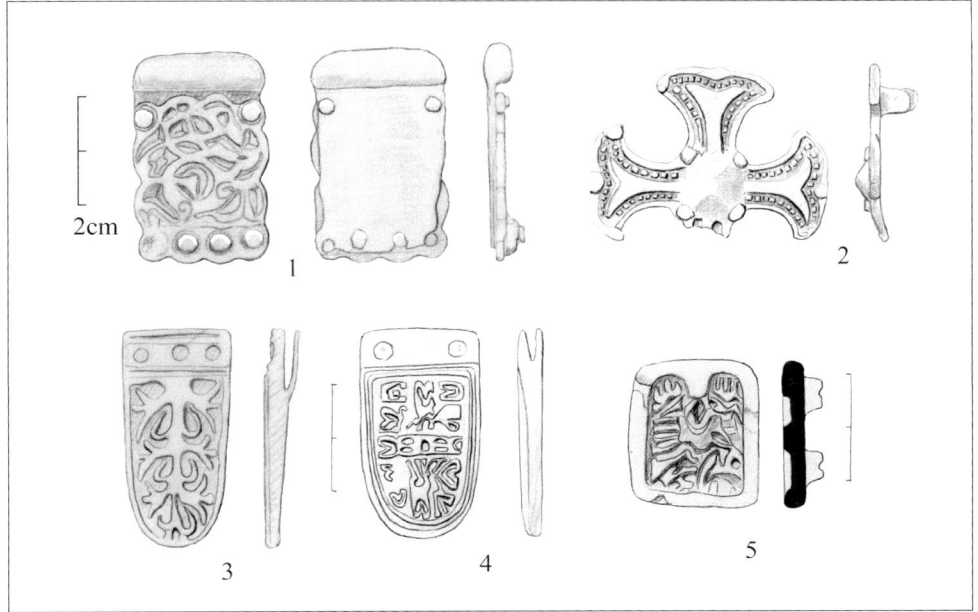

61 Carolingian metalwork from Lindsey.
    1: Copper-alloy strap end with silver rivet. The deeply cut decoration of this important object is
       typical of Anglo-Carolingian metalwork of the eighth century, Kelsey Moor.
    2: Copper-alloy cross brooch of continental type, South Ferriby.
    3: Copper-alloy Carolingian strap end with leaf decoration, Laughton.
    4: Copper-alloy Carolingian style strap end, Whitton.
    5: Copper-alloy Carolingian mount, Scotton.
Drawings by Kevin Leahy

was so large that it is likely to have come from something like a pitcher or large
storage vessel. A sherd of Ipswich ware was found on the site of Humberston
Abbey near Grimsby.

Coins

There has, in recent years, been a revolution in our knowledge of the early medieval
coinage of Lindsey, the number of pre-Viking coins rising from 25 in 1983 to 168
in 1991 and now to more than 360. In addition to these we have 204 later Saxon
coins recorded on the Portable Antiquities database and Early Medieval Coin
Index. These are a tribute to the work of the metal detector users who have found
them, and to Mike Bonser, Mark Blackburn and the Finds Liaison Officers who
have recorded them. There will be coins that I don't know about but, hopefully,
we now know enough for the main trends to have appeared (*63*).

    Coins were never issued by the kings of Lindsey, the silver *sceat* bearing the
inscription 'ALDRID REX' must now alas be attributed to Aldfrith of Northumbria

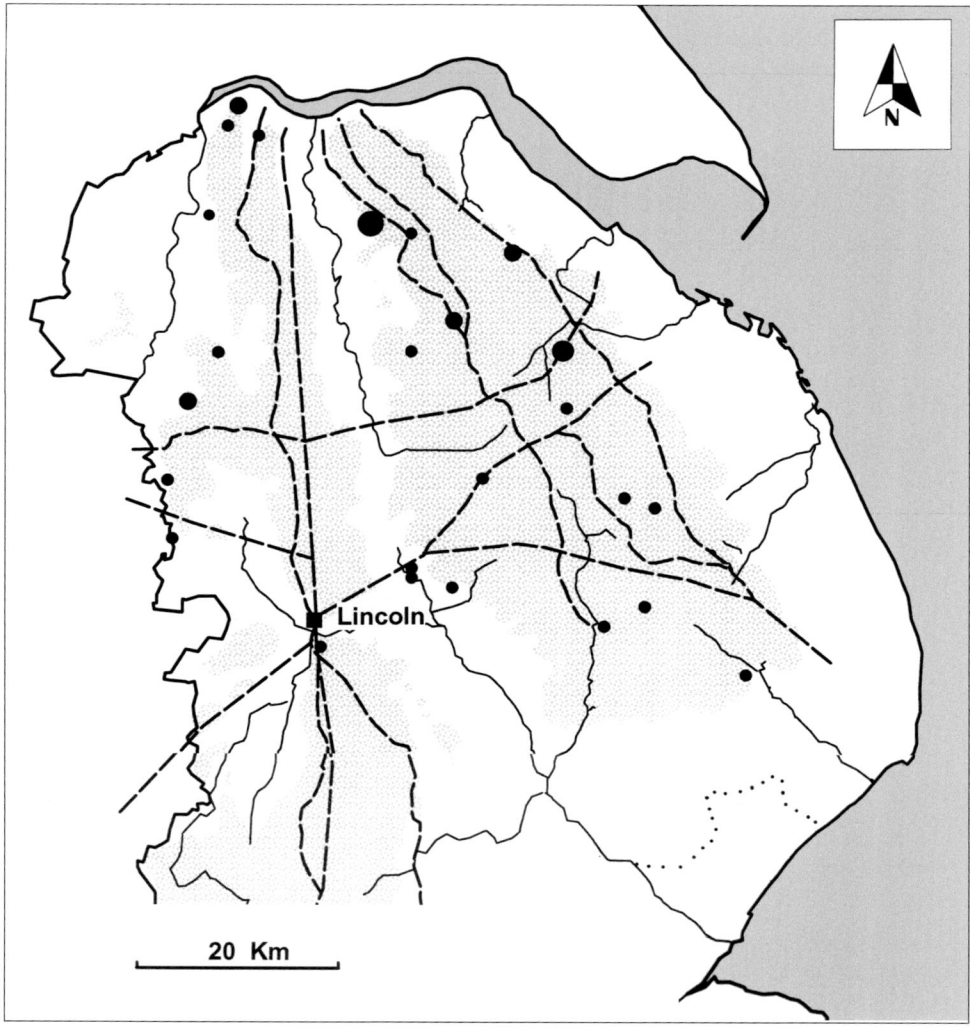

62 Distribution map of material imported into Lindsey during the eighth and ninth centuries. *Digital mapping by Mike Hemblade*

(685-704) not to Aldrið of Lindsey. Lindsey, therefore, relied on coins brought in from elsewhere. There were a lot of *sceattas* or 'proto-pennies' imported from northern Europe and coins of types that were circulating in eastern and southern Mercia. The earliest post-Roman coins found in Lindsey are eight Merovingian gold 'tremissis', including contemporary forgeries, and two gold 'shillings', which date from the seventh century. Some of these come from areas that were later to become important: Louth, Riby, Torksey, Barton and Lincoln. A site near Sleaford, and just outside Lindsey, has yielded early gold coins and is likely to have been the

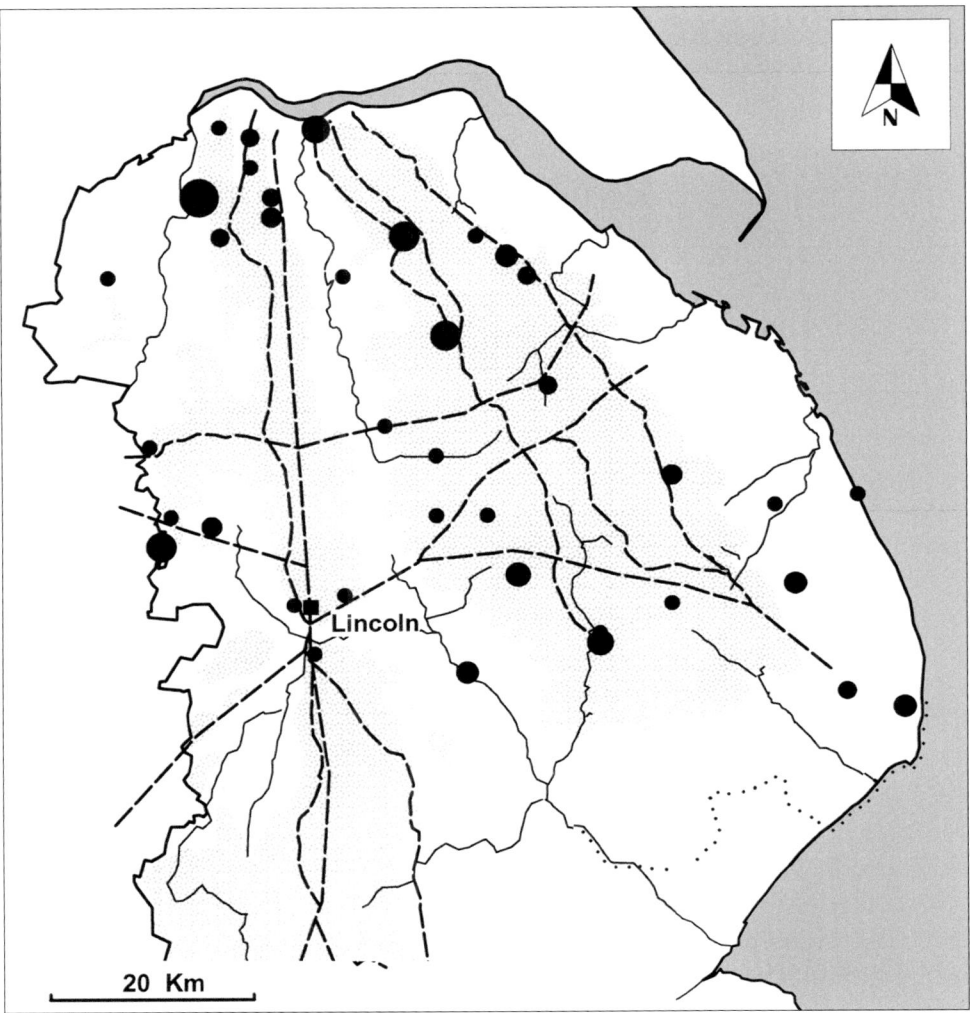

63 Distribution map of Anglo-Saxon and continental 'sceatta' coinage in Lindsey. *Digital mapping by Mike Hemblade*

site of a trading station which must have played a part in the economy of the early kingdom. Coins only really come into use with the appearance of the small silver coins we know as '*sceattas*' (singular '*sceat*') which the Anglo-Saxons themselves almost certainly called pennies (but we know better). We have 123 of these coins, the distribution of which is shown on figure 63. Finds are concentrated on the large 'productive sites' that are a feature of the Middle Saxon period in Lindsey and elsewhere. The concentration of these sites, and single finds along lines of communication, show the importance of trade and communication.

We have early *sceattas* dating from before 700 but in Lindsey the coinage only really gets going in the first half of the eighth century, from which we have around 100 finds. More than 63 of these coins are the continental coins of Series E and D that were discussed above. There are also *sceattas* from other Anglo-Saxon kingdoms: five from Northumbria, four probably from Kent and six East Anglian. The most important source (other than the continent) was Mercia, from which 33 coins came. The low number of Northumbrian *sceattas* suggest that Lindsey was economically divorced from Northumbria by this time.

Only 27 coins have been found that can be dated to the second half of the eighth century, a pattern that occurs elsewhere in Anglo-Saxon England, perhaps due to a fall in the availability of silver. We have few late *sceattas* but things do seem to pick up at the end of the century with 15 broad pennies of King Offa of Mercia. Broad pennies were a new coin based on a continental type which replaced the small, thick *sceattas,* but are much less common. We have 144 coins from the first half of the ninth century but of these 84 are '*stycas*'; small, heavily debased coins of minimal artistic merit which were issued in large numbers in Northumbria. There are 75 coins of the second half of the ninth century, of which 24 were *stycas*, most of the others being silver 'lunettes', pennies of Alfred of Wessex and Burgred of Mercia (one of the Viking weights on *colour plate 23* is set with a lunette penny). The distribution of *stycas* is concentrated along the Trent with 97 from Torksey and 22 from Flixborough. These finds have been attributed to the Viking Great Army over-wintering at Torksey in 872-3 but I would be cautious in attributing all these coins to a single event. *Stycas* occur elsewhere in Lindsey and it is possible that Torksey had been acting as a point of exchange between Lindsey and Northumbria for some time. The use of *stycas* in Lindsey is interesting; they were very debased, some of the later issues being made of brass, but as small change they reflect an active economy looking, at least in part, to the north. Interestingly, a significant number of the *stycas* found in Lindsey are irregular copies of official issues.

Mark Blackburn has written an interim account on the 69 coins found at Flixborough and found that, in general, the pattern of coin use at Flixborough resembles that of the rest of Lindsey. The number of coins fell drastically in the mid-eighth century, to recover around the middle of the ninth century with lunette pennies and relatively large numbers of Northumbrian *stycas*. The earliest coin found on the site was a Series D *sceat* dating to around 700-15 and the main sequence ends with lunette type pennies of King Alfred of Wessex struck around 874-5, but there is also a single late tenth-century penny of King Edward the Martyr. There was also one Carolingian coin, a denier of Peppin the Short, (751-68) issued at the great trading centre of Quentovic on the River Canche in France.

The Viking conquest and Anglo-Scandinavian Lindsey

The first recorded Viking raid on Lindsey was in 841 when the *Anglo-Saxon Chronicle* recorded that '… Ealdorman Hereberht was killed by heathen men and many men with him in the Marsh [probably Romney Marsh in Kent]; and later in the same year [many men] in Lindsey, East Anglia, and Kent were killed by the enemy'. This appears to have been followed by a lull in raids on eastern England, although this may only reflect our inadequate historical sources for the period as Viking activity continued elsewhere. In 865 the Vikings returned with the arrival, in East Anglia, of the Great Army led by Ivar the Boneless and his brother Halfdan. Having ravaged the area for 12 months and acquiring horses they moved up to Northumbria in the Autumn of 866 and on 1 November they captured York. Northumbria was at that time enjoying a civil war and some months passed before the two rival kings united their forces, storming York on 21 March 867. They fought their way into the city but unfortunately both kings and eight of their ealdormen were killed in the attack. The Northumbrians were forced to buy peace and the Vikings installed a puppet king.

The Great Army then moved south, waging a series of campaigns, taking up winter-quarters each autumn and going back into the field the following spring. They were back in Northumbria in 872 but soon afterwards moved south into Lindsey, over-wintering at Torksey on the River Trent. The Vikings had clearly got control of Northumbria by 869 and may have taken over Lindsey. After 12 months at Torksey the Great Army moved into the heart of Mercia, fighting a campaign that led to the flight of King Burgred, in whose place the Vikings appointed Ceolwulf. The *Anglo-Saxon Chronicle* described him as 'a foolish king's thegn' who 'swore oaths to them and gave hostages that it [the kingdom of Mercia] should be ready for them on whatever day they wished to have it'. The winter of 873-4 was spent at Repton where excavations by Martin and Birthe Biddle revealed a massive ditch associated with the Great Army's camp.

Late in 874 the Great Army divided, one part going to Cambridge and the rest travelling north to the Tyne, eventually settling in Yorkshire. In August 877 the southern group, whose attack on Wessex had been repulsed, returned to Mercia and reminded Ceolwulf of his oath. The Anglo-Saxon Chronicle recorded: 'Then in the harvest season the army went away into Mercia and shared out some of it, and gave some to Ceolwulf'. The term 'shared out' suggests that it was a controlled act and not a free for all, but we lack any details. It is assumed that the area the Vikings took was Lincolnshire because of the concentration of Danish place-names in the county and that it forms a discrete entity on the edge of Mercia. The succession of bishops of Lindsey seems to have been broken around this time with no bishop being known between 862 and 953.

In the following year, 878, King Alfred defeated the Vikings at the Battle of Edington, stabilising the military situation. Under the terms of the Treaty of Wedmore, negotiated in the aftermath of the battle, England was divided into two; the area to the north and east of a line between Chester and London was ceded to the Vikings, with the English retaining control of the rest. Unlike the Vikings of York, the Mercian Vikings do not seem to have been united but consisted of a loose federation, based around the Five Boroughs, a weakness that the English kings were able to exploit. The early tenth century saw the gradual reconquest of the southern Danelaw by the English, led by Alfred's son Edward the Elder and his daughter Æthelflæd, the 'Lady of the Mercians'.

The date at which Lincoln was retaken by the English is not known; it could have been around 918-20 but, if Lindsey was under the control of the Vikings of York, the English may not have regained control until the fall of Northumbria in 927. Mark Blackburn has found that the coins from Lincoln show links with the Vikings of York which is supported by Evison and Stocker in their study of the sculpture of the period (see below). During their years of control the Vikings had made a great impact. Lincoln, apparently after years of decay, woke up and became an important trading city (*84*). Elsewhere in the countryside other changes occurred, which we still see and hear today.

Lindsey was in the Danelaw, where Scandinavian people were governed by their own laws and customs, as were set down in the strongly Scandinavian 'Wantage Law Code', accepted for use in the Danish 'Five Boroughs' (Derby, Leicester, Lincoln, Nottingham and Stamford) by King Æthelred in 997. 'Lawmen' were appointed in boroughs and other aspects of the administration took on Danish features. In 1066 Lincoln had 12 lawmen who seem, from their names, to have come from the same families. In the Danelaw, land was measured in '*carucates*' instead of the 'hides' used in England. '*Carucate*' is a Latin translation of the Danish '*plogesland*' (ploughland) and they were counted in units of 12 while English hides were counted in 10s. The local administration was based on the Danish '*wapentake*' not the English 'hundred'. Like Yorkshire, Lindsey was divided into three Ridings (*thriðjung*: third); north, south and west. However, the unnatural symmetry of the Lindsey ridings suggests that, unlike the wapentakes, they were a new creation.

SCANDINAVIAN PLACE-NAMES IN LINDSEY

The main evidence for the Danish presence in Lindsey was, for many years, the remarkable number of Scandinavian place-names (*64*). There are 151 place-names ending in -by (farm or village; Bonby, Crosby) which represents 30.7 per cent of the 492 places recorded at Domesday. In addition to this there are 38 -thorpes (secondary or outlying settlement; Scunthorpe, Raventhorpe) representing a further 7.7 per cent of the Domesday vills. In Lindsey, therefore, 38.4 per cent of the Domesday villages had Danish place-names. In most cases the -by and -thorpe is compounded with a Danish personal name, as at Scunthorpe: '*Skúma's* secondary settlement'. Place-names employing the names of individuals are rare in Denmark but common in England, showing the part played by individuals in the settlement of England. These place-names have typical Scandinavian grammatical inflections showing that they were created by people who were speaking Danish correctly. It is thought that these place-names were created in the late ninth century, although Peter Sawyer has rightly emphasised the difficulties of dating place-names and believes that many of them could post date the settlement period. What is significant is that, at whatever date these place-names were formed, they were created by people with Scandinavian names who could speak Danish.

The distribution map of Danish place-names in Lindsey (*64*) shows a major concentration at the southern end of the Wolds and in two lines running up though the northern Wolds. While it might appear that these sites are located along trackways they actually seem to lie on the spring lines. There is a concentration of Danish place-names in the angle between the Trent and Humber and small clusters north of Lincoln. Many of the parishes with Danish place-names (Riby, Laceby, Brocklesby, Irby, Keelby) contain Early Anglo-Saxon cemeteries and must have been renamed. A striking feature of the distribution is the lack of Danish place-names around Lincoln, which was one of the Five Viking Boroughs (*64*). It is likely that, in 877, the leaders of the Great Army settled at Lincoln taking over, for their own use, the estates around the city. The Anglo-Saxon peasants were left in place and the estates not fragmented or renamed. The few early -*h m* place-names that we have in Lindsey are concentrated around Lincoln, again showing that renaming had not occurred. Elsewhere in Lindsey the land was settled by the

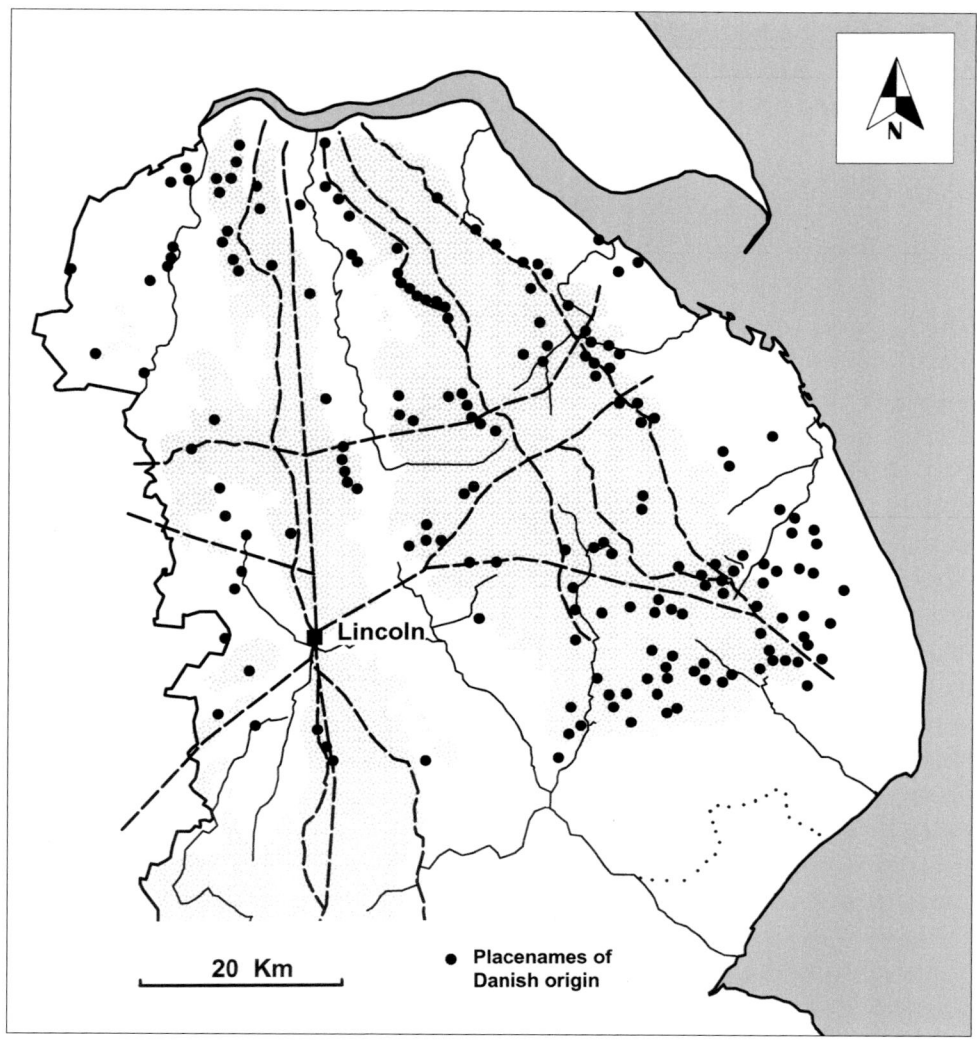

64 Map showing place names of Danish origin in Lindsey. *Digital mapping by Mike Hemblade*

rank and file of the Great Army, the estates represented by the productive sites were fragmented and renamed.

None of the 'productive sites' seem to have survived the Danish takeover as anything other than shadows of what they had been (*65*, cf *46*). It has been suggested on the basis of the pottery that the Flixborough settlement continued through the tenth century. There are, however, only two objects that could be dated to this period, the penny of Edward the Martyr and a lead weight of a type that has, elsewhere, been found on Viking sites (*73*, *2*). As finds dating from

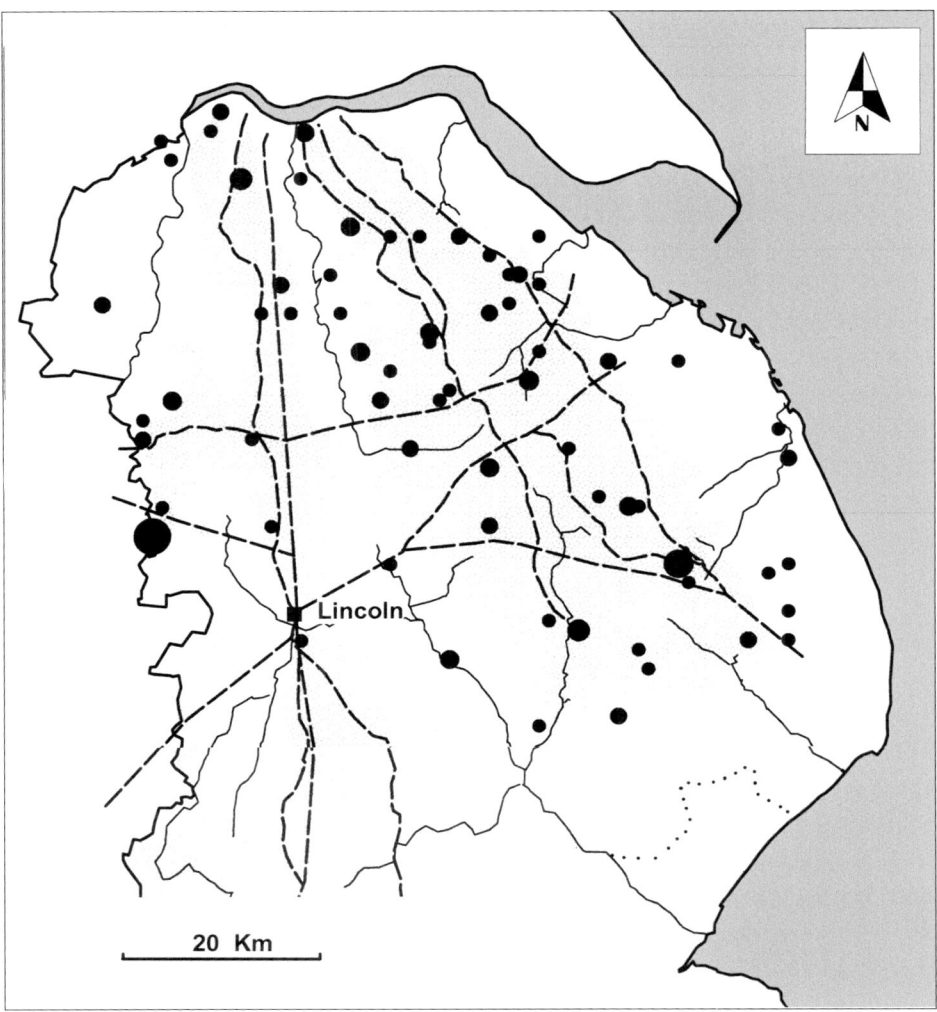

65 Distribution of early Viking (late ninth to early tenth century) metalwork in Lindsey.
Digital mapping by Mike Hemblade

the tenth century are relatively common elsewhere, if Flixborough continued to be occupied it must have been in a much reduced form, as seems to have been the case at Melton Ross.

The Domesday survey records that all of the major landowners in 1066 had Danish names and that Danish personal names were more common than English amongst the rest of the people. The dialect spoken in Lindsey today still uses Danish words to describe the landscape. A stream is not a brook but is a 'beck' from the Danish '*bekkr*'. An island is a 'holme' from the Danish '*holmr*'.

There are 'carr', '*kjarr*' lands, and roads or streets may be 'gate', '*gata*', as in 'Middlegate Lane'. This is a remarkable survival in people's daily lives. A feature of Lindsey at Domesday is the very high numbers of 'sokemen' recorded, with them representing, on average, 54 per cent of the population, rising, in one wapentake, to 70 per cent. This is very different from Essex where sokemen represent only 7.3 per cent of the population. Sokemen were peasants but, unlike villeins, they were free and could dispose of their property. Most sokemen only owned around three bovates, about 45 acres; although they were free, their economic status was low. Caution must be used in interpreting the high numbers of sokemen in Lindsey (we don't know much about the situation before the Danes arrived) but it is likely that these people represented the descendants of the Great Army who settled in 877. Their status had been reduced but they could still remember that grandfather had been a Viking and that they were 'free'. It is interesting to see that in 1086 sokemen were concentrated in those areas of Lindsey where Danish place-names were most common, supporting this interpretation.

VIKING FINDS FROM LINDSEY

Metalwork

While the Danish takeover of Lindsey is not doubted, there has been much debate over what it actually entailed; was it a mass folk movement or just a change in management? Until recently there was very little in the way of archaeological evidence for the Vikings in Lindsey. A few objects had been found during the dredging of the River Witham in the late eighteenth and early nineteenth centuries, but there was nothing from the countryside to say that the Danes had ever been in Lindsey. This did look odd and perhaps there had just been a change in leadership.

The breakthrough came in 1979 when I was going through a metal detectorist's box of scrap metal and found a fragment of a small, crude brooch that had originally had a trefoil shape. It had been found at Keelby and was the first Viking find from Lindsey (*66, 2*). On the strength of this I started to liaise with other metal detector users and record their finds of Viking and Anglo-Saxon metalwork. It soon became clear that there was plenty of evidence for the Danes in Lindsey but it was not what I had expected, and hoped, to see. It consisted, not of weapons, but of small, trashy dress fittings. Many of these came from women's dress and, while there was the occasional fine piece, most of them were of poor quality, cheaply made, using poor materials (*66*). The low quality of these finds is important as it points to an influx of Danish peasant women during the later ninth and tenth century. No Dane is going to be able to give

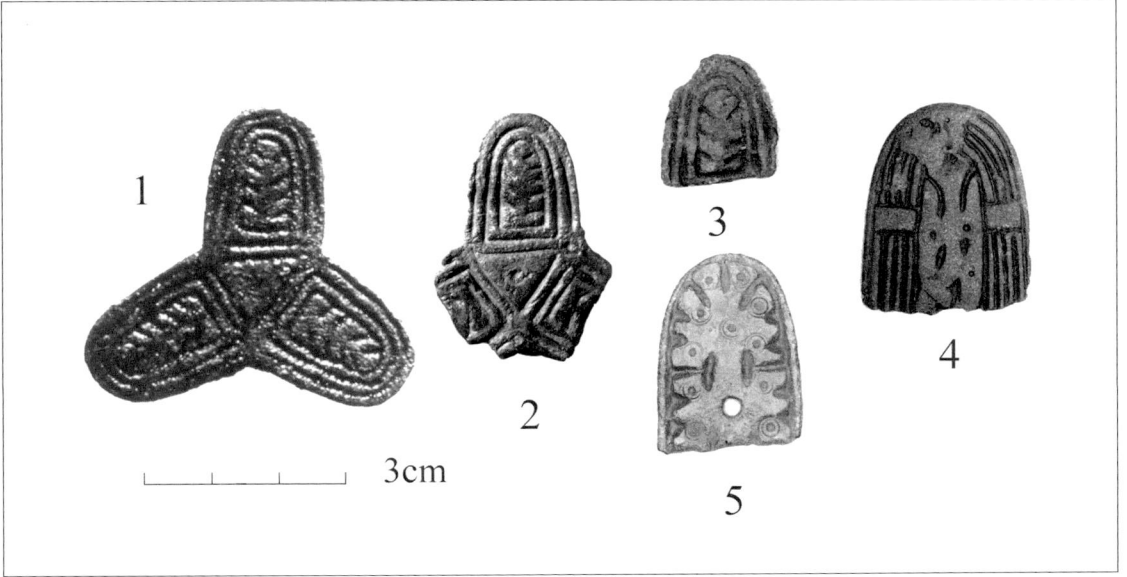

66 Small copper-alloy Viking trefoil brooches. From Winceby (1), Keelby (2), Ketsby (3-4) and Kirmington (5). *Photographs by Kevin Leahy*

his English girlfriend one of these tatty little brooches and expect her to be impressed, a woman needed to be brought up as a Dane and see wearing them as part of her culture. At first I thought that these were locally made copies of Danish brooches; the reference books tended to show only the finest and best, the gold and the silver. It was when Caroline Paterson, with whom I worked on these finds, visited the National Museum in Denmark did we discover that the Lindsey finds were really Viking; the reserve collections in Copenhagen were full of the same tatty little brooches that we were getting.

We now have 274 items of Viking and Anglo-Scandinavian metalwork from Lindsey, of which 139 can be assigned to styles of Viking art, being in general order of appearance:

Borre style	*c.*850-980	59 objects (*67-68, 71*)
Jellinge style	*c.*875-975	8 objects (*70, 71*)
Mammen style	*c.*950-1025	1 object?
Ringerike style	*c.*980-1070	25 objects (*75*)
Urnes style	*c.*1050-1100	47 objects (*75*)

This material is very difficult to date and, as there was also considerable overlap between the styles, the dates given above are only notional. The Borre style

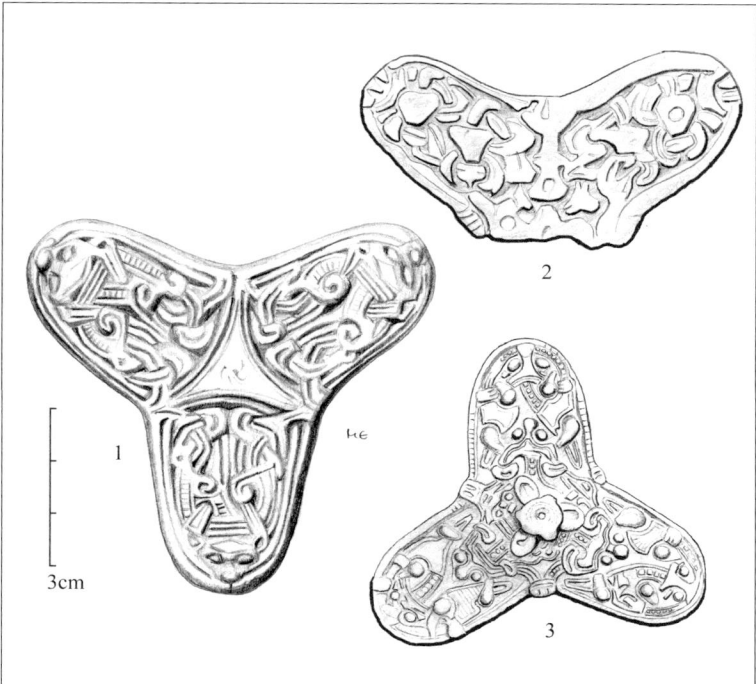

3cm

67 Large Viking trefoil brooches decorated in the Borre style; all in copper alloy.
1: Willoughby
2: Aylesby
3: Stallingborough
Drawing 1 by Marina Elwes, 2 and 3 by Kevin Leahy

appears in Scandinavia around the middle of the ninth century, but we would not expect to see much of it in Lindsey before the Viking Conquest of 877. It occurs on brooches, most of which are small quadrangular type (*71.1*), but we do get the occasional fine example, perhaps the best being the lost brooch from Stallingborough which bore a mass of Borre-style animals of stunning complexity (*67, colour plate 22*). There are also Borre-style strap ends, buckles and stirrup fittings (*68*). The Jellinge style is mostly found on small round brooches but, remarkably, we have a die from Ketsby that was used to make Jellinge-style foils (*71, 6*). Most of Ringerike- and Urnes-style objects are harness fittings from stirrups and strap ends of which we have 20 examples (*75*). It is interesting and significant that the styles of Viking art found in Lindsey seem to stay up to date with what was being used in the Scandinavian homelands, showing that contact was maintained. We are now also seeing some weapons in addition to the weapons found in the Witham; we have a Viking-style spearhead and axe-hammer from Haxey and sword fittings from Calceby, Caistor and Torksey (*69*). This is not a lot, but Viking armies probably numbered, at most, in the low thousands but the settlement of relatively small numbers of people can, if they are well organised, in overall control and concentrated in certain places, have a disproportionate effect on society.

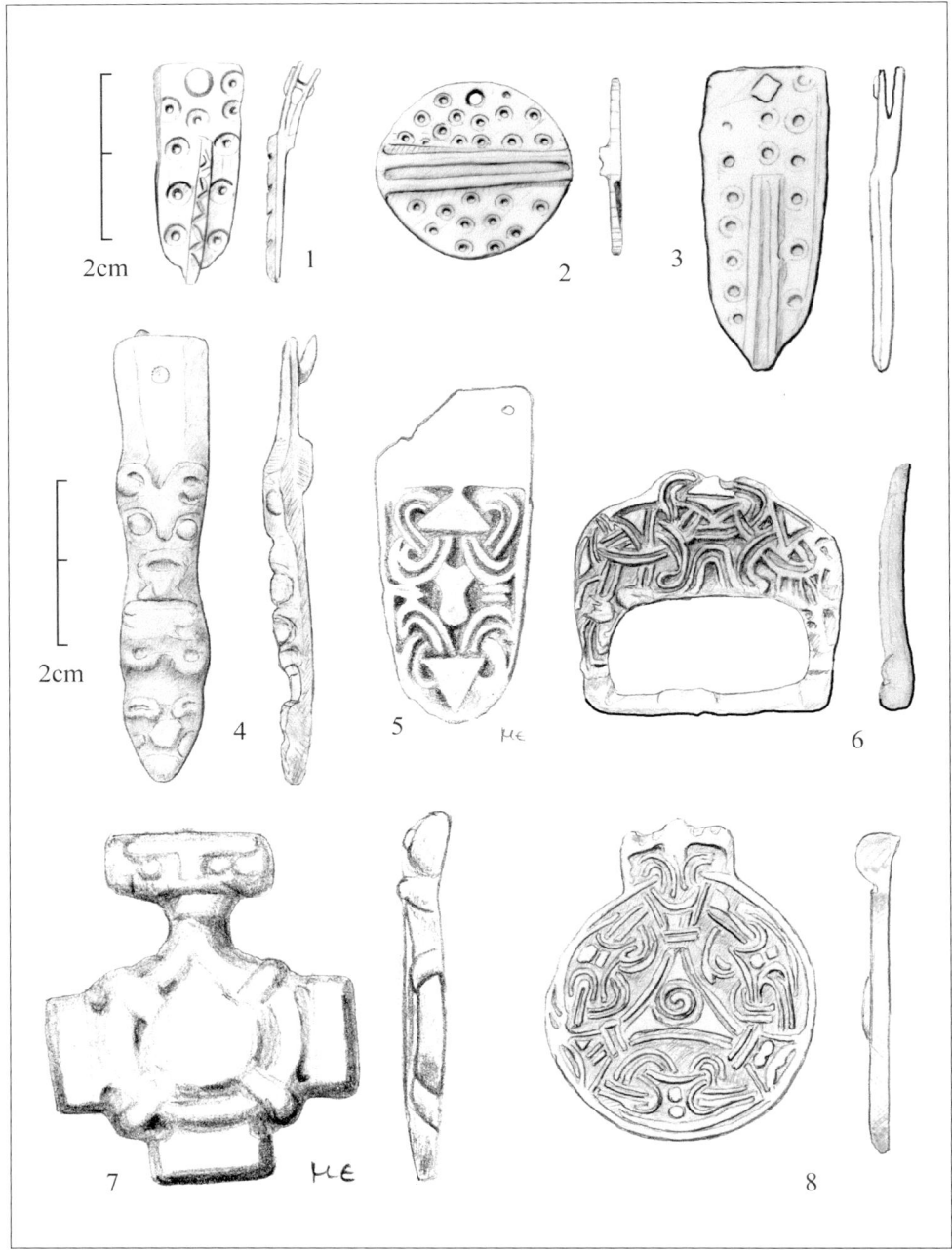

68 Early Viking-period metalwork from Lindsey, all in copper alloy. 1: Tong-shaped strap end, Ketsby. 2: Disc pendant, perhaps made from a strap end like 3, Whitton. 3: strap end, Ketsby. 4: Borre-style strap end, Aylesby. 5: Borre-style strap end, Elsham. 6: Borre-style buckle, Caistor. 7: Borre-style pendant, Swinhope. 8: Borre-style pendant, Tathwell. *Drawings 5 and 7 by Marina Elwes, rest by Kevin Leahy*

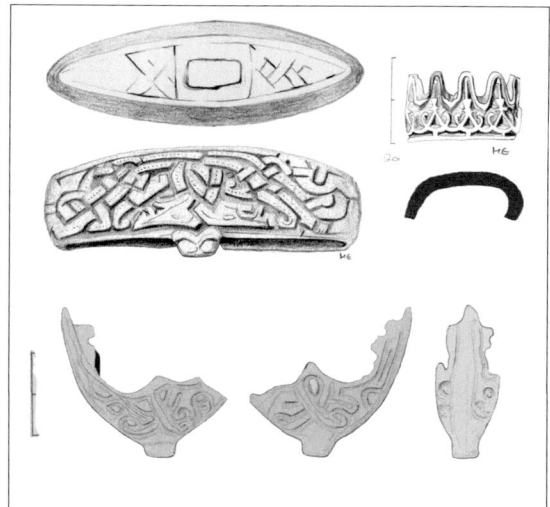

69 Viking sword fragment. Top: Calceby, pommel. Middle: Torksey, gilded copper-alloy hilt ring. Bottom: Caistor, scabbard mount

Left: 70 The Crowle stone. Sadly mutilated by a previous generation's use of it as a lintel over the tower arch, the Crowle stone is still an important piece of sculpture. On one face is a panel of interlace and an animal in the Viking Jellinge style. On the other face are two enigmatic scenes that may represent the Flight into Egypt and Doubting Thomas. The runic inscription is discussed in the main text. Height 2.04m. *Images by Kevin Leahy*

Opposite: 71 Viking small round brooches etc, all in copper alloy. 1: Quatrefoil brooch in the Borre style, Elsham. 2: Borre-style disc brooch, Hibaldstow. 3: Borre-style disc brooch, Ketsby. 4: Jellinge-style brooch, South Ferriby. 5: Decorative mount in the Jellinge style, Nettleton. 6: Die for making Pressblech foil mounts in the Jellinge style, Ketsby. 7: Borre-style brooch, Harpswell. The die (6) is important as it shows that Viking-style metalwork was being made in Lindsey. The dishing on the back of the disc brooch from Harpswell (7) suggests that it is an import while the flat back of the South Ferriby brooch (4) points to it being locally made. *Drawings 1 and 5 by Marina Elwes, rest by Kevin Leahy*

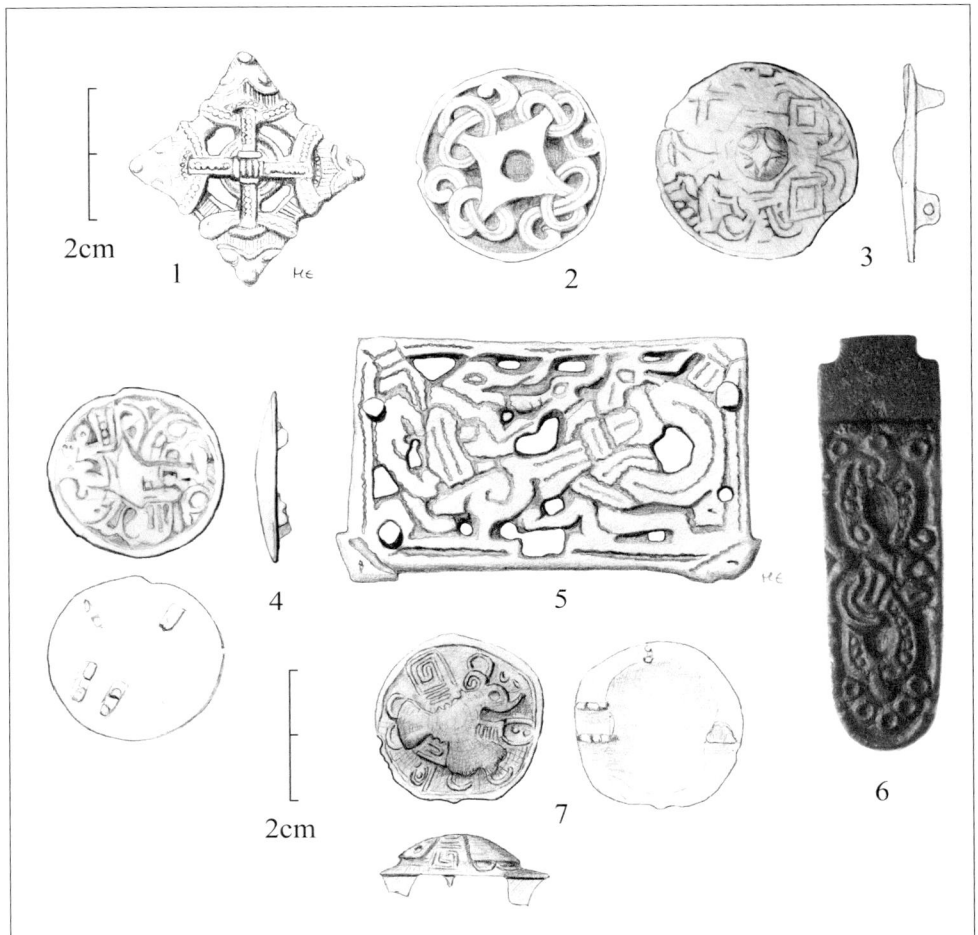

Coins

The distribution of silver pennies of the early Viking period shows them to be concentrated in the areas where Scandinavian place-names are most common, (77, cf 64). Mark Blackburn has commented on the unusual pattern of coin loss in mid to late ninth-century Lindsey. These coins include 35 pennies of King Alfred of Wessex and King Burgred of Mercia, issued 865-875, which present an interesting pattern, with the exception of a small hoard of nine coins from Walmsgate and a small group from Lincoln, they are all single finds. Elsewhere in England these coins tend to be found in hoards hidden to keep them from the Vikings. In Lindsey the Vikings already had the money, it was in the purses of paid-off soldiers who used and spent it, leading to greater usage and greater loss.

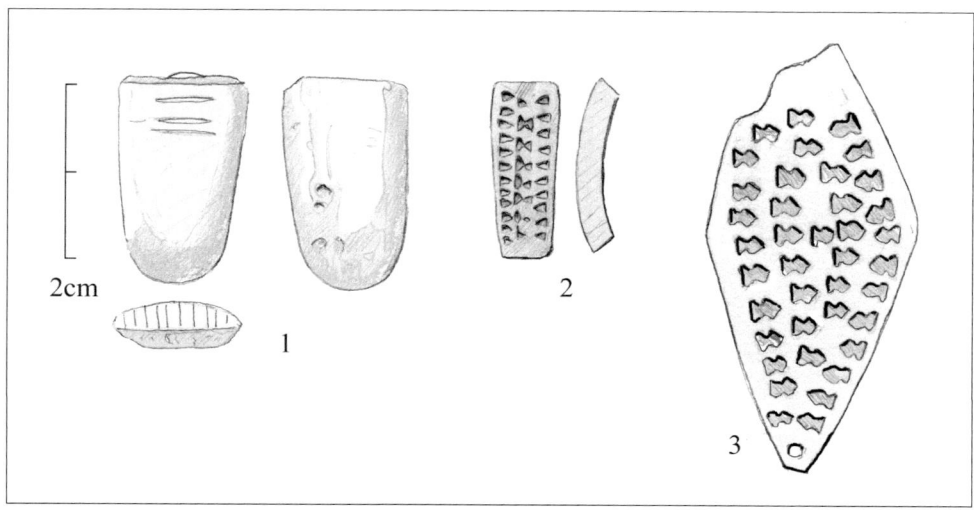

72 Viking silver. 1: Fragment of an ingot, Torksey. 2: Arm ring fragment, South Kelsey. 3: Finger ring (shown flattened) Scotter. The use of heavy stamped decoration is typical of Viking silver work. *Drawings by Kevin Leahy*

We have recorded 23 coins dating from the first half of the tenth century of which 15 are Viking issues, seven from York (as befits Lindsey being controlled by the Vikings of York) four from East Anglia and one each from Ireland, Norway and Denmark. The coin evidence shows that the economy was expanding in the last century of Anglo-Saxon England. We have 42 coins from the second half of the tenth century and 86 from the first 66 years of the eleventh century (*77*). At this time Lincoln was one of the most important of the Anglo-Saxon mints (*colour plate 25*) being second only to London, and there were also small mints at Caistor, Horncastle, Torksey and perhaps Louth.

A group of coins of particular interest are the 55 fragments of Arab '*dirhams*' that have been found at Torksey. These coins are around the size of an Anglo-Saxon silver penny but Mark Blackburn thinks that they may have been broken up for use as bullion. They were minted as far away as al-Basra in Iraq, and Viking trade carried them up the Volga, through Russia into Scandinavia. As yet only a small number of them have been studied in detail, but these show them to be issues dating from the second half of the eighth century through the first half of the ninth century. It is likely that these coins were linked to the over-wintering of the Great Army or its aftermath. Some coins bear peck-marks of the sort made by the Vikings to ensure that the metal was silver all the way through.

While it is likely that Lindsey's productive sites were involved in trade, the strongest evidence we have for a port is on the Trent at Torksey, where large numbers of later Saxon, Viking and Arab coins and metal objects have been

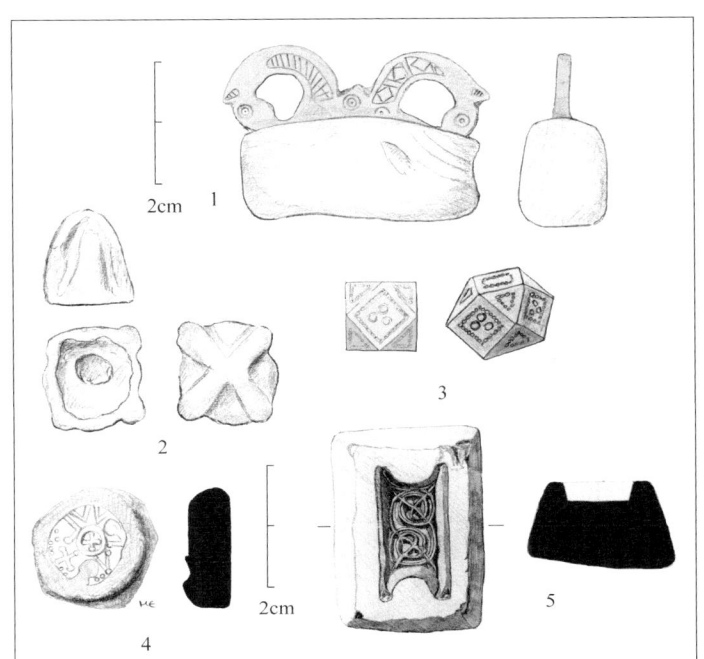

73 Viking weights, lead and copper alloy. 1: Lead weight set with copper-alloy double loop, Theddlethorpe. 2: Lead counter or weight, Flixborough. 3: Polyhedral weight, Torksey. 4: Lead weight set with an Anglo-Saxon silver coin, Scawby. 5: Lead weight set with a piece of Irish gilded copper alloy with interlace decoration, Torksey. The function of these crude weights is not known but they are common finds on Viking sites. *Drawing 4 by Marina Elwes, rest by Kevin Leahy*

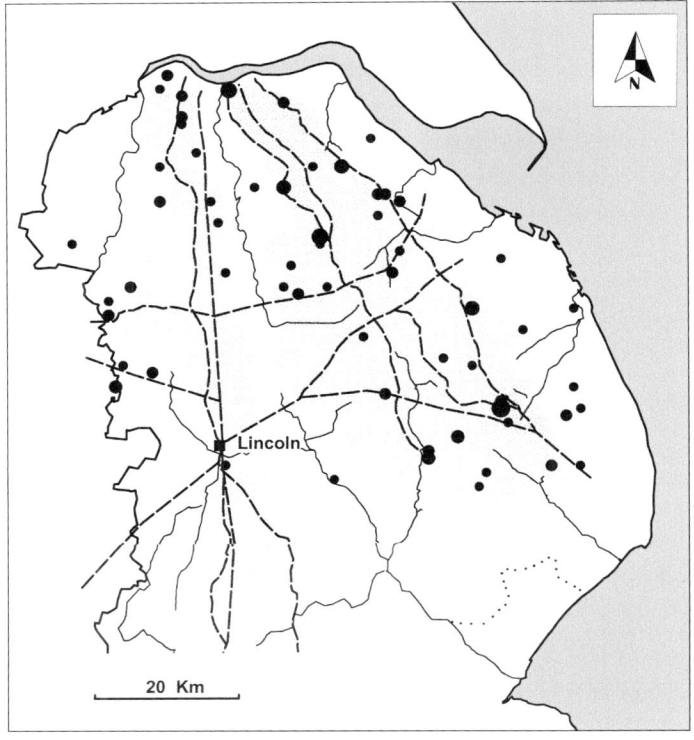

74 Map showing the distribution of later Viking period finds. *Digital Mapping by Mike Hemblade*

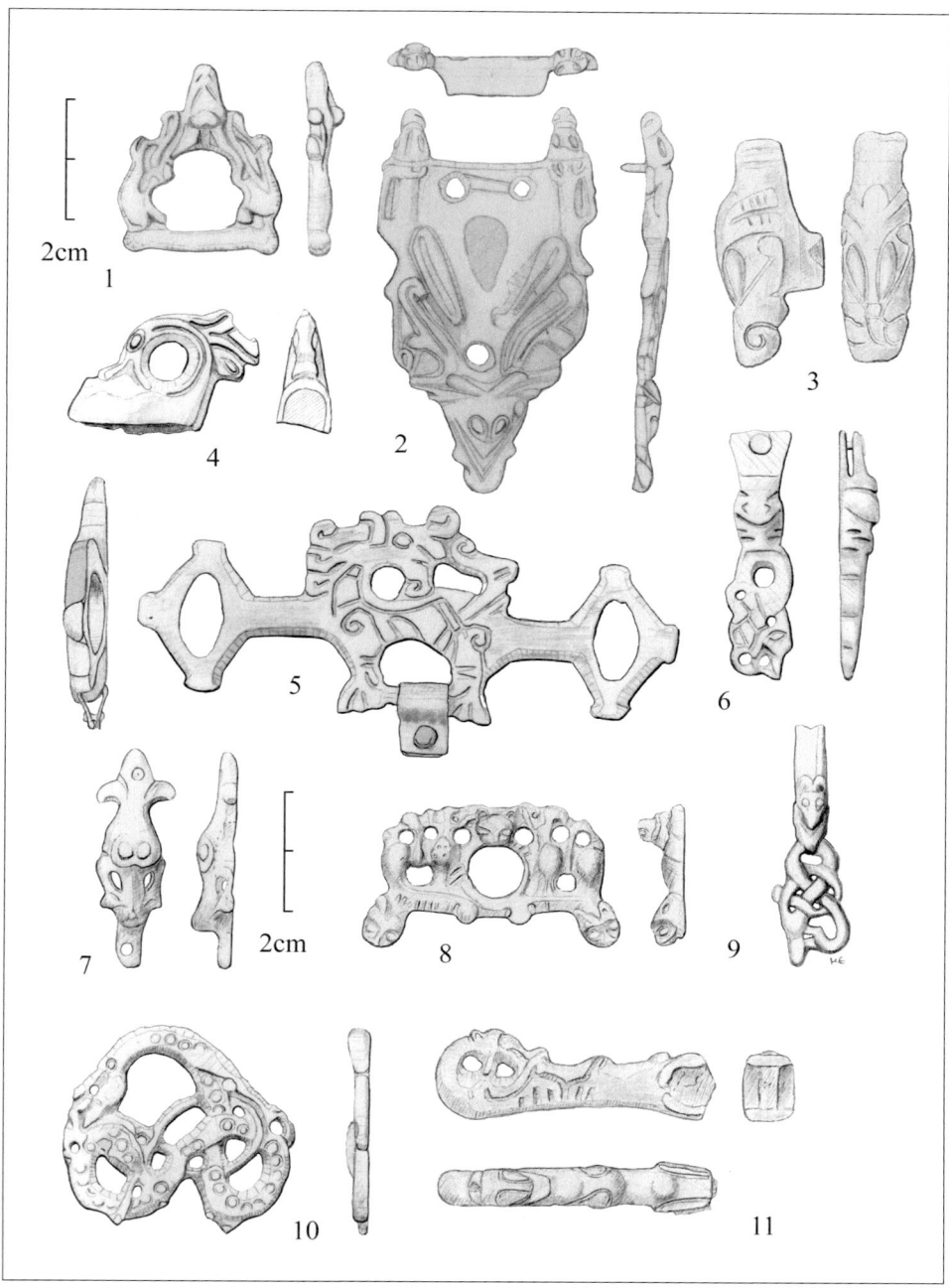

75 Later Viking metalwork, all copper alloy. 1: Ringerike-style buckle, Kirmington. 2: Ringrike-style stirrup mount, Irby on Humber. 3: Urnes-style strap end, Aylesby. 4: Ringerike-style stirrup mount, Ketsby. 5: Ringerike-style bridle fitting, Saxilby. 6: Urnes-style strap end, Ketsby. 7: Urnes-style mount, South Ferriby. 8: Urnes-style mount, Caistor. 9: Urnes-style strap end, Alford. 10: Urnes-style mount, Bardney. 11: Urnes-style mount, Bigby. *Drawings by Kevin Leahy*

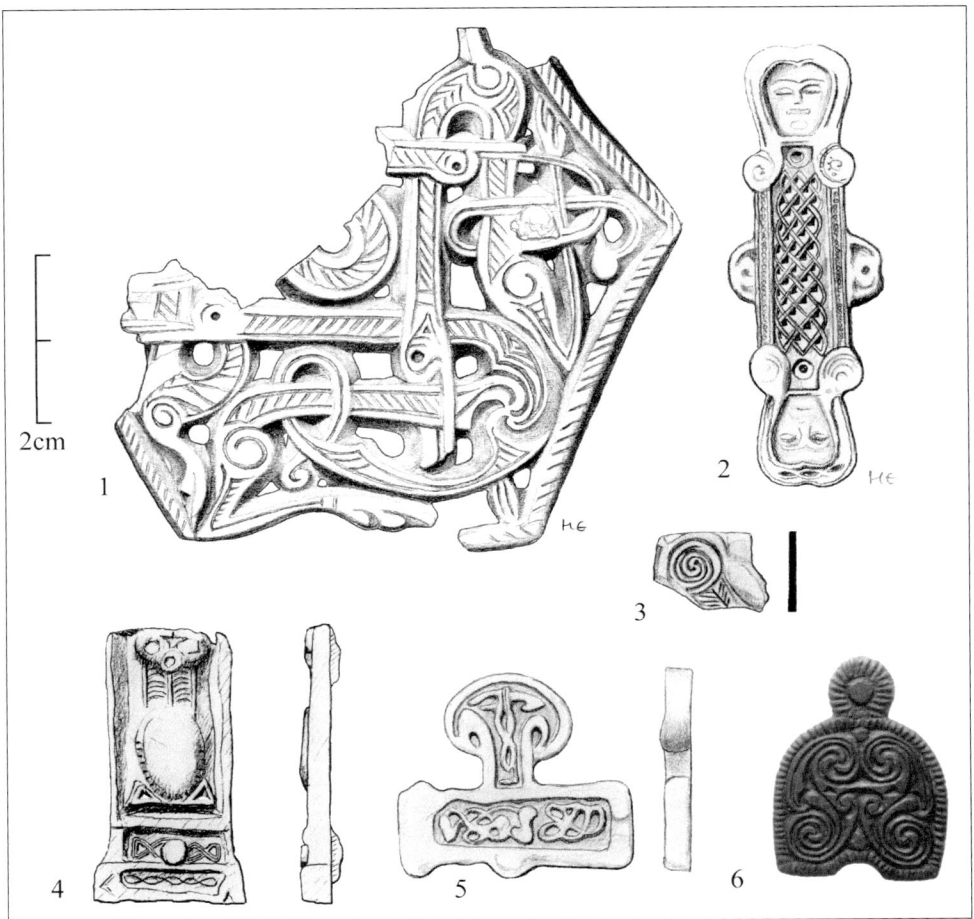

76 Irish metalwork from Lindsey. 1: Mount, copper alloy, Roxby cum Risby. 2: Harness mount, copper alloy, North Owersby. 3: Brooch fragment, silver gilt, Torksey. 4: Harness mount, copper alloy, Ketsby. 5: Harness mount, copper alloy, Welton le Marsh. 6: Pressblech die, Ketsby, seventh century. These objects are decorated using typical Irish designs including net-like interlace. *Drawings 1 and 2 by Marina Elwes, the rest by Kevin Leahy*

found. It may be significant that it was at Torksey, not Lincoln, that the Great Army over-wintered in 873-4. While early Viking metalwork is common at Torksey there is very little of the later styles, suggesting that things had changed, perhaps the port had moved to the now rising Lincoln. The evidence we have for trade in Anglo-Scandinavian Lincoln is suggestive rather than conclusive; the most notable find is a silk head-dress that seems to have been cut from the same bale as a similar cap found at Coppergate York.

During the settlement period the Vikings had a bullion economy, coins were used but only by weight. Examples of Viking bullion have been found in

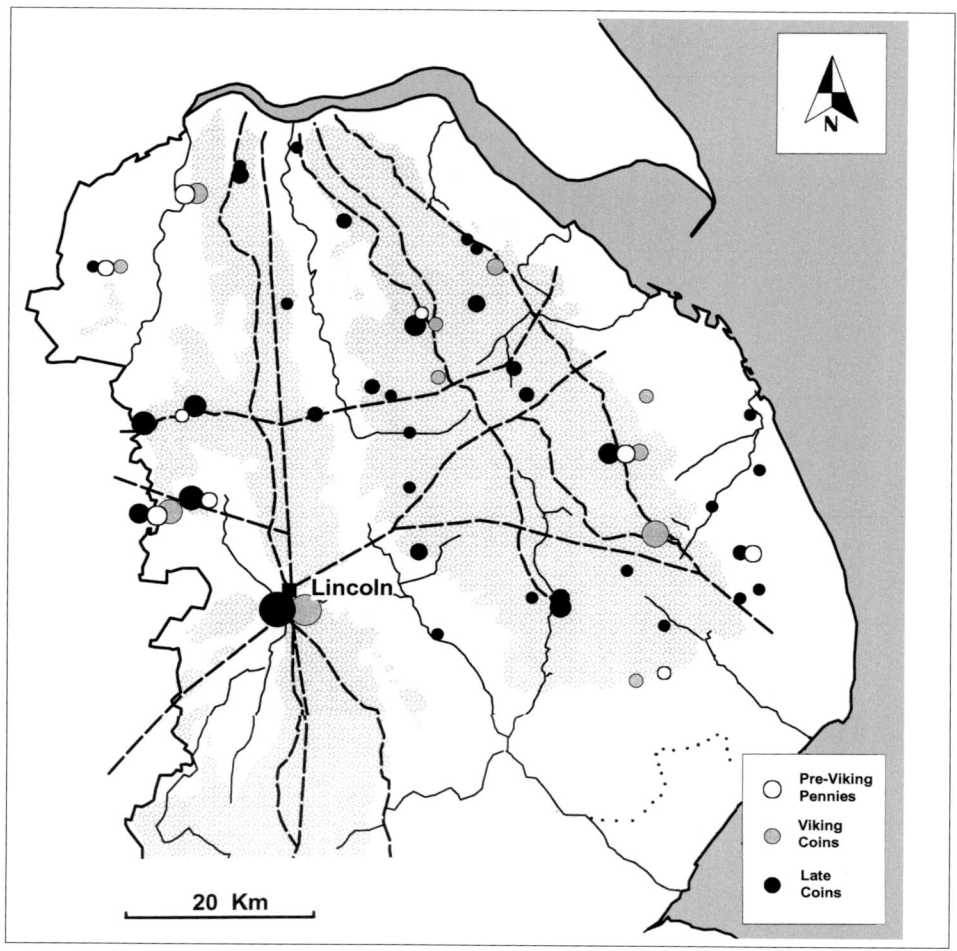

77 Map showing the distribution of Anglo-Saxon silver pennies in Lindsey. *Digital mapping by Mike Hemblade*

Lindsey, fragments of finger-shaped silver ingots cut with a chisel have been found at Torksey and from South Kelsey we have the find of a fragment of a Hiberno-Norse arm ring (*72*). The massive 25mm diameter silver ring from Theddlethorpe is too large for normal wear (*colour plate 24*) and may have been made for use as bullion. Torksey has produced large numbers of small polyhedral weights which may have been used to weigh coins (*73, 3*). More difficult to understand are the lead blocks with coins and pieces of Anglo-Saxon and Irish metalwork set into them. Coins: *sceattas, stycas*, pennies and, in one case, a fourth-century Roman coin, were also set into lead blocks (*73, colour plate 23*). These look too rough to be used for weighing bullion and their function remains in doubt.

Amongst the most unexpected finds is ninth-century Irish metalwork, which at first was assumed to be Viking loot (76). Some objects are clearly loot; the silver fragment from a penannular brooch from Torksey for example (76, 3), but most finds consisted of copper-alloy harness fittings – who would steal this sort of stuff? I think that this points to there being Irish Vikings. Viking is a job description and not an ethnic label, and Danes, Norwegians and Swedes all played their part. A Viking leader, if confronted by a large red-headed man with a battle-axe asking if he could come along 'for the crack', is not going to turn him away. We have other evidence for an Irish presence in Lindsey, as Scotter, Scothern, Scotton and Irby (twice) are all Irish place-names. Of course the word 'Scot' also means a native of 'north Britain' but, as these Gaelic speaking peoples were considered to be the same, it does not matter.

Viking sculpture

Further evidence for the Vikings in Lindsey has been recognised by David Stocker and Paul Everson in their work in the Lincolnshire volume the *Corpus of Anglo-Saxon Stone Sculpture*. They found two groups of Scandinavian stone carvings in Lindsey. The earlier group is small, containing only the stone from Crowle (70) and fragments from Holton le Clay and Thornton Curtis. These resemble the stone crosses found in Yorkshire and are made from millstone grit from the Tadcaster area. A stone cross fragment from Hackthorne and two related grave covers from Lincoln also belong to this group but were made in local stone. These carvings date to the first half of the tenth century, and Everson and Stocker suggested that they represent Hiberno-Norse incomers from the Kingdom of York who wished to emphasise their origins and links.

On the face of the Viking cross shaft from Crowle is a curving band onto which has been cut an inscription in runes. This was badly damaged when the stone was dressed for use as a lintel over the tower door, but David Parsons has read it as:

[…] ælicbæcunæ
which can be transcribed as: ?lic bæcun æ[fter]
which probably means: ? corpse beacon (monument) after (of) …

showing that this was a funerary monument. Although the decoration on the stone is clearly Viking, the inscription uses the English, not the Scandinavian 'C' rune.

The second group of carved stones are the Lindsey grave covers and are much more common. These consist of slabs of stone decorated with a bands of simple interlace set within a cabled frame and date from the second half of the tenth

50cm

78 Lindsey-
type grave slab,
Broughton

century (*78*). They bear no Christian symbols but grave stones with crosses on them may have stood at their head. All 21 known Lindsey-type grave covers are remarkably alike and were probably made in the Lincoln area, where the stone was quarried. These stones are only found in Lindsey and there is no real correlation with important churches; they seem to have been set up around the time that parishes were appearing and may have marked the graves of the founders.

'Danes on their father's side'

The degree of Scandinavian settlement in Lindsey was also reflected in the way in which its people were seen by contemporaries. In 993 the West Saxon version of the *Anglo-Saxon Chronicle* criticised the lack-lustre performance of the men of Lindsey against a Viking army, 'the commanders were first to set the example of flight'. The historian Florence of Worcester explained their heroics by saying that they were 'Danes on their father's side' and, indeed, two of the three commanders had Danish names. Clearly the loyalty of Lindsey to the Anglo-Saxons was not beyond doubt. In 1014, the Danish King Swein died while at Gainsborough. His son, Cnut, stayed on with his army until Easter and the Chronicle says that the people of Lindsey came to the agreement that they would supply him with horses and go on a raid with him. Things went badly wrong, as the Chronicle describes:

> Then, before they were ready, King Æthelred came there with the whole army into Lindsey, and then all humans that could be got at were raided and burned and killed. Cnut himself went out with his fleet – thus the wretched people were betrayed through him …

Cnut later became king of England as well as Denmark but I suspect that the Lindsey branch of his fan club was not large.

LATE SAXON FINDS

In addition to the Viking and Anglo-Scandinavian metalwork we have now recorded 126 items of Late Saxon (tenth- to eleventh-century date) from Lindsey. We have 11 items decorated in the tenth-century 'Winchester style' which uses animal and acanthus leaf motifs. Some of this is good but other pieces are crude imitations (*79*). A feature of this period is the use of lead jewellery, mainly brooches and strap ends (*80, 81*). This is supposed to be copying silver originals (which have so far eluded us) and range in style from the crude to the delightful. We also see a series of small button brooches, often decorated with the backward-looking figure of a lion, but with others occasionally using a design

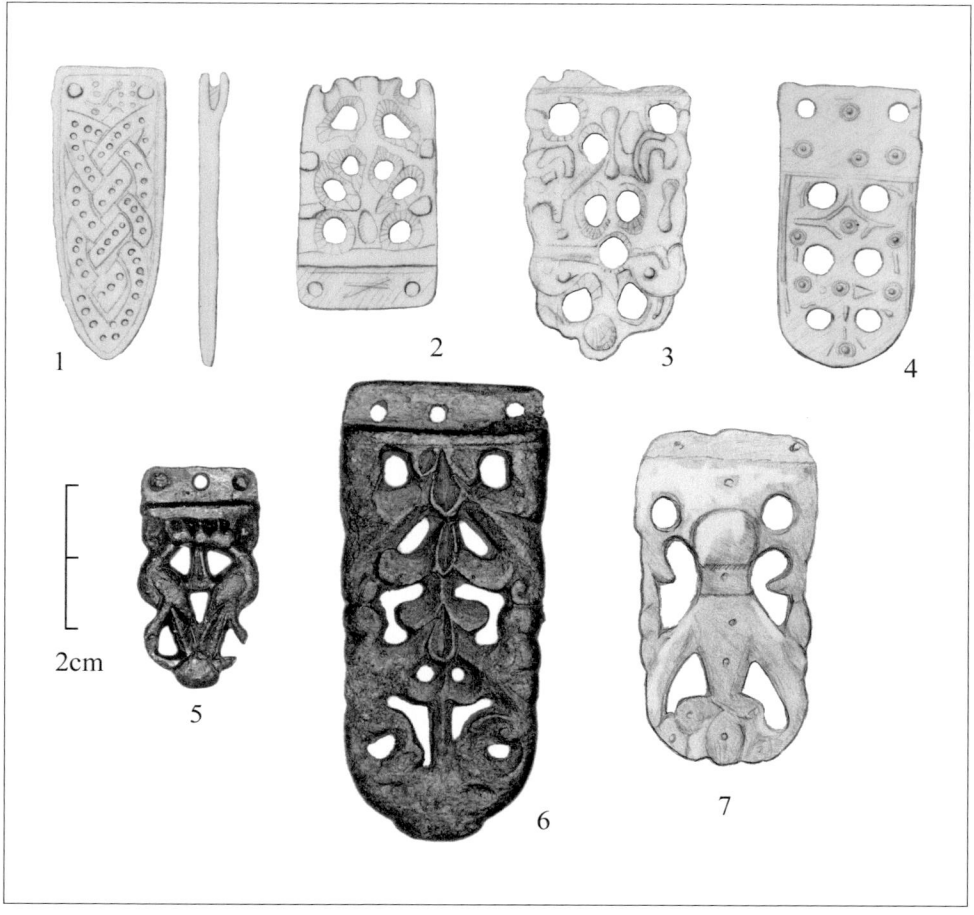

79 Late Saxon copper alloy-strap ends. 1: Maltby. 2: Ravendale, devolved Winchester style. 3: Maltby, Winchester style. 4: Laughton. 5: Brocklesby, Winchester-style birds. 6: Torksey, Winchester style. 7: Caistor. *Drawings and images by Kevin Leahy*

based on a coin (*82*). More elegant is a series of cloisonné enamel brooches; these are gilded and show a high degree of skill in using multiple materials.

From a comparison of the maps in figures *74* and *83* it seems that the distribution of late Viking and Late Saxon finds cannot be separated; both English and Scandinavian metalwork was in use all over Lindsey. This suggests that while the two peoples were living together some were still 'celebrating their diversity'. Attention has already been drawn to the lack of Viking metalwork in the area around Lincoln and the map in figure *83* shows that there is also little in the way of Late Saxon metalwork from this area. This is odd, but as other material is being found by detectorists it seems that this lacuna is real.

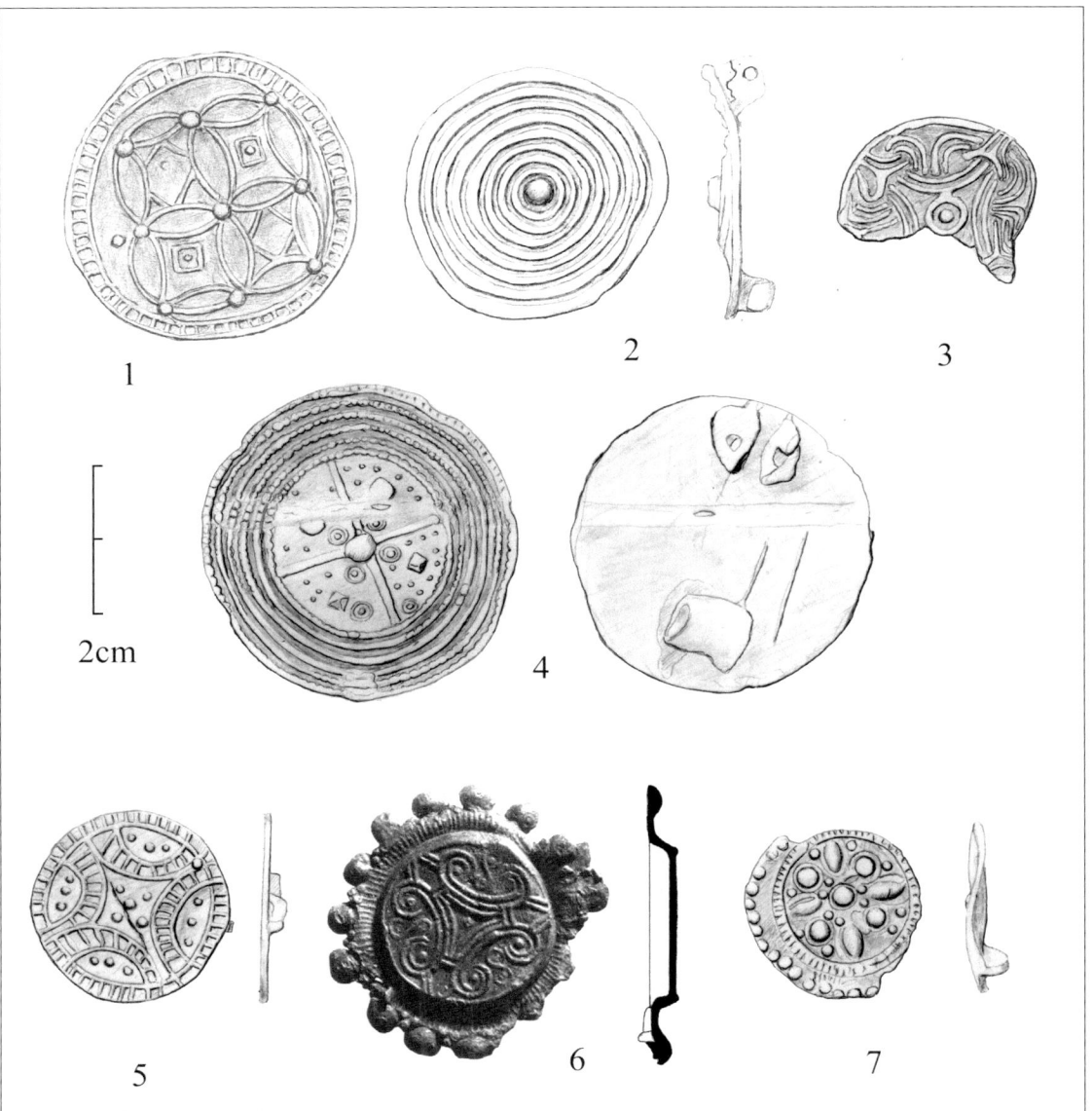

80 Lead brooches.

1: Alford

2: Binbrook

3: North Owersby (this example is in the Borre style suggesting a date in the early tenth century)

4: South Ferriby (note the typical and distinctive fittings on the back. These held an iron pin mechanism)

5: Barrow on Humber

6: Ketsby

7: Ketsby.

Drawings by Kevin Leahy

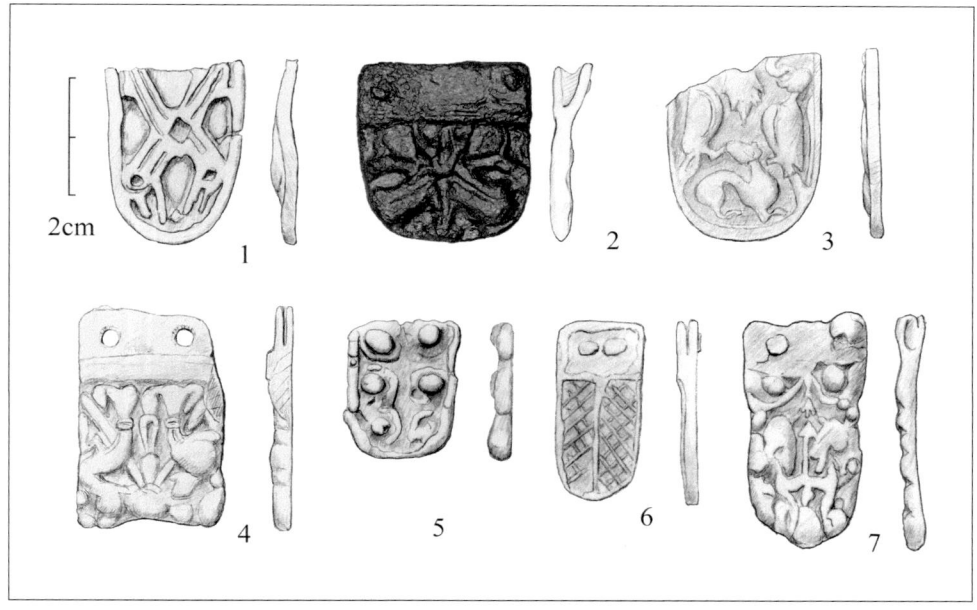

81 Lead strap ends. 1: Owersby. 2: Harpswell. 3: Cadney. 4: Winceby. 5: Sturton by Stow. 6: Gainsborough. 7: Willoughby by Alford (although made of of lead, some of these strap ends are good examples of Winchester style decoration). *Drawings by Kevin Leahy*

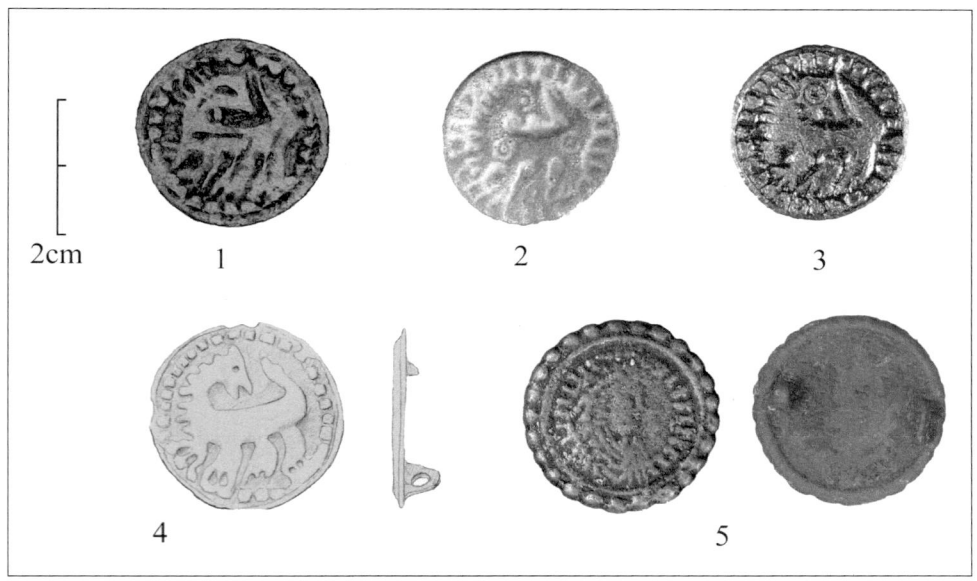

82 Copper-alloy button brooches, tenth century. 1: Swallow. 2: Roxby. 3: South Ferriby. 4: Osgodby. 5: Barnetby le Wold (this brooch is based on a coin of the Carolingian Emperor Louis the Pious). *All images by Kevin Leahy*

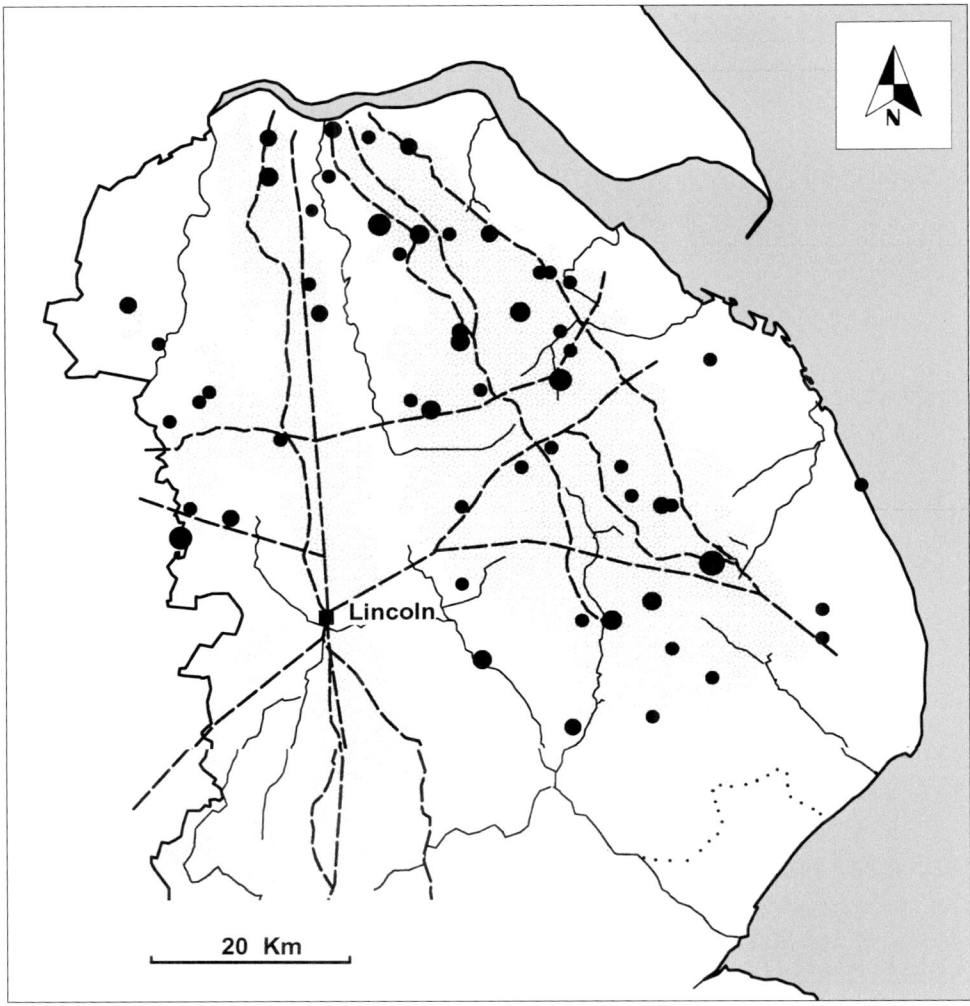

83 Distribution map of late Saxon finds for Lindsey. *Digital mapping by Mike Hemblade*

THE REBIRTH OF LINCOLN

The study of a historic city presents many problems, firstly getting the evidence; Anglo-Saxon and Scandinavian Lincoln lies deeply buried beneath the remains of the medieval and later cities that followed it. Worse still (for Anglo-Saxonists) large parts of these later accretions still survive, and while I might love to know what lies beneath the cathedral, hopefully I will never get a chance to look. In spite of these problems we are starting to see, and even understand, the development of the Late Saxon/Anglo-Scandinavian city. Excavations,

84 Reconstruction drawing of the waterfront at Viking Lincoln. *Drawing by David Vale, courtesy of Friends of Lincoln Archaeological Research*

chance disturbances, records of early finds and analysis of historical sources are allowing us to build up a picture of the city and its rebirth.

Little is known about Lincoln in the Early Saxon period. Alan Vince has plotted the finds of Early Anglo-Saxon pottery and found that they are few and widespread, lacking any focus to reveal a concentration of settlement. The evidence for Lincoln in the Middle Saxon period is also limited. It is likely that the cathedral was somewhere in the city but we cannot be sure. Sherds of Middle Saxon Maxey-type ware have been found on many of the excavations in the city, with a concentration of 69 sherds around the Roman Westgate, now the area occupied by the Lawn. This seems to have been abandoned in the ninth century with settlement moving inside the walls. Maxey-type ware has also been found on excavations at Flaxengate and Saltergate in the lower city.

The excavation at St Paul in the Bail produced a small group of Middle Saxon silver objects decorated in the ninth-century Trewhiddle and Carolingian styles. They were found in a later deposit and may have come from a grave or a small hoard. Four mid-ninth-century silver pennies were also found which might be a small hoard. In spite of the large-scale excavations carried out in the Bail there is no evidence of occupation from the late ninth- to the mid-tenth-century. This area may have had a special function, perhaps as a monastic precinct. In addition to the Middle Saxon burials around St Paul in the Bail at least five graves were found in Silver Street in the south-eastern quarter of the lower city. No grave goods were found but stratigraphy and radiocarbon dates suggest that these burials were Middle Saxon.

It has been suggested that Lincoln's suburb of Wigford, which lies across the River Witham to the south of the city, took its name from 'wic', the word for a trading centre. This term was used at Hamwic, the precursor of Southampton, Ipswich, Lundenwic and Eorforwic (York). Unfortunately, there are no Middle Saxon finds from Wigford to support this and Margaret Gelling has pointed out that the 'wic' element of the place-name is usually the second, not the first element. It should have been 'Fordwic' not Wicford. Early ninth-century Lincoln does not seem to have been a thriving metropolis.

In the popular imagination the arrival of the Vikings should be marked by a discovery of skeletons with axe holes in their heads but, excitingly, the first evidence that things were changing in Lincoln is the appearance of Lincoln gritty ware at Flaxengate. This pottery is locally made and dates from the late ninth to the early tenth century, making it a good chronological indicator. It has not been found in the upper city which may have continued to have an ecclesiastical use prior to the arrival of the Vikings. The cathedral is of late eleventh-century origin but it is likely that there was an earlier church, dedicated to St Mary, on the site. Alan Vince has calculated that the population of Lincoln in 1086 consisted of 1164 households containing around 5238 people. Remarkably, these people were served by 46 churches, that is 25 households (113 people) per church.

As elsewhere, the Danes were a powerful stimulant to the economy and both trade and industry grew with Lincoln (*84*). Manufacture was going on in Anglo-Scandinavian Lincoln, and while this seems to have been on a small scale, a wide range of activities were being carried out. The buildings found had all been built of wood but, unlike York, the deposits were not water-logged and little survived. Earth-fast posts or stakes driven into the ground were used although later they were set in trenches. The posts were 100-200mm in diameter and there is no evidence that they were squared-off or set in pairs across the buildings and linked to form frames. As no trace of daub or cob was found, it is likely that the walls were planked. These buildings would have been short lived, the posts only lasting around 15-25 years.

Within the Flaxengate buildings there was evidence for cross-walls associated with the opposed doorways as seen on medieval buildings. The floors were beaten earth which were covered with a layer of grassy material, burnt during site clearance following demolition. Well-built stone and clay-built hearths were found, around which were stake holes and burnt daub that may have formed ovens or fire backs. Another type of building was found in the Bail area of the upper city. This was dated to the tenth century and consisted of a pit measuring 3.3m x (at least) 4m with a depth of 1.34m, and with what appears to have been a trampled earth floor. Down one of its sides were five post holes, one in a corner and two groups of two

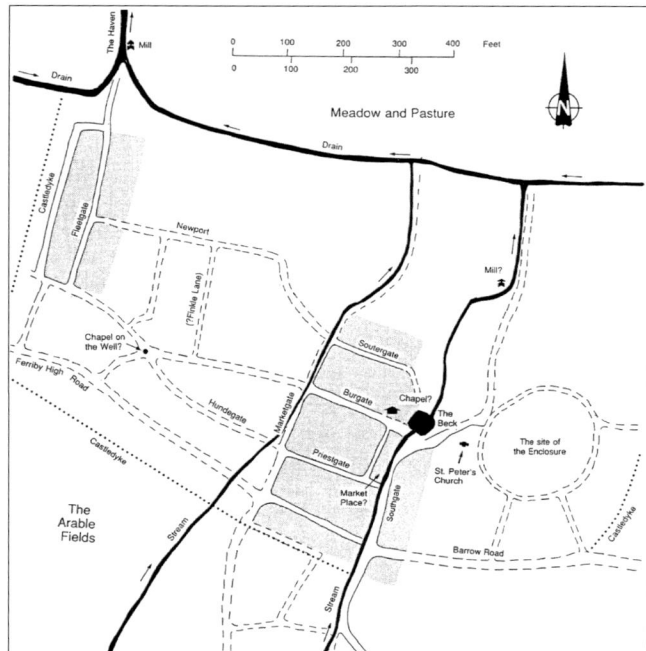

Left: 85 Street pattern in Barton on Humber showing the streets of the possible Saxon town. *Research by Keith Millar, drawing courtesy of Geoff Bryant*

Below: 86 Plan of the late Saxon fortified manor at Goltho/Bullington. *Drawing by Kevin Leahy, based on Beresford*

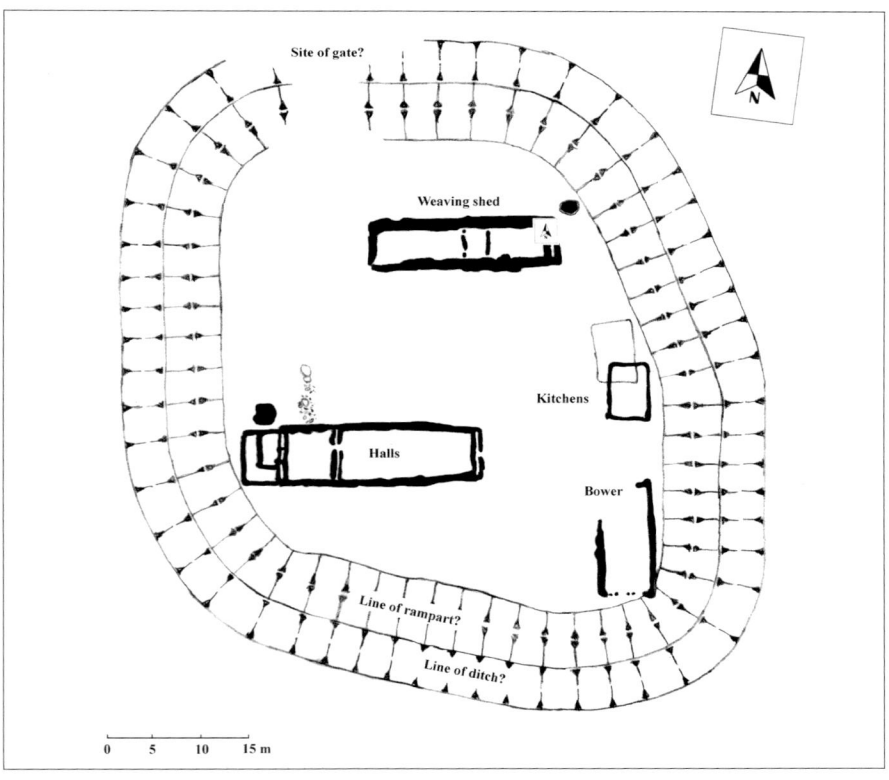

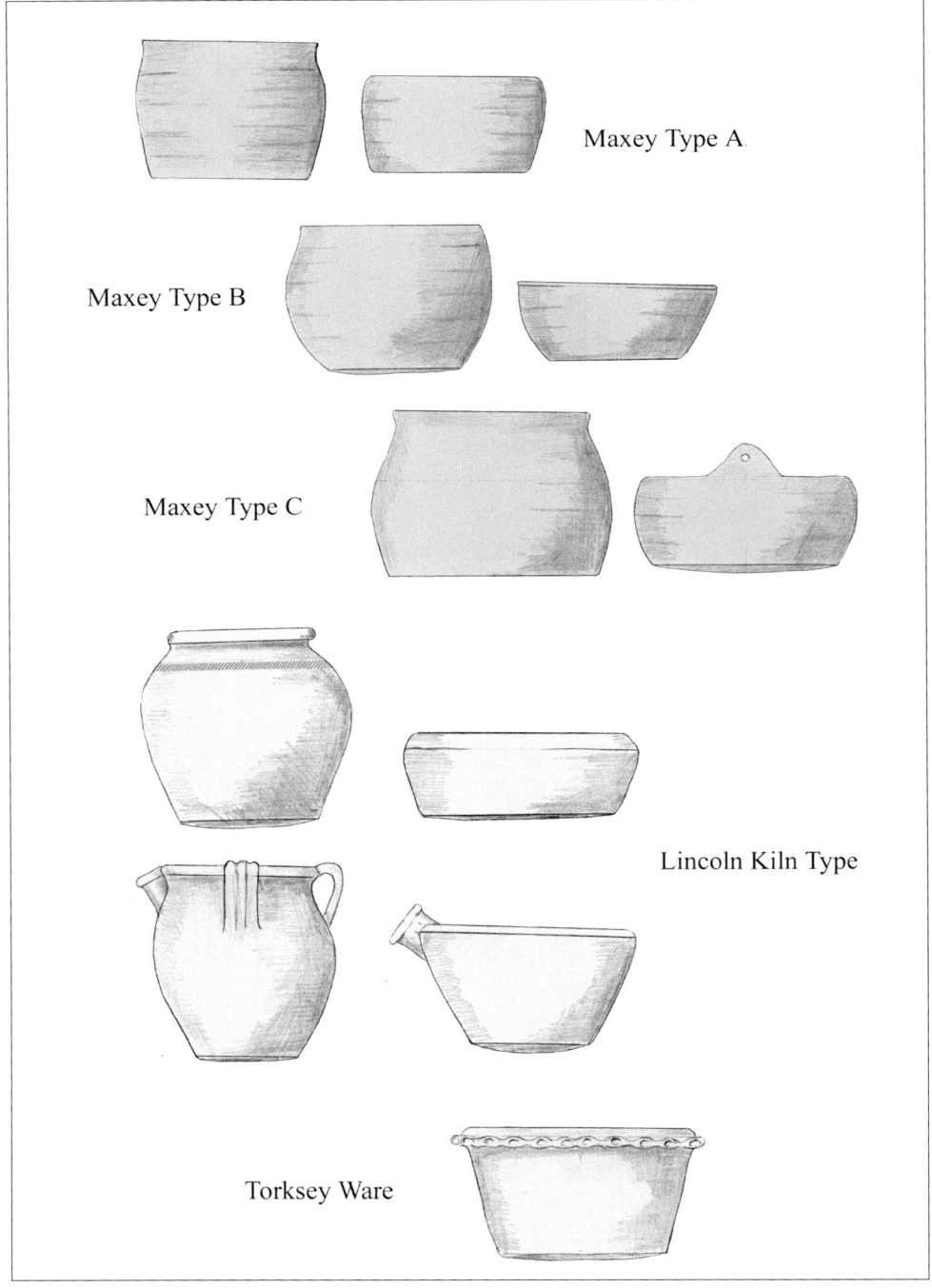

Maxey Type A

Maxey Type B

Maxey Type C

Lincoln Kiln Type

Torksey Ware

87 The forms of Middle and later Saxon pots used in Lindsey. *Drawing by Kevin Leahy, based on the work of Jane Young*

holes. While this might have been a *Grubenhaus,* its depth is reminiscent of the basements of the Anglo-Scandinavian buildings at Coppergate in York.

Building at Flaxengate is likely to have started when a new road system, on a different alignment from that of the Roman city, was laid out. As the periodic demolitions seem to have occurred simultaneously over the excavated area it seems likely that the site was under single ownership. Most of the buildings at Flaxengate were around 5m wide and up to 16m long. Five metres (5.5 yds) is equivalent to one perch – a standard property-width used in the Medieval Period, and possibly earlier. There is evidence for what may be Anglo-Saxon town planning at Barton on Humber (*85*) and Winteringham where Keith Millar has observed that the streets follow a grid layout of the sort seen in Anglo-Saxon planned towns elsewhere in the country.

Our knowledge of the later Saxon pottery in Lincoln and Lindsey is based on studies undertaken by Alan Vince and Jane Young whose work can only be touched on here. The pottery sequence established at Lincoln is sound, but not without its problems. So far no deposits of Early or Middle Saxon date have been found within the city, although pottery dating from these periods has been found incorporated into later layers. Evidence for tenth-century pottery is excellent but there are problems with the early eleventh century. Layers of this date also contain tenth-century pottery leaving some doubts about when the latter went out of use.

The presence of badly fired sherds of Lincoln gritty ware in the Early Anglo-Scandinavian levels at Lincoln suggest that this pottery was being made not far away. In the tenth century, shell-tempered wares, decorated with roller stamp decoration, were being produced by kilns at Silver Street. These pots were made on a wheel and it seems that templates were used to shape the profiles. The products of the Lincoln kilns were mainly jars, but bowls, costrels, funnels, pedestal lamps and drinking cups were also made. Lincoln kiln-type pottery is found thoughout Lindsey but it declined during the middle of the tenth century when it suffered from the competition of Torksey ware and Stamford ware.

Torksey ware is a strong, well-fired pottery which is common in Lindsey (*87*). It first appears in the mid to late ninth century at Flaxengate and kilns have been found and excavated at Torksey. Forms produced consist of a range of jars, bowls and pitchers often with stubby, square rims bearing finger impression 'pie crusting'. Tubular spouts are known, but are rare as are minor forms such as lamps, bottles and lids. While made, not in Lindsey, but in Kesteven, Stamford ware is also common in Lindsey. It was skilfully made on a fast wheel and has a fine clay body which is usually off-white and sometimes bears a yellow or green lead glaze. This represents the first use of glazed pottery in post-Roman Britain. The most distinctive form is the spouted pitcher but jugs, jars and crucibles are also found, the latter being a major product and export.

Agriculture and industry in Anglo-Saxon Lindsey

AGRICULTURE

Lindsey is in a favoured location on the dry eastern side of England which must, to some extent, have protected it from the climatic deterioration of the later fourth century. The rising sea levels around this time would have caused some inland flooding and stress. We have some evidence for woodland regeneration around this time but not enough to suggest an agricultural collapse. Lindsey contains large areas of good farmland and grassland for the rearing of stock. At Domesday there was an exceptional amount of meadow in Lindsey, and Oliver Rackham has calculated that 4.5 per cent of the land (*c*.44,000 acres) was devoted to this use. Stock raising is profitable and in the High Medieval Period good pasture commanded a higher rent than arable. As Lindsey also had access to supplies of salt, it would have been possible to preserve meat for export and sale. Sheep and wool were very important in medieval Lindsey and the finds of sheep bones in graves and urns suggests that interest in sheep rearing started early. Spindle whorls were common in the Cleatham urns and finds from Flixborough suggest that textile manufacture was being carried out on a near industrial scale. At Elsham animal bones were found in 122 urns. Of these, sheep made up 43.6 per cent of the animals, pig 13.6 per cent, horse 22.9 per cent and cattle 10.9 per cent with the ambiguous cattle/horse being in 8.2 per cent of the urns. These are ritual deposits and they may not reflect Anglo-Saxon animal husbandry, horses are probably over-represented.

Sheep provided wool, meat and sometimes milk. The few sheep bones found at Nettleton Top came from animals that had died at between nine months and six years of age, some being slaughtered early for meat but others being retained for wool. At Riby it seems that sheep were being slaughtered early for meat but the most common bones were cattle (51.4 per cent) followed by sheep (31.1 per cent). The numbers of sheep bones at Flixborough may relate to the increasing number of textile working tools found on the site in these phases. The animal bones from Lincoln show that, during the Anglo-Scandinavian period, sheep were being killed early for meat rather than kept as mature animals for wool, as they were following the Conquest. It seems that pigs were usually slaughtered early in Anglo-Saxon Lindsey with only a few animals being kept for breeding.

The small number of cattle whose bones were found on the Early Anglo-Saxon settlement site at Nettleton Top had been slaughtered when immature, or young adults, and were not beasts that had served a long working life. This pattern was also seen at Middle Saxon Belton and in the earlier phases at Flixborough, where 70 per cent of the beasts had been killed before reaching full maturity. In the ninth century the age at which cattle were slaughtered increased both at Flixborough and Riby, which might point to them being raised for traction and diary products. However, at Flixborough the high number of full-grown animals may be due to the site being a manorial centre consuming premium meat raised elsewhere. It seems that the amount of beef being eaten at Flixborough increased during the first half of the ninth century, as did the consumption of chickens and geese which may again point to the high status of the people living there. An interesting feature of the Flixborough cattle was their large size, which suggests they could have come from imported, continental, stock. Few of the Flixborough cattle bones showed any signs of butchery but this was recorded at Riby where vertebrae had been split. The predominance of leg and skull bones at Belton shows that primary butchery, and probably slaughter, were taking place on-site. Amongst the finds from Belton were bones from a butchered horse although this need not have been for human consumption. Six of the Castledyke graves contained the bones of chickens and two the remains of domesticated geese. The fowl were small, being around the size of a modern bantam, and the three that could be sexed were hens. Fowl and goose bones were also found at Riby.

Not all of the flesh eaten came from reared animals and we have some evidence for hunted food. Flixborough was ideally positioned to take advantage of the flood plain of the River Trent and the bones of wildfowl were common. Fish were also being eaten at Flixborough with large numbers of bones from fresh, brackish and saltwater fish being found. Eel and carp bones were found at Belton showing that advantage was being taken of the wetlands around the Isle of Axholme. The bones of roe deer and hare were found at Flixborough, roe and red deer at Belton and a red deer at Riby showing the use of hunted animals. At Goltho the number of deer bones rises in the eleventh century suggesting an increased interest in hunting. The bones of marine mammals; porpoises, dolphins and perhaps pilot whales were found at Flixborough and, although these animals occasionally venture into the Humber where they can be caught or grounded, deliberate hunting may also have been taking place.

Many ancient fields have been recorded on aerial photographs, the difficulty is in recognising what is Anglo-Saxon. At present only the lobe-like enclosures and droveways observed on the Middle Saxon 'Butterwick'-type sites, as found at Melton Ross and Riby, can be identified from the air (*48*). It is likely that these are related to the control of livestock. At Sheffield's Hill, ditches and the holes left by tree roots suggest that the boundaries around the cemeteries were marked by hedges, with some standard trees. Cropmarks on the field resemble those of a Romano-British 'ladder'-type field system and we are probably looking at the survival of an existing field system. If Romano-British fields remained in use at Sheffield's Hill it is likely that this happened elsewhere. In view of the poor fertility of the land at Sheffield's Hill these fields were probably low-grade pasture.

We have some evidence of Early Anglo-Saxon crops, carbonised barley grains were found in the fabric of many of the Cleatham urns and in three of the Castledyke graves, one of which also contained oats. A deposit of carbonised barley mixed with about 1 per cent oats was found on the settlement site at Nettleton top. The 60 cereal grains found at Riby were found to be mixed 80 per cent barley and 20 per cent wheat. Charred wheat and barley were also found in a *Grubenhäus* at South Ferriby. The evidence for the processing of cereals is better, with fragments of lava quern stones being found at Flixborough, Riby and Goltho. Evidence of cultivation consists of an iron ploughshare of probably eighth- or ninth-century date found, with an iron cauldron chain, in a pit at Flixborough. Less spectacular, but more useful, is the evidence provided by 'plough pebbles' which are being found during field walking. Plough pebbles are quartzite pebbles that were driven into holes drilled into the wooden mould boards of ploughs. Wear leaves them with a flat, striated facet on one face. Plough pebbles have been found around Kirton in Lindsey and Elsham, but not, on present evidence, elsewhere.

Perhaps our best source of information on Anglo-Saxon diet comes from the people themselves. Work on the human remains from Early Anglo-Saxon cemeteries in Lindsey shows that the diet was at least adequate, with most people almost achieving their full potential stature. It was notable that the amount of wear on the teeth of the population at Castledyke was low and presence of tartar showed that they were eating a relatively soft food. This could, of course, reflect only the population at Barton on Humber with their access to the Humber and the sea.

CRAFTS AND MANUFACTURE

With the many finds from Anglo-Saxon England the question arises of where all of these things were being made. Unfortunately, it has to be admitted that other than for iron and textile production, which seems to have been going on everywhere, we don't have much evidence. It is said that copper alloy was being worked at Flixborough but during the time that I was involved with the project I saw little evidence. A few crucible fragments were found, but nothing like the big metalworking sites of Scotland and Wales. Nor did I see much evidence for bone working although bone objects were common. Bone and antler were being worked at Anglo-Scandinavian Flaxengate with offcuts of antler and an unfinished comb being found. The most evocative find showing bonework is a comb-case which was found in Lincoln many years ago. This bears an inscription in runes which reads 'Thorfast made a good comb'. There's nothing like advertising.

Excavations at Barrow on Humber produced later Saxon moulds and crucibles but it seems that all that was being made were plain rings of unknown function. In Lincoln, tenth-century evidence for Anglo-Scandinavian metalworking has been found at St Paul in the Bail and Flaxengate where stone and ceramic moulds, crucibles and slag were found. Offcuts of sheet metal showed that sheet metal objects were also being made and small, round, hooked tags were being produced. The discovery of fired clay dishes suggests that the refinement of silver was being carried out. The foot of a small-long brooch, still attached to the casting gate, was found at Winterton which shows that at least some of the brooches found in Lindsey were made within the kingdom

Crucibles used for the melting of glass were found at Flaxengate showing that glass (finger rings and possibly beads) was being worked. A blue glass tessera found at Flixborough represents the way in which glass was distributed from the producers (probably in Ravenna) to the people who would turn it into objects. One of the graves at Sheffield's Hill contained a deposit of broken vessel glass but it is unclear if this was a glass scrap for reworking, or an amulet.

TEXTILE PRODUCTION

This was one of the most important industries and there is a lot of evidence for textile production. Many of the Cleatham urns contained the burnt remains of the bone, stone or pottery whorls that acted as the flywheels on drop spindles. We also have a few pin-beaters, the tool used to beat up the threads on a loom, and a weaving sword that performed the same function, from Castledyke. It is interesting that these textile-working tools show the way in which the Anglo-Saxons defined gender; the Old English word for woman '*wifman*' is likely to be linked to the word 'weave'. The word often used for man was '*wæpman*' (weapon-person) showing how the male role was viewed. Unfortunately without a bone report we cannot confirm if the Cleatham whorls were being found with women. Tools other than weaving implements are rare in Anglo-Saxon graves.

The other common piece of evidence for textile manufacture are loom weights, the annular clay rings that were used to keep the vertical (warp) threads under gentle tension on a warp-weighted loom. Loom weights were found within one of the *Grubenhäuser* at Nettleton Top. These are a common find which has led to these buildings being interpreted as weaving huts, a function for which they would be quite unsuitable, lacking both the roof height and the good light needed for weaving.

Fragments of 19 Middle Saxon loom weights were found at Riby, most of which were unfired and made of clay containing small chalk pebbles. These weights were of intermediate form, being thicker than the early doughnut-shaped weights and having proportionally smaller holes through them. Like the weights from Nettleton Top, the Riby weights bore marks on their upper faces, which may have served to mark ownership or mass. Two of the Riby loom weights were found on the floors of excavated *Grubenhäuser* and a fragment of a loom weight and a bone spindle whorl were found in one of the Belton buildings. The use of unfired clay loom weights was common on Early Anglo-Saxon sites but later, most weights were fired. While actual evidence has not survived it has been suggested that the use of a particular weave known as a 'three shed twill' shows the use of the Roman type of two-beam loom. As three shed twills have been recorded at Cleatham it could show the survival of Romano-British technology.

The Flixborough excavation produced large amounts of evidence for textile manufacture, with more than 200 loom weights being found together with spindle whorls, pin-beaters and iron heckle teeth. There appears to have been a distinct zoning of textile production, with finds representing the stages of manufacture being found in different parts of the site. It has been observed that the loom weights at Flixborough become lighter during the ninth century which may point to the manufacture of finer cloth. The presence of shears and needles shows that garments were being made.

At Goltho a series of buildings were found that were interpreted as weaving sheds on the basis of the finds from around them. These consisted of 13 spindle whorls, 14 wool-comb teeth, six pin-beaters, one shear board hook and a needle. The whorls were associated with the halls and bowers, which seems appropriate for something that was probably a constant female occupation. The wool-comb teeth and pin-beaters were found on the northern part of the site in the area around the weaving shed. No loom weights were found, which supports the tenth-century dating for the site; the warp-weighted loom had gone out of use during the later ninth century when it was replaced by the two-beam loom. The pin-beaters from Goltho are of the long, single-ended type that were used on a two-beam loom, a form that was also found at tenth-century Flaxengate where spindle whorls were common finds, but where loom weights were absent.

IRON SMELTING AND SMITHING

Iron work and working was very important in Anglo-Saxon England and we are fortunate in having good evidence from Lindsey. Large numbers of iron objects have been found on the cemetery sites like Cleatham and Castledyke and we have a prodigious number of finds from Flixborough, where iron objects were both numerous and well preserved. The site yielded 303 knives, 34 pairs of shears and a wide range of iron tools, fittings and fragments (88-90).

North Lincolnshire is still one of the centres of iron smelting in Britain with a major works at Scunthorpe. Iron ores are widespread in Lindsey although they are no longer used due to their low grade. This low iron content makes it unlikely that an early furnace would get much out of them, but a good source of high-grade raw material existed in the bog iron that formed around the pools on Manton Warren and in the marshes flanking the Trent. There is, as we have seen, evidence for Roman iron smelting in the area and extraction continued into the Anglo-Saxon period. The Cleatham cemetery was surrounded by ancient slag heaps known as the 'Cinder Hills' and dense scatters of slag have been found on field walks. Many of the urns at the Cleatham cemetery had crushed slag incorporated into their fabric. While most of the 189kg of slag found on the Flixborough excavation came from forging iron some smelting slag was found, suggesting that some extraction was taking place near, but not on, the site.

Smithing slag, showing that iron was being forged into objects, was also found at Riby and Nettleton Top and it is likely that iron working was being carried out on most Anglo-Saxon settlement sites. Hammer scale and unfinished objects were found at Flaxengate showing that iron was being worked in a proto-urban environment. Some basic smithing could have been done by a handyman but other iron objects must have been made by specialists; early shield bosses were forged in one piece which called for a great deal of skill. The two swords from Sheffield's Hill have pattern-welded blades in which strips of iron were twisted and welded together for decorative effect in a *tour de force* of craftsmanship.

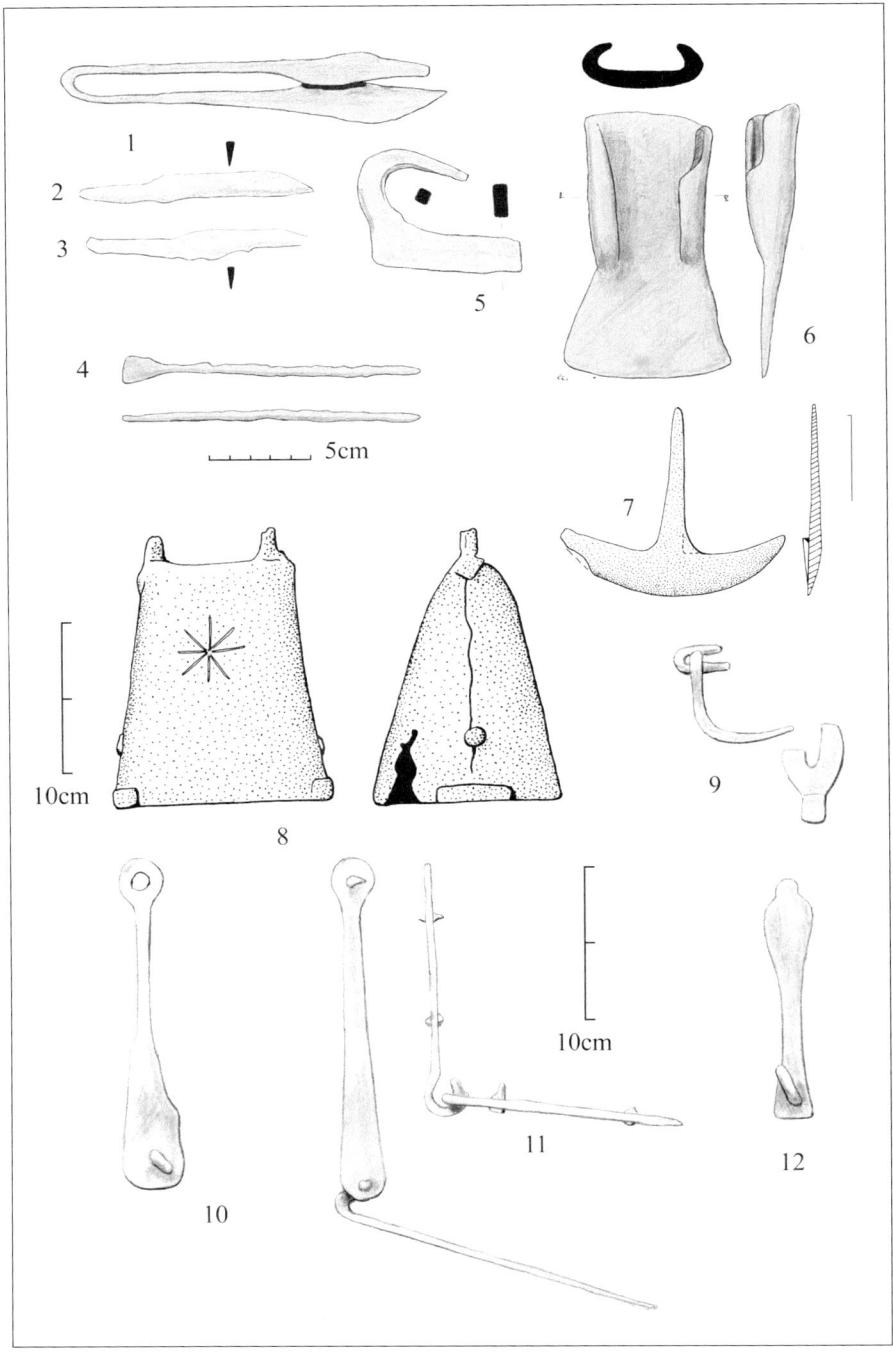

88 Crafts and tools in Lindsey, all from Flixborough. 1: Shears. 2: Knife. 3: Knife. 4: Iron stylus. 5: Iron fire steel. 6: Mattock head. 7: Crescent-bladed knife. 8: Bell from the carpenter's tool hoard. 9-12: Iron chest/coffin fittings. *Drawings by Kevin Leahy*

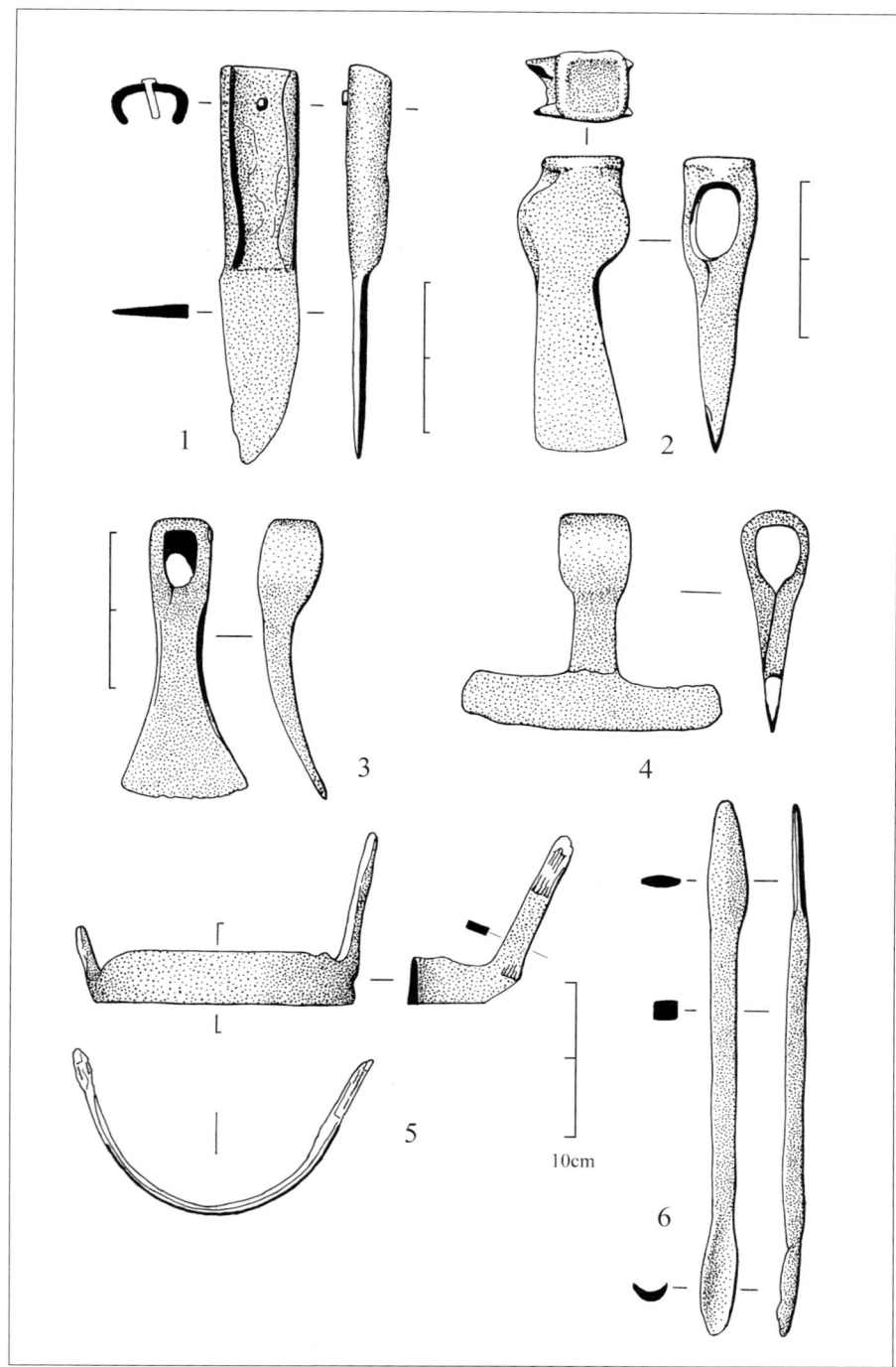

89 Tools from Lindsey, all from Flixborough. 1: Bill for clearing scrub. 2: Felling axe. 3: heavy adze. 4: Smoothing axe. 5: Spoke shave. 6: Spoon bit. *Drawings by Kevin Leahy*

Many of the small iron knives from the early cemeteries have steeled blades, representing a difficult process that would have called for a specialist.

Tool hoards

We are fortunate that Lindsey has produced two hoards of tools and iron objects together with the metalworker's grave from Tattershall Thorpe. The Flixborough hoard is probably eighth or ninth century, the Torksey hoard is likely to be tenth century and David Hinton dated the Tattershall Thorpe smith's grave to the seventh century. Each of the three finds makes a contribution in two ways, the tools show how wood and metal were worked and are, in themselves, examples of the smith's craft. Some tools have changed little over the centuries, the metal-cutting shears and pincers from Tattershall Thorpe would not be out of place in a modern tradesman's tool box (*90*, 1–5; *7*). Other objects have changed, the T-shaped axes from Flixborough and Torksey are of a type that seems to have been in use from the seventh to the eleventh centuries; the spoon-shaped drills are of a type that went out of use early in the last century (*89*). Both of the woodworkers' hoards contain only tools for doing heavy carpentry, there are no chisels or gouges for doing fine work. This is typical of the Anglo-Saxon period when it seems that little fine joinery was being done. The Flixborough hoard consisted of 19 tools: axes, adzes, spoke-shaves and spoon-bits (for drilling holes), everything needed to build a house or a ship.

Interestingly, both the Tattershall Thorpe grave and the Flixborough hoard contained bells (*88*, 8), which have also been found with tools in early medieval hoards, such as the Mästermyr hoard from Sweden. Travelling craftsman may have used these bells to announce their arrival and availability to trade. Tools like these may not have even been made in Lindsey and it seems that the Tattershall Thorpe smith had foreign connections as the grave contained a set of decorative studs of continental type. No gold or silver was found in the grave but there were a small number of cut garnets of the sort set in cloisonné jewellery.

SALT EXTRACTION

While we have no evidence for Early Saxon salt extraction in Lindsey, it would be surprising if this valuable resource was ignored, particularly as large-scale extraction was carried out in the Roman period and earlier. Evidence for a Late Saxon saltern has been found at Marshchapel. This proved interesting, the method being used to extract the salt from seawater resembling the Iron Age/Roman open-pan process, in which the brine was boiled to evaporate the water. In the medieval process the salt was washed out of sand collected from the shore

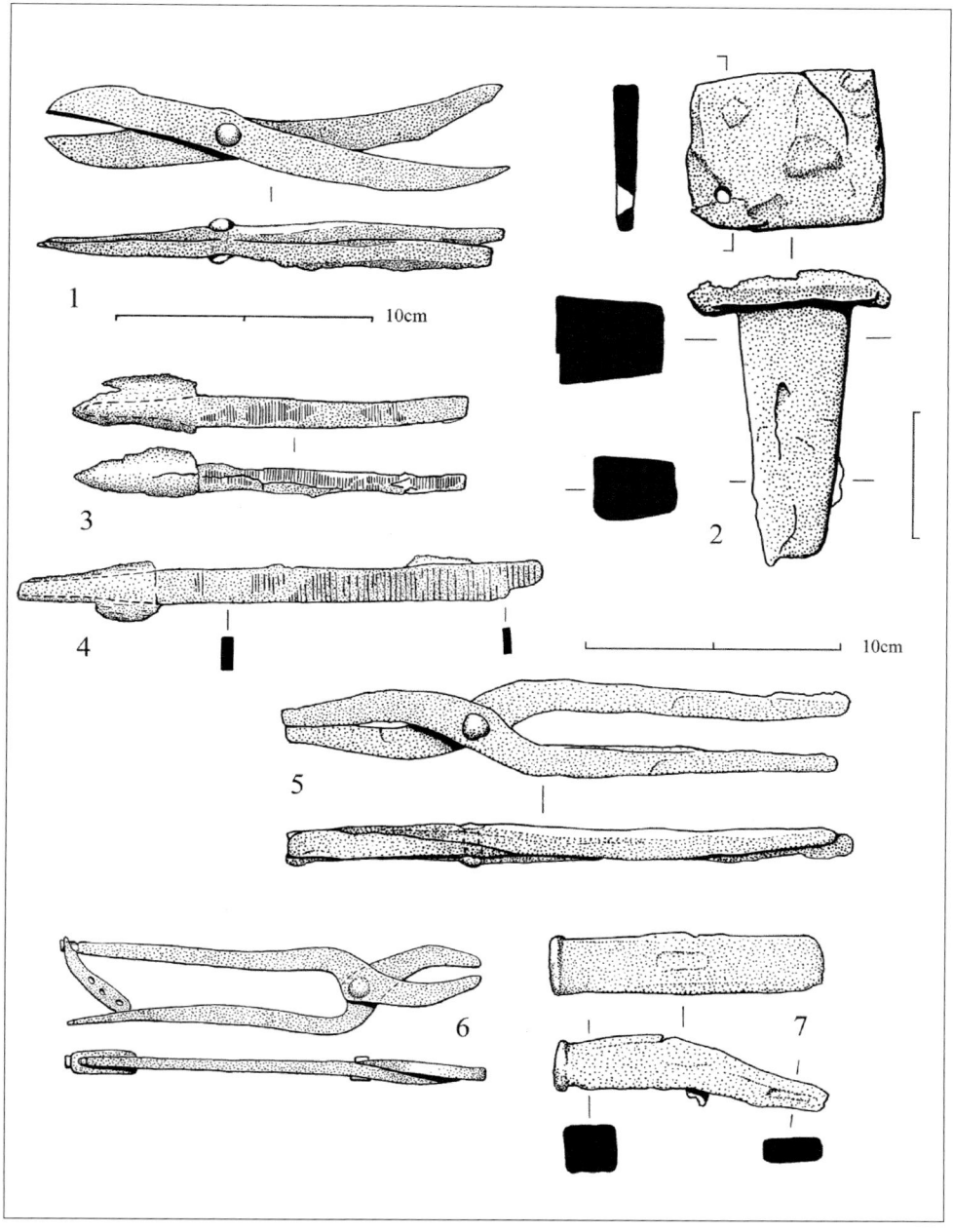

90 Metalworking tools form Lindsey. 1: Shears for cutting metal, Tattershall Thorpe grave. 2: Stake anvil, Tattershall Thorpe grave. 3: File, Tattershall Thorpe grave. 4: File, Tattershall Thorpe grave. 5: Tongs, Tattershall Thorpe grave. 6: Hand vice, Flixborough. 7: Hammer head, Tattershall Thorpe. *Drawings by Kevin Leahy*

and the concentrate then boiled. At Marshchapel it appears that the seawater was channelled into pits and then boiled in lead tanks as a sort of hybrid process. In the Domesday survey of 1086, over 260 extraction sites, *salinae*, were recorded along the Lincolnshire coast.

LEAD VATS

The Flixborough hoard was enclosed in two cylindrical lead vats, one of which had been inverted over the other to form a closed container (*colour plate 21*). In addition to the two vats found at Flixborough, a lead tank was found in a ditch during the excavation of the Riby site and two more were found in a ditch at Bottesford, just outside Scunthorpe, all of which had been squashed flat before burial. They were made from cast lead sheet with soldered joints and, where the sides survive, they had been fitted with small iron rings for carrying. These rings are too small to hold, but could have engaged hooked iron rings like those found in the Flixborough hoard, allowing two people to carry a tank suspended from a pole. The finish on these vats is very poor; the Riby find was badly cast and had a number of patches on it covering casting defects. Its surface was rough and none of the flashing and blobs left by the casting process had been removed. One of the two tanks from Flixborough was decorated with a six-pointed star and some ribbing, the smaller of the Flixborough vats had been made in one piece. The Flixborough vats are not the only examples to have contained tools, the Stidriggs, Dumfries, tank contained tools, as did the tank from Westley Waterless, Cambridgeshire. Jane Cowgill has discussed the function of these tanks and drew attention to two examples from near Garton on the Yorkshire Wolds. These bore traces of sooting on their bases and plugged holes where the lead had melted. It appears that they were used for boiling water but why others are associated with tools remains a mystery. We do have some evidence for the date of these vats as the two from Garton were found in association with Anglo-Scandinavian iron and bone objects. Wood found with the Stidriggs hoard gave a radiocarbon date of 775-892 at one standard deviation, and an example from Warwickshire bore decoration that allowed it to be dated to the ninth century.

The Anglo-Saxon churches of Lindsey

This is the one area where increasing knowledge has led to a reduction in the amount of evidence. Until recently Lindsey, along with the rest of Lincolnshire, was thought to contain one of the densest concentrations of standing Anglo-Saxon churches in England. Unfortunately, David Stocker and Paul Everson have convincingly argued that the 29 Anglo-Saxon towers of 'Lincolnshire type' are of post-Conquest date, reducing the number to four (five with St Paul in the Bail). Not all, however, is lost; in almost all cases the Norman towers were added to a standing building. Their lower stages have only three walls, two of which butt-up against the west wall of the nave up to its roof line, above which the wall of the tower was built on top of the nave wall. These towers may be Norman but the small, rectangular churches they abut could be pre-Conquest.

ST PETER, BARTON ON HUMBER

The most important later Saxon church in Lindsey is St Peter's at Barton on Humber. It was here, in the early years of the nineteenth century, that Thomas Rickman demonstrated that Anglo-Saxon architecture really existed (*colour plate 26*). Before the publication, in 1817, of his book *An Attempt to Discriminate the Styles of Architecture in England,* there were two schools of thought on Anglo-Saxon stone buildings. There were those who thought that there were none (the Anglo-Saxons only built in wood) and those who thought that everything with a round arch was Anglo-Saxon. Looking at St Peter's Rickman realised that if the upper part of the tower was Norman then everything below it must be earlier, and therefore Anglo-Saxon. At St Peter's he was able to define the features by which an Anglo-Saxon church could be recognised; string courses, long and short quoins forming

91 The original form of St Peter's Church, Barton on Humber. *Drawing from Baldwin Brown, 1916*

the corners and certain types of doors and windows (*colour plate 26*). This church has continued to be important in our understanding of Anglo-Saxon buildings. Following it being declared redundant, it was taken over by the Department of the Environment (now English Heritage) and in 1978 a long campaign of recording, excavation and research started, which is still (2007) ongoing.

At St Peter's only the tower and the annex to the west of it are Anglo-Saxon, the rest of the building is medieval and the excavation revealed the long sequence of building and rebuilding that preceded what we see today. To the east of the tower, where the great church now stands, was a small chancel that would have held the altar (*91*). This was demolished and replaced soon after the Conquest. At St Peter's the Anglo-Saxon nave consisted of just the tower. The decorated face of the tower arch faces into the tower so that it would have framed an altar standing in the small chancel (as at Broughton (*92*)). Carved on a stone above the tower arch is a face which probably belonged to a depiction of Christ in Majesty. It is likely that the western annex was a baptistery.

ST MARY, BROUGHTON

The other example of a tower-nave in Lindsey is St Mary's church at Broughton near Brigg. This also has decorations on the inside of the tower arch (*92*) and the remains of a small chancel were found beneath the floor of the medieval church. An additional feature at Broughton is a stair turret attached to the western face of the tower. This contains a spiral stairway built in a manner unlike that used on medieval stairs, where the steps are carved in one piece. At Broughton a helical concrete tunnel was cast, leaving the impression of the wooden shuttering on its roof. Flat stones were set into the floor of the tunnel to form the steps. This arrangement is also found at Brixworth, Northamptonshire, and Hough on the Hill in Kesteven. A feature of St Peter's, Barton; St Mary's, Broughton and other churches along the Humber is the use of massive blocks of stone, giving the walls a cyclopean appearance. These stones are millstone grit from the Pennines to the west. Some bear lewis holes, slots cut by Roman masons to allow large stones to be handled, and at Winteringham Church some decorated Roman stones were used. These must have come from the demolition of important Roman buildings somewhere up river, such as York, Doncaster or Castleford.

These two tower naves are both very small, Geoff Bryant has calculated that the Domesday population of Barton was around 1000, which could not have fitted into the 58m sq area of the tower base. The area of St Mary's tower is only 30.5m sq and these buildings are more likely to be chapels for the aristocracy than parish churches. The dating of St Peter's is something of a problem. Surviving timbers have been radiocarbon dated giving dates in the late tenth century and Richard Gem has proposed that its construction could have been related to Bishop Æthelwold acquiring the Barrow monastic estate in 971. It has also been suggested that these churches date from the early eleventh century when, after that Last Judgement failed to happen at the millennium, it was decided that it was worth building in stone after all!

ST MARY, STOW BY LINCOLN

Lindsey has one surviving Anglo-Saxon great church, St Mary's at Stow by Lincoln. This is a truly magnificent building; with a simple cross-shaped plan and an aisle-less nave and chancel of Norman date. The two transepts and the crossing are Anglo-Saxon and show two phases of building which are of majestic proportions, the piers supporting the large fifteenth-century tower actually stand inside its Anglo-Saxon predecessor, although it is likely that the four arches over the crossing are Norman. It is likely that the Stow church we see

92 The tower arch at St Mary's Church, Broughton, seen from the inside of the tower. *Drawing from Baldwin Brown, 1916*

today has very much the feel of its eleventh-century predecessor. The church at Stow was probably founded by Bishop Ælfnoth of Dorchester (fl. 975). Florence of Worcester recorded that Stow church was built by Eadnoth (probably Eadnoth II) who was bishop from 1034 to 1050. It likely that the earliest surviving work in the transepts dates from this time. Around 1054 Leofric and Godgifu (the Lady Godiva of legend) endowed and refounded St Mary's and more building work was undertaken. The chancel, nave and crossing arches date from after 1091 when Bishop Remigius refounded Stow as an abbey. Excavations carried out by Naomi Field revealed that the original Anglo-Saxon nave was shorter than its Norman successor and had a north 'portacus' or side chapel. The Anglo-Saxon nave cut through 17 burials from an earlier church and a portacus cut through a path that covered still earlier graves.

ST PETER AND ST PAUL, CAISTOR

The other potentially early church is St Peter and Paul at Caistor. This is a complex and mystifying building, the nave of which appears to be Anglo-Saxon. This structure, however, was built up against what is now the base of the tower, as can be seen from the massive thickness of the tower arch, which is made up of two parallel walls. The tower shows signs of having been greatly modified over the centuries, a door and windows being inserted and Norman and medieval upper stages being added. What is clear is that its lower part predated the Anglo-Saxon nave. At the east end of the church, and unconnected to the Anglo-Saxon nave, is the chancel. Set against its walls are tall half-columns that extend up to the roof and make little sense. It has been suggested that these are the remains of a crossing, where the transepts were joined to the body of the church as is seen at Stow. In view of the possible monastery at Caistor and the discovery of the fragment of a monumental inscription (45) this should cause no surprise.

Finally, we have increasing amounts of evidence for Christian burial taking place in the villages of Lindsey prior to the construction of the parish churches. In these cemeteries the bodies are all extended and aligned west-east, there are no grave goods but some burials were in coffins with iron fittings, or in stone cists. To date, burials of this sort have been found at Barrow, Belton, Frodingham, Haxey, Fillingham, Waddingham and Whitton with burials from Whitton giving seventh- to eighth-century radiocarbon dates. These burials suggest that in Lindsey the villages had started to appear far earlier than we suspected.

Endnote

The Kingdom of Lindsey is no more, its unity gone and its existence forgotten for all but a few sad people like me. Even after it was joined by Holland and Kesteven in the eleventh century it kept something of its integrity. At first Lincolnshire may only have consisted of Lindsey, with Kesteven being administered from Stamford as part of the short-lived county of 'Stamfordshire'. By 1066 the three Parts had been amalgamated and Lincolnshire took the form that it kept until recent times. Eventually, having survived the Mercian conquest, the Viking conquest and the Norman Conquest it was subjected to something more terrible than them all, twentieth-century bureaucracy in the form of the 1974 Local Government Reorganisation Act. Lindsey was divided between the new counties of Humberside and Lincolnshire.

This has not been an easy book to write and I am only too aware of its limitations. There is no right way to organise material of this sort but many wrong ways. For all this I hope that it will at least make some of the early medieval material I have recorded over the years available and perhaps make Lindsey a little less overlooked.

As a child I always wanted to be an archaeologist, discovering lost civilisations as a precursor to Indiana Jones. During the 1950s our horizons were more limited, the annual family holiday consisting of a week on the Lincolnshire coast. Little did I know, as we drove down the long road from the Midlands that I would become an archaeologist but that my lost civilisation would not be in a tropical rainforest. It was marked by a sign on the roadside that we passed each year, 'District of West Lindsey'. It was here and waiting.

Bibliographical notes

This short essay can only start to touch on the large number of things that have been published on Anglo-Saxon Lindsey. For reasons of space it has only been possible to cite the longer texts, I have tried to acknowledge the shorter references in my text but I may have missed someone. All that I can do is to humbly and gratefully acknowledge the help given to me by fellow students of Lindsey over many years.

INTRODUCTION AND BACKGROUND

Lindsey has been well served by the studies of some excellent historians who have done wonders with the sparse evidence. In particular see the works of:

Sawyer, P.H. 1998 'Anglo-Saxon Lincolnshire, A history of Lincolnshire' volume 3, Lincoln, The Society for Lincolnshire History and Archaeology

Stenton, F.M. 1971 *Anglo-Saxon England*, 3rd edition, Oxford University Press

Stafford, P. 1985 *The East Midland in the Early Middle Ages*, Leicester University Press

Yorke, B. 1993 'Lindsey: The Lost Kingdom found?' in A. Vince ed. *Pre-Viking Lindsey*, Lincoln, City of Lincoln Archaeological Unit 141-150

Details of early discoveries appear in:

Phillips, C.W. 1934 'The present state of archaeology in Lincolnshire' part II, *Archaeol J* 91, 97-187

Meaney, A. 1964 *A gazetteer of early Anglo-Saxon burial sites*, London, Allen and Unwin

Finds recorded by the Portable Antiquities Scheme can be found on the Scheme's web site www.finds.org.uk

THE LAND OF LINDSEY

Maps showing the geography of Lindsey appear in:

Eagles, B.N. 1979 *The Anglo-Saxon settlement of Humberside*, Brit Archaeol Rep Brit Series, 68, i & ii, Oxford and in Hill, D. *An Atlas of Anglo-Saxon England*, Oxford, 1981

The boundaries of the kingdom are considered in:

Stenton, F.M. 1970 'Lindsey and its Kings', in Stenton, F.M. ed. *Preparatory to Anglo-Saxon England*, 127-35, previously published in *Essays presented to Reginald Poole Lane* ed. Davis, H.W.C., 1927, 136-50 and in Eagles, B.N., 1989 'Lindsey', in *The origins of the Anglo-Saxon Kingdoms* ed Bassett, S., Leicester University Press 202-12

A good discussion of the Humber appears in:

Ellis, S. and Crowther, D. eds. 1990 *Humber Perspectives – a region through the ages*, Hull University Press

THE ENVIRONMENT IN THE ANGLO-SAXON PERIOD

The early medieval environment is discussed in:

Dark, P. 2000 *The Environment of Britain in the First Millennium* AD, London, DuckworthHill, 1981 *ibid*

More detailed information is available in:

Lamb, H. 1981 'Climate from 1000 BC to 1000 AD' in M. Jones and G. Dimbleby eds. *The Environment of Man: the Iron Age to the Anglo-Saxon Period*, Brit Archaeol Rep British Series 87, 53-65

Sea level changes have been reviewed in:

Long, A.J. and Roberts, D.H. 1997 'Sea level change' in M. Fulford, T. Champion and A.J. Long eds *England's Coastal Heritage*, London, English Heritage 25-49 and flooding in Waddelove A.C. and Waddelove E. 1990 'Archaeology and research into sea-level during the Roman era: towards a methodology based on highest astronomical tide' *Britannia* 21, 253-66.

Flooding around the Wash is also discussed in Hayes P.P. and Lane T.W. 1988 'Roman to Saxon in the South Lincolnshire Fens' *Antiquity* 62, 321-6

Deposits around the Humber are described in:

J.B. Whitwell 1988 'Late Roman settlement on the Humber and Anglian beginnings' in J. Price and P.R. Wilson eds, *Recent Research in Roman Yorkshire, Studies in Honour of Mary Kitson Clark (Mrs Derwas Chitty)* Brit Archaeol Rep, Brit Ser 193, 57; Van de Noort R. and Davies P. 1993, Wetland Heritage: an Archaeological Assessment of the Humber Wetlands, Hull, 39; Buckland P.C. and Saddler J. 1985 'The nature of late Flandrian alluviation in the Humberhead Levels', *East Midlands Geologist* 8, 239-51

Catastrophic environmental change has been discussed in:

Dark, op. cit. 22-5 and Baillie, M.G. 1995 *A Slice through Time*, London Batsford, 81-94

The amount of woodland surviving in Anglo-Saxon Lindsey has been reviewed in:

Rackham, O. 1986 *The History of the Countryside*, London, Dent, Darby H.C. 1977, Domesday England, Cambridge and Hill, op. cit.

Woodland regeneration is discussed in:

Van de Noort and Ellis, op. cit. and Van de Noort and Davies op. cit.

The dates of trees felled by the Anglo-Saxons come from:

Tyres, I., Hillam, J. and Groves C. 1994 'Trees and woodland in the Saxon period: the dendrochronological evidence', in J. Rackham ed., *Environment and Economy in Anglo-Saxon England*, CBA Research Rep, 89, 12-22

THE FOUNDATIONS OF LINDSEY: LATE ROMAN BACKGROUND

The significance of the *Rescript of Honorius* is discussed in:

Esmonde Cleary A.S. 1989, *The Ending of Roman Britain*, London, Batsford. 138

Reviews of the archaeological evidence for Anglo-Saxon Lindsey appear in:

Eagles, B.N. 1979 *The Anglo-Saxon Settlement of Humberside*, Brit Archaeol Rep Brit
    Series, 68, i and ii, Oxford

Loughlin, N. and Miller, K.R. 1979 *A Survey of Archaeological Sites in Humberside*,
    Humberside Libraries and Amenities, Hull

Whitwell, J.B. 1970 *Roman Lincolnshire, A History of Lincolnshire Vol 2*, Lincoln, Soc
    Lincs Hist and Archaeol

Whitwell J.B. 1982 *The Coritani, Some Aspects of the Iron Age Tribe and the Roman Civitas*,
    Oxford, Brit Archaeol Rep, Brit Series, 99

There are discussions of the Romano-British settlement patterns in:

Bewley, R. ed. 1998 *Lincolnshire's Archaeology from the Air*, Society for Lincolnshire History
    and Archaeology/Royal Commission on the Historical Monuments (England)

Lindsey's Roman pottery kilns have been listed in:

Swan, V.G. 1984 *The Pottery Kilns of Roman Britain*, RCHME Suppl Ser 5

ROMAN LINCOLN

The most up-to-date accounts of Roman Lincoln are:

Mick Jones *2002 Roman Lincoln, Conquest, Colony and Capital*, Stroud, Tempus

Jones, M.J., Stocker D. and Vince, A. 2003 *The City by the Pool, Assessing the Archaeology
    of the City of Lincoln*, Lincoln Archaeological Studies 10, Oxford, Oxbow

Accounts of the later years of Roman Lincoln appear in:

Jones, M.J. 1993 'The latter days of Roman Lincoln', and Stean, K. and Vince A. 1993
    'Post Roman Lincoln: archaeological evidence for activity in Lincoln in the 5th-9th
    centuries' both of which appear in Vince, A. ed., 1993 *Pre-Viking Lindsey*, Lincoln,
    City of Lincoln Archaeological Unit

THE DEFENCE OF ROMAN LINDSEY

The lost 'Saxon Shore Fort' at Skegness is discussed in:

Whitwell, J.B. 1970 op. cit, 51-2

The defences of Horncastle are discussed in:

Field, F.N. and Hurst, N. 1983. 'Roman Horncastle', *Lincs Hist Archaeol* 18, 47-88

Late Roman Belt fittings were first discussed in:

Hawkes, S.C. and Dunning, G. 1961 'Soldiers and settlers in Britain, 4th-5th century',
    Medieval Archaeol 5, 1-70

Finds from Lindsey were reviewed in:

Leahy, K.A. 1984 'Late Roman and Early Germanic metalwork from Lincolnshire', in
    F.N. Field and A. White, eds, *A Prospect of Lincolnshire: Essays in Honour E.H. Rudkin*,
    Lincoln 23-32. See also Leahy K.A. 'Soldiers and settlers in Britain, fourth to fifth
    century, revisited' in M. Henig and T.J. Smith eds, *Collectanea Antiqua; Essays in
    Memory of Sonia Chadwick-Hawkes*, Archpress, 2007

THE END OF ROMAN LINDSEY

The Balkan scenario for the end of Roman Britain will be discussed by Stuart Laycock in a forthcoming Tempus volume.

THE ANGLO-SAXON SETTLEMENT OF LINDSEY

The cremation cemetery at South Elkington was published in:

Webster, G. and Myres, J.N.L. 1952 'An Anglo-Saxon urnfield at Elkington, Louth, Lincolnshire', *Archaeol J* 108, 25-64

There is a short discussion of the finds from West Keal in:

Thompson, F.H. 1956 'Anglo-Saxon sites in Lincolnshire: unpublished material and recent discoveries', *Antiq J*, 36, 181-99

I am grateful to Miss Freda Berisford and Mr Chris Knowles for my information on the Elsham cemetery. The Cleatham cemetery appears in:

Leahy, K.A. 2007 'Interrupting the Pots; the Excavation of the Cleatham Anglo-Saxon Cemetery', CBA Research Rep 155

Accounts of the smaller Anglo-Saxon cremation cemeteries appear in:

Eagles, B.N. 1979 *The Anglo-Saxon Settlement of Humberside*, Brit Archaeol Rep Brit Series, 68, i and ii, Oxford

Meaney, A. 1964. *A Gazetteer of Early Anglo-Saxon Burial Sites*, London, Allen and Unwin

CEMETERY LOCATIONS

The locations of Anglo-Saxon cemeteries on parish boundaries is discussed in:

Goodier, A. 1984 'The formation of boundaries in Anglo-Saxon England: a statistical study' *Medieval Archaeol*, 28, 1-21

The location of the Elsham cemetery is discussed by Leahy, K.A. 2003 'Middle Saxon Lincolnshire: an emerging picture' in T. Pestell and K. Ulmschneider eds *Markets in Early Medieval Europe; Trading and 'Productive Sites', 650-850*, Macclesfield, Windgather Press

Howard Williams has done intensive work on the relationship between Anglo-Saxon cemeteries and earlier monuments:

Williams, H. 1997 'Ancient landscapes and the dead: the reuse of Prehistoric and Roman monuments as early Anglo-Saxon burial sites' *Medieval Archaeol*, 41, 1-32

Williams, H. 1998 'Monuments and the past in early Anglo-Saxon England', *World Archaeology* 30 (1), 90-108

The relationship between Anglo-Saxon cemeteries and Lincoln is discussed in:

Leahy, K.A. 1993 'The Anglo-Saxon settlement of Lindsey' in A. Vince, ed. 1993, 29-44

Bassett, S. 1989, ed. *The Origins of the Anglo-Saxon Kingdoms*, Leicester, University Press

LINKS BETWEEN CREMATION CEMETERIES

The urns made by the 'Sancton-Elkington potter' are discussed in:

Myres, J.N.L. and Southern, W.H. 1973 *The Anglo-Saxon cremation cemetery and Sancton, East Yorkshire*, Hull Museum Publication No. 218, 19

Myres, J.N.L. 1969 *Anglo-Saxon pottery and the settlement of England*, Oxford University Press, 238, fig 46

For the work of the Sancton-Baston potter see:

Myres, J.N.L. 1977 *A corpus of Anglo-Saxon pottery of the pagan period*, 2 vols. CUP, 343-4, fig 347. This group of urns is analysed in more detail by Arnold, C.J. 1983 'The Sancton-Baston potter', *Scottish Archaeol Rev*, 2, 17-30

ROMAN FINDS FROM CLEATHAM

For the Roman type urns from Newark see:

Kinsley, A.G. 1989 *The Anglo-Saxon Cemetery at Millgate, Newark on Trent, Nottinghamshire*, Nottingham Archaeological Monographs 2, Nottingham, Dept of Classical and Archaeological Studies, University of Nottingham

The Great Casterton Roman pot appears in:

Corder, P. ed., 1951 *The Roman Town and Villa at Great Casterton, Rutland*, University of Nottingham

An excellent account of the Castledyke cemetery appears in:

Drinkall, G. and Foreman, M. 1998 *The Anglo-Saxon Cemetery at Castledyke South, Barton on Humber*, Sheffield Excavation Reports, 6

For a survey of Roman finds from Anglo-Saxon graves see White, R. 1990 'Scrap or substitute: Roman material in Anglo-Saxon Graves' in Southworth, E. ed., *Anglo-Saxon Cemeteries: a Reappraisal, Proceedings of a Conference held at Liverpool Museum 1986*, Stroud, Alan Sutton, 125-52

THE INHUMATION CEMETERIES

For a survey of the Anglo-Saxon cemeteries of Lindsey see Leahy, K.A. 1993 'The Anglo-Saxon settlement of Lindsey' in A. Vince, ed. 1993, 29-44

Published cemeteries are:

Castledyke South, Barton on Humber, Drinkall and Foreman 1998, op. cit; Fonaby Cook, A.M. 1981 *The Anglo-Saxon Cemetery at Fonaby, Lincolnshire*

Occasional papers in *Lincs Hist and Archaeol*, 6, Sleaford; Cleatham, Leahy 2007 op. cit.

There is an interim account of the Sheffield's Hill cemeteries in Leahy, K.A. and Williams, D.J. 2001 'Sheffield's Hill, two Anglo-Saxon cemeteries', *Curr Archaeol*, 175, vol. 15; 7, 310-3

THE FINDS FROM THE GRAVES

As Catherine Mortimer's work is not generally available Anglo-Saxon cruciform brooches still continue to be classified into the groups proposed in:

Åberg, N. 1926 *The Anglo-Saxons in England in the Early Centuries after the Invasion*, Cambridge, Heffer and Sons

For Anglo-Saxon dress see:

Owen-Crocker, G.R. 2004 *Dress in Anglo-Saxon England*, Cambridge University Press

Great square-headed brooches have now been classified in:

Hines, J. 1997 *A New Corpus of Anglo-Saxon Great Square-Headed Brooches*, Soc Antiq London, Woodbridge, Boydell

Sleeve clasps by Hines, J. 1993 *Clasps Hektespenner Agraffen, Anglo-Scandinavian Clasps of Classes A-C of the 3rd to 6th Centuries* AD. *Typology, Diffusion and Function*, Stockholm, Almqvist and Wiksell

Amulets have been studied by Meaney, A. 1981 *Anglo-Saxon Amulets and Curing Stones*, Brit Archaeol Rep Brit Series 96, Oxford

Anglo-Saxon spearheads have been classified in:

Swanton, M.J. 1973 *The Spearheads of the Anglo-Saxon Settlements*, London, Royal Archaeological Institute

Heinrich Härke has done important work on Anglo-Saxon weapon graves, see:

Härke, H. 1989a 'Early Anglo-Saxon weapon burials: frequencies, distributions and weapon combinations' in S.C. Hawkes ed., *Weapons and Warfare in Anglo-Saxon England*, Oxford University Comm for Archaeol, Monograph 21, 49-61, Oxford

Härke, H. 1989b 'Knives in Early Anglo-Saxon burials: blade length and age at death' *Medieval Archaeol*; 33, 144-8: Härke, H. 1990. 'Warrior graves? The background of the Anglo-Saxon burial rite', *Past and Present*, 126, 22-43

COMPARISONS WITH OTHER REGIONS

The position of bodies in the graves and the use of brooches in East Anglia and Lindsey has been examined in:

Fisher, G. 1995, 'Kingdom and Community in Early Anglo-Saxon England' in Lane Anderson Beck ed. *Regional Approaches to Mortuary Analysis*, New York, Plenum Press, 147-66

ARCHAEOLOGICAL EVIDENCE FOR BRITISH SURVIVAL

These penannular brooches were first discussed in:

Fowler, E. 1963 Celtic metalwork of the Fifth and Sixth centuries AD: a reappraisal, *Archaeol J*, 120, 98-160

A more recent summary appears in:

Youngs, S. 1989 *The work of angels, masterpieces of Celtic metalwork, 6th-9th century* AD, London, The British Museum

THE SEVENTH-CENTURY 'FINAL PHASE' CEMETERIES

The 'Final Phase' cemeteries were first discussed in:

Lethbridge, T.C. 1931 *Recent excavations in Anglo-Saxon cemeteries in Cambridgeshire and Suffolk*, Cambridge Antiquarian Society, Quarto publications, new series vol. III

Lethbridge, T.C. 1936 *A cemetery at Shudy Camps, Cambridgeshire: report on the excavation of a cemetery of the Christian Anglo-Saxon period in 1933*, Cambridge Antiquarian Society, Quarto publications, new series vol. V

Lethbridge's ideas were taken further in Leeds, E.T. 1936 *Early Anglo-Saxon art and archaeology*, Oxford, Clarendon Press

Excavated Final Phase cemeteries are discussed in:

Meaney, A. and Hawkes Chadwick, S. 1970 'Two Anglo-Saxon cemeteries at Winnall' Soc. Medieval Arch, Monograph No. 4

Hyslop, M. 1963 'Two Anglo-Saxon cemeteries at Chamberlain's Barn, Leighton Buzzard, Bedfordshire' *Archaeol J* 120, 160-200

A more up to date synopsis of them appears in:

Boddington, A. 1990 *Models of burial, settlement and worship: the Final Phase reviewed*, in Southworth, E. ed. 1990

SINGLE GRAVES

Anglo-Saxon single graves have been discussed nationally in:

Shephard, J. 1979, 'The social identity of the individual in isolated barrows and barrow cemeteries in Anglo-Saxon England', B.C. Burnham and J. Kingsbury eds. *Space, Hierarchy and Society* Brit Archaeol Rep Int Ser 59, Oxford

Single graves in Lindsey have been listed and discussed in:

Everson, P. 1993 'Pre-Viking settlement in Lindsey', in Vince, A. ed. op. cit. 91-100

We have a good contemporary description of the Caenby finds in:

Jarvis, E. 1850 'Account of the discovery of ornaments and remains, supposedly of Danish origin, in the parish of Caenby, Lincolnshire', *Archaeol J*, 7, 36-44

HANGING BOWLS

Full accounts of the hanging bowls from Lindsey appear in:

Bruce-Mitford, R. 1993 'Late Celtic hanging bowls in Lincolnshire and South Humberside' in Vince, A. ed. op. cit. 45-70

Bruce-Mitford, R. 2005 *A Corpus of Late Celtic Hanging Bowls, with an account of the Bowls found in Scandinavia*, Oxford University Press

The discovery of the St Paul in the Bail bowl is described in detail in:

Steane K. with Darling M., Jones, M.J., Mann J., Vince A. and Young J. 2005 *The Archaeology of the Upper City and the Adjacent Suburbs*, Lincoln Archaeological Studies 3, Oxbow, Oxford

The inscription on the Cleatham hanging bowl is discussed in:

Hines, J., 1990 'The runic inscriptions of Early Anglo-Saxon England' in A. Bammesberger and A. Wollmann eds *Britain 400-600: language and history*, Heidelberg, Carl Winter

Hines, J. 1991 'Some observations on the runic inscriptions of Early Anglo-Saxon England' in A. Bammesberger *Old English runes and their continental background*, Heidelberg, Carl Winter

THE EARLY HISTORY OF LINDSEY

The best account of the genealogy of Aldfrið is in:

Foot, S. 1993 'The kingdom of Lindsey' in A Vince ed. *Pre-Viking Lindsey*, Lincoln, City of Lincoln Archaeological Unit 141-150

The *Tribal Hidage* is discussed in Dumville, D. 1989 'The Tribal Hidage: an introduction to its texts and their history' in, S. Bassett ed. *The Origins of the Anglo-Saxon Kingdoms*, Leicester University Press, 225-30

The issue of the Humbrenses was reviewed in:

Myres, J.N.L. 1986 *The English Settlements*, Oxford, Clarendon Press, 174-5

PLACE-NAMES

An excellent summary of Lincolnshire place-names appears in:

Cameron, K. 1998 *A Dictionary of Lincolnshire Place Names*, Nottingham, Engl Place-name Soc

The place-name 'Lindsey' is discussed in:

Gelling, M. 1989 'The name Lindsey', *Anglo-Saxon England*, 18, 31-2

The origin of the name 'Trent' has been discussed in:

Rivet, A.L.F. and Smith, C. 1979 *The place-names of Roman Britain*, London, Batsford

Early Anglo-Saxon place-names have been discussed in:

Cox, B. 1973 'The significance of the distribution of English place-names in *-h m* in the Midlands and East Anglia', Engl Place-name Soc, 5, 15-93

The origins of the place-name 'Wyham' and other pagan shrines are discussed in:

Gelling, M. 1975. 'Further thoughts on pagan place-names' in K. Cameron ed., *Place-name Evidence for the Anglo-Saxon Invasion and Scandinavian Settlements*, Engl Place-name Soc, 99-114

Further analysis was included in Wilson D. 1992, *Anglo-Saxon Paganism*, London, Routledge

PSEUDO-HISTORY

Articles discussing the placing of the Arthurian legends in Lindsey appear in:

Green, T. 'Lincolnshire, Yorkshire and Arthurian Legend', www.arthuriana.co.uk, 1-16

Reavill, J.B. 2003 'Lincolnshire in the Dark Ages' *Lincolnshire Past and Present*, No 33, 3-4

A useful account of the main Arthurian texts appears in:

Alcock, L. 1971 *Arthur's Britain*, London

The quotes that I have used from Geoffrey of Monmouth's '*The History of the Kings of Britain*' come from the translation by Lewis Thorpe 1966, Penguin Classics

Stukeley quotes are from: Stukeley, W. 1776 *Itinerarium Curiosum*

The significance of the place-name 'Yarborough' is discussed in:

Cox, B. 1994 'The pattern of Old English burh in early Lindsey', *Anglo-Saxon England*, 23, 35-56

Yarborough Camp is discussed in:

Leahy, K. 2003 'Middle Saxon Lincolnshire: an emerging picture' in Pestell, T. and
    Ulmschneider, K. eds *Markets in early Medieval Europe, Trading and 'Productive Sites',*
    650-850 Windgather Press, Macclesfield, 138-154
Ken Dark's discussion of sub-Roman earthwork sites in north and western Britain
    appears in:
Dark, K. 2000, *Britain and the End of the Roman Empire*, Stroud, Tempus

CHRISTIANITY IN LINDSEY

The references to the early history of Christianity in Lindsey are drawn from the
    historical sources listed at the start of this section.
The Walesby 'font' and the Caistor 'box' are discussed and illustrated in:
Whitwell, J.B. 1970 *Roman Lincolnshire, A History of Lincolnshire Vol 2*, Lincoln, Soc
    Lincs Hist and Archaeol, 72, 129

MONASTERIES IN LINDSEY

The location of Lindsey's Anglo-Saxon monasteries has been analysed in:
Stocker, D. 1993, 'The Early Church in Lincolnshire: A study of the sites and their
    significance' in A. Vince ed. 1993 *Pre-Viking Lindsey*
An authoritative account of the lost Caistor stone appears in:
Everson, P. and Stocker, D. 1999 *Corpus of Anglo-Saxon Sculpture, vol v: Lincolnshire*, The
    British Academy, Oxford
The Barrow on Humber Charter has been published in:
Everson, P. and Knowles, G.C. 1993 'The Anglo-Saxon bounds of *Æt Bearuwe*' EPNS
    Journal 25, 19-37
An interim account of the Flixborough site was published in:
Loveluck, C. 2001 'Wealth, waste and conspicuous consumption, Flixborough and its
    importance for Middle and Late Saxon rural settlement studies' in H. Hamerow and
    A. MacGregor eds, *Image and Power in the Archaeology of early Medieval Britain, Essays*
    in Honour of Romemary Cramp, Oxbow, Oxford
See also:
Leahy, K. 1999 'The Middle Saxon site at Flixborough, North Lincolnshire' in
    J. Hawkes and S. Mills eds *Northumbria's Golden Age*, Stroud, Sutton
The Anglo-Saxon finds from Whitby are described in:
Peers, C.R. and Radford, C.A.R. 1943 'The Saxon monastery at Whitby' *Archaeogia*, 89,
    27-88
David Roffe's identification of Stow Green as *Ætheldreðestowe* appears in Roffe D. 1986
    'The seventh century monastery at Stow Green, Lincolnshire' *Lincs Hist Archaeol*. 21,
    31-3

For Donemuthan see:
Parker, M.S. 1985 'An Anglo-Saxon monastery in the Lower Don valley', *Northern*
    History, 21, 19-32

SETTLEMENTS AND 'PRODUCTIVE SITES'

The Melton Ross site has been published in:
Leahy, K. 2003 'Middle Saxon Lincolnshire: an emerging picture' op. cit.
For a comparable site to the north of the Humber see:
Leahy, K. 2000 'Middle Saxon metalwork and coins from South Newbald and the productive site phenomenon in Yorkshire' in H. Geake and J. Kenny *Early Deira, Archaeological Studies of the East Riding of Yorkshire in the fourth to ninth centuries* AD, Oxford, Oxbow, 51-82
Butterwick-type sites were defined in:
Stoertz, C. 1997 *Ancient Landscapes of the Yorkshire Wolds, Aerial Photographic Transcription and Analysis*, Royal Commission on Historic Monuments, England, Swindon
The excavation of the Riby site was published in:
Steedman, K. 1994 'Excavation of a Saxon site at Riby Lincolnshire' *Archaeological Journal* vol. 151, 212-306
References to the Lincolnshire Domesday come from:
Foster, C.W. and Longley, T. 1921. *The Lincolnshire Domesday and the Lindsey Survey*, Lincoln Record Society, Vol. 19

THE VIKING CONQUEST

The quotations from the *Anglo-Saxon Chronicle* come from:
Colgrave, B. and Mynors, R.A.B. 1969 *Bede's Ecclesiastical History of the English People*, Oxford University Press
Other historical evidence is drawn from the sources listed at the head of this section.
For the Repton encampment see:
Biddle, M. and Kjølbye-Biddle, B. 2001 'Repton and the great heathen army, 873-4' in Graham-Campbell, J., Hall, R., Jesch, J., and Parsons, D. *2001 Vikings and the Danelaw, Select Papers from the Proceedings of the Thirteenth Viking Congress*, Oxbow, Oxford, 45-96
A discussion of the Viking settlement of Lindsey appears in:
Leahy, K. and Paterson, C. 2001 'New light on the Viking presence in Lincolnshire: the artefactual evidence, ibid. 181-202, and in Leahy, K. 2004 'The Lincolnshire Vikings' *Current Archaeology*, No 190, 462-5
Mark Blackburn's discussion of the Early medieval coins from Lindsey appears in:
Blackburn, M. 1993 'Coin finds and coin circulation in Lindsey, *c*.600-900', in Vince ed. op. cit.
The Viking sculpture from Lindsey is catalogued in Everson, P. and Stocker, D. 1999, *Corpus of Anglo-Saxon Sculpture, vol v: Lincolnshire*. The British Academy, Oxford

THE RE-BIRTH OF LINCOLN

Work on early Medieval Lincoln appears in a number of sources, see in particular:
Jones, M., Stocker, D. and Vince, A. 2003 *The City by the Pool*, Lincoln Archaeological Studies 10, Oxbow, Oxford

Pering, D. 1981 *Early Medieval Occupation at Flaxengate Lincoln*, The Archaeology of
Lincoln vol. ix-1, Lincoln Archaeological Trust, CBA, London

Steane, K. et al 2005 *The Archaeology of the Upper City and Adjacent Suburbs*, Lincoln
Archaeological Studies No 3, Oxford, Oxbow

Vince, A. 2001 'Lincoln in the Viking Age', in Graham-Campbell, J. et al 2001

RURAL BUILDINGS AND SETTLEMENTS

Accounts of the publication of Anglo-Saxon settlements and buildings are summarised in:

Everson, P. 1993 'Pre-Viking settlement in Lindsey' in A. Vince ed. op. cit.

See also:

Salmonby: Everson, P. 1973 'An excavated Anglo-Saxon sunken featured building and
settlement at Salmonby, Lincolnshire, *Lincs Hist Archaeol* 8, 61-72

Nettleton Top: Field, F. and Leahy, K. 1993 'Prehistoric and Anglo-Saxon remains at
Nettleton Top, Nettleton', *Lincolnshire History and Archaeology*, vol. 28, 9-38

Belton: Abramson, P. ed. 2001 Unpublished Developer Report on Archaeological
Fieldwork on the Hatfield Gap Pipeline carried out by Northern Archaeological
Associates for Scottish Power PLC, North Lincolnshire Sites and Monuments
Record

Riby: Steedman, K. 1994 'Excavation of a Saxon site at Riby, Lincolnshire' *Archaeol J*
vol. 151, 212-306

Flixborough: Loveluck, C. 2001 op. cit.

Goltho: Beresford, G. 1987 *Goltho: the Development of an early Medieval Manor c.850-1150*,
English Heritage

WARFARE AND DEFENCES

A plan of Barrow Castles appears in:

Atkins, C. 1983 'The 'Castles, Barrow on Humber' *Lincs Hist Archaeol* 18, 91-3

For 'burh' sites see:

Cox, B. 1994 op. cit., 35-56

Both the Barton ditch and evidence for town planning appear in:

Bryant, G. 1994 *The Early History of Barton on Humber*, 2nd edition (revised), The
Workers' Educational Association, Barton on Humber Branch

LINDSEY'S ECONOMIC BASE

For early Anglo-Saxon pottery in Lindsey see:

Leahy, K. 2007, op. cit.

Later Anglo-Saxon pottery is discussed in Young, J. and Vince, A. 2005 *A Corpus of
Anglo-Saxon and Medieval Pottery from Lincoln*, Lincoln Archaeological Studies No. 7,
Oxford, Oxbow

Some of the forms of Maxey type ware can be seen in:

Addyman P.V. and Whitwell J.B. 1970 'Some middle Saxon pottery types from
Lincolnshire' *Antiquaries J*, 50, 96-102

A range of Torksey ware forms appear in:

Barley, M.W. 1964 'The Medieval Borough of Torksey: Excavation 1960-2', *Antiquaries J*, 44, 165-187

Salt extraction at Marshchapel is described in:

Fenwick et al in Ellis, S., Fenwick H., Lillie, M. and Van de Noort 2001 *Wetland Heritage of the Lincolnshire Marsh: An Archaeological Survey*, Hull, University of Hull, 137-58; 236-7

CRAFTS AND CRAFT WORK

Accounts of hoards and craft work appear in:

Hinton, D. 2000 *A Smith in Lindsey, The Anglo-Saxon Grave at Tattershall Thorpe, Lincolnshire*, Society for Medieval Archaeology Monograph 6

Leahy, K. 2003 *Anglo-Saxon Crafts*, Tempus, Stroud

Mann, J.E. *Early Medieval Finds from Flaxengate, I: Objects of Antler, bone, stone, horn, ivory, amber and jet*, The Archaeology of Lincoln Vol. XIVl-1, Council for British Archaeology, London

THE ANGLO-SAXON CHURCHES OF LINDSEY

Baldwin Brown, G. 1925 *The Arts in Early England, Vol 2, Anglo-Saxon Architecture*, Murray, London

Pevsner, H., Harris, J. and Antram, N. 1989 *The Building of England: Lincolnshire*, Penguin, London

Stocker, D. and Everson, P. 2006 *Summoning St Michael, Early Romanesque Towers in Lincolnshire*, Oxbow, Oxford

Taylor, H.M. and Tayor, J. 1979 (pb edition) *Anglo-Saxon Architecture*, Cambridge University Press

Index

Important references and main entries appear in bold, figures are in italics.

Ackthorpe Top see South
  Elkington
Ælfnoth Bishop of Dorchester 205
Æthelberht II King of Kent 99
Æthelreðestowe (Stow Green?) 142
Æthelflæd (Lady of the Mercians)
  162
Æthelheard, abbot of Louth 126
Æthelhild, abbess 120, 124, 140
Æthelred King of Mercia 7, 99,
  102, 122, 124
Æthelred II King of England 132,
  162, 179
St Æthelthryth (Etheldreda) abbess
  119, 141
Æthelwine, Bishop of Lindsey 120
age at death **78-9**
Alcock, Leslie 108
Aldfrið, King of Northumbria 99,
  157
Aldfrið, King of Lindsey **97-99**,
  105, 115
Alexander, Bishop of Lincoln 110
Alford 75, 80
Alfred, King of Wessex 136, 160,
  162, 171
Alftham see West Halton
Alkborough 14, 15, 103, 127, 128,
  136
  Countess Close 112, 136
amulets 44, 63-64, *26*
Ancholme, River 11, 15, 16, 17,
  24, 64, 103, 110, 113, 126, 130,
  134, *40*
Anglian Collection 97
Anglo-Saxon Chronicle 161-162,
  179
animal bones with burials 56, **72-3**
animals (wild fauna) 75, 190-191
Arles, Council of 21, 25, 117
Arthur 'King of the Britons' 107-
  110
Asgarby 91
Atkins, Caroline 136
St Augustine, Archbishop 114
Aylesby *58*, 67, 68, 75

Axholme, Isle of 14, 15, 105, 127,
  135, 190
bag rings, ivory 48, *25*
Bardney
Monastery 14, 102, 120, 121, **122-4**,
  126, 132, 139, 143
finds *57, 58*, 75
'King's Barrow' 91
Barnetby le Wold (see also Melton
  Ross) 16, 49, 130, 132-134, 135
Barrow on Humber, monastery
  14, 121, 124, 126, 215, *6, 80*
earthwork 136
metalworking 192
Barton on Humber 126, 133, 158,
  188, *85*
St Peter's Church, **201-2,** *91, colour
  plate 26*
defensive ditch 136, *colour plate 27*
Barton Street 135
Basra, Iraq 172
Baumber 109
beavers 64
Bede 7, 14, 97, 100, 102, 103, 114-
  7, 120-124, 126
Belton 127, 128, 135, 138, 190,
  193, 205
Beresford, Guy 136
Berisford, Freda *37, 77*
Bernicia 97, 102, 119, 121
Biddle, Martin and Birthe 161
Beilby *58*
Bigby 22
Binbrook *80*
Biscop 99
bishops of Lindsey 7, 110, 114, 115,
  117, 119-121, 124, 162
Roman 21, 25, 117
Blackburn, Mark 129, 157, 160,
  162, 171-2
Blæcca, 'Præfectus' of Lincoln 114,
  115
Blinkhorn, Paul 156
Boddington Andy 88
Bolingbroke 49, 91
Bonby 163

Bonser, Mike 157
Borre style 167, 168, *67, 68, 71*
Bottesford 41, 199
Boundaries, sites on 49, 75, 90, 132
Bracebridge Heath grave 85, 93
Bracteates 63, *26*
Brigg 16, 24, 109-111
Brixworth, Northants 203
Brocklesby 163, *79*
Bromwich, Rachel 110
brooches 41, 44, 57, 59, 64-66
alloys used 66
annular 64, 66, 72, 85, 86, 88, *23, 31*
ansate 155, *60*
'C2' brooches 66, 101
coin 179-180, *82*
cruciform 57, 61, 66, 86, 91, *22,
  colour plate 7*
end of use 86
how worn on dress 59
Late Saxon, disc 179, *82*
Late Saxon, lead 179, *80*
Late Saxon, enamel 180
penannular 83-4, 105, 113, *37, 38*
quoit 66
radiate headed 67
saucer brooches 61
small-long 63, 66, 86, 192, *24*
square headed 61, 63, 66, *colour
  plate 8*
supporting arm 32
swastika 66
tutulus 32
Viking 166-71, *66, 67, 71*
Brooks, Nicholas 100
Broughton, St Mary's Church 203,
  78, 92
Brown, Michelle 140-141
Bruncliffe, Derbys imported jug
  88
Bucellarii 31
buckles
Early Anglo-Saxon *25*
Late Roman *6*
Middle Saxon *58*
Viking *68, 75*

buildings 128, 129, 132, 135, 137, 138-139, 185, 188, 193, 201
Bullington see Goltho
Burgh on Bain 136
Burgh le Marsh 'Cock Hill' 91, 136
Burgred, King of Mercia 160, 161, 171
Burhs 113, 136
Burnham 105
Burton upon Stather, Bagmoor 40
Burwell 136
Butterwick-type sites 132, 135, 136, 191, *48*
Cabourn 64, 88, 93
Cadney *81*
Cadwallon King of Gwynedd 101, 110, 119
Cædbæd 98, 105
Caenby, 'royal' burial 93-96, *35, 36*
Caister 16, 24, **26-29**, 30, 50, 54, 57, 59, 104, 105, 112, 118, 121, 168
Anglo-Saxon cemeteries 50, 57, 59, 104
Churches of Ss Peter and Paul 205
defences 26, 29, 105, 112
finds 168, *57, 68, 75*
inscription 126, 139, 205, *45*
lead vessel 118
mint 172
monastery 121, 139
sword fitting 168, *69*
Caistor High Street 24
Calceby 168, *69*
Camelot 111
Cameron, Kenneth 102
Carolingian metalwork 155, 160, 184, *61, 62*
carucates 162
Castledyke South, Barton on Humber 52, 54, 55, 57, 58, 72, 75, 77, 78, 79, 82, 90
finds 52, 54, 56, 61, 63, 64, 66, 67, 69, 70, 72, 73, 88, 90, 190, 191, 193, *25, 31,32, 33, colour plate 5*
graves 71, 72, 73, 75, 90, *30*
prehistoric ditch 50, 75
population 78-79, 82
health, disease and injury 77, 79-81
diet 82, 191
hanging bowls 85, 90, *32*
'Celtic' burials 85-86
Cecesey, monastery 126
Ceolwulf, King of Mercia 161-162

cereals 191
St Chad, Bishop of Mercia and Lindsey 119, 124
Chamberlain's Barn, Beds 88
Charlemagne, Emperor of the Franks 155
'Charnwood' pot fabric 51
Cheddar, Somerset 143
Cherry Willingham 128
Christianity 88, 90, 110, **114-115, 118-126**
Roman **117-118**
churches in Lindsey **201-205**
Cingulum 30
Claxby 22
Cleatham 35, **37-41**, 48, 50, 54, 56, 57, 59, 64, 66, 75, 82, 84, 85, 86, 91, 96, 104, 105, 127, 189, 194
animal bones 56
'Celtic' burial 85
Final Phase graves 86-90, *31*
finds from graves 57, 59, 66, 67, 69, 72, 81, 85, 101, *20, 22, 23, 24, 25, 26, 27, 28, 31*
finds from urns **44-48**, 54, 57, 64, 66, 67, 84, 85, 189, 192, *13, 14, 15*
graves 54, 57, 59, 71-73, 75, 86, *21*
health, disease and injury 77, 79-81
horse burials 54, 56
location 48-49, 105
plan *9*
population 59, 78-79, 82-83
rituals associated with urns 54-6, *18*
round barrow? 49-50
'Roman' pots 52-54, 86, *17*
urns 41-44, 50, 51, 52, 55, 56, 191, 194, *10, 11, 12, 16, 18, Colour plates 3, 5*
Clixby *7*
Cnut, King of England 179
Coenwulf, King of Mercia 132
coins, **157-160**
Denier of Peppin 160
Dirhams 172
lunettes issues 160, 176
Magnentius 118, *43*
mints, see below
pennies 132, 160, *77, Colour plate 25*
Roman 25, 33
sceattas 132, 155, 158-160, 176, *63*
stycas 132, 160, 176
tremissis 158
Viking period 171

Coldingham, Yorks 141
combs, bone 41, 44
Comitatenses 31
Corieltauvi 14
Corringham wapentake 49
coral beads 48, 56
Counters, bone 44
Cowgill, Jane 199
cowrie shells 48, 57, 64
Cox, Barrie 104, 136
crafts **192**
cremation cemeteries **35-56**, Map *8*
Crosby 163
Crowle 15, 177, *70*
Cumberworth, lead plaque 141
St Cuthbert, bishop 44, 88, 121
Danelaw 162
Dark, Ken 113
Da Vinci Code 109
Deda, abbot of Partney 114, 116
defences, Anglo-Saxon **136**, *86, colour plate 27*
Deira 50, 97, 100, 101, 102, 119, 121
De la Pryme, Abraham 142
demography 78, **82-3**
De Ross, Robert 134
diet 82
Diuma, Bishop of Mercia 119
Domesday Survey Map 11, 19, 49, 83, 104, 130, 132, 133, 135, 163, 165, 166, 189, 199, 203, *3*
Donemuthan 143
Doncaster 24, 203
Don river 14, 143
Dragonby 22, *6*
Dumville David 99
Dunning, Gerald 29
Eadhæd, Bishop of Lindsey 119
Eadnoth II, Bishop of Dorchester 205
Eagles, Bruce 21
Ealdwine, abbot of Bardney 120
Early Anglo-Saxon Pottery Project *9*
East Anglia 64, 66, 71, 156, 160, 161, 172
East Ravendale 37
East Riding of Yorkshire, Deira 21, 31,
East Wykeham 104
Ecgfrið, King of Mercia 98
Ecgfrið, King of Northumbria 101, 119, 124, 141
Edgar, Bishop of Lindsey 120, 138
Edgar, King of England 120, 126

Edlington 32
St Edmund King of East Anglia, chapel of 96
Edward the Martyr, King of England 160, 164
Edwin, King of Deira 99, 101, 110, 114, 119
Elmet 99, 100
Elsham 32, 35, **37**, 38, 54, 55, 59, 67, 82, 86, 105, 155, 127, 191
animal bones 56, 189
cremation deposits 77
finds 48, *68*, 71
location 48, 49, 113, 133-4, *40*
place-name 104
population size 78-9, 82
urns 50-51, 55
English Heritage 202
Epworth 15
Ermine Street 15, 22, 24, 95, 105
Essex 99, 166
Ethelburga, wife of Edwin of Northumbria 114
Everson, Paul 116, 137, 177, 201
feeding bottle 67, *colour plate 5*
Field, Naomi 136, 205
Fillingham 205
Final Phase burials **86-90**
Fisher, Genevieve 64-65
Flixborough 15, 122, 129, 130, 136, **137-143,** 164, 191, 192
animal bones 138, 189-190-191
buildings 138-139, *colour plate 17*
burials 80, 129, 138-139
coffin fittings 138, *88*
coins 155, 160
finds 130, 138, 140, 143, 147-8, 151, 156, 164-5, 189, 191-194, *50, 51, 52, 55, 58, 73, colour plates 18, 20*
lead plaque 140-141, *59*
lead vats 199, *Colour plate 21*
productive site 129, 130
tool hoard 197, 199, *88, Colour plate 21*
Florence of Worcester 179, 205
Foederati 29, 30, 31
Fonaby 50, 57, 58, 66, 71, 77, 86, 101, 104
Foot, Sarah 99
Fossdyke, cannel 24
Fowler, Elizabeth 83
Francisca 40, 69
Froddingham 15
Gainsborough 95, 136, *81*
Garton, East Yorkshire, 199
Gelling, Margaret 142, 185

Geoffrey of Monmouth 109
Gifle 100
Gildas 105, 108, 118
girdle hangers 25
Glentworth 22
Goltho, Bullington 136-7, 155, 190, 191, 193, *86*
Grainthorpe 26, 105
graves, see inhumations
Great Casterton, Rutland 52
Great Limber 41
Green, Tom 107
Greenland ice cores 16
Greetwell, near Lincoln 22, 25
Grimsby
  Humberston Abbey 157
  Weelsby Avenue 112
Grubenhäuser 128, 129, 132, 135, 188, 193, *49*
Habrough 136
Halfdan, Viking leader 161
Hall Hill, see West Keal
-h m place-names 104-105
Hamwic 156, 185
hanging bowls **84-85**, 91, 93, 105, 116, *31, 34, 39, 54*
Härke, Heinrich **69-71**
Harman, Mary 37, 77
Harrison, Alan 33
Harpswell 95, 136, *58, 71, 81*
Hartlepool 139, 143
Hatfield 14, 18, 99, *50*
  Chase, battle of 101, 102
Hawkes, Sonia 29
Haxey 15, 168, 205
health disease and injury **79-81**
Hemswell 95
Here paeð 95
St Herefrith of Louth 120, 139
Hibaldstow 30, 32, 54, 91, 121, 126, *6, 71*
Hicce 100
Historia Brittonum 108, 110
Hoddom 139
Holland (Parts of Lincolnshire) 7, 14, 100, 130, 208
Holton le Clay 156, 177
Holton le Moor mounts 93, *colour plate 11*
Horkestow 22, 118
hooked tags *58*
Horncastle 124, 29, 30, 59, 105, 121, 147, *5, 50, 51*
  Anglo-Saxon graves 59
  boar's head mount 93, *colour plate 16*
  Late Roman fortification 26-29,

105, 112
mint 172
pendant *colour plate 13*
Hough on the Hill, Kesteven 203
Hull, River 17
human remains **76-82**, 191
Humber Estuary 11, 14, 17, 19, 22, 24, 26, 30, 31, 66, 67, 99, 100-101, 103, 105, 109, 110, 113, 115, 127, 130, 141, 142-3, 156, 163, 191, 203
Humber Field Archaeology 138
Humber Head Levels 14, 15, 16, 17, 18
Humberside 21, 207
Humberside Archaeological Unit 138
Humberside Sites and Monuments Record 137
Humbrenses **100-101**
Hwicca 99
St Hygbald, abbot 126
imported material 34, 48, 84, 155, *88*
Ine, King of Wessex 72
Ingham 30, *6*
inhumation cemeteries **57-76**
cross-gender burials 59, 81
vessels in Graves 52, 67, 73
weapon graves **67-71**, *27*
body positions **71-72**
burial structures **73-76**
'Celtic' burial rites **85-6**
inscriptions 85, 118, 121, 126, 141, 177, 192, *26, 31, 45, 70*
Ipswich ware 154, 155, **156**
wic 156
Irby on Humber 75
Ireland 18
Irish metalwork 151, 176, 177, *76*
Irish monks 119, 120
Irish Vikings 177
iron working **194-197**
Ivar the Boneless, Viking leader 161
ivory rings 48
James the Deacon 119
Jarrow 143
Jellinge Style 167, 168, *70, 71*
Jones, Mick 117
Keelby 67, 163, 166, *6, 66*
Kemble, JM 41, 110
Kent 30, 88, 97, 99, 100, 114, 119, 156, 160, 161
Kesteven (Parts of Lincolnshire) 7, 14, 100, 130, 142, 203, 207, 208

Ketsby *66*, 68, 71, 75, 76, 80

Kingerby 136

Kirkdale, Yorkshire 141

Kirmington 22, 24, 29, 31, 32, 33,
54, 84, 111, 112, 113, *6, 7, 26, 37,
40, 66, 75*

Kirmond le Mire 22

Kirton in Lindsey 22, 37-38, 49,
52, 121, 127, 191

soke of 37, 49, 54, 96

Mount Pleasant Villa 69, 75, 84

knives 44, 69-70, 72, 91, 194, 197,

Knowles, Chris 37, 77

Laceby 163

Langworth, river 16

Laughton *61, 79*

Laycock, Stuart 30, 34

lead vats 199, *colour plate 21*

Lethbridge Tom 88

Leeds, ET 88

Leofric (Earl of Mercia) and
Godgifu 'Godiva' 205

Leland, John 26, 122

Liber Eliensis 141-142

Limitanei 31

Lincoln 8, 11, 12, 14, 15, 24, 102,
109, 110, 121, 143, 153, 155, 158,
162, 163, 175, *6*

Anglo-Saxon city 138, 183

bishop from 21, 25, 117

Cathedral and churches 121, 185

coins from 158, 172

'Dark Earth' deposits 25-26, 33,

Flaxengate 188, 192, 194

gravestones made at 177, 179

pottery from 185-188, *87*

lawmen 162

mint 172

place-name 102-103, 105, 163

survival 83, 105

relationship with cremation
cemeteries 50, 59, 82, 105

Roman city 14, 17, 22, 24-26, 30,
33, 115

St Paul in the Bail, dating 84, 115-
116, 117, 139, 184, *39, 42*

hanging bowl 84-85,

sunken floored building 138

St Paulinus preaches 114-5

Viking city 162, 171, 175, 177, 180,
183-188, 190, 192

manufacture 179, 192

Wigford 103, 185

Lincoln Edge (Cliff) 14, 15, 22, 24,
48, 127

Lincolnshire Rising 113

Lindsey, Kingdom of
boundaries **11-14,**

churches **201-205**

environment **16-19, 189**

finds, maps of

Anglo-Saxon, Early *19*

Anglo-Saxon, Late *83*

Anglo-Saxon, Middle *46*

Celtic *38*

coins, Early *63*

coins, Later *77*

cremation cemeteries *8*

imports *62*

Late Roman *4*

Viking, Early *65*

Viking, Late *74*

genealogy of kings **97-99**

industries 24

Lindsey Survey (AD1115-18) 14

Linnuis 108

part of '*Humbrensia*' 100-101

Map *1, 2*

place-name 102-103

Prouinciæ Lindissi 115

rainfall and temperature 18-19

ridings 163

topography **14-16**

water supplies **14-16**

woodland 19

livestock 189-190

Lindisfarne 121

Littleborough 22

loom weights 22, 128, 135, 137, 193

Louth 35, 49, 121, 126, 139, 158,
168, *50, 52*

Loveden Hill, Kesteven 38, 50, 75

Ludbough 136

Ludford 22, 103, 113

Loveluck, Christopher 138

Mablethorpe *52, 55*

Maltby 79

Malton, East Yorkshire 29, 31, 130

Mammen style 167

Manley, wapentake 49

Manton 37, 49, 52, 91, 93, 126,
127, *60*

iron smelting 52, 194

Gilliate's grave 52, 55, 56, 72

hanging bowl 84, 91

'warrior grave' 69, 91

Market Rasen sword 93, *colour
plate 15*

marshes 11, 12, 14, 15, 16, 17, 24,
91, 95, 99, 103, 104, 105, 110,
126, 141, 142, 194,

Marshchapel 103, 197

Mästermyr, Sweden 197

Maxey-type ware 128, 135, 153-5,
184, *87*

May, Jeffrey 22

Mayen lava 155, 191

Meaney Audrey 8

Melton Ross/Barnetby site *40*

crop marks 132, 191, *47*

finds 57, 82

productive site **130-135, 143,** 165

decorative mount **139,** *47*

furc (gallows) 134

sword fitting 143, *47*

Mercia 7, 71, 97, 100, 102, 119, 121,
124, 136, 158, 160, 161, 162, 208

metalworking tools *90*

Middle Anglia 119, 130

Middlegate Lane 24, 37, 105, 130,
133, 155, 166, *40*

Middle Street 24

Millgate, Newark 48, 52, 54

Millar, Keith 21, 188

monasteries 114, 117, 120, **121-126,**
129, 139, 140-143, 205, *44*

Morden, Robert 143

Mortimer, Catherine 66

Myres, J.N.L. 35, 99-101

Navenby 86

Nennius see *Historia Brittonum*

Nettleton 59, 104, 128, *71*

Nettleton Top 54, 104, 128, 189-
190, 191, 193, 194, *49*

Newball 32, 120, *7, colour plate 14*

Newton on Trent 12-14

Normanby le Wold 128

North Conesby 137, 142

Northern Archaeological Associates
135

North Lincolnshire Museum 127

North Owersby 76, 80, 81

Northumbria 7, 11, 71, 97, 99-102,
114, 119, 132, 136, 143, 160,
161, 162

North Gyrwe 100

Norton, Cleveland 66, 67

Notitia Dignitatum 31

Nottinghamshire 21, 31, 130

Offa, King of Mercia 98, 122, 155,
160, 166

Offa's Dyke 136

Okasha, Elisabeth 14

Osgodby *6, 55, 82*

Osthryth, Queen of Mercia 102,
120, 122

St Oswald, King of Northumbria
101, 119, 102, 122, 124, 139

Oswiu, King of Northumbria 102, 119
Ouse, river 11, 130
Owen, Arthur 120
Owmby 22, 24, 113
Owston Ferry 127
Parker, M.S. 143
Parkin, Gary 132
Partney (Skendleby?) monastery 14, 114, 120, 124, 140
Paterson, Caroline 167
pathology see human remains
St Paulinus, Bishop of Northumbria 21, 99, 101 **114-115** 116, 117, 119
Peacock, Edward 41
Peada, son of King Penda of Mercia 119
Penda, King of Mercia 101-102, 110, 119
Peterborough Abbey 126
pin-beaters 44, 192, 193, 194,
pins 86, 130, 135, 143, 147, 148, **151**, *31, 47, 50, 51, 55,*
Phillips, C.W. 8
place-names in Lindsey 102-105
Danish place-names 163, *64*
plough pebbles 191
pollen 17
Portable Antiquities Scheme 8, 30, 147, 157
productive sites **129-135**, 164
prone burials 72
Quentovic, coin from 160
Quern stones 155, 191
Rackham, Oliver 189
Raventhorpe 163
Redbourne 126, 139
Reightlin comb 41
Reavill J.B. 107
Remigius, Bishop of Lincoln 121, 205
Riby Park 88, 90, 163
Riby Cross Roads 133, **135**, 163, 191
finds 51, 55, **135**, 139, 148, 155, 156, 158, **190**, 193, 194, 199, *52*
Richards, Julian 54
Richardson, Thomas 50
Rickman, Thomas 201
Ringerike Style 167, 168, *75*
Roman coins from urns 54
Roman Lindsey 14, **21-34**
buckles and strap ends **29-32**, 34, 54, 113, *4, 6*
coins **33-34**, *43*

communications 14, 17, **22-24**
defences **26-32**
end of Roman Lindsey **32-34**
environment 16-19, 21,
erosion 17, 22
flooding 17-18
industry 24, 34
Roman survival? 82-83
rural settlement 15, **17-22**, 113
villas (listed) 22
Roxby cum Risby 22, 76, 82
Salmonby 128
salt extraction **197-198**
Sancton/Baston potter 50-51, 101
Sancton/Elkington potter 50, 101
Sandtoft 18
Sawyer, Peter 120, 121, 123, 163
Saxilby 75
Saxon Shore Forts 26, 30
Scampton 22, 32, *colour plates 7, 8*
Scawby 126, *73*
Scothern 177
Scotter 177, *72*
Scotton *61*
sculpture 126, 177-9, *70, 78*
Scunthorpe 8, 15, 24, 163, 194
Scutiform Pendants 63
sea level change 16, 17
Searby 67, 88
Seax 69, 91
Sewerby, East Yorks 66, 67
Sewara and Sewenna 141
Sheffield's Hill, Roxby 57, 58, 71, 77, 128, 191, *colour plate 6*
coffins 73
Final Phase graves 86-90
finds 67, 69, 70, 84, 86, 93, 121, 192, 194, *colour plate 9, 10*
ring ditches 73
grave structures 73, 75
gold pendants 121, *Colour plate 12*
layout 21, 76, 86, 191, *29*
swords 93, 194
shields 67, 69, *27, 34 colour plates 9, 10*
Simeon of Durham 24
Sincil Dyke, Lincoln 103
single Graves **90-96**, *35, 36*
Skegness 26
Sleaford (Kestern) 130, 158
sleeve clasps 44, 52, 63, 86, *25*
Snape, John 142
Society of Antiquaries of London *35*, 54
sokemen 166
South Elkington **35-6**, 40, 48, 49,

50, 59, 82, 86
South Ferriby 16, 17, 24, 33, 66, *61*, 71, 75, 80, 82
South *Gyrwe* 100, 141
South Kelsey 126, 176, *61, 72*
South Newbald, Yorks, East Riding 130, 132
'Southumbria' 11
spearheads 69, 72, 73, 82, 91, 93, 143, 168, , *27, 28, 34*
Spilsby *60*
spindle whorls 44, 189, 192, 193, 194
Spital in the Street 95
Spong Hill, Norfolk 38, 48, 51,
Stallingborough 135, 136, 168, *57, 67, colour plate 22*
Stamford, Kesteven 162, 208
Stamfordshire 208
Stamford ware 132, 154, 188
strap ends 151
Carolingian 155, *61*
Final Phase *31*
lead 179, *81*
Trewhiddle style 153, *57*
Viking 168, *68, 75*
Winchester style 179, *79, 81*
Stenigot 91
Stenton, Sir Frank 98, 99
Stickford 151, *6, 50*
stirrup fittings 75
Stidriggs, Dumfries 199
Stocker, David 116, 121, 122, 124, 125, 126, 143, 162, 177, 201
Stow by Lincoln 121, 203-5
Stukeley, William 112
Sturton by Scawby 22
Sturton by Stow *81*
Styli 140, *88*
Sub-Roman, see Roman survival?
Sussex 7, 99
Sutton Hoo 77, 84, 93, 95
Swallow 103, *55, 82*
Swan, Vivien 24
Swein, King of Denmark 179
Swinhope *68*
swords 67, 86, 93, 94, 194, *32, 34, 56, 69*
Syddensis civitas 121
Tamworth, Staffordshire 19
Tathwell *68*
Tattershall Thorpe 197
Taylor G.V. 37
Tennyson, Alfred Lord 14, 114
textile working 137, 189, 190, **192-194**

Till Bridge Lane 22
Tiowulfingacæstir (Littleborough?)
 115
Theddlethorpe 176, *73, colour
 plate 24*
Theodore, Archbishop 119
Thorne 14, 18
Thornton Curtis 112, 177
Thwing, East Yorkshire 113
Tondberht, ealdorman 141
tool hoards **197** *88, 89, 90*
Torksey 24, 155,
 coins 158, 160, 172
 finds *57, 58, 72, 79*
 Irish brooch 177, *76*
 sword fitting 168, *69*
 tool hoard 197
 Vikings at 161, 175
 weights 176, *73, colour plate 23*
Torksey ware 132, 188
Trent, River 11, 12, 14-17, 22, 24,
 95, 105, 114, 127, 128, 130, 142-
 3, 163, 190
 Battle of 7, 102, 124
 place-name 103
 Vikings on 161, 172
Thorpe, Lewis 109
Trewhiddle style 153, 184, *55,
 56, 57*
Tribal Hidage 7, 14, 97, **99-100**,
Trollope, Edward *37, 50*
Twigmore 49
Tyrani 105
Ulmschneider, Katarina 130
University of Sheffield 134
Urnes Style 167, 168, *75*
Vicarius of Britannia 31
Vikings
 Anglo-Scandinavian 49, 113,
 179-180
 bullion economy 175, *72, 73*
 coins **171-172**
 conquest of Lindsey 114, 136, **161-
 163**, 168, 185
 Danelaw 162
 Danish words in Lindsey dialect

 165-166
 finds **166-168**, *65, 66-75*
 Five Boroughs 162, 163
 Great Army 160, 161, 175
 Irish links 151, 175-176, 177, *55*
 lawmen 162
 lead weights 160, 164, *73, colour
 plate 23*
 Lincoln 175, **183-188** 192
 place-names 163, 171
 raids 126, 143, 161, 179
 sculpture **177-179**, *70, 78*
 Viking art, see Borre style, Jellinge
 style, Mammen style,
 Ringerike style, Urnes style
 Wantage Law Code 162
Vince, Alan 51, 117, 155, 184, 185,
 188
Waddingham 205
Walh 103
Walcot, Alkborough 103
Walesby 22, 58, 81, 117
Walmsgate 171
Wansdyke 136
wapentakes 49, 113, 163
warfare 70-71
weapon graves **67-71**
Webster, Graham 35, 40,
Welbeck Hill, Irby on Humber 57,
 58, 64, 67, 71, 72, 128, 163, *26*
Wellingore 121
Welton le Marsh 143, *51, 57, 76*
West Halton 142-143
West Heslerton, East Yorks 127
West Keal 35, **36-7**, 48, 49, 82, 91
West Ravendale 50, 51, 60, 79
West Wykeham, 104
Westley Waterless, Cambs 199
Welton by Lincoln 59
whelk shells 64
Whetstones 44
Whithorn 139
Whitton 205, *61, 68*
Whitwell JB 21
wics (trading centres) 156
Wich m place-names 103-4

Wigford see under Lincoln
St Wilfrid, Bishop of Northumbria
 119, 141
Williams, Howard 49
Willoughby by Alford *67, 81*
Willoughton 128
Winchester style 179
Winfrith Bishop of Mercia 119,
 125
Winghale Priory, South Kelsey
 126
Winnall, Hampshire 88
Winteringham 22, 99, 141, 188,
 203, *6, 37*
Winterton 15, 22, 33, 99, 118, 192,
 6, 57
Winsby *66, 81*
Withcall *60*
Whitby 139, 143
Worlaby 58, 64, 69, 71, *25*
William I, King of England 121
Witham, River 12, 13, 15, 16, 17,
 103, 122
 bowl 147, *54*
 pins 147, 148, *colour plate 19*
 sword *56*
 Viking finds 166
Woden 98
Wold Newton 41
Wolds 14-15, 16, 19, 22, 24, 48, 91,
 111, 127, 130, 136, 163
Woodland 15, 19, 83, 189
woodworking tools *88, 89*
Wrawby 134, *53*
Wulfhere, King of Mercia 102,
 124, 126
Wyham place-name 105
Wykeham, Nettleton 104
Yarborough Camp, Croxton 29,
 105, **111-114**, 134, 135, 136, *40, 41*
Yeavering 143
York 18, 31, 101, 109, 117, 121, 132,
 156, 161, 162, 172, 175, 185
Yorke, Barbara 100
Young, Jane 51, 188